Becoming a Teacher in a Field-Based Setting

An Introduction to Education and Classrooms

Donna L. Wiseman
UNIVERSITY OF MARYLAND

Stephanie L. Knight
TEXAS A&M UNIVERSITY

Donna D. Cooner
COLORADO STATE UNIVERSITY

THOMSON
— ✳ —
WADSWORTH   Australia • Canada • Mexico • Singapore • Spain • United Kingdom • United States

THOMSON

★

™

WADSWORTH

Education Editor: Dan Alpert
Development Editor: Tangelique Williams
Assistant Editor: Jennifer Wilkinson
Editorial Assistant: Erin Worley
Technology Project Manager: Barry Connolly
Marketing Manager: Dory Schaeffer
Marketing Assistant: Annabelle Yang
Advertising Project Manager: Tami Strang
Project Manager, Editorial Production: Jennie Redwitz
Print/Media Buyer: Judy Inouye

Permissions Editor: Bob Kauser
Production Service: Melanie Field, Strawberry
    Field Publishing
Text Designer: Adriane Bosworth
Photo Researcher: Myrna Engler
Copy Editor: Carol Lombardi
Cover Designer: Lisa Delgado
Cover Image: © LWA-Dann Tardif/CORBIS
Compositor: Stratford Publishing Services
Text and Cover Printer: Webcom

Printed in Canada
1 2 3 4 5 6 7   08 07 06 05 04

For more information about our products,
contact us at:
Thomson Learning Academic Resource Center
1-800-423-0563

For permission to use material from this text or
product, submit a request online at
http://www.thomsonrights.com.

Any additional questions about permissions
can be submitted by email to
thomsonrights@thomson.com.

Library of Congress Control Number: 2004102455

ISBN 0-534-27425-0

Thomson Wadsworth
10 Davis Drive
Belmont, CA 94002-3098
USA

Asia
Thomson Learning
5 Shenton Way #01-01
UIC Building
Singapore 068808

Australia/New Zealand
Thomson Learning
102 Dodds Street
Southbank, Victoria 3006
Australia

Canada
Nelson
1120 Birchmount Road
Toronto, Ontario M1K 5G4
Canada

Europe/Middle East/Africa
Thomson Learning
High Holborn House
50/51 Bedford Row
London WC1R 4LR
United Kingdom

Latin America
Thomson Learning
Seneca, 53
Colonia Polanco
11560 Mexico D.F.
Mexico

Brief Contents

Contents

2 *Educational History and Philosophy*   34

5 *The Status of Contemporary Students*   128

6 Classroom Learning Theory   158

7 Successful Classroom Environments   202

School Contexts, Organization, and Leadership 282

Preface

*A life in teaching is a stitched-together affair, a crazy quilt of odd
pieces and scrounged materials, equal parts invention and imposi-
tion. To make a life in teaching is largely to find your own way,
to follow this or that thread, to work until your fingers ache, your
mind feels as it will unravel, and your eyes give out, and to make
mistakes and then rework large pieces. It is sometimes tedious and
demanding, confusing and uncertain, and yet is as often creative
and dazzling: Surprising splashes of color can suddenly appear
at its center; unexpected patterns can emerge and lend the whole
affair a sense of grace and purpose and possibility.*

—W. Ayers, *To Teach: The Journey of A Teacher*

*T*he act of teaching has multiple and complex dimensions, and teachers
must therefore be smart, altruistic, and ready to develop habits of lifelong learning. Teaching is a profession where change is the norm and not
the exception. Teaching is affected by the world we live in: Factors such as
student demographics, corporate economics, and federal and state policies add to complexities of teaching. If you are seeking a career that is free
from the challenges and confrontations of contemporary life, then teaching is not for you. However if you are looking forward to making a difference in the lives of children, adolescents, and young people, then you have
chosen the right profession. This book will help you prepare for this
uniquely rewarding career.

This text is for students who are taking the first steps toward learning
to be a teacher in a formal preparation program. You are involved in university classroom discussions, readings, and writings and are starting to
make your first classroom observations. As you continue your preparation

program, you will spend more time learning about teaching and learning from professors, mentors, teachers, and students. You will continue to learn about teaching as you gain experience and practice new teaching skills. However, teaching is much more than learning from books or learning from classroom experiences. Experience in the absence of reflection will not guarantee growth. Reflection, both individually and as a shared process, is an important part of your development as an educator. Discussions with peers, teachers, mentors, university professors, and elementary and secondary school students will enable you to see and evaluate your experiences through different lenses. As you mature as a teacher, reflecting on your experiences will allow you to interface more effectively with colleagues and professionals so you can learn to work with children and families, deliver instruction to diverse learners, use technology in classroom instruction, and create an environment of mutual trust between you and your students. This book offers ideas and opportunities to practice all of these skills.

The third edition of *Becoming a Teacher in a Field-Based Setting* provides you with an introduction to the education profession—its history and current contexts, the complexities of teaching and learning, and the dynamics of the classroom. The ideas and experiences in this text will introduce you to the profession and allow you opportunities to reflect on your own and others' current practices.

Features in the Third Edition

The following elements in this textbook will help you get the most from your class and advance your personal development as a teacher:

GUIDING YOUR READING Each chapter begins with a set of questions to help you read for important concepts and ideas. At the end of the chapter, answers to the questions are provided to help you check your understanding of the major points.

FIELD-BASED ACTIVITIES The Field-Based Activities—a vital part of your preparation—include reflective and observational small-group activities, technology experiments, and journal exercises. Some of the activities suggest development and collection of portfolio artifacts; others encourage you to demonstrate your development as a teacher using technology as a tool. Your supervisor or university professor will help you select and personalize the activities that will be most useful to your professional growth. Each of the activities is linked to INTASC standards for preparing new teachers and will help you develop your understanding of the teaching profession.

VOICE OF A TEACHER To help you understand the ideas of other teachers as you learn about becoming a teacher yourself, we have included examples and descriptions written by beginning and experienced teachers to illustrate the ideas in this text. These excerpts provide an insider account and let you hear the sound of teachers' voices (Shulman, 1992). These classroom narratives evolved from interviews and written responses and occasionally include the views of children, parents, principals, and others. The stories provide clarification and interpretation of topics presented in the text.

SELF-REFLECTION EXERCISES You will become a professional by observing, doing, inquiring—and then by reflecting on teaching and learning. These short quizzes assess your own attitudes, monitor your learning, identify further areas of interest and needed study, and help you understand chapter concepts. Each chapter has suggested activities and guidelines for discussions with classroom teachers, your peers, and university instructors. Cultivating interactions with others and sharing ideas will enable you to solve problems collaboratively.

PORTFOLIO REFLECTIONS These activities are more than course requirements—they are designed to engage you in the important process of reflection and will serve as a measure of your growth in this important first phase of becoming a teacher. The Portfolio Reflections provide suggestions for exhibits based on field experiences, and the suggested activities are associated with topics presented in each chapter. You can use the suggestions as a starting point for creating exhibits that demonstrate your development as a teacher. Often our suggestions provide ways for you to present your reflections and perceptions related to teaching and learning.

E-PORTFOLIO EXHIBITS Because many programs require them, suggestions for e-portfolios appear in each chapter. We encourage you to use multimedia when possible.

INFOTRAC® COLLEGE EDITION If you want to know more about a topic presented in the text, the InfoTrac College Edition activities and Internet references in each chapter provide a good place to begin your inquiries.

APPENDIX: YOUR PROFESSIONAL PORTFOLIO This section offers cogent suggestions about compiling and organizing your own portfolios for various uses. Specific ideas for this very important digest will help you decide what to include and how to present it.

The Field-Based Setting

Learning about teaching includes several important components. Your university experiences form the foundation of your professional training. Content knowledge, understanding of child and adolescent development, and pedagogical processes make up the basis of your university experience. However, we believe that the field-based setting is a crucial place to learn about teaching, and we hope your preparation program includes several opportunities for you to work in schools and with students. The experiences you have in the schools are planned by university professors and classroom teachers through a partnership between the school and the university. The school–university partnership that accompanies your teacher education program connects university and school-based perspectives. The best way to learn to teach combines learning from university-sponsored research and theory while integrating the practical knowledge that teachers have gained from their own classroom experience (Zeichner, 1992).

Sometimes theory and practice collide. The things you read about in a textbook and talk about in university classrooms may not match what you are seeing in the school setting. When this happens, it is important to talk about the differences and establish a balance between educational theory and classroom practice. Some educators ignore the role of theory and feel practice is the best way to learn to teach. We believe both aspects of teacher training are important. You may become impatient with university coursework and focus more on your field and clinical experiences. But to be a professional, you must understand both the theories and the practices of teaching.

A Special Profession

Teaching is a lifelong learning process, and you will have different needs as you gain experience. Your needs as a beginning teacher will be quite different from those of experienced teachers. The first steps of learning to teach are both exciting and daunting. There will be days that you feel challenged but, as William Ayers points out in the opening quote, you will experience times when "surprising splashes of color appear . . ." that will leave you humbled and strengthened as you grasp the impact a teacher has on all learners. As you become a teacher, you will realize that you are not the first to experience insecurities and challenges. It is part of the lifelong learning process of becoming a teacher.

Acknowledgments

We continue to learn from the many teachers who work with us and the students in our university classrooms. The ability of teachers to manage the change and challenges associated with educating children, adolescents, and young people provides many new lessons about flexibility, teaching, and researching. Our students who want to be teachers bring a never-ending commitment, excitement, and needed freshness to our work and provide the basis for much of our own learning. We are constantly amazed at what individuals who are committed to their students can accomplish in the classroom.

We would like to thank the following reviewers for their suggestions:

Mary Lee Bass, Monmouth University

Ted Bulling, Nebraska Wesleyan University

Willie Ennis, III, Southeastern Louisiana University

Kathy Finkle, Black Hills State University

Christopher P. Halter, University of California, San Diego

Catherine Lux, University of Arkansas

Melvin J. Pedras, University of Idaho

Michael C. Petrowsky, Glendale Community College

Elena J. Scambio, Bloomfield College

The Thomson Wadsworth editors and staff provided support and encouragement to help us complete this project. Dan Alpert's vision, support, and enthusiasm for the project inspired us to push our ideas further and try new text features. Melanie Field, Jennie Redwitz, and Carol Lombardi worked with us to make sure that all was acceptable and gently maintained the pace of production in spite of our diversions. Many thanks to all of these people.

Donna L. Wiseman
Stephanie L. Knight
Donna D. Cooner

REFERENCES

Epigraph: Ayers, W. (2001). *To teach: The journey of a teacher* (2nd ed., p. 1). New York: Teachers College Press.

Shulman, J. (1992). *Case methods in teacher education.* New York: Teachers College Press.

Zeichner, K. (1992). Rethinking the practicum in the professional development school partnership. *Journal of Teacher Education,* 43(4), 296–307.

Personal View of Teaching

I teach who I am. What I value and believe arises from my personal background and experience—whom I have loved and who has loved me; what has encouraged and hurt me; and the idealistic quests involving myself, other people, and American society. My identity as a teacher was formed through parents, family, friends, successes, and failures. What I decide is true and necessary for my students and me, in both the anxiety-filled nights and clear daylight, comes from my no-longer-negotiable identity, character, and philosophy.

My background helps explain my teaching.

—Stephen Gordon in *What Keeps Teachers Going?*

In This Chapter

- Impact of Personal Biography on Teaching
- Reasons for Becoming a Teacher
- Characteristics of Good Teachers
- Teaching as a Lifelong Learning Process
- The Formal Steps of Learning to Teach
- Learning to Teach in a Field-Based Setting

Guiding Your Reading

1. Why do I want to be a teacher?

2. What experiences have shaped my ideas about teaching?

3. What is a good teacher?

4. How do teachers learn how to teach?

*G*ood teachers touch learners' lives and captivate students' attention, motivating them to learn and encouraging them to do their best. They demonstrate passion about a content area while caring for and respecting their students. At the same time, good teachers are capable of critiquing their schools and understanding the impact of state and local requirements on classroom instruction. Teachers interact with parents and community leaders from all walks of life. They play an important role in the community and know how to use the resources available to them to benefit their students. They are able to understand five-year-olds' explanations of important life events and adolescents' defense of their favorite rock music. In sum, they are lifelong learners who focus their varied skills and abilities on working with other learners.

The teaching profession is complex and challenging. To meet these challenges, future teachers need experiences that will help them acquire and later refine their skills and abilities. Your formal preparation will provide you opportunities to gain skills and abilities related to good teaching and help you grow through reflective analysis of what you read, learn, and experience. The reflection encouraged in your formal teacher preparation will serve as a model for learning throughout your teaching career. Many of the activities suggested in this textbook are designed to help you reflect.

Impact of Personal Biography on Teaching

Teachers' past and present life experiences have an impact on their attitudes and definitions of teaching and influence their identities as teachers (Knowles, 1992). Personal and professional biography becomes a rich source of information that helps clarify teachers' dispositions and behaviors and accounts for some of their ability to be socialized into the world of teaching. Childhood experiences, early teacher role models, teaching experiences, personal knowledge and beliefs, and significant relationships make important contributions to an individual's definition of and approach to teaching (Calderhead, 1996; Crow, 1987; Knowles, 1992).

Childhood Experiences

Many teachers can recall when, as a child, they set up a school in their backyard and enlisted their brothers and sisters as students. Although not every child who plays teacher in his or her early years becomes a teacher, teaching is something that we observe and know about early in our lives. These

© Donna Wiseman

Teachers explain that they have entered the profession because they want to have a positive impact on students' lives. Many believe that becoming a teacher is more than a career choice—it is a calling.

early observations and feelings about school and teaching contribute to the ways we think about teaching and what we do in our classrooms.

Even those childhood experiences that occur away from the classroom can become a part of how teachers identify their roles. Personality development, socialization patterns, and ways of interacting with others are some of the same traits developed during early experiences that ultimately become integral parts of teachers' identities. For example, our notion of intelligence as a factor that can change (or not) may develop in response to the way our parents and early teachers regarded intelligence.

Family members provide a great deal of input in how we think about teaching. Those who grow up with parents who teach will likely be influenced by their parents' careers. If parents are teachers and talk about their work during family interactions, their philosophy and framework can easily become a part of their own children's philosophy. Dinnertime discussions about teaching and schools have the potential to remain with teachers throughout their career.

In addition, family expectations and rules contribute to teacher identity. Behaviors learned as a child, as well as patterns of interaction and family values, can have an impact on teaching behaviors. Parental expectations about work, learning, play, creativity, and other important issues are reflected in our teaching careers. Such personal attributes as work habits established as a young child stay with the adult teacher.

Role Models

Positive influences from one's own teachers may provide a clear view of what it means to be a teacher. As Kristen, a future teacher, shares, "I have impressions in my mind of some of my favorite teachers. I want that same impression of myself in my students' minds." Obviously, favorite teachers can be significant in helping individuals decide to become teachers. Teachers may recognize a particular talent and encourage their students to pursue a teaching career. Our own school experiences also contribute to our perception of the teacher's role. Even negative experiences can result in a clearer conception of teaching: If we did not have good experiences in the classroom, then we may have a different view of how to handle students. For example, those who experienced a very structured school may have difficulty developing spontaneous instructional patterns and open classroom responses. Studies of teachers' biographies demonstrate that positive school environments encourage positive role identification with teachers as well as positive preservice teacher behaviors (Knowles, 1992).

Teachers at the university level also contribute to one's ideas about teaching. These contributions are most influential during the preservice stage of your career, as you begin to form your explicit views of teaching.

Early Teaching Experiences

Working with learners in informal and formal learning environments before deciding to become a teacher also provides motivation for becoming a teacher. Experiences in church school, baby-sitting, after-school tutoring, Boys and Girls Clubs, youth sports, art, theater, and summer programs are ways future teachers discover that they have a special talent or preference for interacting with children and adolescents.

Specific lessons are learned in these first encounters with teaching. Early teaching experiences provide frameworks for dealing with students, planning instruction, selecting strategies, and feeling comfortable in the classroom. Teachers' early experiences using small groups or discussion activities in church school might influence the use of some of the same techniques in their own classrooms. Tutoring experiences teach future teachers how to use one-on-one strategies effectively in classroom settings. Early experiences with teaching help individuals understand and use interpersonal skills needed in teacher–student interactions.

Preservice teachers can easily relate to practices in classrooms that are like their images of teachers' work. You may find that you reflect on your early experiences as you begin to learn to teach. When faced with difficult experiences or important classroom decisions, new teachers often revert to behaviors they learned during previous teaching experiences (Knowles, 1992). When your university professor talks about a certain strategy, such as cooperative grouping, it may remind you of times that you were involved in such a strategy. Early experiences are useful as a foundation for reflection, but it is important to do more than remember the experiences. You also should question why a teacher used the strategy, how students responded, and how you might change or adapt that strategy. Recognizing and analyzing memories of early teaching or learning opportunities can convert past experiences into a strong influence on your own teaching decisions.

Life-Changing Decisions

A recent trend is for individuals to enter the teaching profession after participating in another career or life endeavor—perhaps after retirement from business or military, involvement in volunteer activities, or caring for children or other family members. A sense of commitment to our nation's youth, a desire to match the schedule of one's school-age children, a response to teacher shortages in specific areas, or a need to improve economically are among the reasons why adults make the life-changing decision to become a teacher. Some professionals learn skills in other careers that lend themselves particularly well to teaching. A school librarian who has been around elementary and high school students will adapt quickly to a school environment. A military or business person who has been involved in human development activities will quickly relate to teaching and learning processes. Experiences offered in various career paths have the potential to offer creative and innovative approaches to the teaching profession after appropriate preparation.

University preparation is becoming more flexible to reflect the differing needs of individuals who are learning to teach. Several institutions offer teacher education programs designed to target the specific needs of experienced military professionals or Peace Corps volunteers pursuing teaching as a second career. Other teacher education programs are fast track, allowing college graduates in other fields to complete their certification quickly. Online teacher education programs are also increasingly popular. Creative programs preparing teachers for shortage areas (such as mathematics, science, and special education) are emerging in many university settings.

FIELD-BASED ACTIVITY

1.1

Develop an autobiographical timeline that traces who or what influenced your decision to become a teacher. Form small working groups made up of classmates and identify common themes and factors across the data. Identify categories by writing group responses on three-by-five-inch cards and organizing them according to similar features. After agreeing on common characteristics, label each group of cards and discuss them.

INTASC Principle 9*

Reasons for Becoming a Teacher

The most compelling reason given for becoming a teacher involves the interpersonal interactions with children and young people. Specifically, teachers mention that they like to work with children and youth, make a difference in students' lives, and see the look of joy when a learner finally "gets it" (Metropolitan Life Survey, 1995). These teachers view teaching as a special mission and consider teaching a valuable service and a way to make a lasting contribution to society. One teacher explained her career choice by saying, "I want to be a difference in somebody's life. I want to mean something . . . change something. I would choose teaching again in a minute if I had the chance. It's what I want to do."

Other reasons people mention when discussing their decision to teach include ease of entry, exit, and reentry into the profession; flexibility of time; and material benefits (Lortie, 1975; Metropolitan Life, 1995). The teaching career is accessible to individuals who start their careers in other fields and develop a second career. Parents enjoy the hours that parallel their children's hours, including the time off during holidays and in the summer. Satisfying salaries, job security, and benefits certainly attract individuals into teaching careers. Nevertheless, without fail, surveys continue to demonstrate that "love of teaching" is the primary reason that teachers state for continuing in their chosen profession (Metropolitan Life Survey, 1995).

---

*Each Field-Based Activity will refer to one or more standards published by the Interstate New Teacher Assessment and Support Consortium (INTASC), which establishes guidelines for preparation and certification of educators. Many teacher education programs use INTASC principles to guide their course development, field experiences, evaluation, rubrics, and portfolio assessments. These references may therefore help you understand why certain activities are suggested and assist you as you develop portfolio evidence or complete other self assessment processes. The complete list is available in Figure 3.1 (page 81).

FIELD-BASED ACTIVITY

1.2

Either form a panel of teachers and professors working in your schools or interview your mentor or supervising teacher and ask about early influences on their career decisions. Ask why they became teachers and remain in teaching. Work with your classmates to compile the responses. Using your notecards from Activity 1.1, compare the reasons given by these experienced teachers with the categories generated by you and your classmates. How do they compare? Prepare a chart, graph, or diagram that depicts differences between beginning and experienced teachers. Compare your chart with material from this chapter and see if your class has discovered findings similar to those of researchers in other settings.

INTASC Principle 9

Perhaps due to the influences of family discussed in the previous section, teaching often becomes a family tradition. One future teacher in five reports a mother or father who taught at one time or is still teaching. As one future teacher wrote, "I never had the opportunity to have my Dad as a teacher, but I have always heard wonderful things about him from his ex-students. . . . I guess you could say I am in the 'family business.'"

Despite the statistics, some parents may not support their children's decision to become teachers. Many beginning teachers report that family members tried to dissuade them from entering the teaching profession. Future teachers are often aware of the negative perceptions associated with a teaching career but are not daunted by them. One future teacher admitted, "When I made it to college—graduating at the top of my high school class—my whole family said I shouldn't go into teaching. 'You're too smart to teach,' they said. 'You need to be a doctor or lawyer and make some money.' I was the only one in my extended family to ever get a degree, so everyone was pushing me to do different things. I looked at business, but nothing excited me like teaching."

Characteristics of Good Teachers

Everyone has a vision of a good teacher or can tell a story of an exceptional teacher and the impact that teacher had on our lives. Even as early as first grade, children have opinions on what makes a good teacher and produce delightful ways of expressing those opinions. Even though definitions of a good teacher may vary depending on one's perspective, the responses in Figure 1.1 provide a composite profile of what is honored and regarded as good teaching.

We may be more sophisticated than these first-graders when we describe what makes a good teacher, but it is possible to recognize their views in the most academic presentation. Clearly, a good teacher has a long-term impact on student achievement and behaviors. In an often-quoted study completed in Tennessee, researchers (Sanders & Rivers, 1998) convincingly demonstrate that effective teachers produce high achievement for all students and for lowest-achieving students in particular. This research clearly demonstrates that the effect of good teachers is long lasting and can be felt up to two years after a student leaves their classrooms.

The characteristics of high-quality teachers have been debated and discussed for decades. Recent research attempting to identify these char-

---

FIGURE 1.1 **First-Graders Describe a Good Teacher**

The original spellings in these excerpts add to the charm of their descriptions.

A good teacher is nice, smart, and has good handwriting. And in order. And gets her stuff dun on time. —Zach, age 7

A good teacher is someone Who makes good disishons [decisions]. A good teacher is nice. —Manuel, age 8

A good teacher helps you lurn! —Elizabeth B., age 7

A good techer helps. A good techer has a plan. some techers giv you a good plan. A good good techer love all the cis [kids] in hr clas. A good techer givs you in st stuchins [instructions] all the time. a techer hast to have a room and qostivachin [positive action]. —Beth Ann, age 7

I think that the qualities of being a good teacher is the importance of the children learning. You really feel good when you are a teacher. The main thing is to help the kids learn. I think being a teacher is a good job. you should try! —Dustin, age 8

Teachers sould have a good atutood [attitude] and be a little pushy. The teachers jobs are teaching math and siens [science] and arithmatick, acsedera acsedera [et cetera, et cetera]. A teacher wants to be a teacher because they jost wont to be by kids! —Stacy, age 8

acteristics recognized that strong verbal and math skills, deep content knowledge, and teaching skill all contribute significantly to teaching effectiveness (Haycock, 1998). The document that sets forth the national standards for teaching lists the fundamental requirements for proficient teaching as a broad grounding in the liberal arts and sciences; knowledge of the subjects to be taught, of the skills to be developed, and of curriculum and materials; knowledge of methods for teaching and of learner development; skills in understanding the diverse needs of students; and ability to employ such knowledge in the interest of students (National Board for Professional Teaching Standards, 1997). The standards also describe five propositions necessary for good teaching. Let's look at each in detail.

You may learn more about the National Board for Professional Teaching Standards at this Web site:

http://www.nbpts.org/

URLs may change over time. For up-to-date links to relevant Web sites, visit our Companion Web site:

http://education.wadsworth.com/wiseman3e

Commitment to Students and Their Learning

Good teachers make the assumption that all students can learn and are willing to act on that belief. Good teachers internalize knowledge about student development and learning processes. The work of social and cognitive scientists that applies to teaching is integrated with teachers' personal theories of learning and development. Good teachers recognize, accept, and rejoice in their students' differences. They demonstrate the ability and willingness to adopt teaching methodologies that take differences into account. An acceptance of differences and an understanding of personal development and learning processes prod good teachers to provide opportunities for all students in their classrooms to receive attention. To do so, teachers repress biases about ability differences, handicaps, disabilities, social or cultural backgrounds, language, race, religion, or gender. A good teacher constantly struggles to meet the needs of all students in personal and social learning, academics, interpersonal skills, and character development.

Knowledge of Subjects and of How to Convey Content to Students

Good teachers are committed and enthused about the subject matter they present to their students. They have a general understanding of how the content is organized and can integrate and connect related content areas. Recent federal policy links high-quality teacher characteristics very closely

One of the most important attributes of good teachers is dedication and commitment to the students in their classrooms.

with content knowledge. Schools are mandated to assure parents that students are taught by teachers who are highly qualified and are knowledgeable in the subject area they teach. Teachers are required to possess degrees in the subject areas they teach and, in some situations, are required to take a test to demonstrate this content area knowledge. To meet these mandates, your teacher preparation program most likely requires evidence of a strong academic background and a testing process that assesses your content knowledge.

In addition to an understanding of the content, effective teachers also possess an understanding of the specialized knowledge of how to convey the subject to a student. In other words, it is not enough to know science; a teacher also must know how to present science content in an appropriate way to the learner. Use of materials and resources is considered part of knowing the pedagogical content. Good teachers possess large repertoires of curriculum resources, teachers' guides, videotapes, computer software, and music recordings that can be used to teach their content. Various resources are used to generate multiple paths to knowledge.

Shulman (1987) describes knowledge of content in three ways:

1. Subject matter knowledge. This is a deep understanding of the content—for example, what a science major would know about plant phyla.

2. Curriculum knowledge. This refers to a teacher's knowledge about what is to be taught, what materials are to be used in the classroom, and what students already know about the subject.

3. Pedagogical knowledge. This refers to how subject matter can be presented to students—the strategies used by the teacher.

Taken together, knowledge of these three types constitute pedagogical content knowledge.

The concept of pedagogical content knowledge is one of the most important ways to identify good teachers. Good teachers understand the content and also understand the best way to teach that content to whatever age students they teach. Pedagogical content knowledge, although most often discussed in relation to high school teachers, is equally important to elementary teachers.

Ability to Manage and Monitor Student Learning

Good teachers have appropriately high expectations for all their students and see their job as facilitating students' learning. They are able to use a wide range of methods to meet instructional goals and to help students learn based on student strengths and weaknesses. Teachers encourage student engagement by managing learning in varied arrangements, including small groups, large groups, individuals, and pairs. This often requires that teachers control and manage behavior of students while encouraging social interaction and engagement. As teachers manage and monitor their students' learning, they are regularly assessing students' progress toward the principal learning objectives.

Ability to Think about Teaching and Learn from Experiences

Thinking about teaching includes understanding the decisions and actions that occur in classroom settings. This kind of decision making is one factor that makes teaching so complex. Good teachers must make difficult decisions that test their judgment, often while engaging in ongoing instruction. Part of the decision-making skill comes from what they know about teaching through their own experiences, and part comes from the advice of others. In addition, teachers can draw on educational research and participate in teacher research to constantly improve their practice. Through the very act of teaching, teachers model what it is like to be an educated person and how one can practice lifelong learning.

Participation in Learning Communities

Even though much of their work is done in isolation with groups of young people, teachers are not solo performers. Good teachers contribute to school effectiveness by collaborating with their colleagues. They participate in the joint establishment of goals for learners, development of school curriculum, coordination of instruction, interpretation of state and local goals and objectives, and implementation of student services. Good teachers cooperate with their administrators, share their knowledge and skill with others, and participate in the ongoing development of strong school programs. In addition, teachers must work collaboratively with parents and take advantage of community resources.

Several ideas can be taken from this review of effective teaching. First, as in any complex endeavor, there are multiple ways to be good or excellent. Although it may not be easy to measure a good teacher, the processes that contribute to good teaching can be described. A review of these processes reveals the enormous responsibility of a good teacher. Often, these descriptions make teaching appear to be an almost impossible endeavor. Teaching will never be simple or easy, but skills acquired by beginning teachers can be refined through reflection on experience. Becoming a good teacher is a lifelong process.

The knowledge base about teaching and learning is growing steadily and provides an understanding about what it takes to be a good teacher.

FIELD-BASED ACTIVITY

1.3

Work with your classmates and develop a questionnaire or interview designed to use with Pre–K-12 students to discover what they think makes a good teacher. Individually, administer the questionnaire to one or more classes or use it to interview several students. Bring your findings to class. In pairs or small work groups, compare students' models of good teaching with this text's descriptions of good teaching. Label and describe the findings. Develop a representation (picture, narrative, music, poetry, collage, computer-assisted visuals, Internet collage) of a summary of the results of interviews about what it takes to be a good teacher and present it to your classmates.

INTASC Principle 9

All the definitions of good teaching include certain common elements, although they may organize or emphasize different aspects of the teaching process (see, for example, Borko & Putnam, 1996). A teacher is molded by both formal and informal experiences in and out of classrooms. Various individuals and experiences contribute to the dynamic socialization and learning of future teachers. However, learning to be a good teacher results from conscious reflection on biographical events, professional training, personal experiences, reading, and other contextual contributions.

Teaching as a Lifelong Learning Process

Good teachers are lifelong learners. A teacher's career is influenced by personal life experiences such as his or her personal environment, family situation, positive life incidents, crises, individual dispositions, interests, and life stages. Becoming a teacher requires several years of formal preparation, but the concentrated university training that prepares a person to be a teacher is not the end of understanding about the profession. Successes and failures in the classroom, the adult development that occurs naturally through life experiences, and the continued formal learning that the job offers all contribute to the professional development of teachers. School regulations, management styles of supervisors, public trust of schools, societal expectations, professional organizations, and unions add to teachers' career development (Fessler & Christensen, 1992). As a result of life experiences, maturation, and normal development, teachers will progress through several stages of teaching. The following section explores these stages in some detail; Figure 1.2 provides one example of phases typically experienced as a teacher matures.

The Preservice Years

Individuals who are involved in formal, intensive university preparation are said to be in the preservice phase of their careers. Initial preparation offered by universities includes courses and field experiences planned by professional teacher educators.

Preservice teachers typically need to be socialized into the profession, become comfortable with the methods and processes of teaching and learning, develop instructional and interpersonal strategies to cope with the complexities of teaching, learn to work collaboratively in a professional setting, and understand the purposes of schools and how they work. Nevertheless, not all of those in the preservice stage have exactly the same needs.

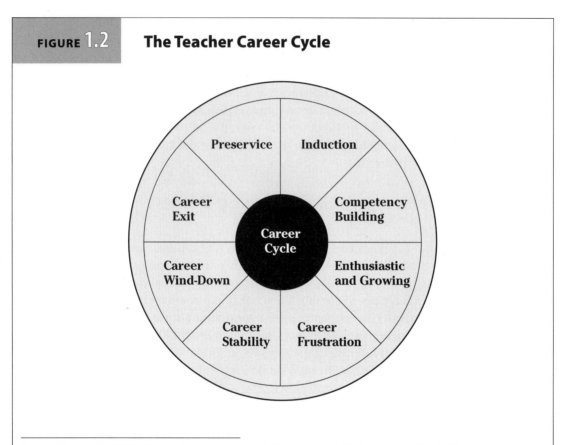

FIGURE 1.2 **The Teacher Career Cycle**

Preservice

Induction

Competency Building

Enthusiastic and Growing

Career Frustration

Career Stability

Career Wind-Down

Career Exit

Career Cycle

Source: Fessler, R. (1992). The teacher career cycle. In R. Fessler & J. C. Christensen (Eds.), *The teacher career cycle: Understanding and guiding the professional development of teachers* (pp. 21–43). Boston: Allyn & Bacon. Reprinted by permission of the author.

The period of life when you decide to enter the preservice stage of your career can make a great difference in how you learn and respond to university preparation. If you are a young adult, your family may provide financial support. Older students may have the responsibility of a family and their own expenses. Depending on your age, you may be planning a marriage, raising young children, or caring for aging parents. Some of you may be entering the profession after several years in another career. You may have experienced responsibilities in workplaces that may or may not have been related to education. You may want to teach because outside interests connected you with teaching. Working with scouts, clubs, or in childcare may have provided you with experiences that suggested teaching as a career.

Preservice experiences planned by universities often include several common elements, but they may differ in the way that courses and experiences are delivered. Traditionally, courses and experiences have been provided on university campuses. Increasingly, programs include courses and experiences that take place in school settings. Preservice experiences have the potential to greatly influence the way you think about teaching and about the skills and abilities you acquire at this stage of your career.

Societal attitudes, expectations, and needs also may affect your attitude toward teaching. For example, your experiences in dealing with students who are poor, suffer emotional trauma, or speak different languages may affect how you approach teaching. Take time now to complete the Self-Reflection exercise (on page 19) and to think about what you have learned.

Beyond the Preservice Years

Classroom experiences as well as additional learning opportunities and personal development activities may result in different ways of thinking about teaching. One way is to think about moving through distinct stages (Fessler & Christensen, 1992) as shown in Figure 1.2. As with any outline of human development, these stages are not exact but only a suggestion of what a person might expect during the progression of a career in teaching.

Induction

The induction stage occurs during the first few years of teaching and is the time when teachers are socialized into the profession. During this period, the new teacher works for acceptance and attempts to become comfortable with teaching on a day-to-day basis. This may be when the beginning teacher finds where he or she "fits." Teachers may move from building to building or grade to grade until they find a situation where they feel most comfortable. The stress of beginning a new profession may be compounded by other events in individuals' lives (Head, Reiman, & Thies-Sprinthall, 1992). New teachers are usually adjusting from viewing themselves as students to having a full-time job and getting to know a new community. They are dealing with issues related to personal relationships, finances, and activities outside of work. It is an exciting time for new professionals, albeit a busy and stressful one.

During this stage, many school districts provide support in the form of experienced mentor teachers to help induct new teachers into the profession. Mentors provide new teachers with a support system by acting as peer coaches, helping with planning, sharing ideas, introducing school routines, judging appropriateness of assignments, and explaining the context of specific teaching situations (Evertson & Smithey, 1999; Theis-Sprinthall, 1990).

Should I Be a Teacher?

Put T for true or F for false in the space provided as you think about each of these statements.

_____ **1.** When I think of people I admire the most, many of them are teachers.

_____ **2.** A teacher is born, not made.

_____ **3.** I am really proud of my decision to be a teacher.

_____ **4.** One of the advantages of teaching is that I would not have to work in the summer.

_____ **5.** As a child, I liked playing school.

_____ **6.** If I had to choose a summer job, I would rather work in a store or an office than with students.

_____ **7.** I would prefer to teach in a culturally diverse setting.

_____ **8.** Teaching is something I can do if other career choices do not work out.

_____ **9.** I want to teach, even though I was advised to do something more challenging.

_____ **10.** All that is needed to teach is knowledge of your subject area.

_____ **11.** Liking what I do is more important than making a lot of money.

_____ **12.** I enjoy learning about the subject that I plan to teach.

Scoring

Give yourself one point for each true answer on the odd-numbered items _____

Give yourself one point for each false answer on the even-numbered items _____

Tally the total number of points _____

Six or above. You seem to be comfortable with your decision to be a teacher; however, you may want to look at the items that received no points and reflect on how your response may affect your teaching commitment. For example, if you did not receive points for Items 1, 3, or 9, you may want to reflect on your attitudes toward the status of teaching compared with other professions.

Below six. You may want to investigate the teaching profession in greater depth and plan for ways that you can experience what it is like to be a teacher. Talk to teachers, become involved with children, and read books such as Esme Raji Codell's (1999) account of her first year of teaching.

Teacher education students learn a great deal from working with experienced teachers. Teacher preparation is greatly enhanced when future teachers participate in school activities, plan lessons, and interact with students under the supervision of an experienced teacher.

Mentors ease new teachers into the profession and increase the possibilities that they will stay in the teaching field for a longer period of time. This is an important role for an experienced teacher, because 40 to 50 percent of new teachers leave teaching after seven years or less (Huling-Austin, 1989). New teachers who receive appropriate mentoring during their first year or two in the profession continue to learn, grow, and develop more positive attitudes toward the profession (Head, Reiman, & Thies-Sprinthall, 1992).

Competency Building

The competency building stage is an exciting time when teachers are growing and becoming more secure in their teaching processes. During this time, teachers begin to feel comfortable with teaching and seek out new materials, methods, and strategies. Teachers may continue their professional development by attending workshops, conferences, and enrolling in graduate programs. This stage is characterized by a great deal of experimentation, innovation, and continued learning.

Enthusiasm

As teachers continue to work and gain experience, they begin to develop a high level of competency. The confidence resulting from positive experiences in a classroom leads to enthusiastic support of the teaching profession. Experienced, enthusiastic teachers look forward to each day of teaching, enjoy interacting with students, and search for new ways to teach and improve their practice. They often become important contributors to the learning of others—in their district and their school—by sharing what works for them and by designing innovations to be tried by others.

Frustration

As with most careers, almost all teachers suffer some level of frustration and disappointment. Although stress may be expected, various strategies can help teachers overcome burnout and view their work with renewed attention, enthusiasm, and excitement. Returning to school, changing schools, or working on an innovation can renew and encourage an experienced teacher who is feeling less than positive about the profession. Overall, today's teachers maintain a positive attitude toward the teaching profession. More than three-quarters of teachers surveyed agreed with the statement "I love to teach," and most would encourage a young person to pursue a career in teaching (Metropolitan Life Survey, 1995). Individuals who are just starting their teaching careers rate having a "satisfying job" their top reason for entering teaching.

Stability

Experienced teachers achieve confidence and pride in their teaching and enter into a period of stability marked by increased expertise, leadership development, and student success. By this time, teachers have identified those strategies that are comfortable for them, understand their students, and can manage behavior and classroom activities effectively. They continue to refine and perfect teaching strategies and may become "experts" in a particular strategy, approach, or philosophy. This period may be marked by continuing professional education, education and experiences that lead to administration, or involvement in curriculum development and other projects. It is generally during this stage that teachers feel that they can contribute to the development and design of programs and experiences for new teachers by serving as mentors and supervisors in preservice programs.

Winding Down

This stage may occur when teachers reach a certain age, develop other interests, or recognize that their life goals have made it necessary for them to move on to other jobs or situations. A spouse's retirement, a parent's illness, or another life event may cause an experienced teacher to consider retirement. Teachers who feel that it is nearly time for them to exit their careers may engage in reflection on different aspects of teaching. They begin to gather information to help them consider what their next career step will be. In the process, they may remember individual students and the stories that accompanied their classroom experiences. Some teachers look forward to a career change or retirement, consider it a natural event, and begin to make plans for the future, whereas others struggle with leaving the profession. Depending on the action planned by a teacher who has decided to exit the profession, this stage may take from several months to several years.

Career Exit

Teachers exit their careers with different plans and patterns. Some teachers leave teaching with the expectation that their absence will last only a few years while they are raising children, caring for parents, or exploring another career. Experienced teachers not ready for retirement may leave teaching to become principals or administrators. Teachers closer to retirement age may avoid full retirement and look for opportunities for part-time teaching and other ways to ease out of the profession they love. Other teachers may close the doors on the classrooms where they have spent many years and never return.

These career stages illustrate that teaching is dynamic and that anyone entering the profession can expect to go through periods when they experience different needs based on where they are in the career cycle. At this point, most of you are involved in the preservice stage of your career and learning about teaching is your primary focus.

The Formal Steps of Learning to Teach

Informally, your first exposure to teaching may be working with learners at church, in youth groups, during after-school tutoring, coaching, summer camps, baby-sitting, or other types of childcare that involve untrained individuals. One's first formal learning about teaching is usually embedded

FIELD-BASED ACTIVITY

1.4

Choose a book, movie, or television series that features a practicing classroom teacher (for example, *Mona Lisa Smile, Dead Poet's Society, The River Is Wide, Stand and Deliver, Mr. Holland's Opus, Ferris Bueller's Day Off, Boston Public*). Briefly describe the teacher portrayed. Can you place each teacher appearing in the book or movie in one of the career stages identified in this section? Do you see overlap across stages? Share your analysis with your classmates.

INTASC Principle 9

in the college experience upon entering a teacher preparation program during the last two years of undergraduate study or a year of intensive study after receiving a degree in a content field. Ideally, the teacher preparation program will extend prior experiences; provide new experiences related to teaching; and give you opportunities to test your teaching ability, receive feedback, and learn to be an effective teacher.

Teacher Education: The Theory

The preservice stage of teaching is guided by university curriculum. The goals of teacher preparation include the presentation of a connected and integrated professional program of (1) general and professional studies, (2) observations of practice, and (3) supervised teaching experience (Goodlad, 1990). Training is not a dramatic event in which a preservice teacher becomes as confident as an experienced teacher. Rather, it is the beginning of a process that will be ongoing for many years. Preservice professional educational experiences should help you make the transition from being a university student to becoming a teacher. One of the major changes that happen during this transition is that you will become socialized into the profession.

Socialization into the profession means that teachers learn what they should know and be able to do in their profession. Your own early experiences as a student offer many examples and impressions about schools, teaching, and education. An important part of the socialization of preservice teachers is the opportunity to learn about schools through a guided sequence of activities introducing the culture of teaching. Preservice programs offer a continuous framework for reflection and learning about teaching while experiencing the schooling process. Access to the instructional context of schools during this process is a key element. Formal preservice experiences should be carefully orchestrated between school and university. Ideally, the contexts where preservice teachers are socialized should be positive and represent the most current examples of teaching and learning. Occasionally, however, schools may offer preservice teachers a more negative aspect of school socialization. During your preservice experience, you may observe events and processes that are not the most beneficial for students and that do not fit within the theoretical frameworks discussed in your university classes. When you observe striking and contrasting events, your program should offer you the opportunity to talk with university professors and schoolteachers about what you are seeing.

A future teacher may take many courses in English and understand the content in that subject area very well, but knowing the content is not enough. Teacher education attempts to offer you a glimpse of some of the issues, questions, possible solutions, and strategies needed to move beyond content area proficiency. For example, teacher education helps future teachers learn about society at large—the social, political, and institutional connections that have an impact on schools. Future teachers can benefit from understanding the connections between the organizational frameworks of schools and the historical and cultural roots of those schools. Future teachers learn about families, communities, and societies other than their own and how diversity enriches our lives.

One of the striking features of teaching noted in earlier research on schools is the abruptness with which a person must take responsibility for a classroom (Lortie, 1975). Preservice teachers often move from positions of limited responsibility for students during their internship to sole responsibility during their first year of teaching with little attention paid to the demands of the transition. School–university programs in which experienced teachers work with university faculty to provide mentoring for new teachers provide a logical scaffolding for teacher preparation and provide needed support and structure. Practicing teachers are increasingly involved in the development and implementation of early field experiences offered to preservice teachers. In general, teacher education has changed significantly in the past twenty-five years—in practices and contexts as well as in definitions of what it means to be a teacher (Griffin, 2000).

Overall, university curriculum goals typically focus on providing opportunities necessary to move teachers into the induction or novice stage of their career. Many professional educators will take part in teacher preparation programs that prepare and induct teachers into the profession. This textbook and the course you are in right now will help you begin establishing the framework for continued learning during your preservice program. Teacher education programs that are jointly developed and delivered by

Becoming a teacher is a lifelong learning process. Professional development activities that present new ideas and help teachers learn new skills and abilities are important at all stages of career development.

classroom teachers and administrators and university teacher educators provide an ideal opportunity to link theory with practice.

Teacher Education: Linking Theory and Practice

One purpose of preservice education is to develop scaffolding between the content understanding of individuals and the study of pedagogy (Hilty, 1992). To develop stronger collaboration between the schools and universities, many teacher education programs have developed a partnership that provides high-quality preparation for new teachers. These partnerships vary widely in their approach and arrangement. No two partnerships are the same; each partnership has its own personality and character, reflecting the strength and uniqueness of the school's staff and the strengths and diversity of the university faculty. In field-based programs, at least a portion of your preservice coursework will be taught on the campus of a local school by a combination of school and university faculty. You will become familiar with the school and with students, teachers, and parents from a wide range of cultural backgrounds. To take full advantage of the field-based setting, some of your class assignments will focus on meeting with teams of teachers, participating in varied field experiences, collecting data from teachers and students, and becoming comfortable with and using technology in instruction.

School–University Collaboration

Although collaborative teacher education classes are not available at every university, most good programs contain elements of school–university partnerships. A collaborative teacher preparation program provides opportunities for university professors, public school teachers and administrators, university graduate and undergraduate students, public school students, and others to learn from each other.

The most complex collaboration between universities and schools has produced a concept called Professional Development Schools (PDS), wherein a formal written agreement sets forth the methods by which the university and the schools work together. Any number of activities may be included in the agreements, which tend to focus on (1) preparing new teachers, (2) improving preservice teacher preparation, (3) providing opportunities for experienced teachers to continue their learning, (4) changing the curriculum for young people so that they are able to achieve at the highest level possible, and (5) encouraging inquiry and research about teaching and learning. PDSs may provide new models of teacher education and development by serving as exemplars of practice, builders of knowledge, and vehicles for communicating professional understandings among teacher educators, future teachers, and veteran teachers (Byrd & McIntyre, 1999; Darling-Hammond, 1994; Holmes Group, 1990).

Partnerships between schools and universities in teacher education tend to provide opportunities for more exposure to schools for a longer period of time. Future teachers become immersed in PDSs and will often spend a full year in the schools. The preservice stage of a career may be completed entirely on a public school campus. By definition, preservice teachers will spend a substantial number of hours each week in the field. Public school teachers are usually involved in mentoring, teaching, or supervising a portion of the teacher preparation program.

Many who have experienced teacher education in PDSs find it difficult to think that teacher preparation would be done in any other manner. After a decade and a half, PDS are a fixture in many teacher education programs. Many PDSs have not been able to incorporate all of the characteristics traditionally associated with school–university partnerships (McIntire,

1995), but different models have emerged to meet the needs of schools and universities that establish the relationships. Other obstacles remain: Establishing partnerships is difficult because PDS involve combining the contrasting cultures of universities and public schools. These two settings often use different terms, rely on different funding sources, possess contrasting reward systems, and think about scheduling and workdays in very different ways (Knight, Wiseman, & Smith, 1992). Additionally, teachers and administrators worry that involvement in PDS activities (and resulting focus on training preservice teachers) may direct their attention away from students in their own classroom. Often, university faculty resist getting involved in partnership work because universities do not reward them for their efforts (Winitzky, Stoddart, & O'Keefe, 1992). Even so, most would agree that a close partnership between universities and schools is an effective way to prepare new teachers.

University and Public School Contributions

Almost all the teachers and university professors who work in school–university partnerships share the goal of effectively teaching young people in a school setting. They typically find common ground in their love of teaching and learning and concern for students and their learning. But aside from those commonalities, they bring different offerings to the preservice teachers, as follows:

University professors of education generally focus on research and theories about teaching and teacher preparation, learning theory, and content area learning. Although most of them were public school teachers at one time, they now focus on research and development of ideas associated with learning and teaching. Their schedules are flexible; they may write during the early morning hours, come into work late in the morning to advise and teach adult students and participate in university-based meetings, and teach graduate classes at night. University professors possess expertise in adult learning and spend a great deal of time writing, researching, and reading about education in general as well as about their specific areas of expertise. Areas of expertise may include diverse topics such as metacognitive strategies, mental imagery, children's literature, gender issues in education, social and cultural foundations of learning, and content area pedagogy. University professors are usually experts in a single area of educational expertise and receive promotion and tenure based on how they represent their knowledge in publications, presentations, and research activities. They also focus on the development of preservice and inservice teachers. They will use their knowledge of teacher education to contribute to the blend of activities planned by schools and universities. They may become involved in presenting readings, theories, and research findings connected to what is going on in the schools. Professors may work with teachers to develop research projects that address instructional issues in the classroom.

Teachers in schools focus on the young people in their classrooms. They possess expertise in such areas as child and adolescent development, classroom management, and motivational techniques related to teaching and learning. In addition, teachers typically have a wealth of practical knowledge about children and young people and the nature of teaching. They know what the state requires of teachers, techniques for organization, and management of classrooms. Their daily routine requires that they walk halls, bend over small desks, supervise lockers, stand on playgrounds, monitor busy hallways, and remain on their feet for long periods during a structured teaching schedule. They work from morning to midafternoon and have little time for any personal business during their workday. If and when they do research, it focuses on classroom issues related to children and young people. Teachers are rewarded by their students' achievement in the classroom, administrator and parental feedback, and other recognition programs in their district. Depending on whether they teach in elementary or secondary classrooms, they are usually experts in child or adolescent development as well as in specific content areas and possess a large repertoire of knowledge linking content areas with day-to-day happenings.

In the PDS context, university teacher educators and Pre K-12 teachers take on different roles and responsibilities related to teacher education, and both the schoolteacher and the university professor have valuable experiences and knowledge to share with beginning teachers, as follows:

Traditionally, university professors are responsible for planning the preservice teacher curriculum, participating in the delivery of the curriculum, and researching the results of what happens in preservice education. One of their major responsibilities is to increase the knowledge associated with teacher development and preparation and to integrate that new knowledge into the curriculum and experiences planned for preservice teachers. University professors are also expected to disseminate their findings to others in the field of teacher education.

Practicing teachers take on broad and varied roles in preparing future teachers. Experienced teachers serve as role models, provide mentorship, and share information and strategies. They offer suggestions to improve future teachers' teaching abilities and help evaluate the effectiveness of their lessons and teaching approaches. They help future teachers reflect

Voice of a Teacher

My work with the school–university partnership is a great deal of additional work added to my duties as a first-grade teacher. I am the person that university teacher educators contact at our school to talk about collaborative activities, field experience arrangements, and other connections that link the school and the university together. I occasionally teach a class on my own or with a university professor who is offering a class at my school. Sometimes my job requires me to do activities that seem to lack professionalism, like sitting on the floor, singing, coloring, and going out to recess. When I work with future teachers and university professors, I feel a great deal of respect for what I do, and I know I am making a difference. I enjoy sharing my teaching practices with future teachers, and they always give me new ideas and help me reflect on my own teaching.

on their teaching by offering alternatives, asking questions, or providing support or justification for teaching activities. Experienced teachers can be crucial to how future teachers learn and reflect as they plan, discuss, debate, and work together in the school setting.

Preservice teachers are heavily influenced by the teachers in the schools where they observe and where they complete their internships. When given a choice, preservice teachers admit to allegiance to their cooperating teachers and not their university connections (Hollingsworth, 1998). Preservice teachers are quickly caught up in the day-to-day activities of the schools and perceive that they need a great amount of knowledge about the practical aspects of teaching. Emotional and social bonds notwithstanding, school and university perspectives offer a preservice teacher a balanced view of education, and the roles of both are important to the beginning teacher.

Learning to Teach in a Field-Based Setting

The formal teacher education program will guide you as you enter the profession. You have different needs as a preservice teacher than you will have at any other phase of your career (see previous section on the career cycle).

Learning to be a teacher in a school–university setting will provide you with the opportunity to learn where theory and practice are connected in relevant and meaningful ways. This experience is one of many that will shape your beliefs, prepare you to interact with children and young people, and introduce you to instructional strategies.

Reflection in Teacher Education Programs

Preservice teacher activities should help future teachers build an image of good teaching. However, experience is only one component required. Analysis and discussion of ongoing events as well as readings and writings featuring alternate perspectives are necessary to enable future teachers to focus on a fuller range of instructional practices and promote effective learning from them. Reflective processing is therefore vitally important to the creation of good teachers.

Importance of Developing a Personal Philosophy

There is more to teaching than caring about students, knowing content, and implementing instructional procedures. The decisions you will make in your future classrooms will have an impact on your future students' lives and will contribute to reshaping schools, families, universities, and churches. Your actions and decisions are based on how you know and understand the world (Clark, 1995). Your own philosophy of life and way of thinking about education account for your unique teaching style, educational decision making, and interactions with learners. Your beginning experiences should help you understand your teaching philosophy and how your beliefs affect your teaching.

Developing a personal philosophy of education involves clarifying educational issues, justifying educational decisions, interpreting educational data, and integrating that understanding into the educational process (Meyers & Meyers, 1995). Although your personal philosophy will influence much of what you do, your expectations for children and adolescents' learning are an important component of your beliefs. The development of a personal philosophy requires self-examination and honest consideration of what we are about as teachers. Such development is a continual process that requires seeking answers to hard questions over a long period of time.

PORTFOLIO REFLECTIONS AND EXHIBITS

You will complete a series of Field-Based Activities in each chapter. The activities will serve as the basis for a portfolio representing what you've learned in each chapter. For each chapter, you may choose one of the Field-Based Activities suggested in the text or develop an alternate exhibit that represents what you have learned. Your responses to the activities (or your alternate exhibit) can become part of your teaching portfolio, or you may follow the alternate suggestion presented here.

Suggested Exhibit 1: Personal View of Teaching

A portfolio representation for this chapter might include these items:

1. A summary of all Field-Based Activities in this chapter including references to the text and other readings.

2. Identification of one Field-Based Activity in this chapter that is most important to you.

3. A representation of your own decision to become a teacher. Consider the impact of your own biography on your choice to become a teacher. Use the different influences described in this chapter to guide the development of an autobiography of your career choice. Illustrate your childhood experiences, teacher and family influences, and teaching experiences that contributed to your decision to become a teacher. You can develop a portfolio representation of your biography in many ways. A narrative, poetry, music, artwork, or collage can represent your decision to become a teacher.

E-Portfolio Entry 1

Think about an introduction to your e-portfolio. Perhaps you will want to develop a representation of your own decision to become a teacher. Work through the tutorial (http://soe.cahs.colostate.edu/cttec/PDF/Powerpoint/e-portfolio.pdf) on creating PowerPoint slides to create a multimedia, interactive e-portfolio. Create a six-slide presentation that demonstrates your journey to becoming a teacher.

INTASC Principles 9 and 10

ANSWERS TO GUIDING YOUR READING

1. Why do I want to be a teacher?

The reasons for becoming a teacher are many. Family histories of teaching and early experiences working with children lead many to the teaching profession. People may become teachers because they want to make a difference in the lives of children, adolescents, and young people or because of the ease with which one can enter and exit teaching as a first or second career. Parents may teach because schedules and holidays work well with raising families. Even though a multitude of reasons contribute to why teachers teach, the most compelling reason recalls the positive feelings that teachers receive from making a difference in their students' lives.

2. What experiences have shaped my ideas about teaching?

We begin forming ideas about teaching from childhood experiences, interactions with role models, and teaching experiences outside the classroom. Those who enter teaching as a second career may bring ideas about teaching from former occupations or experiences working with people in noneducational contexts. Initial ideas about teaching are expanded as we complete a teacher preparation program that provides opportunities to read, learn, and reflect on our own teaching experiences.

3. What is a good teacher?

Good teachers are first and foremost committed to students and their learning. They are well educated, possess knowledge of the subjects they teach, and know best how to teach content to their students. Good teachers develop the ability to manage and monitor student learning, think and reflect on their teaching experiences, and constantly learn from their classroom experiences. Finally, a good teacher understands how to work with others—students, other teachers, administrators, families, and communities—to develop a learning community where their students can learn effectively.

4. How do teachers learn how to teach?

Learning to teach is a lifelong activity. A university teacher preparation program designed to induct an individual into the profession is where most start the process of learning to teach. Almost all teachers enter the profession by experiencing a combination of university coursework and field-based experiences. Teacher education programs help future teachers scaffold content understanding and knowledge about how to teach. University programs have a strong connection to the elementary, middle, and secondary schools and involve future teachers in classroom activities where they work with and observe experienced teachers. However, no preparation program is complete without opportunities to reflect, analyze, discuss, and learn from the many events associated with learning to teach.

INFOTRAC COLLEGE EDITION EXTENSION

InfoTrac College Edition provides online access to hundreds of scholarly and popular periodicals to extend the depth and breadth of your knowledge and to facilitate individual and group projects. To use the feature, log on to the InfoTrac College Edition Web site and type in the password provided on the card that accompanies your text. Familiarize yourself with the search procedures by viewing the introduction and the major search categories described in the Help feature. When you feel comfortable with the system, access these topics through the suggested search modes below:

1. Using a subject search, type in one or more of the following topics:

   reflective practice

   teacher effectiveness

2. Using a keyword search, type in the following topics:

   national teaching standard!

   professional development school!

   good teacher!

   (The wildcard [!] enables you to find titles that contain either the singular or plural form.)

3. Using the PowerTrac search, find a recent journal article that the authors of this text published about Professional Development Schools.

RELATED READINGS

The following books provide more information about some of the topics and ideas presented in this chapter:

Bullough, R. V., & Baughman, K. (1997). *"First-year teacher" eight years later: An inquiry into teacher development.* New York: Teachers College Press.

In their description of Kerri Baughman's struggles and successes in learning to teach, the authors show the evolution of her beliefs and the importance of professionalism. This book illustrates the ten-year development of an experienced teacher and the role of teacher learning in the process.

Clark, C. M. (1995). *Thoughtful teaching.* New York: Teachers College Press.

Dr. Clark believes that what teachers think, believe, and do (inside and outside the classroom) will ultimately affect their students' learning. Teachers' personal and professional development, career paths, relations with colleagues, working conditions, rewards, and interaction with the leadership in their schools all affect the quality of instruction they deliver. He describes teaching as syntheses of reason and emotion, of feeling and thinking.

Codell, E. R. (1999). *Educating Esme.* Chapel Hill, NC: Algonquin.

This first-year teacher's diary is an often brutally honest description of the leadership, politics, tears, and joy experienced in a fifth-grade classroom in the Chicago projects. At times, Esme is unconventional in her approach to teaching, but she cares deeply about her students. Ms. Codell gained media attention as a result of this book's publication.

REFERENCES

Epigraph: Gordon, Stephen (2003). In Sophia Nieto (Ed.), *What keeps teachers going?* (p. 30). New York: Teachers College Press.

Borko, H., & Putnam, R. (1996). Learning to teach. In D. Berliner & R. Calfee (Eds.), *Handbook of educational psychology* (pp. 673–708). New York: Macmillan.

Byrd, D., & McIntyre, D. (1999). Research on professional development schools. *Teacher Education Yearbook VII.* Thousand Oaks, CA: Corwin.

Calderhead, J. (1996). Teachers' beliefs and knowledge. In D. Berliner & R. Calfee (Eds.), *Handbook of educational psychology* (pp. 709–725). New York: Macmillan.

Christensen, J. C., & Fessler, R. (1992). Teacher development as a career-long process. In R. Fessler & Clark, C. (1995). *Thoughtful teaching.* New York: Teachers College Press.

Codell, E. R. (1999). *Educating Esme.* Chapel Hill, NC: Algonquin.

Crow, N. A. (1987). Preservice teachers' biography: A case study. Paper presented at the annual meeting of the American Educational Research Association, Washington, DC.

Darling-Hammond, L. (1994). *Professional development schools: Schools for developing a profession.* New York: Teachers College Press.

Evertson, C., & Smithey, M. (1999). Supporting novice teachers: Negotiating successful mentoring relationships. In R. Stevens (Ed.), *Teaching in American schools* (pp. 17–40). Upper Saddle River, NJ: Merrill.

Fessler, R., & Christensen, J. C. (1992). Summary and synthesis of career cycle model. In R. Fessler & J. C. Christensen (Eds.), *The teacher career cycle: Understanding and guiding the professional development of teachers* (pp. 249–268). Boston: Allyn & Bacon.

Goodlad, J. I. (1990). *Teachers for our nation's schools.* San Francisco: Jossey-Bass.

Griffin, G. (2000). Changes in teacher education: Looking to the future. In G. Griffin (Ed.), *The education of teachers* (pp. 1–28). Chicago: National Society for the Study of Education.

Haycock, K. (1998). Good teaching matters: How well-qualified teachers can close the gap. *Thinking K-16, A Publication of The Education Trust,* 3(2), 1–14.

Head, F. A., Reiman, A. J., & Thies-Sprinthall, L. (1992). The reality of mentoring: Complexity in its process and function. In T. M. Bey & C. T. Holmes (Eds.), *Mentoring: Contemporary principles and issues* (pp. 5–21). Reston, VA: Association of Teacher Educators.

Hilty, E. B. (1992). Teacher education: What is good teaching and how do we teach people to be good teachers? In J. L. Kincheloe & S. R. Steinberg (Eds.), *Thirteen questions: Reframing education's conversation.* New York: Peter Lang.

Hollingsworth, S. (1998). Making field-based programs work: A three-level approach to reading education. *Journal of Teacher Education,* 39(4), 28–36.

Holmes Group. (1990). *Tomorrow's schools of education.* East Lansing, MI: Author.

Huling-Austin, L. L. (1989). Beginning teacher assistance programs: An overview. In L. Huling-Austin, S. J. Odell, P. Isshler, R. S. Kay, & R. A. Edelfelt (Eds.), *Assisting the beginning teacher* (pp. 3–18). Reston, VA: Association of Teacher Educators.

Johnston, S. (1994). Experience is the best teacher: Or is it? An analysis of the role of experience in learning to teach. *Journal of Teacher Education,* 45(3), 199–208.

Knight, S. K., Wiseman, D. L., & Smith, C. W. (1992). School-university partnerships: The reflectivity-activity dilemma. *Journal of Teacher Education,* 43(3), 269–277.

Knowles, J. G. (1992). Models for understanding, preservice and beginning teachers' biographies. In I. F. Goodson (Ed.), *Studying teachers' lives* (pp. 99–152). New York: Teachers College Press.

Lortie, D. C. (1975). *School teacher: A sociological study.* Chicago: University of Chicago Press.

McIntire, R. G. (1995). Characteristics of effective professional development schools. *Teacher Education and Practice,* 11(2), 36–49.

Metropolitan Life. (1995). *The Metropolitan Life survey of the American teacher, 1984–1995: Old problems, new challenges.* New York: Louis Harris and Associates, Inc.

Meyers, C. B., & Meyers, L. K. (1995). *The professional educator: A new introduction to teaching and schools.* Belmont, CA: Wadsworth.

National Board for Professional Teaching Standards. (1997). *What teachers should know and be able to do.* Detroit: Author.

Sanders, W., & Rivers, J. C. (1998). Cumulative and Residual Effects of Teachers on Future Students' Academic Achievement. Knoxville, TN: Value-Added Research and Assessment Center, University of Tennessee.

Shulman, L. S. (1987). Knowledge and teaching: Foundations of the new reform. *Harvard Educational Review,* 57(1), 1–22.

Theis-Sprinthall, L. (1990). *Becoming a teacher educator: A curriculum guide.* Raleigh, NC: Department of Curriculum and Instruction, NCSU.

Winitzky, N., Stoddart, T., & O'Keefe, P. (1992). Great expectations: Emergent professional development schools. *Journal of Teacher Education,* 43(1), 3–18.

2

Educational History and Philosophy

People are asking what is the criterion of a teacher. The first requisite and the last criterion of a teacher is to be a true follower of the Great Teacher, not so much in professing as in living . . . it means a right attitude toward the profession, toward each subject taught, toward the home, the community and the child. It means to possess knowledge and the ability to interpret it to right uses so that it becomes a power for good in the life of a child.

To be a teacher, many methods of approach are necessary in reaching the minds and hearts of growing boys and girls: these at the levels of the child's abilities to pursue and achieve. And when such happy team work is obtained the teacher continues to walk beside the developing mind and soul; pressing a little here, guiding, directing thoughtfully, prayerful, ever keeping the goal of a perfected character as the objective sought. . . .

Someone had said to be educated meant to bring forth and train up all the faculties and powers of the mind and body to their highest possible use. To accomplish this makes it mandatory to live in such manner of thought and activity as will make the whole world better for our having lived in it.

—Sarah Gillespie Huftalen (writing in 1865), "To Be a Teacher"

Guiding Your Reading

1. How have past education events influenced current trends?

2. How have modern reform efforts affected traditional schooling?

3. What roles have minorities played in educational history?

4. What philosophical roots can be linked to contemporary education?

*W*hen you are studying to be a teacher, you tend to want to focus on the here and now, learning how to deal with the students in the classrooms where you are learning to teach. It may seem difficult to take time out and reflect on the past, but there are reasons for you to do just that. The foundations of teaching—philosophy and history—are with you in each classroom you enter. Little about teaching, learning, and children was discovered just yesterday. History can illuminate contemporary issues and provide insights into common problems. An understanding of the history of education and how it connects with the present can help us interpret the present and perhaps help us avoid repetition of past mistakes. Cicero (106–43 B.C.) declared that "persons who are ignorant of history will remain forever children" (Power, 1991, p. ix), and educated future teachers have the responsibility to understand what their contribution will be to the continuum of education.

Knowledge of educational history places current educational issues in context, and philosophy provides a tool for educational decision making. Philosophical beliefs affect how teachers make decisions, interact with children, and approach their careers. Traditionally, well-developed philosophies of education include statements about what education should and should not do: in other words, what the goals, content, and methods should or should not be. Analysis of the aims of education and the dispositions to be fostered in students, determination of the rationale for the dispositions, recommendations about the means of fostering the dispositions, and discussions of the line of argument used to support use of particular means provide a basis for discussing different philosophies (Frankena, 1974). In

FIELD-BASED ACTIVITY

2.1

Before you read the chapter, write down your answers to these questions, which will help you build a personal philosophy of education.

1. What should the purpose of education be in the United States? In your classroom?

2. What do you want your future students to be able to do or be as a result of their experiences in your class? Why?

3. What kinds of teaching approaches and strategies will most likely help your students meet these goals?

Share your ideas with another preservice student. How do your philosophies differ? How are they similar?

INTASC Principle 9

addition, these elements suggest guidelines for development of more personal definitions of the means and ends of education. As you develop your own philosophy of teaching, you may want to compare your beliefs about what education should or should not do with those of philosophers (past and present).

A Brief History of American Schools

European Precursors

CALVIN AND LUTHER Events in Europe had a major impact on early American education. John Calvin (1509–1564) and Martin Luther (1483–1546) were active reformers who believed schools should serve many purposes, including teaching as many people as possible to read so that they could read and interpret the Bible. John Calvin's educational approach established mandatory and strict obedience to the church and a belief in God. He stressed civic training and rigorous discipline for all classes of the population. Luther articulated a plan to educate children of all classes in Germany. As part of the plan, he turned authority for education over to the city mayors and aldermen. His theory connected the religious and civic purposes of education and, in its modern form, still fuels educational debate. The greatest legacy of this time was the concept of education for everyone, which became an important component of the American education system.

LOCKE AND ROUSSEAU During the Age of Enlightenment (1700–1800), European philosophers emphasized the power of the human mind. Philosophers such as John Locke and Jean-Jacques Rousseau believed the way to a better life was through an educated mind, but they differed greatly in their approaches. John Locke (1652–1704) challenged both theological and humanistic conceptions of human nature and focused on the importance of learners' experiences (Power, 1991). Locke believed children began as a blank slate, a *tabula rasa* (Smith, 1979). Children subsequently experienced events, developed simple ideas, and eventually replaced initial thoughts with more complex ideas based on experiences. The purpose of education, Locke thought, was to help children to experience a healthy, virtuous, and successful life.

Rousseau (1712–1778) believed education should conform to a child's individual needs and that young children learn by acting on natural impulses. "Society," he declared, "should reject any commission to teach persons or direct their scholastic course. Its role should be passive; nothing more than an environment wherein the natural impulses of autonomous persons can find full satisfaction" (Power, 1991, p. 202). He believed all children were good and needed to be allowed to grow naturally. Although Locke and Rousseau held very different views of the role of education, they are considered the fathers of modern child psychology, and their theories are the basis for much of modern-day child development. Their ideas spread to the Colonies before the end of the eighteenth century and formed the basis of schooling, but it was not long before the new country produced thoughtful educators and uniquely American educational processes.

Colonial Schools of the Early 1600s

From the earliest European settlement in North America during the first half of the 1600s, schools played an important role in establishing the new society. Occupying a savage new world and working long hours on their new homesteads, busy pioneer parents looked to schools as a way to transmit civilized behavior to their children (Perkinson, 1991). Settlers faced ambiguities related to learning and teaching. On one hand, they wished to protect the new culture they were developing; on the other hand, they were anxious to promote the intellectual, moral, and religious values they had inherited (Power, 1991).

The earliest colonial schools were established to provide young people with the opportunity to study religion. Gradually, religious education began to give way to the idea that the purpose of education was to provide knowledge that would help future citizens uphold democracy. At varying times in different states, laws were passed requiring that everyone become literate and that communities be responsible for establishing schools.

As early as 1642, Massachusetts had a compulsory education law that held parents responsible for the education of their male children (Perkinson, 1991). Other colonies replicated the Massachusetts law. Even colonies that had no laws requiring schooling established schools and put schoolmasters in place to educate their male children. The first laws passed in Massachusetts supporting compulsory education mandated that all boys be instructed in reading, although it did not matter if that occurred at home, in school, or elsewhere. The Old Deluder Satan Act of 1647 required towns of fifty households or more to hire a schoolmaster capable of teaching reading and writing. Common elementary schools were established in Massachusetts to provide basic education in reading, writing, and math. Boys usually attended the one-room schools from about ages five through fourteen.

Attitudes of elitism about who should be educated were transported with the colonists' European roots. During the early days of the Colonies, education was based on the social class system (Timm, 1996). Those who were poor could not afford for their children to attend schools, and at first there was almost no educational opportunity offered poor children, children of slaves, or young girls. Slowly, educational opportunities became available to more and more children, as young women and a few boys attended the dame schools taught by women and held in private homes. Although these schools were not highly regarded, they became the main educational system for girls during the 1700s. The mostly female students would study reading, writing, religion, and the rudiments of arithmetic while their teachers, who were also homemakers, worked in the kitchen and around the house.

Boys from higher socioeconomic status levels would continue in Latin grammar schools and learn under the classical system as they prepared for religious or civic careers. Such schools were first established in colonial America during the seventeenth century and were taught by ministers who relied on strict discipline and rote memorization to teach logic, rhetoric, and Latin. The Latin grammar schools were essentially the first secondary schools, whose course of study prepared colonial boys for colleges—usually Harvard or Yale. Only a small percentage of children attended these grammar schools, and, of course, there was no need for girls to attend them, because colleges of that time did not admit women.

Contributions of Jefferson and Franklin

As the post-Revolutionary government was established in the late 1700s to rule the new society, educating all its citizens became more and more important. The ideas of Locke and Rousseau and the attitudes of the new country helped Thomas Jefferson (1743–1826) and Benjamin Franklin (1706–1790) frame the views of American education to focus on freedom of expression and universal public education.

Franklin was a Puritan who did not receive formal schooling but underwent an apprenticeship. His first writings, *Poor Richard's Almanac,* became popular reading in America in the early 1800s. In addition to being an author, Franklin was a scientist, inventor, philosopher, and educator. Franklin accepted Locke's philosophy of education but extended educational ideas to include all classes and those who had not been involved in the system thus far. As early as the 1760s, Franklin wrote that African Americans were equal to whites and appealed for better treatment of Native Americans.

Franklin supported the study of basic skills, religion, the development of high moral character, logical reasoning, integrity, self-discipline, and some study of classics (Smith, 1979). In *Proposals Relating to the Youth of Pennsylvania,* an essay outlining the academy he had established, he called for a "well-stocked library (complete with maps, scientific instruments, and diagrams); a frugal diet and regular physical exercise for the scholars; training in such practical skills as penmanship, drawing, accounting, and gardening; and courses in arithmetic, geometry, astronomy, English grammar, and modern foreign languages" (McMannon, 1995, p. 17). Franklin's Puritan background influenced his ideas about school, and he wrote that spending too much time with the classics was wasteful and that the core of educational studies should be derived from what is useful and should meet the practical needs of the local communities. He viewed schools as a way to prepare young Americans for business or professions. One of Franklin's major contributions was his attempt to establish a permanent school, an academy, that would reflect stability (Perkinson, 1991). Imagine his disappointment when his academy eventually became a Latin grammar school, embodying many of the aristocratic and wasteful studies he abhorred.

Thomas Jefferson attended formal schooling (in contrast to Franklin) and demonstrated great personal abilities in languages and literature. He was also highly talented in music and the arts and was an inventor, farmer, scientist, and architect. He was a student of Locke and Rousseau and believed there should be a government-sponsored educational system so that all citizens could have equal educational opportunities (Smith, 1979). He founded the University of Virginia based on this belief and worked to propose a system of schooling that would provide the most basic schooling to all children in the state. His plan, which was presented to his state legislature but was not successful, provided for three years of elementary school. He envisioned an educational system designed to preserve the democracy by producing well-educated, capable leaders and citizens. Schools were to create a populace that would advance the common interest and protect the young democracy from tyranny or dictatorship (McMannon, 1995).

The 1800s

In the beginning of the 1800s, schools refined the force that shaped U.S. society, and connections between education and government became more explicit (Perkinson, 1991). Americans began to argue for an educational system that was common across the states, standardized in content and duration, and offered to all children equally. By 1860 almost all states had some form of public school system, and some of the ideas that we see in our schools today began to evolve.

Many of our ideas about how children learn were influenced by the ideas of European educators. The famous Swiss educator Johann H. Pestalozzi (1746–1827) felt that men were neither good nor evil but shaped by their experiences (Button & Provenzo, 1989). Like Rousseau, he argued for child guidance based on caring, nurturing, and providing children opportunities to be actively involved in learning, as opposed to learning by rote memorization. Pestalozzi honored the role of mothers and believed affection was the basis of obedience. In his philosophy, a good teacher was like a good mother. He believed women were well suited for teaching, especially because of their nurturing, caring attitudes and natural affinity for teaching, especially for young children (McMannon, 1995).

By the early 1800s, our educational system had acquired many characteristics that are still in place. Horace Mann, crusading for common, or public, schools, proposed a state board to exercise control over public schools and insisted that the purpose of schooling was to educate the citizenry, not to focus on religion. He supported a practical curriculum aimed at developing moral character and effective citizenship. He was one of the first American educators to suggest that teachers should possess specific qualifications. One of Mann's lasting contributions to the U.S. educational system was to transfer Prussia's graded school levels to the United States. Classification of students was seen as advantageous over the one-room schoolhouses because it provided the teacher with the opportunity to address lessons to appropriate levels for students.

In the decades before the Civil War, educational efforts were almost all focused on elementary schooling. Schools provided free and universal elementary education to all children, including those who were poor, with the hopes that education would improve their lives. In 1820, because of a commonly held belief that democracy could not be totally run by those educated in common elementary schools, secondary schools began to emerge. Secondary school studies were more comprehensive than those offered by the early Latin schools, which concentrated on classical education. History, bookkeeping, geometry, surveying, and algebra curricula began to evolve from the first secondary schools. During the last half of the century, the clamor for a more practical curriculum led to manual training courses in existing secondary schools and new manual training high schools. Training students for specific skills such as farming or wood- or ironworking was perceived as too narrow and intellectually limiting. Instead, manual training focused on the practical training of the eye and the hand and on such skills as perception, observation, practical judgment, visual accuracy, manual dexterity. Manual training schools were the precursors of modern vocational schools.

Given the rapid expansion and experimentation with curricula, high schools were very different from each other. Educators were split on questions defining the purpose of secondary schools. Should they offer curricula to prepare students for college or to train youth for jobs? In the wake of this controversy, in 1892 the National Education Association appointed a task force known as the Committee of Ten to study secondary school curriculum and make recommendations. The committee, made up of scholars and chaired by the president of Harvard, called for efforts to ensure that all students take a similar core of academic courses. The high school curriculum they suggested was designed for the exclusive purpose of preparing students for college-level work. As such, it was one of the first "back-to-basics" movements in education (Angus & Mirel, 1995). Their suggested curriculum was challenged by people who argued that high school should prepare students to enter the workforce. As a result of the debate, a report was issued in 1911 calling for high schools to produce individuals who were committed to basic American values and capable of making contributions to the country.

In the first three decades of the 1800s, a great deal of attention was given to common schools and secondary schools, but colleges began to gain attention. In particular, the evolution of state colleges was strong during the second half of the 1800s. Colleges began to add professional, technical, and scientific curricula to their traditional focus on religion and social graces. By the mid-1880s, an entirely new component of learning emerged with the establishment of agricultural, industrial, mining, and engineering units. Women gained access to private universities, and coeducation soon became accepted in state-supported colleges and universities. By the beginning of the 1900s, nearly one-fourth of the students in college were

TEACHER'S CONTRACT.

It is Hereby Agreed, By and between School District No. *77*.....Township No.*13*......,Range No. *5*.....
County of. *Lincoln*.........., Territory of Oklahoma, and.. *Ephraim Wall*..............
the holder of a Territorial and County Certificate, this day in force, that said teacher is to teach, govern and conduct
the public schools of said district to the best of h*is*.......ability, follow the course of study adopted by the District
Board, keep a register of the daily attendance and studies of each pupil belonging to the school, make all reports
required by law, and such other reports as may be desired by the County Superintendent of Public Instruction, and
endeavor to preserve in good condition and order the school house, grounds, furniture, apparatus, and such other district property as may come under the immediate supervision of said teacher, for a term of......*3*..........school
months, commencing on the...*8*..............day of.....*November*..................., A. D. 189*7*..
for the sum of.. *Twenty-seven*.........Dollars per school month, to be paid at the end of each month;
PROVIDED, That in case said teacher shall be legally dismissed from school, or shall have h*is*......certificate legally
annulled, by expiration or otherwise, then said teacher shall not be entitled to compensation from and after such dismissal or annullment: PROVIDED, FURTHER, That the wages of said teacher for the last month of the school term shall
not be paid unless said teacher shall have made the reports hereinbefore mentioned.

And the said school district hereby agrees to keep the school house in good repair, to provide the necessary fuel,
school register, and such other supplies as may be necessary.

IN WITNESS WHEREOF, We have hereunto subscribed our names, this. *13*...day of.*September*....
A. D. 189*7*..

.................*W. C. Yoder*...Director or Treasurer.

.................*Ephraim Wall*....Teacher.

ATTEST: *Henry Bergdorf*....Clerk or ~~Treasurer.~~

REMARKS:---This Contract shall be made out in duplicate, and one copy given to the teacher, and the other placed on file in the District Clerk's office. The
law does not authorize the Board of Directors to make a contract with a teacher, or to pay his salary, for any time during which his certificate is not in force.

© Donna Wiseman

Teaching has changed a great deal since the late 1890s. Teachers may
have attended only eight years of grammar school, and the responsibilities outlined in this contract (signed by one author's grandfather) were
quite different from those of today's teachers.

women (Power, 1991). Even so, women were not encouraged to attend college and, when they did enroll, they were offered different experiences and
less academic content than what was offered to their male counterparts.

The U.S. school systems grew rapidly during the 1880s, and theories of
teaching and learning began to proliferate. Nevertheless, education was
still not equally available to all citizens.

MINORITIES In the early 1800s, education was not an expectation for
minorities. Even though there was some movement to include African
American students in formal educational experiences, children of slaves
did not have equal access to education. During the 1700s and until after
the Civil War, African Americans were treated as property, and their educa-

tion was limited to technical skills needed for their contribution to the economy of their owners (Timm, 1996). Some owners did provide opportunities for African Americans to learn to read the Bible, but this did not continue after the American Revolution. The Puritans allowed a few of their slaves to be tutored, but for the most part African Americans were left out of early Colonial educational endeavors. In Boston during the early 1800s, African American parents began to establish separate school systems for their children and requested integrated educational systems. Abolitionists were in favor of education for African Americans, and a school opened to educate black Americans in Philadelphia in 1820. Education for slaves was still opposed in the South.

Some African Americans, albeit very limited numbers, had access to higher education during the 1880s. Oberlin College was one of the first universities to admit both black and white students (Timm, 1996). Soon, African American educators began taking leadership roles in the educational process. Booker T. Washington, who was born into slavery, was educated at Hampton Institute, and he founded Tuskegee Institute, a showplace that provided vocational training for blacks. He viewed Tuskegee as a way for blacks to win acceptance in the white world. His philosophy was to

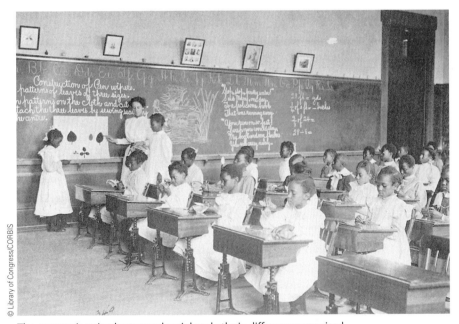

The country's attitudes toward racial and ethnic differences required many cultural and ethnic groups to establish their own schools. School segregation continued until after the civil rights movements of the 1950s and 1960s.

encourage educated blacks to do good work and win the approval of the white world by helping others.

A very different approach was taken by the educator W. E. B. Du Bois, who sought a liberal education for African Americans. He was born a free man and, after becoming the first African American Ph.D. in the United States, taught at Wilberforce College and Atlanta University before he took over the leadership of the newly formed National Association for the Advancement of Colored People (NAACP). His approach was much more aggressive than Washington's, and he advocated equal rights for African Americans in the United States. Du Bois viewed himself as an activist who fought for the rights of black Americans (Perkinson, 1991).

As late as 1860, Asian Americans were also prohibited from attending public school. As did African Americans, Asian Americans began to establish segregated schools for their children. The first schools that taught in Chinese were in San Francisco in the 1870s. Even after a law was enacted to end Chinese immigration, the education of Chinese children continued. The Japanese did not begin to immigrate until the second half of the century, and their schools were established mainly in Honolulu. These Asian Americans established the importance of education for the more recent immigrants from Vietnam, Laos, Cambodia, and Thailand.

Native Americans were not always treated fairly in the emerging educational system. Groups of people who were not Native American were intent on controlling the process for Native American children, and these groups ignored family and tribal cultures. As early as 1720, President Monroe provided money to Protestant missionaries so they could establish elementary and secondary tribal schools where Native Americans could receive a Christian education. The schools offered lessons and curriculum that attempted to teach Native Americans to be subservient, to abandon their tribal ways, and to adopt the white culture. Native Americans recognized that the white culture's education would cause them to surrender their own culture and lifestyle. For the most part, Native Americans ignored these attempts to educate them in the way of the Christian Americans and conveyed the message that their own learnings and way of doing things met their needs (Button & Provenzo, 1989). Nevertheless, Native American children were greatly affected by the white man's culture.

Tribal schools for Native Americans were closed during the Civil War and replaced with boarding schools, which removed children from their homes and families and did not provide parents input in the educational process of their children. Some schools offered narrowly defined content focusing only on training Native Americans for manual labor associated with the agricultural economy. Students educated in boarding schools were often lonely and missed their families, who resented the fact that their children were forced to leave home to receive an education.

Notable exceptions were some schools that were created at the request of the tribes and monitored by the tribal leaders. In the mid-1800s, the Choctaw and Cherokee Nations in the Oklahoma territory established an intensive education program relying on boarding schools built and maintained with tribal initiative and funding. Tribal leaders worked intimately with the heads of the schools to ensure the children were taken care of and taught useful skills as well as American history and English. Children were expected to study hard and learn well so they could, in turn, teach others. Many graduates of these tribal schools became teachers themselves and opened day schools near their homes.

Two of these schools became model schools and have had a lasting impact on Native American educational systems. One was the Red Cloud Indian School, founded as the Holy Rosary Mission in 1888 at the request of Chief Red Cloud of the Oglala Sioux at the Pine Ridge Reservation. Another Indian boarding school, which is still in use today, is the Theodore Roosevelt School in northeastern Arizona. It was first attended by local Navajo and Apache students. When new schools were built in Arizona, Navajo and Apache students began attending local schools and Theodore Roosevelt then became a boarding school for children of many tribes.

The Mexican War of 1854 brought the first Hispanic students recorded in the U.S. educational system in the Southwest. Language instruction was one of the first concerns, and, almost immediately, laws were passed that recognized English as the language of instruction. In many states, legislation was designed to eliminate the Spanish language entirely. The discussions of language framed a bias against Mexican American students on the part of school officials. Many Mexican American parents avoided issues of language and cultural bias by sending their children to private Catholic schools.

EXPANDING SCHOOL SYSTEMS While elementary and secondary schools were establishing policies dealing with race and culture that would remain for years, the higher education system continued to evolve with the help of the federal government. The Land Grant College Act of 1862 was the first federal aid to higher education and offered states a means to establish public colleges. States were given land that they were to sell to finance the building and establishment of new colleges. However, states did not always use the money as intended, and much of the money acquired by selling the property was used to build canals and bridges (Button & Provenzo, 1989). Normal schools (which later evolved into schools of education) were established to prepare elementary teachers, and universities developed programs to train secondary teachers. Two-year normal programs were open to students who were sixteen and wished to be teachers. Future teachers studied early forms of psychology and theories of teaching.

The ever-increasing immigrant population of the 1800s put demands on the U.S. educational system. The immigrants needed specific skills and dispositions to succeed in their adopted country and, as a result, the number of schools increased. During this expansion of public schools, a law was passed to levy taxes that would support elementary and secondary schools—thus establishing the precedent of a publicly funded educational system.

The 1800s marked many advances in U.S. education. Early educational processes established precedents, beliefs, and attitudes that remain in our current system. In the 1880s and 1890s, schools felt the impact of social and political changes in the nation (McMannon, 1995). Economic depression, political turmoil, and tense racial relations affected schooling throughout the country. Jobs became important resources, and schools were seen as one way to gain economic advantage. The most significant movements at the end of the century were free schooling, creation of educational systems that began with schooling young children and continued through a university system, and establishment of policies and governance systems to oversee the educational system.

The 1900s and the Progressive Era

As the new century began, the educational system was reviewed and found guilty of providing ineffective educational experiences for children. Educators criticized the traditional curriculum, textbooks, and materials that had been used during the 1800s (Button & Provenzo, 1989). Philosophies and purposes of education were questioned, and new ideas and theories began to emerge. Progress in government was connected to school reform. Progressives—those who identified the importance of linking progress and education—encouraged adoption of a variety of educational strategies, some newly developed, others transported from abroad, and still others reconstituted from the past.

The Progressive movement encouraged the schools to develop a new role as liberator, helping children realize their talents and potential so that they could make contributions to political life, enriching the quality of democracy (Perkinson, 1991). Progressive educators began to shift curricula from subject-centered schools to child-centered schools, where students' interests were considered when planning educational experiences. Two American theorist-philosophers, Francis Parker (1837–1902) and John Dewey (1859–1952), criticized the traditional education of the 1800s and proposed new ways of thinking about education. Among other things, Parker advo-

 © Donna Wiseman

In the early 1900s, one-room schoolhouses were still common in rural communities, and teachers needed only one or two years of college to teach children of various ages. This teacher (mother of one of the authors) conducted classes in a one-room school in Oklahoma.

cated doing away with the old books and curriculum and bringing in current magazines, newspapers, and student accounts of their experiences.

Dewey developed a comprehensive American educational philosophy known as pragmatism. He based his theory on discovery in an environment that encouraged learning. He believed a human's interaction with the environment was the basis for intellectual development (Tanner, 1997). Although often grouped with progressive educators such as Pestalozzi, Dewey resisted being known as a progressive educator. He believed that change in education is inevitable and that curriculum must constantly be reformed. He based his curriculum on problem-solving activity and experiences in natural settings. He joined the faculty at the University of Chicago and established an on-campus experimental laboratory school, where his teaching ideas could be practiced. Dewey's laboratory school is considered a forerunner to the school–university partnerships in which teachers and university professors collaborate.

 www You can learn more about John Dewey at this Web site:

http://www.siu.edu/-deweyctr/index2.html

URLs may change over time. For up-to-date links to relevant Web sites, visit our Companion Web site:

http://education.wadsworth.com/ wiseman3e

The early 1900s were marked by attempts to make an exact science of education, which inspired development of research and testing techniques to that end (Button & Provenzo, 1989). Educational research would ultimately have a huge impact on schooling in many ways: Methods of preparing teachers underwent major change, as increasing numbers of colleges offered courses in pedagogy. Scholars and teachers began to build a community of educators who studied and practiced the best of teaching. Significant research focused on testing and measurements. The study of teaching and learning resulted in viewing curriculum construction as dependent on knowledge of subject specialties and child development.

Like all public institutions, schools were affected by major national and international events. During the Great Depression, many schools, especially in the South, became impoverished. Teachers' salaries began to diminish, and many teachers were laid off. The Depression was followed by World War II, which once more changed the way Americans thought about schools. Economy, labor, and the needs of the workforce began to influence what happened in our schools. Schools were seen as a way to prepare the workforce and as a result the education of students became highly valued. The end of the war was followed by the baby boom (a large increase in birthrates from 1946 to 1950), the children of which began to fill schools in the 1950s.

From the 1950s to the 1980s

The middle of the twentieth century may have seemed calm on the surface, but there were foreshadowings of the changes that were to influence education and society by the end of the 1900s. Research and development

FIELD-BASED ACTIVITY

2.2

Imagine you are a child in the United States in the early 1860s. Based on the readings, what kind of education would you receive? What family characteristics would facilitate or hinder your access to education (for example, race or ethnicity, gender, family economic level)? As a class, tally the percentage of students in your class who would receive an education based on school attendance in the United States at that time. Ask those who would receive an education to explain what they would study and how they would be taught.

Now do the same for the early 1900s. How do the percentages change? Are the content and methods similar to those of the early 1800s?

INTASC Principles 2 and 9

began to have an impact on medicine, technology, and economics (Nichols & Good, 2000) and suggested changes for every aspect of American culture, including educational processes. The ethnic and racial makeup of the country was beginning to shift, and civil rights issues were emerging as important and controversial problems throughout the country. The wealth of the nation was also changing from an agricultural and industrial base to a more technologically centered one. The youth of the mid-1900s were portrayed as obedient, clean-cut family members who were home for dinner every evening. That picture was also about to change.

Probably no event characterizes the current educational context as clearly as the Russian launch of the satellite *Sputnik* in 1957. Americans were shaken out of their complacency when their archcompetitors managed to blast the first unmanned rocket into space. This event inspired much faultfinding and finger-pointing as Americans looked for someone to blame and for ways to explain why our research and development efforts had been outdone by a communist country. Eventually the blame centered on schools and their so-called failure to educate children and youth to be the thinkers needed for the modern competitive world. Soon after *Sputnik*'s launch, amid calls for education to be restructured to make our students more competitive, the federal government provided large grants to schools and universities to develop curricula that focused on math, science, and technology. New ways of teaching subjects and innovative practices in education were implemented. The entire nation felt a sense of urgency to prepare our children to win the international competition for technological bragging rights in the "race for space."

As mentioned above, one result of *Sputnik* was increased educational focus on technology development. During the 1950s, televisions were just beginning to appear in living rooms, and computers were increasingly used in research endeavors by universities and businesses. The computers of the 1960s and 1970s, although not as impressive as the ones that sit on our desks in the 2000s, began to make a difference in the way we lived and educated our children (Button & Provenzo, 1989). Technology revolutionized communication, changed jobs, provided new ways to spend leisure time, and affected transportation and manufacturing.

Not everyone had access to the good life, particularly African Americans, and as the century progressed, equality and civil rights became major issues. The 1954 Supreme Court decision in *Brown v. Board of Education* (see Chapter 4) began a three-decade movement to achieve equal rights in education. During the late 1950s and early 1960s, schools were the site of confrontations between supporters of civil rights and segregationists. Television newscasts, now appearing in everyone's living room, showed African American students being accompanied by security guards and police as they entered schools over the objections of state governors and others. The quiet times of the 1950s gave way to a more activist period that would change the very nature of schools and our nation.

Activism that may have begun over civil rights expanded and became more violent in response to U.S. participation in the Vietnam War. During the 1960s, America's nerves were frayed by war protests; urban riots; and the assassinations of President John F. Kennedy, his brother Robert, and civil rights leader Martin Luther King Jr. Media changed the way we learned about these events and assimilated the changes in our society. History was occurring right before our eyes, leaving schools and their teachers no other choice than to deal immediately with what was happening in their neighborhoods, the country, and the world. The sedate, picturesque view of American life in the 1950s transformed into the tumultuous, frightening, but exciting 1960s—in which new technology, civil rights, and media-provided instant information all had an impact on educational settings. These changes also contributed to the current educational context, which is the subject of discussion in Chapter 3.

Twenty Years of Educational Reform, 1980–2000

The 1980s began an era of reform that over the years took several forms (Myers & Myers, 1995). In the early 1980s, several national reports warned that U.S. schools were in trouble. One was *A Nation at Risk,* released in 1983 by the National Commission on Excellence in Education. This report contributed to a national attitude of concern for our schools that continues in 2004. It cited an alarming weakening and mediocrity of teaching and learning, suggested that the state of our schools would put the entire country at risk, and issued dire predictions about the future of our country. The report stated that lower standardized test scores, lower SAT scores, higher illiteracy rates, lower graduation requirements, and more students in remedial college courses were indicators that our educational system was not working. This document was a major critique of education in our country, framing many citizens' concerns and focusing issues on a condensed set of statements. The report recommended (1) an increased amount of content taught at schools, (2) higher standards and expectations for students, (3) increased time for learning, (4) higher standards for teachers, and (5) increased leadership from elected officials and fiscal support from government.

These public concerns prompted politicians to establish goals to build a national commitment to education. Formulation of these goals began with the Republican administration of President Reagan and continued into the Democratic administration of President Clinton. The original effort was outlined by state governors, who worked to develop national goals

Classrooms of the 2000s are diverse and represent a wide range of cultures because of desegregation policies and ever-changing immigration patterns. Compare this picture with the those on pages 43 and 47.

designed to guide educational reform. The goals, known as "Goals 2000: Educate America" and passed by Congress in 1994, included resolutions about preparing young children for school; assuring success for all students; focusing on literacy, mathematics, and science; and emphasizing drug-free, orderly school environments.

Soon after the 1983 publication of *A Nation at Risk,* a second wave of change was initiated, primarily at the state level. Teaching processes became the focus of attention, and reformers suggested teacher and student testing as measures of accountability for student learning. Recommendations from the second round of educational reports, funded by foundations and the federal government and occurring in the mid-to-late 1980s, included a more subject-centered curriculum; a back-to-basics approach; a greater focus on mathematics and science instruction; and a strong connection between testing, promotion, and graduation. The reports also called for alternative and flexible ways to educate teachers and included plans for merit pay, increased workloads, and longer school days. As a result, teachers' salaries increased, principals and teachers received leadership training, and states specified required competencies for students and teachers.

The reform efforts of the 1980s were confusing and rather disjointed.

Some programs tried to control what teachers taught; others suggested that decision making should be decentralized and based in the school settings (Apple, 1996). A series of isolated innovations, including attempts to structure the teaching process into isolated behaviors and leadership training encouraging site-based decision making, came and went with regularity. In spite of the 1980 reform efforts, problems and concerns associated with educational change simply worsened. The reforms did little to change the content of instruction, failed to directly involve teachers in the reform process, and were unsuccessful in altering the practices related to teaching and learning (Smith & O'Day, 1991). This period was extremely stressful for teachers, who felt neither involved in the change processes nor recognized for their efforts on students' behalf.

Toward the end of the 1980s and the beginning of the 1990s, reform movements began to take on a different tone from earlier calls for change. Innovations became more comprehensive, and themes related to basic values and recognition of family began to emerge (Hlebowitsh & Tellez, 1997). The development of standards for student achievement and teacher preparation became the focus of many reform movements. Change efforts also attempted to connect requirements for student learning with teacher preparation and professional development of experienced teachers. Schools made efforts to provide more educational choices to students and their parents and worked to be more flexible.

The state educational agencies played an important role in facilitating educational change. For example, in 1990 the Kentucky Education Reform Act facilitated a complete rebuilding of the school systems (Holland, 1997). The new school system was developed around three major areas: administration, curriculum, and finance. The changes included "establishing elected councils of educators and parents to run local schools, reorganizing the lower elementary grades into primary school classrooms that included children of different ages and abilities, and setting up a high-stakes accountability system that rewarded or sanctioned teachers and principals according to students' test scores" (Holland, 1997, p. 265). State officials reported that, as a result of the law, more than 92 percent of the state's 1,400 schools improved student achievement between 1992 and 1996 (Rothman, 1997). But the law mandating the complicated changes is still hotly contested, and most agree that it is not yet possible to determine whether improved student learning can be maintained. As happens in many school reform movements, Kentucky moved beyond their 1990 Reform Act into a new era by adopting the Comprehensive School Reform Demonstration program in 1998. The program provides state-mandated resources for local schools to implement comprehensive school reform programs that are based on reliable research and effective practices. The model programs include an emphasis on basic academics and parental involvement.

School reform activity in the early to mid-1990s was widespread and extremely varied (Shields & Knapp, 1997). Even though students were taking more difficult courses and the school dropout rate had stabilized, SAT scores had not increased substantially, college professors were still complaining that students were not ready for university curriculum, and employers still believed high school graduates were unprepared for the workplace (Jennings, 1995). After nearly twenty years of intense change effort, it is clear that attention to school reform is no guarantee of improved learning opportunities for children and young people. Calls for American education to reinvent itself still make news.

In the early 2000s, reform efforts focused on increasing the flexibility and variety of educational opportunities. Changes in educational funding allow the states to take more control of their resources, and some state governments encouraged local districts to allow students to choose where they attend school. Reforms also attempted to link change efforts and, in doing so, become more comprehensive and focused on students who were overlooked by past reforms by taking special steps to address the needs of poor and culturally diverse populations (Jackson, 2000). Unfortunately, a wide achievement gap between minority, English-as-a-second-language, low-socioeconomic-status students and white, middle- and high-socioeconomic status students persisted.

www

For more information about the achievement gap, review the following Web sites:

http://www.ed.gov/nclb/accountability/achieve/edpicks.jhtml?src=qc

http://www.ncrel.org/gap/what.htm

http://www.edweek.org/sreports/gap.htm

URLs may change over time. For up-to-date links to relevant Web sites, visit our Companion Web site:

http://education.wadsworth.com/wiseman3e

Education reformers engineered changes in teaching, assessment, and accountability of teachers, administrators, and in ways to meet the goals set forth by particular reform movements. But, because large groups of children were still not academically successful, a general consensus developed among the public that the basic structure of schools still needed to change. Even after years of modern reform efforts, general discontent with educational systems existed, and calls for dramatic changes became more intense. Public dissatisfaction about education influenced platforms of national political candidates and inspired new federal legislation. As you will read in Chapter 3, educational reform in the 2000s began an era of stronger national involvement in education.

▶ Philosophies of Education

Educational history offers descriptions and stories that recount changing venues, people, and contexts, but educational questions remain relatively constant. Educators have constantly struggled with philosophical questions about education: the purpose of education, the nature of the learner, what constitutes knowledge, and what is worth knowing; the strategies associated with teaching; and the struggle between religion, basic education, and liberal approaches. Educational philosophies have evolved around these timeless struggles.

Contemporary philosophies, which to a large extent have evolved from historical philosophies, form the basis for understanding the purposes of education and help develop theories about what should be taught and how students learn. Most philosophies can be traced to one of four major historical stances: Idealism and realism, two of the oldest philosophical positions, and pragmatism and existentialism, both newer philosophical systems, all have had an impact on educational thought (Myers & Myers, 1995). In most cases, philosophies do not reflect only one view but represent an evolution of thinking that has guided decisions and theory building.

Idealism

The intellectual roots of educational philosophy can be traced back to ancient Greece and Rome. Socrates (469–399 B.C.) made contributions to teaching and the value of knowledge by searching for basic meanings and truth and by bringing others together to do the same (Power, 1991). He attempted to educate social and political leaders by connecting knowledge and civic duty, and he used probing questions to explore the worth of human acts. Socrates' questions disturbed the status quo and upset those who held and accepted common assumptions. His constant questions became unpopular because they were viewed as revolutionary and an affront to the authority of those in power. As a result, he was eventually tried for corrupting Athenian youth with antiestablishment ideas, found guilty, and forced to commit suicide by drinking poison. Socrates is best remembered for his process of constant questioning (the Socratic method) as a teaching tool. He was a master at creating a series of questions that helped his students develop an awareness of their own thought processes.

Socrates' philosophy and his teaching methodology are widely known to us through his student, friend, and constant companion, Plato (427–347 B.C.). Many feel that all educational philosophy originated with Plato's ideas. He suggested that societies and the character of societies are highly dependent on the humans who exercise authority within that society. He was convinced that good citizenship and intellectual accomplishment were closely connected and that strong social structures were dependent on the education of citizens, although he had a clear preference for educating only the elite to provide leadership (Power, 1991). Plato's philosophy states that the purpose of education is to develop students' abilities so they can serve society (i.e., increase their abilities to improve society through work, intellectual pursuits, economic endeavors, and leadership). Plato is the founder of idealism, a philosophy that focuses on the spiritual and intellectual development of the individual.

Idealism includes ideas that go beyond the physical or concrete world. Idealists attempt to describe ideas, mind, consciousness, form, thought, energy, and other nonmaterial concepts. Ideals reside in the mind, and reality is identified through the subconscious. Idealism reflects Plato's ideas and his belief that education is necessary for an individual's freedom and limitless creative growth. In this philosophy, conservation of existing traditions, political arrangements, and customs is valued in personal and social life.

Today's classrooms may reflect idealism in several ways. Teachers encourage students to recognize and emulate the thoughts and actions of great people. Knowledge is viewed as unchanging, and students are encouraged to hone their reasoning skills to better get at "truth." Teachers still use questioning strategies and ask students to learn for the sake of learning—regardless of the practical application of the knowledge.

Schools that reflect modern interpretations of idealism may focus on "back to basics," and the literature used in their classrooms tends to be traditional classics. History and science classes focus on the Euro-American experience and thus offer limited interpretations or perspectives. Many proponents of Christian and other current religious education movements draw on idealist philosophies to provide a rationale for the goals and content of education. However, applications of idealist philosophies do not necessarily have a religious focus. Mortimer Adler's (1982) Paideia Proposal establishes ten principles to guide educational processes. The curriculum advocates a strong, integrated core curriculum for all students, including fine arts, music, foreign language, and the manual arts, featuring study of the great books, and is consistent with an idealist view of what constitutes important knowledge.

Realism

Aristotle (384–322 B.C.) studied in Plato's academy for seventeen years and introduced a novel educational philosophy—scientific empiricism—which became the basis for the philosophy known as realism. Aristotle felt that dialogue and questioning were too emotional and personal and that the process failed to make good use of data. He considered the question methodology of Socrates and Plato a waste of valuable learning time because it depended too much on personal experiences. Instead, he believed that student learning occurred by writing and used descriptive prose as a teaching technique. His philosophy emphasized the importance of habit and instruction, which he viewed as the bases of happiness.

Realism, antithetical to idealism, holds that objects and happenings exist regardless of how we perceive them. The universe does not depend on our minds for interpretation; everything comes from nature and is subject to natural law. Scientific method is honored, and each content area is precisely structured. Learning and teaching are viewed as a science based on hard facts. Realists focus on skills of reasoning and believe the major purposes of education are to promote thinking and to understand subjects. Pestalozzi, Locke, Jefferson, and Mann were all realists. The current drive for accountability is based on a philosophy of realism (Myers & Myers, 1995). Aristotle's emphases on the virtues required and nurtured by the good life have strongly influenced contemporary advocates for character education (Noddings, 1997).

In today's classrooms, realism is often represented in science and environmental studies. Instruction reflecting a realist philosophy may focus on the environment and its influence on humans. Realist methods apply a specific theory and truth to understand the world. Teachers who maintain realism as a philosophy are usually subject matter specialists who focus on reason and thinking. Because idealism and realism share the view that reality and truth are unchanging, they are often combined in educational practice. Teachers who maintain that there is a common core of knowledge and skills that should be taught to learners, even if they cannot agree on the nature of this core knowledge, would feel most comfortable with the philosophies of idealism and realism.

Pragmatism

The theory of pragmatism constantly questions what is viewed as truth. John Dewey, founder of pragmatism, established experimental education and influenced notions of educational research. In this philosophy, knowledge is obtained and developed through experiences and interactions with the environment (Tanner, 1997). Humans become increasingly complex as they gain experiences and interact with the universe. Therefore, students need opportunities to act on their environment and undergo the consequences of that action. This experimentation goes beyond mere trial and

© Bettmann/CORBIS

John Dewey is recognized as one of the most distinguished philosophers and educational theorists of the twentieth century. He based his philosophy, which is the foundation for experienced-based education, on what he learned at a Laboratory School he established at the University of Chicago. His work of the early 1900s was so influential that it continues to affect modern educational practices.

error or mindless activity; it requires reflection on the connections between the action and its consequences.

From this perspective, education is defined as the reconstruction or reorganization of experiences (Dewey, 1916). A teacher who is a pragmatist will help students understand that what is known is changeable, that there are a number of ways to interpret events, and that there is no absolute truth. As noted previously, Dewey often avoided identification with popular notions of progressive education, but he identified certain common principles shared by progressive schools. An example of the differences between pragmatist and idealist or realist classrooms can be seen in the changes in teaching and learning history that occurred during the Progressive Era. Previously, teachers stressed lecture, recitation of facts, and notetaking by students as appropriate history instruction. Dewey, through influence on the Committee on Social Studies of 1916, reconceptualized the study of history as embedded in a social studies curriculum that was more student-appropriate, relevant, and active than previous approaches (Brophy & VanSledright, 1997). Among other hands-on instructional techniques, student discussions, project development, and recreations began to dominate teaching and learning processes. The struggle between philosophically opposing conceptions of the substance and goals of history reemerged in 1994, when the National Standards for History was published (National Center for History in the Schools, 1996) amid considerable controversy over what the history curriculum should look like (Brophy & VanSledright, 1997).

At the heart of the issue was whether history consists of an unchanging set of facts to be learned or whether these "facts" are relative to time, place, and people. The controversy continues, particularly as the federal government plays a stronger role in guiding our curriculum. (See Chapter 3 for more discussion on this topic.)

Discovery learning and child-centered learning are themes associated with the pragmatist philosophy, which promotes inquiry and uses reflective thinking to solve problems. Classrooms implementing the pragmatic philosophy may be child-centered, discovery-based, cooperative, and motivated by student interests. Tasks are more likely to be "authentic" in that they reflect the world outside the classroom and can be directly applied to situations that students might encounter outside of school. Problem-based learning, project approaches, and community-based learning are all consistent with a pragmatic philosophical approach.

Existentialism

Existentialism, a relatively recent philosophy emerging after World War I, focuses on the individual and interprets the world through feelings, anxiety, and choice. Existentialist thought believes reality and humans to be too complex and unpredictable to fit into a neatly predictable system. Truth is subjective. Based on the writings of educational theorists influenced by the writings of Sartre, Nietzsche, Ortega, and Jaspers, existentialism has little to offer to educational philosophy and may even destroy education as it currently exists (Baker, 1974; Morris, 1963). However, Martin Buber (1957) has explicitly connected his general philosophy with an existentialist philosophy of education. From his perspective, teachers are in a position to impose their views of reality and truth on their students but choose instead to merely present their perspectives and allow students to develop their own views. Developing a capacity to love, appreciate, and respond emotionally are important elements of this philosophical stance. Values, arts, and multiple perceptions are used to explain events and to interpret concepts. Self-actualization and self-realization are themes often associated with this view of existentialism.

A classroom of today that reflects an existentialist philosophy focuses on individuals and their perceptions of events. Students are encouraged to build meaning from their own experiences. A classroom interpretation of existentialism encourages students to accept responsibility for their actions and focuses on respecting one's own ideas as well as the ideas of others. Perhaps the best-known example of existentialist applications in education was the experiment at Summerhill, which emphasized student choice and was based on the conviction that students will make good choices about their own learning (Neill, 1960). Schools that follow the Summerhill model tend to forgo any set curriculum and feature activities and experiences that revolve around student interests and questions. Curriculum is personalized, and teachers emphasize personal interaction among teachers and students above facts and ideas. Given the emphasis on educator accountability related to student testing in today's schools (see Chapter 3), existentialist approaches to education are not as prevalent in public schools today as they were in the 1960s.

Current Systems

Philosophers from the past inform contemporary philosophies that influence today's schools directly. As a result, many contemporary philosophies—although unique in outlook or focus—are outgrowths of the four basic categories of philosophy.

Recently, a more critical stance has played a role in educational philosophy. Critical philosophers focus on how and why society and schools oppress some people and not others and on how political issues are influenced by oppression. Racism, sexism, religion, and economics form the basis of their critical analysis of curriculum, instructional strategies, and attitudes in the schools (Piner, 1998). They encourage teachers to question their classroom actions and to understand how teachers contribute to the students' success or failure based on the students' gender, ethnicity, or economic status.

Over time, despite the influences of formal philosophy, most teachers develop their own versions of educational philosophy and theory, which are deeply rooted in their own beliefs about the nature of knowledge and of the learner as well as their own experiences with learning and with what works in their classrooms. Teachers' educational philosophy will determine how comfortable they feel with innovations (see Chapter 3) and how

FIELD-BASED ACTIVITY 2.3

With your classmates, list as many past and present educational issues or controversies currently being debated as you can think of. Can you and your classmates identify educational disagreements that are clashes of basic philosophies? Ask teachers or administrators in your school to join the class discussion and review some of these educational issues. What philosophies do you recognize? Write a summary paragraph of the ideas you identified during the discussion.

INTASC Principles 3 and 9

Divide into small groups. Each group should choose one of the four philosophical approaches described in this section and prepare a vignette or concrete description of an activity in a classroom that exemplifies that particular approach. Have a representative from your group read your vignette to the rest of the class and ask them if they can identify the philosophical approach.

INTASC Principles 3, 4, and 9

willing they are to change what they do in the classroom. For example, teachers who feel more comfortable with idealist and realist notions of the enduring quality of knowledge and reality will be less likely to adopt constructivist approaches to education (described in Chapter 6). Teachers who feel more comfortable with existentialist views of student choice, responsibility, and freedom will feel frustrated by externally imposed accountability systems. Understanding and reflecting on learning theories, teaching methodology, classroom management, and curriculum helps teachers understand their own philosophy of education. Teachers can learn about their philosophy through their own teaching experiences and by comparing their beliefs and actions to principles embodied in established educational philosophies. Take time now to complete the Self-Reflection exercise and to think about what you have learned.

SELF-REFLECTION

What Is Your Educational Philosophy?

Review and consider how strongly you agree or disagree with the following statements. Use this scale to indicate your level of agreement with each item: 5 = Strongly agree, 4 = Agree, 3 = Neutral, 2 = Disagree, 1 = Disagree strongly.

_____ **1.** The most important role of a teacher is to be a model for intellectual and moral excellence in the classroom.

_____ **2.** By studying humans in their natural settings, we can discover universal moral laws.

_____ **3.** Although truth is changeable, we can discover it using the scientific method.

_____ **4.** The main question teachers should ask students is, "What does this idea or content mean to you?"

_____ **5.** Although vocational studies have their place, most students should be required to have a strong liberal arts education.

_____ **6.** The most important task for a teacher is to promote reasoning within a particular content area.

_____ **7.** The role of the teacher is to engage students in active problem solving applied to social and personal problems.

_____ **8.** Truth is subjective and based on personal experiences and beliefs.

_____ **9.** There are enduring and unchanging truths and values in all subject areas that students need to understand.

_____ **10.** To learn facts and truth in a content area, teachers may need to use considerable drill and practice.

_____ **11.** Use of the scientific method is a major goal of education.

_____ **12.** The teacher's primary role is to enable students to create their own values.

_____ **13.** Students learn best when they study the ideas and the works of great people.

_____ **14.** There are enduring truths in all subject areas that students can discover by careful reasoning.

_____ **15.** When deciding what curriculum should be emphasized for students, educators should base their decisions on real-life usefulness of the content.

_____ **16.** If forced to choose between covering the content and exploring personal perspectives, a teacher should choose personal exploration.

_____ **17.** Time-tested great literary works should be required reading for all students even at the expense of more popular readings.

_____ **18.** The curriculum should be based on "the basics" and rely on drill and memorization as learning strategies.

_____ **19.** The most important role of the teacher is to facilitate reflection and use the scientific method to solve problems.

_____ **20.** The most important concepts to explore with students in the classroom revolve around love, freedom, responsibility, death, and values.

(_continued_)

Transfer your scores to this chart and add each column.

A	B	C	D
1. _____	2. _____	3. _____	4. _____
5. _____	6. _____	7. _____	8. _____
9. _____	10. _____	11. _____	12. _____
13. _____	14. _____	15. _____	16. _____
17. _____	18. _____	19. _____	20. _____

How much did you agree or disagree with the educational philosophies discussed in this chapter? Each column represents one of the philosophies of learning: A = idealism, B = realism, C = pragmatism, and D = existentialism. The more points you have in each column, the more your own philosophy matches with established philosophies. The highest possible score in any column is 25, and the lowest score is 5. A score of 20 or above in any column indicates strong agreement, whereas a score of less than 10 indicates little agreement. Where are your highest scores, and where are your lowest? Is your own philosophy highly representative of the classical ways of thinking about education, or do you have a tendency to embrace more than one philosophical stance?

PORTFOLIO REFLECTIONS AND EXHIBITS

Prepare an exhibit that illustrates what you learned as you read and discussed the concepts in this chapter. Your responses to the activities and to these suggestions will provide you with some ideas that might contribute to a professional portfolio.

Suggested Exhibit 2: Philosophy of a Preservice Teacher and Plans for Providing Appropriate Experiences

1. Review your response to Activity 2.1. Use the response as the first step to identify your own philosophy of teaching. Prepare a demonstration of your philosophy. Write a poem; develop a collage, picture,

or essay; or identify a life story that helps you illustrate your perspective on education. Make reference to the established history and philosophy presented in this text and other readings.

2. Share your philosophy and evaluation of your experiences with your college professor and classroom teacher mentor. Allow them to provide you with feedback.

E-Portfolio Entry 2

Build on the slide presentation from E-Portfolio Entry 1 (on page 62). Add two more slides that represent your emerging philosophy of teaching. Develop a short written statement to accompany a visual developed from computer graphics, Internet connections, or simulations. (Assume that you will continue to add to this entry as you learn more about teaching and learning, because a well-developed philosophy statement is usually required for university assignments throughout your program and when you apply for jobs after you have completed your university experience.) As you complete your coursework, observe and work with students in classrooms, read this and other texts, and reflect on your growth as a teacher, you will continue to add and amend your philosophy.

INTASC Principles 4 and 9

ANSWERS TO GUIDING YOUR READING

1. How have past education events influenced current trends?

   Almost any contemporary "innovation" can be traced to a past event, person, or situation. Debates and reform movements that occur today can be traced back to early educators' dilemmas and philosophies. For example, many of Dewey's progressive ideas, which were highly questioned in the early 1900s, are still the basis for debate and proposed reform.

2. How have modern reform efforts affected traditional schooling?

   Reform in education is a consistent theme throughout the years. Modern reform efforts have attempted to provide equitable access to education for all students, increased the role of accountability and testing, encouraged the establishment of standards for teaching and learning, supported the professionalization of teaching, and increased options for school choice. It is difficult to measure the full impact of reform, and some say that education and schooling have not changed much, regardless of continuous efforts.

3. What roles have minorities played in educational history?

In almost every case, minorities have struggled to experience high-quality educational opportunities in American schools. Many minorities in our society, such as Native Americans and Chinese Americans, did not have equal access to schooling until the 1960s. In many cases minorities first attended segregated schools that were established especially for their cultural or ethnic group. Segregated schools often operated with unequal resources and reduced support from state and federal government. The struggle for equal access to education by American minority groups has resulted in inclusive schooling that is constantly striving to provide equal education for all students.

4. What philosophical roots can be linked to contemporary education?

There are many ways to discuss philosophical roots related to education, but most philosophies can be traced to one of four major stances. Education and schooling can still be connected to Socrates' and Plato's idealism, Aristotle's realism, Dewey's pragmatism, and Buber's existentialism.

 INFOTRAC COLLEGE EDITION EXTENSION

Log on to the InfoTrac College Edition Web site and use it to find out more about programs exemplifying the philosophies that were introduced in this chapter. If you still need information to help you understand them, try Item 1 below. If you feel comfortable with your level of knowledge about each philosophy, try Item 2.

1. Using the subject guide search, type in the name of one of the philosophies discussed in this chapter. On the next screen, choose "View Reference Book Excerpts." Read one or two of the excerpts to deepen your philosophical understanding. Repeat the process with another philosophy.

2. Using the keyword search, type in the name "Mortimer Adler." Read an article that explains his great books program.

RELATED READINGS

The following books will help you understand more about the topics discussed in this chapter:

Cuban, L. (1993). *How teachers taught: Constancy and change in American class-rooms 1880–1990.* New York: Teachers College Press.

>This book looks at the past century of American teaching to describe how elementary and secondary classrooms are influenced by history, sociology, and education. Cuban uses observations of teachers to provide "snapshots" into classrooms to identify both continuity and change.

Postman, N. (1997). *The end of education: Redefining the value of school.* New York: Alfred A. Knopf.

>Postman questions some of the assumptions and values on which current educational practices are built. He presents narratives and metaphors that help us consider different ways to think about schools.

Tanner, D. (1997). *Dewey's laboratory school: Lessons for today.* New York: Teachers College Press.

>Tanner explains how teachers developed and implemented curriculum in Dewey's Laboratory School. She relates Dewey's teaching and learning philosophies to modern trends and issues. This book is a good introduction to Dewey.

REFERENCES

Epigraph: Huftalen, Sarah Gillespie. (1992). To be a teacher. In M. H. Cordier (Ed.), *Schoolwomen of the Prairie and Plains* (pp. 175–209). Albuquerque: University of New Mexico Press.

Adler, M. (1982). *The Paideia proposal.* New York: Macmillan.

Angus, D. L., & Mirel, J. E. (1995). *The failed promise of the American high school: 1890–1995.* New York: Teachers College Press.

Apple, M. W. (1996). *Cultural politics and education.* New York: Teachers College Press.

Baker, B. F. (1974). Existential philosophers on education. In J. Park (Ed.), *Selected readings in the philosophy of education* (4th ed., pp. 128–138). New York: Macmillan.

Brophy, J., & VanSledright, B. (1997). *Teaching and learning history in elementary schools.* New York: Teachers College Press.

Buber, M. (1957). *Between man and man.* Boston: Beacon Press.

Button, H. W., & Provenzo, E. F. (1989). *History of education and culture in America.* Englewood Cliffs, NJ: Prentice-Hall.

Dewey, J. (1916). *Democracy and education.* New York: Macmillan.

Frankena, W. K. (1974). Model for analyzing a philosophy of education. In J. Park (Ed.), *Selected readings in the philosophy of education* (4th ed., pp. 139–144). New York: Macmillan.

Hlebowitsh, P., & Tellez, K. (1997). *American education: Purpose and promise.* Belmont, CA: Wadsworth.

Holland, H. (1997). KERA: A tale of one teacher. *Phi Delta Kappan,* 79(4), 264–271.

Jackson, J. F. (2000). What are the real risk factors for African-American children? *Phi Delta Kappan,* 81(4), 308–312.

Jennings, J. (1995). School reform based on what is taught and learned. *Phi Delta Kappan,* 76(10), 765–769.

McMannon, T. J. (1995). *Morality, efficiency, and reform: An interpretation of history of American education.* Work in Progress Series, No. 5. Seattle: Institute for Educational Inquiry.

Morris, V. C. (1963). *Selected readings in the philosophy of education* (2nd ed., pp. 551–552). New York: Macmillan.

Myers, C. B., & Myers, L. K. (1995). *The professional educator: A new introduction to teaching and schools.* Belmont, CA: Wadsworth.

National Center for History in the Schools. (1996). *National standards for history: Basic edition.* Los Angeles: UCLA.

Neill, A. (1960). *Summerhill: A radical approach to child rearing.* New York: Hart.

Nichols, S. L., & Good, T. L. (2000). Education and society, 1900–2000: Selected snapshots of then and now. In T. L. Good (Ed.), *American education: Yesterday, today, and tomorrow, ninety-ninth yearbook of the National Society for the Study of Education,* Part II (pp. 1–53). Chicago: University of Chicago Press.

Noddings, N. (1997). Character education and community. In A. Molner (Ed.), *The constructions of children's character* (pp. 1–16). Chicago: NSSE and University of Chicago Press.

Perkinson, H. J. (1991). *The imperfect panacea: American faith in education 1865–1990.* New York: McGraw-Hill.

Piner, W. E. (Ed.). (1998). *Curriculum: Toward new identities.* New York: Garland.

Power, E. J. (1991). *A legacy of learning: A history of western education.* Albany: State University of New York Press.

Rothman, R. (1997). KERA: A tale of one school. *Phi Delta Kappan,* 79(4), 272–275.

Shields, P. M., & Knapp, M. S. (1997). The promise and limits of school-based reform: A national snapshot. *Phi Delta Kappan,* 79(4), 288–294.

Smith, S. (1979). *Ideas of the great educators.* New York: Barnes & Noble.

Smith, M. S., & O'Day, J. (1991). Systemic school reform. In S. Fuhrman & B. Malen (Eds.), *The politics of curriculum and testing* (pp. 116–133). Philadelphia: Falmer Press.

Tanner, D. (1997). *Dewey's laboratory school: Lessons for today.* New York: Teachers College Press.

Timm, J. T. (1996). *Four perspectives in multicultural education.* Belmont, CA: Wadsworth.

An Era of Accountability and Change

Accountability has become a much over-worked word, and in some cities, it's become anathema to teachers. That's because many parents, acting out of frustration, blame teachers for the failure of schools. Their code term is that we should hold teachers "accountable." As we've already begun to see, though, if there's anyone who doesn't deserve to be blamed, it's the teachers. On the other hand, there is a need for a clear system of monitoring performance and behavior in every large organization and school systems are no exception. Too often, the more centralized school systems are breeding grounds for poor performance and outright dishonesty. . . .

When people get interested in school reform—as many are today—they tend to focus first on accountability. They start with a preconceived notion that schools are lax. . . . Putting two and two together, they conclude that if you get tough on principals and teachers, the problems of education will be solved. Unfortunately, it isn't that easy. . . .

—William Ouchie, *Making Schools Work*

Guiding Your Reading

1. What are the educational agendas and mandates that affect teaching and learning in current classrooms?

2. What are characteristics of successful educational programs that address needed changes in teaching and learning?

3. What effects do you think reform movements will have on your teaching?

4. What are some of the reasons people resist educational change?

*T*eachers who begin their careers during the twenty-first century are likely to experience continuing change. Educators, parents, corporate and other community members, banking and business people, and politicians are continuously engaged in discussions about improving education. Different groups and individuals have various educational agendas. Politicians and policymakers impose standards and mandates for accountability. In response, educators "reinvent" and develop new strategies for teaching and learning. Business, industry, social organizations, and educational institutions are constantly developing new ways to work and need a workforce capable of adapting to new practices. New technologies require that we use different instructional tools. Rapidly changing demographics bring different perspectives to educational contexts. Constant mandates, suggestions, and discussions require educators to respond, consider, and change teaching and learning strategies. Schools and the teaching that goes on within the schools have been "scrutinized, criticized, eulogized, and 'reformed'" (Myers & Myers, 1995, p. 25).

Most would agree that the more complex requirements of our society—federal and state mandates; the rapid influx of technology; the diversity of our population; and the number of children, youth, and adolescents living in poverty—require that schools change to meet new demands. However, different stakeholders hold different views about the direction that changes and restructuring should take. An overview of some of the

Pay attention to radio, television, and newspaper reports about education and note the nature of the topics discussed. Are they primarily critical of education? Are there calls for change? Criticism of current practice? Reports of what is or is not working in education? Relate current issues to concerns and practices in your school setting. Share these with your classmates.

INTASC Principle 9

issues, challenges, and successes of educational reform provide a context for understanding the nature of modern schooling and the environments in which new teachers will begin their careers.

Current Directions of Reform

When all the dust settled from the public's discussions about education from the 1980s through 2000, a wide variety of topics emerged, ranging from reforms in school funding to students' rights. Despite the quantity and diversity of proposed issues and innovations, one area held constant: a desire for accountability, standards for students and teachers, and assessment to ensure mastery of standards. Related issues, including equitable education for all students, school choice, professionalization of teaching, teacher quality, school restructuring, and innovations for teaching and learning, were recast to fit under the umbrella of the accountability movement.

Equitable Education for All Students

Student diversity and a wide range of economic stratification among children have forced the topic of educational equality into the forefront of educational issues. All students—including the poor, non-English speaking, and disabled—deserve a quality education. Central to quality education is a highly qualified teacher in every classroom. To provide equitable education for all students, teachers must consider how diversity affects the way students respond to schooling, recognize that differences influence learning, and take those differences into account when planning instruction.

One way to view equity issues is to explore how teachers perceive the potential achievement of their students. Differences such as culture, race, family status, and socioeconomic background have historically been related

Schools are required by law to modify teaching approaches and change the structure of school buildings so that all students, regardless of their physical differences, are able to experience equal access to learning. Teachers will modify teaching approaches, provide necessary monitoring, and provide assistance to students who may have special physical or emotional requirements.

to success or failure in schools, but some students' learning difficulties arise from teachers' expectations. Teachers often believe, for example, that students who are poor or who speak English as a second language will not succeed in school. Life situations do affect learners' achievement, but it does not mean that they are doomed to failure. One of the first steps teachers can take to eliminate learning difficulties is to accept all students and honor their differences; a very wise teacher will go one step further and use these differences to enrich schooling experiences for all students.

Equity issues are particularly glaring when school funding is considered. U.S. students who live in rich communities have schools that are better funded than those in poor communities. Combined with the poverty of some students' families, differences in school funding generate large disparities in student achievement (Payne & Biddle, 1999). A broader discussion of educational equity and equality is presented in Chapter 5.

Although individual teachers are important to providing equitable education, recent legislation has recognized the need for a more global approach to the challenge. The No Child Left Behind (NCLB) Act of 2001

(Pub. L. 107–110, NCLB) became law in January 2002. The act substantially revises the Elementary and Secondary Act of 1965 (ESEA) in a manner designed to provide all of America's public school students with the opportunity and means to achieve academic success. Some of the major provisions include:

- Accountability for results
- Expanded state and local flexibility
- Expanded school choices for parents
- Focused resources on proven educational methods, particularly in reading instruction
- Strengthening of teacher quality
- Confirmation of student academic progress and measurement of "adequate yearly progress"
- Promotion of English proficiency

Implications of NCLB for teaching and learning at all levels are profound. Testing is a prominent feature in state educational programs and drives curriculum and instruction in individual schools. Teacher quality provisions require a highly qualified teacher in every public school classroom by 2005. (Highly qualified teachers hold a bachelor's degree with majors in core areas taught in schools and demonstrate competency in subject matter knowledge—usually measured by tests.) Initial teacher preparation programs and professional development for experienced teachers need to meet the requirements of NCLB. All educators need to understand the new NCLB requirements related to accountability and testing.

You can learn more about No Child Left Behind at the following Web sites:

http://www.ed.gov/nclb/landing.jhtml

http://nclb.ecs.org/nclb/

URLs may change over time. For up-to-date links to relevant Web sites, visit our Companion Web site:

http://education.wadsworth.com/wiseman3e

Accountability and Testing

Declining test scores, rising rates of illiteracy, and demands for greater accountability from schools contributed to the public support for NCLB. The public feels that it is the schools' responsibility to provide an education to students and wants some evidence that schools and teachers are effective. Criticism of what graduates know and are able to do have prompted many U.S. citizens and leaders to demand that students pass a series of standardized tests. The emphasis on testing as a way to hold schools accountable reflects the perspective that good teaching is measured by students' achievement (Clark, 1995). As a result of this emphasis, particularly in light of NCLB, states have developed curriculum requirements and companion standardized tests that are administered at predetermined intervals during primary and secondary schooling.

Historically, the major tool for holding educators responsible for student learning is testing. During the last few years, it has played a major role in what is being taught in the classroom. Testing of students' learning is a major influence on the teaching processes in modern classrooms because test results are used to measure the effectiveness of teaching. Every school uses standardized achievement tests to document students' achievement and growth over time. Tests are used for comparative, administrative, and political reasons, but few teachers accept the idea of measuring their students' growth and achievement with only one test score. Tests are a sampling of students' abilities and may not represent the full range of students' knowledge, skills, and abilities.

Proponents of the testing movement suggest that there is general agreement among education professionals about just what should be taught to each and every student. However, despite NCLB, the ideas associated with

© Stephanie Knight

Demands for greater accountability in schools has lead to a widespread acceptance of testing as a way to measure school and teacher effectiveness. Educators agree that testing is necessary, but many are concerned about the over-emphasis on testing and the negative teaching and learning processes that may result from over-reliance on the results.

testing and the accountability movement are highly debatable. How success should be measured can be viewed in very different ways. Some would argue that the definition of educational excellence has been the same for many years. Others suggest that different learners may need different content, presented in different ways, depending on their needs and their past experiences (Piner, 1992). For example, some people would include African and African American knowledge (that is, history and literature) in the school curriculum. Others disagree and say that the curriculum basics should come from traditional (that is, Eurocentric) topics and approaches.

Despite some disagreement over the content and form of testing, few would argue the merits of evaluation in general. Teachers must assess what students know to plan for instruction. Testing helps teachers discover what concepts students understand and what experiences they need to continue effective learning. When teachers know their students, they are able to plan more effective, motivating activities and interactions. Continuous and long-range assessment identifies growth patterns and results from teacher–learner experiences. However, it is not entirely clear whether the tests associated with the accountability trends provide educators with that needed information.

Reliance on standardized tests may also produce undesirable results (Falk, 2000). Due to perceived pressures from administrators and parents, teachers may "teach to the test"—that is, they allow tests to guide curricular and instructional decisions. Another danger is that the tests may affect students' perceptions about their own ability to learn. Teachers may expect less from students who do not perform well on a test.

Standardized tests are not in themselves a deterrent to learning if they are used with caution. Testing, or any other single effort, cannot constitute an accountability and evaluation system. A school creates effective evaluation and assessment policies and procedures by using various tools that inform teachers, administrators, parents, and community members about how student learning contributes to educators' decision making, and provide the basis to respond to students' strengths and needs (Hlebowitsh & Tellez, 1997). When teachers know their students and use multiple methods to assess and evaluate learning, interpretation of achievement will be more effective and improve instruction for all students. Tests affect more than individual classroom teaching and learning. The results of testing are often identified as a catalyst for large-scale change and reform in education. For example, current national educational reform efforts are in place because of the persistently low test scores of groups of students. We must understand the contributions and potential dangers of standardized testing to truly understand reform and change movements in our schools.

Standards for Teaching and Learning

One of the benchmarks of recent educational change is the development and implementation of standards. Standards are frameworks that focus on academic behaviors and assessments, and their purpose is to encourage high academic performance (Cohen, 1995). The modern era of standard-setting began with Goals 2000, the education goals that guided three presidents and encouraged the development of national standards in several areas. The NCLB focus on confirmation of educational progress, teacher quality, and accountability for results perpetuates the heightened interest in standards. A variety of state-based frameworks (many in existence before the passage of the NCLB legislation) list the expectations for what teachers teach and students learn.

The Illinois Learning Standards (Illinois State Board of Education, 1997) are similar to other state standards that help design state assessment programs, guide school curriculum development, assess student progress, focus school improvement plans, and communicate the purpose and results of schooling to the community. Developed with the input of teachers, administrators, parents, employers, community leaders, and representatives of higher education, standards were created for English language arts, mathematics, science, social science, physical development and health, fine arts, and foreign languages for early elementary, late elementary, middle/junior high school, early high school, and late high school. As you can see from the excerpt of the English language arts standards in Table 3.1, the first goal is that all students "read with understanding and fluency." The framework then presents learning standards and the benchmarks that would indicate that appropriate student learning has occurred. Statewide achievement tests were developed to assess compliance with the learning standards shown.

You can learn more about the Illinois Standards at this Web site:

http//www.isbe.state.il.us/ils/

URLs may change over time. For up-to-date links to relevant Web sites, visit our Companion Web site:

http://education.wadsworth.com/wiseman3e

In addition to state efforts, educators have developed or reevaluated existing standards in many subject areas. Standards for specific content areas exist at national and state levels. Sometimes standards are developed though collaborative efforts, linking the state and national efforts together, but more often they are developed separately without articulation between the two. For instance, during the 1990s, professional organizations such as the National Council of Teachers of English, National Council of Teachers of Mathematics, and the National Science Foundation conducted a series of discussions and studies to determine what should be taught to students of different ages. Specific content area goals and standards evolved from these national discussions and often serve as the basis for the development of state standards.

Some content area standards developed by professional organizations generated concerns and disagreements from parents and other interested groups. As outlined in Chapter 2, the subject of history or social studies was particularly contentious and widely debated. Social studies educators interpreted standards from a broad perspective and accepted the history and culture of multiple perspectives as valid and desired. Their interpretation of social studies recognized different perspectives based on gender, race, culture, and religion. For example, the history of the western United States settlements included the role of women in the wagon trains. Of course, including such diverse views will change the stories and narratives associated with important events. The new standards emphasized the importance of including roles of minorities in history and including minority literature. However, some educators and parents believed their schools should focus on traditional aspects of history and geography. In many cases, parental beliefs regarding the content and subject matter taught reflect their own cultural and language experiences. The resulting disagreements were reported on the national news and delayed the approval of the new standards in many settings.

www You may access professional organizations and learn more about subject area standards at these Web sites:

National Council for Teachers of English
http//www.ncte.org

National Council for Social Studies
http://www.ncss.org

National Council of Teachers of Mathematics http://www.nctm.org

International Reading Association
http://www.reading.org

URLs may change over time. For up-to-date links to relevant Web sites, visit our Companion Web site:

http://education.wadsworth.com/wiseman3e

The Professionalization of Teaching

Several education reformers suggest that one of the problems in education is the lack of professionalism among teachers. Generally, "professionalism" refers to teachers' ability to regulate their profession, the provision of a qualified educational workforce, and effective professional development for all educators. However, as used in reform recommendations, "professionalism" usually focuses on how to hold teachers accountable for what they do in the classroom.

The standards movement has therefore affected classrooms in two ways: standards for students and standards for teachers. As discussed above, learning standards require testing students to be sure they've acquired the specified knowledge, and the results are also used to evaluate the quality of teaching.

TABLE 3.1

Illinois Learning Standards/English Language Arts

State Goal 1: Read with understanding and fluency.

As a result of their schooling, students will be able to:

LEARNING STANDARD	EARLY ELEMENTARY	LATE ELEMENTARY
1.A.1a Apply word analysis and vocabulary skills to comprehend selections.	**1.A.1a** Apply word analysis skills (e.g., phonics, word patterns) to recognize new words. **1.A.1b** Comprehend unfamiliar words using context clues and prior knowledge; verify meanings with resource materials.	**1.A.2a** Read and comprehend unfamiliar words using root words, synonyms, antonyms, word origins and derivations. **1.A.2b** Clarify word meaning using context clues and a variety of resources including glossaries, dictionaries and thesauruses.
B. Apply reading strategies to improve understanding and fluency.	**1.B.1a** Establish purposes for reading, make predictions, connect important ideas, and link text to previous experiences and knowledge. **1.B.1b** Identify genres (forms and purposes) of fiction, nonfiction, poetry and electronic literary forms. **1.B.1c** Continuously check and clarify for understanding (e.g., reread, read ahead, use visual and context clues, ask questions, retell, use meaningful substitutions). **1.B.1d** Read age-appropriate material aloud with fluency and accuracy.	**1.B.2a** Establish purposes for reading; survey materials; ask questions; make predictions; connect, clarify and extend ideas. **1.B.2b** Identify structure (e.g., description, compare/contrast, cause and effect, sequence) of nonfiction texts to improve comprehension. **1.B.2c** Continuously check and clarify for understanding (e.g., *in addition to previous skills,* clarify terminology, seek additional information). **1.B.2d** Read age-appropriate material aloud with fluency and accuracy.

Note: Examples are designated by "e.g." and enclosed in parentheses. They are meant to guide the teacher as to the general intent of the standards and benchmarks, not to identify all possible items.

WHY THIS GOAL IS IMPORTANT: Reading is essential. It is the process by which people gain information and ideas from books, newspapers, manuals, letters, contracts, advertisements and a host of other materials. Using strategies for constructing meaning before, during and after reading will help students connect what they read now with what they have learned in the past. Students who read well and widely build a strong foundation for learning in all areas of life.

JUNIOR HIGH SCHOOL	EARLY HIGH SCHOOL	LATE HIGH SCHOOL
1.A.3a Apply knowledge of word origins and derivations to comprehend words used in specific content areas (e.g., scientific, political, literary, mathematical). **1.A.3b** Analyze the meaning of words and phrases in their context.	**1.A.4a** Expand knowledge of word origins and derivations and use idioms, analogies, metaphors and similes to extend vocabulary development. **1.A.4b** Compare the meaning of words and phrases and use analogies to explain the relationships among them.	**1.A.5a** Identify and analyze new terminology applying knowledge of word origins and derivations in a variety of practical settings. **1.A.5b** Analyze the meaning of abstract concepts and the effects of particular word and phrase choices.
1.B.3a Preview reading materials, make predictions and relate reading to information from other sources. **1.B.3b** Identify text structure and create a visual representation (e.g., graphic organizer, outline, drawing) to use while reading. **1.B.3c** Continuously check and clarify for understanding (e.g., *in addition to previous skills,* draw comparisons to other readings). **1.B.3d** Read age-appropriate material with fluency and accuracy.	**1.B.4a** Preview reading materials, clarify meaning, analyze overall themes and coherence, and relate reading with information from other sources. **1.B.4b** Analyze, interpret and compare a variety of texts for purpose, structure, content, detail and effect. **1.B.4c** Read age-appropriate material with fluency and accuracy.	**1.B.5a** Relate reading to prior knowledge and experience and make connections to related information. **1.B.5b** Analyze the defining characteristics and structures of a variety of complex literary genres and describe how genre affects the meaning and function of texts. **1.B.5c** Evaluate a variety of compositions for purpose, structure, content and details for use in school or at work. **1.B.5d** Read age-appropriate material with fluency and accuracy.

Continued on next page

TABLE 3.1 **Illinois Learning Standards/English Language Arts** (*continued*)

State Goal 1: Read with understanding and fluency.

As a result of their schooling, students will be able to:

LEARNING STANDARD	EARLY ELEMENTARY	LATE ELEMENTARY
C. Comprehend a broad range of reading materials.	**1.C.1a** Use information to form questions and verify predictions. **1.C.1b** Identify important themes and topics. **1.C.1c** Mark comparisons across reading selections. **1.C.1d** Summarize content of reading material using text organization (e.g., story, sequence). **1.C.1e** Identify how authors and illustrators express their ideas in text and graphics (e.g., dialogue, conflict, shape, color, characters). **1.C.1f** Use information presented in simple tables, maps and charts to form an interpretation.	**1.C.2a** Use information to form and refine questions and predictions. **1.C.2b** Make and support inferences and form interpretations about main themes and topics. **1.C.2c** Compare and contrast the organization of selections. **1.C.2d** Summarize and make generalizations from content and relate to purpose of material. **1.C.2e** Explain how authors and illustrators use text and art to express their ideas (e.g., points of view, design, hues, metaphor). **1.C.2f** Connect information presented in tables, maps and charts to printed or electronic text.

JUNIOR HIGH SCHOOL	EARLY HIGH SCHOOL	LATE HIGH SCHOOL
1.C.3a Use information to form, explain and support questions and predictions.	**1.C.4a** Use questions and predictions to guide reading.	**1.C.5a** Use questions and predictions to guide reading across complex materials.
1.C.3b Interpret and analyze entire narrative text using story elements, point of view and theme.	**1.C.4b** Explain and justify an interpretation of a text.	**1.C.5b** Analyze and defend an interpretation of text.
1.C.3c Compare, contrast and evaluate ideas and information from various sources and genres.	**1.C.4c** Interpret, evaluate and apply information from a variety of sources to other situations (e.g., academic, vocational, technical, personal).	**1.C.5c** Critically evaluate information from multiple sources.
1.C.3d Summarize and make generalizations from content and relate them to the purpose of the material.	**1.C.4d** Summarize and make generalizations from content and relate them to the purpose of the material.	**1.C.5d** Summarize and make generalizations from content and relate them to the purpose of the material.
1.C.3e Compare how authors and illustrators use text and art across materials to express their ideas (e.g., foreshadowing, flashbacks, color, strong verbs, language that inspires).	**1.C.4e** Analyze how authors and illustrators use text and art to express and emphasize their ideas (e.g., imagery, multiple points of view).	**1.C.5e** Evaluate how authors and illustrators use text and art across materials to express their ideas (e.g., complex dialogue, persuasive techniques).
1.C.3f Interpret tables that display textual information and data in visual formats.	**1.C.4f** Interpret tables, graphs and maps in conjunction with related text.	**1.C.5f** Use tables, graphs and maps to challenge arguments, defend conclusions and persuade others.

Source: Illinois State Board of Education (1997). *Illinois Learning Standards*. Springfield: Illinois State Board of Education.

Another effect of the standards movement is that new standards for teaching may mandate additional initial training and expanded requirements for maintaining certification. Since the early 2000s, federal policy has required states to demonstrate that teachers are qualified by imposing statewide tests that teachers must pass before they are certified or licensed. The federal policy includes the stipulation that teacher preparation programs publish their graduating students' pass rates in handbooks and college Web sites. Currently, state governments have a great deal of control over the regulations that define who will teach and who will be licensed. State certification is usually guided by state standards of competence and establishes the labels and descriptions of professionalism accepted by the state educational community. Thus new teachers may face differing requirements depending upon where they decide to work.

NATIONAL BOARD FOR PROFESSIONAL TEACHER STANDARDS (NBPTS)
The focus on establishing national standards to recognize and encourage excellence in experienced teachers led to establishment in the late 1990s of the National Board for Professional Teacher Standards (NBPTS). To receive certification from NBPTS, teachers must demonstrate their competence in five different areas: commitment to students and learning, knowledge of subject matter, ability to manage and monitor student learning, willingness to engage in reflective practice, and the propensity to participate in learning communities. For experienced teachers to be recognized as NBPTS teachers, they must undergo an intensive one-year evaluation process that requires them to develop a portfolio, be observed while teaching, take part in interviews, and pass a comprehensive subject area exam. It is an expensive process, but most teachers who complete the process feel that it increases their professionalism and acknowledges their efforts to improve their practice. A few states, such as Virginia, help teachers defray the cost of taking the test, and other states and districts may offer merit pay for teachers who complete the process. Most school districts have yet to recognize teachers who have completed the process by raising salaries when they become NBPTS-certified. The impact of NBPTS is still being assessed in the profession, but the future teachers should monitor the evolution of this certification process.

www You can learn more about the National Board for Professional Teacher Standards (NBPTS) at this Web site:

http://www.nbpts.org/

URLs may change over time. For up-to-date links to relevant Web sites, visit our Companion Web site:

http://education.wadsworth.com/ wiseman3e

INTERSTATE NEW TEACHER ASSESSMENT AND SUPPORT CONSORTIUM (INTASC) A similar process exists for beginning teachers. The Interstate New Teacher Assessment and Support Consortium (INTASC) establishes guidelines for preparing, licensing, and certifying educators. INTASC comprises ten standards (Figure 3.1) and also requires a new teacher to establish a portfolio and take a test at the end of the preparation program. Some states use INTASC assessment or similar processes to certify new teachers as they enter the profession. Check your state agency Web site or ask an advisor in your teacher education program about the requirements for

---

FIGURE 3.1   **INTASC Standards**

Principle 1: The teacher understands the central concepts, tools of inquiry, and structures of the discipline(s) he or she teaches and can create learning experiences that make these aspects of subject matter meaningful for students.

Principle 2: The teacher understands how children learn and develop and can provide learning opportunities that support their intellectual, social, and personal development.

Principle 3: The teacher understands how students differ in their approaches to learning and creates instructional opportunities that are adapted to diverse learners.

Principle 4: The teacher understands and uses a variety of instructional strategies to encourage students' development of critical thinking, problem solving, and performance skills.

Principle 5: The teacher uses an understanding of individual and group motivation and behavior to create a learning environment that encourages positive social interaction, active engagement in learning, and self-motivation.

Principle 6: The teacher uses knowledge of effective verbal, nonverbal, and media communication techniques to foster active inquiry, collaboration, and supportive interaction in the classroom.

Principle 7: The teacher plans instruction based upon knowledge of subject matter, students, the community, and curriculum goals.

Principle 8: The teacher understands and uses formal and informal assessment strategies to evaluate and ensure the continuous intellectual, social, and physical development of the learner.

Principle 9: The teacher is a reflective practitioner who continually evaluates the effects of his/her choices and actions on others (students, parents, and other professionals in the learning community) and who actively seeks out opportunities to grow professionally.

Principle 10: The teacher fosters relationships with school colleagues, parents, and agencies in the larger community to support students' learning and well-being.

new teachers in your state. You may find that you can use the Portfolio suggestions (at the end of each chapter in this text) as part of state- or university-required portfolio systems.

Another issue related to professionalism is set forth by those who feel teachers should have more control over their profession. Critics of the national standards movement feel that standards, assessment, and accountability—as set forward in the United States in NCLB and Title II—actually reduce the professionalism of teachers by maintaining control of the profession by nonteachers through licensing and testing. Because teachers do not have a great deal of control over licensure and evaluation and testing, many argue that standards, testing, and accountability created and administered by nonteachers do not contribute to professionalism. Those who hold this view suggest that professionalism of teachers is directly proportional to the amount of control teachers have over the establishment and maintenance of standards and testing. The role of federal and state politics in establishing licensure and testing procedures and the resulting benefits to the testing industry fuel much debate in educational settings.

You can learn more about the Interstate New Teacher Assessment and Support Consortium (INTASC) at this Web site:

http://www.ccsso.org/projects/interstate_new_assessment_and_support_consortium/780.cfm

URLs may change over time. For up-to-date links to relevant Web sites, visit our Companion Web site:

http://education.wadsworth.com/wiseman3e

Although opinions differ about national standards and the status of the teaching profession, no one doubts that teaching is moving toward a "higher, more complex, demanding plane" (Myers & Myers, 1995, p. 616). The debates over teacher controls, standards establishment, and how teachers are held accountable are necessary before the profession can be perceived as credible and fully effective. Redefining a profession is an evolutionary process influenced both by those in the profession and by external events. Future teachers will make major contributions to the struggle toward professionalism that is a constant theme in today's teaching environment.

SALARY CONCERNS Most people enter teaching to work with children and young people or because they enjoy and are excited about a certain subject area, but salaries are traditionally an important issue in the teaching profession. Although low in comparison to many other professions, teacher salaries have steadily improved in most regions. The average salary for teachers rose in the last decade to $38,500—a 20 percent increase since 1980 (Sadker & Sadker, 2000). Salaries are higher in larger school districts and in urban areas and tend to be lower in the southern states. Public school teachers are paid more than are private school teachers. Although teachers, like most professionals, might like to receive higher salaries, most say they entered the profession for other reasons.

School Choice

In an effort to recognize parental opinions and desires, particularly in the context of NCLB, several innovations increasing school choice are currently popular. Parents have the right to select the school they wish their children to attend. They no longer have to send their children to schools that do not exhibit expected test results or have been designated as a dangerous school. One of the reasons behind the popularity of school choice is the market-based belief that schools will then compete for students and attempt to attract students by providing the best educational experiences possible. Most school choice programs provide for redirection of funds based on parents' decisions about where to educate their children. Although the concept of school choice is often debated, choice makes a notable difference in parent satisfaction. A recent government survey indicates that parents who had some say in their children's schools were more satisfied with teachers, academics, order, and discipline than were parents of children attending assigned public schools (National Center for Educational Statistics, 1999).

VOUCHERS Vouchers are proposed as a way to further increase the choices parents have in selecting schools. Instead of providing tax money to neighborhood schools, states would issue tuition vouchers to parents, who can then enroll their children in a school of their choice, whether it be public or private. The chosen school would then collect state funds based on the number of students enrolled. Supporters argue that parents have the right to send their children to any school of their choice. Others argue that using vouchers would dramatically change the concept of public schooling, enabling private schools to compete with traditional public schools and greatly reduce funding to public schools.

CHARTER SCHOOLS The development of charter schools is another innovation evolving from the desire to expand school choice. Charter schools are newly created, state-funded public schools offering a specific educational concept or theme, such as service learning, art or music, or a back-to-basics approach to teaching. Museums, communities, businesses, individuals, teachers, and even for-profit organizations may develop a charter for a school as long as a local school board or the state department of education approves the educational plan. Arkansas lawmakers have even conceptualized and supported the idea of a virtual charter school, where students will be taught online. The first charter school was established in Minnesota in 1991, and in the 2000–2001 school year 1,993 charter schools were reported. Most of the schools are elementary, and half of the schools were located in Arizona, California, and Michigan (National Center for Education Statistics, 1999). As of August 2002, the National Education Association (2001) reported there were more than 2,300 public charter schools serving more than 500,000 students nationwide.

There are many different charter school themes and arrangements. Existing charter schools have evolved around traditional basic skills, home-schooling, storefront programs, distance learning, and computer-based learning (Oliva, 1997). Some charter schools target low achievers or at-risk students and attempt to raise achievement by innovative and creative teaching and learning environments. Students must demonstrate achievement on statewide accountability measures, but because the teachers and administrators are not held to state requirements and curricula, charter schools are seen as a way to accomplish two things: (1) encourage innovation and (2) force traditional schools to change their approaches to compete for and maintain their student populations.

You can learn more about charter schools at this Web site:

http://www.charterschools.org

URLs may change over time. For up-to-date links to relevant Web sites, visit our Companion Web site:

http://education.wadsworth.com/wiseman3e

FOR-PROFIT EDUCATORS One important choice available to both schools and parents is the option of privatized and for-profit educational services. Many private-sector companies, such as Sylvan Learning Systems, are filling a niche as providers of specialized services, such as tutoring. Large for-profit ventures also have targeted other school functions during the past few years. One of the best known, the Edison Project, is attempting to establish a successful franchise based on assuring student success. The Edison Project will manage schedules, hire teachers, purchase equipment and supplies, maintain transportation, and make other important educational decisions. Several large public schools have transferred resources to the Edison Project, hoping that the for-profit organization can change their schools into places in which all children succeed. Some of the for-profit educational systems are struggling to stay in business, and their effectiveness has yet to be demonstrated. Supporters of the idea believe that schools can be run like a business and that privatization is cost-efficient and academically effective. Critics include the National Education Association and the American Federation of Teachers, who raise concerns about making a profit from the education of children. Future teachers will face and consider these issues during their careers.

HOMESCHOOLING Homeschooling has emerged as a choice that many parents make for educating their children, and the number of children who are taught in their homes by their parents, relatives, or close friends is approximately 850,000 (NCES, 1999). Parents decide to take over their children's education for many reasons, usually because they feel that the public or private school system cannot provide the type of education they want for their children. The desire to include a religious component in a child's learning process is one of the most common reasons for homeschooling. Other parents may want to provide their children with art, music, or other experience-based educational approaches. Still other parents do not feel the schools in their community provide a safe environment or effective education for their children. The industry of homeschooling is growing rapidly: Parents can access curricula from private companies, the Internet, or their churches. In many cases, parents homeschool for the early years of elementary school and then send their children to public school for middle and high school. The critics of homeschooling cite the uneven quality offered by untrained educators and the reduced opportunities for children to become socialized by being around other children as drawbacks. Nevertheless, many children who are homeschooled and receive individualized instruction in a supportive home-based environment do quite well.

Here is one example of the many Web sites devoted to homeschooling:

http://www.home-school.com

URLs may change over time. For up-to-date links to relevant Web sites, visit our Companion Web site:

http://education.wadsworth.com/wiseman3e

Whether school choice improves the overall educational process is still debated among educators, politicians, and community leaders. Studies looking at the effectiveness of school choice are inconclusive at best. Many parents who support the idea of school choice believe that, if they can transfer educational resources paid by the government to any school of their choice, then their children will be guaranteed the best education possible. But many critics feel that it simply helps families with adequate resources to improve their situation and works against families with limited resources. For example, the neediest students may be left behind in schools that have reduced support and underfunded programs because parents with additional resources have chosen to leave neighborhood schools. Barriers that prevent lower-income parents from choosing where they send their children to school may be as basic as lack of transportation. Issues of school choice are bound to have an impact on teaching and teachers in the future.

▶ Success in Times of Change

Change is often very difficult, stressful, expensive, and time-consuming for all involved. Despite these challenges, educational reform has made a difference for many children and youth. Several successful programs for comprehensive school reform have led to improved conditions and provide models of success for all students. The programs outlined in the following sections have had their successes documented by extensive research.

Successful schools where all students can achieve academic success share several characteristics that focus on organization, administration, and support systems. Successful schools are often described in terms of their teachers—who are enthusiastic about teaching, care about their students, accept student diversity, and are knowledgeable about their subject matter and the students they teach.

Theodore Sizer: Essential Schools

Theodore Sizer takes on the mountain of issues and problems associated with secondary schools and has established a network of high school–university partnerships across the country to improve secondary school teaching and learning. In Sizer's program, changes in high schools are made based on nine common principles that help the schools set clear and simple goals about intellectual skills and knowledge for their students. Schools that adopt his model establish a vision of integrated, comfortable, trusting environments that focus on collaboration (Sizer, 1992, 1996).

You can learn more about the Coalition of Essential Schools at this Web site:

http://essentialschools.org/

URLs may change over time. For up-to-date links to relevant Web sites, visit our Companion Web site:

http://education.wadsworth.com/wiseman3e

Schools following Sizer's model focus on helping all adolescents to master skills and use their minds as opposed to merely memorizing content. Teachers involve students in hard work and become the coaches as their students work to learn. Students are not separated by age and are judged successful on the basis of exhibitions or demonstrations of their learning. Sizer's Essential Schools movement uses larger blocks of time for instruction than are traditionally scheduled and puts students in smaller, more manageable working groups so that instruction can be more personalized.

Robert Slavin: Success for All

Robert Slavin determined that many of the instructional interventions designed to help hard-to-teach students (for example, pullout programs, special education, reduced class size) actually have had a detrimental effect on school achievement and attitudes (Slavin & Madden, 2000). As a result, he and his colleague developed an intervention model that focuses on helping students before they drop behind. His model focuses on self-paced instructional procedures and goals that use cooperative learning techniques (see Chapter 7). Tutors, schoolwide curriculum, family support teams, and facilitators who work with teachers are important components of the Success for All program. His first efforts focused on instructional methods in reading, writing, and language arts from kindergarten to grade six. Recently, he has added Roots and Wings, a mathematics, social studies, and science curriculum (Slavin, Madden, & Wasik, 1996). Several Spanish bilingual adaptations of the program are also available.

Teachers who work in schools that adopt the Success for All model believe they contribute to students' success and that it is their responsibility to prevent students from falling behind. Teachers are trained that

You can learn more about Success for All and Roots and Wings at this Web site:

http://successforall.net

URLs may change over time. For up-to-date links to relevant Web sites, visit our Companion Web site:

http://education.wadsworth.com/wiseman3e

"all children" can learn and, if students are not successful, then it is up to the teacher to be more responsive to individual needs of students and develop ways to involve students in their own learning. Slavin and Madden's (2000) research shows that this program results in consistent, substantial success for all groups of students.

James Comer: School Power

Convinced that educational systems have failed black children, James Comer developed a model for inner-city children that recognizes and addresses cultural heritage and diverse socioeconomic situations (Haynes & Comer, 1990). Comer's model emphasizes nurturing students who are identified as hard-to-teach. He acknowledges the importance of adults in children's lives, and his programs require a great deal of adult involvement. He believes school governance teams are the most important structural component of a school and proposes new methods of school leadership. His schools are governed by teams of ten to fifteen representatives from

You can learn more about James Comer at this Web site:

http://info.med.yale.edu/comer/

URLs may change over time. For up-to-date links to relevant Web sites, visit our Companion Web site:

http://education.wadsworth.com/wiseman3e

all the adults who work with students in the school, including teachers, counselors, principals, parents, and social workers. The team focuses on building strong relationships among the children and adults. His model involves parents and families deeply in everything from school governance to curriculum planning. Instructional activities tend to focus on dual

development of academics and social skills. His model consistently results in improved achievement scores and improved attitudes and behaviors for children who were not succeeding in traditional school organizations (Comer, 1994). He is currently expanding his model to include middle and high school.

Effective Teaching Practices for Linguistic and Cultural Diversity

In today's sound-byte culture, it is extremely popular to use test results as the only measure of school success (Kohn, 2000). However, the pervasive gap between minority students and white students suggests that learners may need content presented in different ways. For these reasons and others, many questions arise about the role of accountability and testing in culturally diverse classrooms.

Instructional strategies specifically tailored for diverse populations may be necessary to address the achievement gaps discussed in Chapter 2. No single approach will solve all educational challenges in diverse classrooms. However, the following strategies have proven successful for diverse populations and serve as examples about how instruction can respond to classroom diversity.

CULTURALLY RESPONSIVE TEACHING This strategy incorporates students' everyday lives into instructional activities. Family, culture, and community issues become markers that help students learn. Classroom learning activities are based on familiar events and build on students' backgrounds. Familiar referents, examples, and descriptions connect students' existing knowledge with new material presented during instructional activities. Culturally responsive teaching makes new subject matter relevant and significant (Peregoy & Boyle, 2000).

INSTRUCTIONAL CONVERSATIONS During instructional conversations (Echevarria, Vogt, & Short, 2004; Tharp et al., 2000), teachers facilitate discussions about the formal content of instruction and draw upon students' prior and background knowledge. During classroom conversations, many ideas are shared based on experiences students have as individuals and in their home and community lives. In addition to focusing on students' cultural knowledge, the approach explicitly targets formulation and expression of subject matter ideas through oral language and is used prior to, during, and after reading and in combination with other approaches. Good instructional conversations may seem spontaneous, but in fact they are not. Instructional conversations are carefully planned to focus on student learning goals. The teacher is thoroughly acquainted with the text and the ideas being discussed. During the interactions, teachers may take the time to provide direct teaching of a skill or concept. Instructional conversations allow students to learn about topics and concepts in a challenging but nonthreatening atmosphere. As students participate in extensive discourse, they develop conceptual understandings and practice complex language and expression related to the topic being discussed.

www You can learn more about programs that are successful with diverse populations from the following Web site:

http://www.crede.ucsc.edu/

URLs may change over time. For up-to-date links to relevant Web sites, visit our Companion Web site:

http://education.wadsworth.com/wiseman3e

One characteristic of many successful schools is parental involvement in school-related activities. When parents and families feel welcome and involved in their children's schools, they will be more likely to contribute to their children's school experiences in a variety of ways.

SHELTERED INSTRUCTION This approach for teaching content to English language learners (ELLs) promotes students' English language development and understanding of subject matter. ELLs receive content-based instruction (such as math, science, or social studies) in simplified English. The language used by the teacher reflects the level of the learners' comprehension, and the texts used for reading make the content accessible to students.

Characteristics of Successful Programs

Effective and successful school programs produce evidence that schools can make a difference and provide positive outcomes for all students. Schools that succeed usually have a staff of enthusiastic and caring teachers who are knowledgeable in subject matter and pedagogy; a cohesive teaching and learning plan that is integrated across all subjects in the curriculum; recognition of diversity in students' backgrounds, cultures, and talents; a high level of teacher and student engagement; and strong parental involvement (Smith & O'Day, 1991). Successful programs in today's schools pay particular attention to language and cultural diversity represented in classrooms. Figure 3.2 identifies five standards that define successful programs for diverse populations. Crucial to all of the programs briefly described here is the involvement of caring, trained educators who hold the belief that all children, youth, and adolescents can learn if expectations are high and meaningful.

Characteristics of successful programs offer some ideas about the ideal results of school reform, especially because they can easily be transferred to most educational systems. Most successful schools are small organizations with fewer students than the average enrollment expected in today's schools. In successful schools, teachers work together to plan for

---

FIGURE 3.2 **Five Characteristics of Successful Programs**

The Center for Research on Diversity and Excellence in Education (CREDE) has identified five standards for teaching and learning that define the characteristics of successful programs for diverse populations (Tharp et al., 2000, 2002).

1. *Teachers and students producing together.* Teachers and students work collaboratively toward a common product or goal.

2. *Developing language and literacy across the curriculum.* A focus on language development and learning is an important aspect of curriculum for diverse groups of students.

3. *Making meaning—connecting school to students' lives.* Effective teachers help students integrate new learning and previous learning and experiences and make relevant connections to families and cultural and geographic communities.

4. *Teaching complex thinking.* Effective teaching for diverse classrooms does not preclude teaching of basic skills, but goes beyond the skills level to involve students in use of facts and skills to think analytically and engage in problem solving.

5. *Teaching through conversation.* Teaching through dialogue is an instructional strategy that relies on authentic teacher and student questions and sharing of knowledge and ideas within a classroom "community of learners."

Further information is located at http://www.crede.ucsc.edu/research/pdd/5stand_evidence.html.

teaching and learning. The vision, goals, and means of achieving the goals are clearly articulated by teachers and administrators and developed through continuous discussion and reflection. Teachers have professional development and planning time and are encouraged to collaborate and plan integrated approaches that consider language and cultural diversity. Caring for students is an important component of successful school reform. This is particularly true in Comer's model, for example, in which the importance of developing a supportive, caring relationship with the adults in the school is explicit (Rossi & Stringfield, 1995). Innovative learning strategies are incorporated to engage students in motivating, relevant activities. Most successful programs present a "parent and family friendly" school, where many different individuals are welcomed as a caring community (Minicucci et al., 1995).

Successful schools are good for children and for teachers, and the common characteristics of successful programs suggest what new teachers should look for in schools when they begin their careers. Take time now to complete the Self-Reflection exercise (on page 94) and to think about what you have learned about school reform.

The Case against Change

Not everyone agrees that change is needed, and some believe that change efforts are expensive, time-consuming, and detrimental to the educational process. In particular, opponents of high-stakes testing perceive current accountability approaches as deterrents to the kind of schooling that promotes meaningful learning and creativity among teachers and students. One study outlined harmful effects of high-stakes testing, particularly for underrepresented populations (Amrein & Berliner, 2002). Some even suggest that calls for reform are bogus and politically motivated, as in a report from the Sandia National Laboratory that was conducted at the onset of the accountability movement and concluded that the nation's educational system did not need an overhaul (Carson, Huelskamp, & Woodall, 1993; Tanner, 1993). This report suggested that the data used in support of accountability reform had been skewed to justify the need for change. Authors asserted that the call for change was generated by businesses that saw testing and for-profit schools as a moneymaking endeavor. Berliner and Biddle (1996) and Bracey (2000) made the case that many of the criticisms of education were myths that have actually damaged public schools. They claim that test results in the United States are holding steady in international assessments and that "school bashing" has been a popular sport for years. As Berliner and Biddle (1996) admitted, this argument is based on a fundamental difference in values and beliefs of what education is about (see the discussion on philosophies in Chapter 2). However, the arguments about changes in schools during the last few years have gone beyond the typical past disagreements about philosophy and use of successful strategies. They have gained political weight and appear in the rhetoric of presidential speeches, new laws, federal budget debates, and church pulpits.

The groundwork for recent federal legislation related to school reform was laid in the early 1980s. In President Reagan's 1984 State of the Union address, he urged Americans to return to traditional values in education. "Excellence must begin in our homes and neighborhood schools, where it's the responsibility of every parent and teacher and the right of every child . . . restore discipline . . . encourage the teaching of new basics . . . and put our parents back in charge" (McGraw, 1984, p. 39). In 1989, strategists for the Christian Coalition established the "Contract with the American Family," which supported school vouchers, discouraged teaching history from a multicultural perspective, and advocated eliminating the Department of Education, reducing the arts in schools, and denying or withholding benefits for young unmarried mothers. Eleven years later, the 2000 presidential campaign again focused on education and reiterated the call for reform and excellence in education. The most recent manifestation of political interest in education is the George W. Bush administration's No Child Left Behind legislation, which mandates reform at national and state levels.

Calls for change are often confusing and frustrating for teachers. Most teachers want to focus on their own classrooms and the students who are there to learn. However, some reforms do make a positive difference in the classroom. Future teachers need to remain informed about what and who may have an impact on their work.

There will always be calls to make changes in teaching and learning, often accompanied by controversy and blame. They come from parents, community members, politicians, religious groups, and business. Many proposals about education result from differing philosophical stances (see Chapter 2), others from new information and technologies, and still others from the needs of students. But the key factor in the reform movement remains the classroom teacher (Hord, 1992). Teachers who are educated in ways that encourage them to support all students' learning will benefit from and promote changes in their classrooms that support their students' successes and achievement.

FIELD-BASED ACTIVITY

3.2

As a class, design several questions that you would like to ask experienced teachers about how reform has affected their careers. Questions such as "List all the reforms or changes that you can remember" or "Which calls for reform have had the greatest impact?" will help you understand the changing nature of the teaching profession. Divide your class into four or five small groups. Each person in your group can interview a teacher using the questions that the class designed. Discuss the results of your interviews with your small-group members. Compare your group's interview results with those of the rest of the class. When comparing the results of your interviews, identify the time span represented by the teachers' perspectives, the reform movements that affected the teachers directly, the concerns the teachers expressed about change, and the benefits and challenges of school change.

INTASC Principle 9

SELF-REFLECTION

Recognizing Reform

In this list of successful school programs, check off those you are familiar with and place a question mark in the second column if you are unfamiliar with the program.

	Familiar	Unfamiliar	Of Interest
School Development Program http://info.med.yale.edu/comer/	_____	_____	_____
Roots and Wings http://www.successforall.net/ curriculum/rwprogdescr.htm	_____	_____	_____
Edison Project http://www.edisonschools.com/	_____	_____	_____
Sheltered Instruction http://www.crede.ucsc.edu/	_____	_____	_____
Accelerated Schools http://www.acceleratedschools.net	_____	_____	_____

	Familiar	Unfamiliar	Of Interest
Talent Development High School http://scov.csos.jhu.edu/tdhs/index.htm	_____	_____	_____
Instructional Conversations CREDE/www.crede.ucsc.edu	_____	_____	_____
Modern Red Schoolhouse http://www.mrsh.org/	_____	_____	_____
High Schools That Work http://wvde.state.wv.us/hstw	_____	_____	_____
Expeditionary Learning Outward Bound http://www.elob.org/	_____	_____	_____

Now count the number of check marks. If you score less than six out of ten, visit the Web sites for the unfamiliar programs. After visiting the Web sites, put a check mark in Column Three next to those that really look interesting to you. If you want to know even more about a particular reform program, search InfoTrac College Edition for more in-depth articles.

PORTFOLIO REFLECTIONS AND EXHIBITS

Throughout this chapter you completed a series of Field-Based Activities. The activities may serve as the basis for a portfolio representation, or you may develop your own portfolio representation or complete these suggested portfolio activities:

Suggested Exhibit 3: Educational Reforms

A portfolio representation for this chapter might include these items:

1. Review your responses to the Field-Based Activities in this chapter. Itemize factors that cause change in most educational settings.

2. Develop a "change chart" that illustrates the origin of reform or change movements. Indicate whether the changes are the result of differences within the educational community, diverse ideas about

(continued)

the purpose of education, demands from society, changes in technology, or something else. The chart should illustrate the origin of the reform and include a statement about the impact of outside influences on the teaching profession.

E-Portfolio Entry 3

Research NCLB on the Internet. Develop a list of Web sites that will help you and your classmates understand the impact of NCLB changes on classroom teachers. Annotate the most helpful Web sites and include them as a file on a link in your e-portfolio. The following Web site will help you get started: http://www.edu.gov.

INTASC Principles 9 and 10

ANSWERS TO GUIDING YOUR READING

1. What are the educational agendas and mandates that affect teaching and learning in current classrooms?

The No Child Left Behind Act is affecting current teaching and learning processes and will continue to do so. Despite the quantity and diversity of proposed issues and innovations established by federal legislation, the desire for accountability, standards for students and teachers, and assessment to ensure mastery of standards is an overriding agenda. Other agendas that will continue to affect teaching and learning are equitable education for all students, school choice, professionalization of teaching, teacher quality, school restructuring, and innovations for teaching and learning.

2. What are characteristics of successful educational programs that address needed changes in teaching and learning?

Successful schools are good for children and teachers. Most successful schools are small organizations with fewer students than the average enrollment expected in today's schools. Teachers work collaboratively to meet common goals and plan for teaching and learning. The vision, goals, and means of achieving the goals are clearly articulated by teachers and administrators and developed through continuous discussion and reflection. Teachers have professional development and planning time and are encouraged to collaborate and plan integrated approaches that consider language and cultural diversity. Caring for students is an important component of successful school reform, and parents and families are included in the educational processes.

3. What effects do you think reform movements will have on your teaching?

Teachers entering the profession in the next few years will be greatly affected by the No Child Left Behind Act. This federal legislation puts a great deal of pressure on teachers to make sure their students perform well in the classroom. Teachers will focus on testing and accountability and will work closely with parents and other caregivers to help students succeed.

4. What are some of the reasons people resist educational change?

Critics of current educational changes are particularly concerned about the impact of testing on some groups of students. Others may view mandated requirements as intrusive and a political tool. Still others may resist change because of the increased pressure on teachers and the economic costs associated with needed reforms. Even though it inspires many criticisms, educational reform is here to stay and will always be a part of the teaching profession.

INFOTRAC COLLEGE EDITION EXTENSION

Log on to the InfoTrac College Edition Web site and use it to find out more about current testing issues. Using the subject guide, type in "high stakes testing." Choose an article about testing for either students or teachers. What are the arguments for and against testing of this type?

RELATED READINGS

The following books will provide you with more information about the topics discussed in this chapter:

Cunningham, P. M., & Allington, R. L. (1999). *Classrooms that work: They can all read and write* (2nd ed.). New York: Longman.

Cunningham and Allington describe what works for classroom teachers who care about the literacy development of the children they teach. This book presents a positive view of one of the most contentious topics in elementary school teaching—teaching reading and writing. The authors also explain that change does not happen overnight. If we want to see real differences in the classroom, we must be patient and give it some time.

Ingersoll, R. M. (2003). *Who controls teachers' work? Power and accountability in America's schools.* Boston: Harvard.

This book presents a critical view of recent national and local policies that control what and how teachers teach. Ingersoll describes the political nature of accountability and reform and makes a strong research-based case for leaving the control of the classroom in the hands of teachers.

Sizer, T. (1992). *Horace's compromise: The dilemma of the American high school.* Boston: Houghton Mifflin.

Sizer, T. (1992). *Horace's school: Redesigning the American high school.* Boston: Houghton Mifflin.

Sizer, T. (1996). *Horace's hope: What works for the American high school.* Boston: Houghton Mifflin.

Horace Smith, a fictional teacher, and other characters make Sizer's arguments and suggestions for changing American high schools informative, inspiring, and positive. These three books demonstrate successful educational changes.

Wasley, P. A. (1994). *Stirring the chalkdust.* New York: Teachers College Press.

This book presents an insiders' account of the changes that come about when Sizer's Coalition of Essential Schools processes are put in place. Secondary teachers write about the rewards and challenges of change. The book also presents a description of the most common changes teachers are making.

REFERENCES

Epigraph: Ouchi, William G. (2003). *Making schools work: A revolutionary plan to get your children the education they need* (pp.101, 105). New York: Simon & Schuster.

Amrein, A. L., & Berliner, D. C. (2002). High-stakes testing, uncertainty, and student learning. *Education Policy Analysis Archives,* 10(18).

Berliner, D. C., & Biddle, B. J. (1996). *The manufactured crisis: Myths, fraud, and the attack on America's public schools.* New York: Addison-Wesley.

Bracey, G. W. (2000). The 10th Bracey report on the condition of public education. *Phi Delta Kappan,* 82(2), 133–144.

Carson, C. C., Huelskamp, R. M., & Woodall, T. D. (1993). Perspectives on education in America. *Journal of Educational Research,* 86(5), 259–310.

Clark, C. (1995). *Thoughtful teaching.* New York: Teachers College Press.

Cohen, D. (1995). What standards for national standards? *Phi Delta Kappan,* 76(10), 751–757.

Comer, J. (1994). Home, school and academic learning. In J. I. Goodlad & P. Keating (Eds.), *Access to knowledge* (pp. 23–42). New York: College Board.

Echevarria, J., Vogt, M. E., & Short, D. (2004). *Making content comprehensible for English language learners: The SIOP mode* (2nd ed.). Boston: Allyn & Bacon.

Falk, B. (2000). *The heart of the matter: Using standards and assessment to learn.* Portsmouth, NH: Heinemann.

Haynes, N., & Comer, J. (1990). Helping black children succeed: The significance of some social factors. In K. Lomotey (Ed.), *Going to school: The African American experience* (pp. 103–113). Albany: State University of New York Press.

Hlebowitsh, P., & Tellez, K. (1997). *American education: Purpose and promise.* Belmont, CA: Wadsworth.

Hord, S. M. (1992). *Facilitative leadership: The imperative for change.* Austin, TX: Southwest Educational Development Laboratory.

Illinois State Board of Education (1997). *Illinois learning standards.* Springfield: Author.

Jennings, J. (1995). School reform based on what is taught and learned. *Phi Delta Kappan,* 76(10), 765–769.

Kohn, A. (2000). *The case against standardized testing: Raising the scores, ruining the schools.* Portsmouth, N.H.: Heinemann.

McGraw, O. (1984). Reclaiming traditional values in education: The implications for educational research. *Educational Leadership,* 38(1), 30–42.

Minicucci, C., Berman, P., McLaughlin, B., McLeod, B., Nelson, B., & Woodworth, K. (1995). School reform and student diversity. *Phi Delta Kappan,* 77(1), 77–80.

Myers, C. B., & Myers, L. K. (1995). *The professional educator: A new introduction to teaching and schools.* Belmont, CA: Wadsworth

National Center for Educational Statistics (1999). *Homeschooling in the United States.* Washington, DC: US Department of Education, Institute of Education Sciences.

National Commission on Excellence in Education. (1983). *A nation at risk: The imperative for educational reform.* Washington, DC: U.S. Department of Education.

National Education Association (2002). *Charter schools.* Retrieved February 2004 from www:nea.org/charter/

Oliva, P. F. (1997). *Developing the curriculum* (4th ed.). New York: Longman.

Payne, K. J., & Biddle, B. J. (1999). Poor school funding, child poverty, and mathematics achievement. *Educational Researcher,* 28(6), 4–13

Peregoy, S. F., & Boyle, O. F. (2000). English learners reading English: What we know, what we need to know. *Theory into Practice,* 39, 237–247.

Piner, W. F. (1992). The curriculum. In J. L. Kincheloe & S. R. Steinberg (Eds.), *Thirteen questions: Reframing education's conversation* (pp. 31–38). New York: Peter Lang.

Rossi, R. J., & Stringfield, S. (1995). What we must do for students placed at risk. *Phi Delta Kappan,* 77(1), 73–77.

Sadker, M. P., & Sadker, D. M. (2000). *Teachers, schools, society* (5th ed.). Boston: McGraw-Hill.

Sizer, T. (1992). *Horace's school: Redesigning the American school.* Boston: Houghton Mifflin.

Sizer, T. (1996). *Horace's hope: What works for the American high school.* Boston: Houghton Mifflin.

Slavin, R. E., & Madden, N. A. (2000). Research on achievement outcomes of success for all: A summary and response to critics. *Phi Delta Kappan,* 82(1), 38–67.

Slavin, R. E., Madden, N. A., & Wasik, B. (1996). *Success for all: A summary of research.* Baltimore: Johns Hopkins University.

Smith, M. S., & O'Day, J. (1991). Systemic school reform. In S. Fuhrman & B. Malen (Eds.), *The politics of curriculum and testing* (pp. 116–133). Philadelphia: Falmer Press.

Tanner, D. (1993). A nation truly at risk. *Phi Delta Kappan,* 75(4), 288–297.

Tharp, R. G., Estrada, P., Dalton, S., & Yamauchi, L. (2000). *Teaching transformed: Achieving excellence, fairness, inclusion, and harmony.* Boulder, CO: Westview.

Legal and Ethical Issues

4

. . . By the end of her fifth week, Kay has begun to realize that everything does not depend upon the teacher, that there are many factors that influence what can and will occur. . . . One cannot force children to learn, and learning will not always be fun. Children can contribute to their own learning and observing them is beneficial. . . . Her embryonic theory of teaching and learning is now more apparent, and shows evidence of applying ethical and moral criteria as she questions classroom events. . . .

Equity, fairness, and justice are clear themes that begin to appear in journal entries. . . . Early in the semester Kay has a strong reaction to an offhand jest that Janet makes about giving up on a child:

"At one point after class I asked Janet what to do about Christy, who says no to everything and is constantly causing trouble. She said in jest, 'Oh, I've given up on her.' I know Janet is not totally giving up because I see her deal with her. I really don't want to be the type of teacher that gives up on kids, although I see how hard it is not to when you have 27 other students to think of. Idealistically, I'm saying I'll never give up, but I hope realistically I follow this."

—Frances Schoonmaker, *Growing Up Teaching*

Guiding Your Reading

1. What constitutional rights and responsibilities affect schools?

2. What laws govern the teaching profession?

3. What are the rights of teachers and students?

4. What are the important ethical issues related to teaching, and what dilemmas do they present to teachers?

*T*his example, taken from a ten-year study chronicling teacher development, illustrates the connections between a teacher's actions and her moral and ethical development related to teaching. The young teacher described in the excerpt is recognizing that it is her ethical responsibility to help all students learn. Teachers' classroom behaviors are affected by their own ethical values—the system whereby they judge right and wrong. The legal aspects of education may force teachers to look closely at their own ethics and at the moral standards accepted in the community. Unfortunately, personal ethical dilemmas rarely have the benefit of a law or previous case to guide decision making. The legal and ethical issues emerging in school settings are almost always complex and difficult.

Teachers and their students have rights embedded in the Constitution of the United States. The laws, and less directly the ethics of our society and profession, govern all individuals in the schools, but interpretation of these laws is often more difficult when children and young people are involved.

At one time, contracts with the schools where teachers taught tightly regulated their lives. Their duties were specifically outlined down to the clothes they were required to wear. Men had to wear a jacket and tie, and women had to wear dresses and skirts. Personal lives were also regulated. A female teacher's career was terminated if she married, and teachers were not allowed to drink or engage in any behavior that would not set a good example for their students. All teachers were expected to live up to strict ethical and community guidelines—guidelines not required of most other professionals.

This attitude was maintained throughout the early 1900s, but changes in other aspects of our society from that time forward also changed how teaching and other professions were governed. The Depression, war, and women's rights deeply affected society and the workplace during the 1930s and the 1940s, and policies affecting teachers began to relax. Although the

1960s civil rights movement brought dramatic changes to many of the strict regulations on teachers, they are still not free to act irresponsibly. Because legal and ethical considerations must guide teachers' decisions, behaviors, and words both in class and out teachers need a basic understanding of the issues relevant to their profession. This chapter discusses those issues.

Governmental Authority

The laws that contribute to educational governance are legislated at the federal, state, and local levels. Each level of government has a very different role and responsibility when it comes to school policy.

Federal Authority

Schools are not considered a direct responsibility of the federal government, and federal laws tend to be indirect when dealing with education. Although education is not addressed specifically in the Constitution, several of its provisions are important for education. Through Constitutional interpretation by federal courts and the Supreme Court, the federal government has had a great impact on education (Myers & Myers, 1995). The four Constitutional amendments that most affect what happens in schools are the First, the Fourth, the Tenth, and the Fourteenth (Figure 4.1).

None of these three amendments establish schools, but they each have an impact on education in various ways. When cases about education come before the courts, for example, interpretation of one of these amendments is usually at the core of the case.

The limited power of the federal government granted by the Constitution does not prevent Congress, the president, and the U.S. Department of Education from formulating national policies and guidelines, providing funds to schools, and encouraging school improvement (Myers & Myers, 1995). The George W. Bush administration affected day-to-day operations in schools with its The No Child Left Behind Act of 2001 (Pub. L. 107–110, 115 Stat. 1425), which provides guidelines for many activities, including reading instruction, assessment processes, and parental communication. As this law demonstrates, education has become a major issue in the political arena, and the public looks to the federal government to make such large-scale changes.

Federal governmental authority is also extended in laws that fund education. Congress regularly approves a comprehensive and complex bill, known as the Elementary and Secondary Education Act (ESEA). Since the 1960s, the federal government has made funds available to schools through

FIGURE 4.1 **Constitutional Amendments That Affect Schools**

Amendment I [1791]

Congress shall make no law respecting an establishment of religion, or prohibiting the free exercise thereof; or abridging the freedom of speech or of the press; or the right of the people peaceably to assemble, and to petition the Government for a redress of grievances.

This amendment is the basis of debates over what should be read or discussed at school, the legality of school prayer, and whether topics such as evolution should be taught.

Amendment IV [1791]

The right of the people to be secure in their persons, houses, papers, and effects, against unreasonable searches and seizures, shall not be violated, and no warrants shall issue, but upon probable cause, supported by oath or affirmation, and particularly describing the place to be searched, and the persons or things to be seized.

This amendment is often at the heart of debates over privacy issues related to searching school lockers and students' backpacks for drugs, weapons, or other items.

Amendment X [1791]

The powers not delegated to the United States by the Constitution, nor prohibited by it to the States, are reserved to the States respectively, or to the people.

This amendment assigns the process of establishing schools to the states.

Amendment XIV [1868]

Section 1. All persons born or naturalized in the United States, and subject to the jurisdiction thereof, are citizens of the United States and of the State wherein they reside. No State shall make or enforce any law which shall abridge the privileges or immunities of citizens of the United States; nor shall any State deprive any person of life, liberty, or property, without due process of law; nor deny to any person within its jurisdiction the equal protection of the laws.

This amendment states that all citizens and people within the jurisdiction of the United States have a right to all privileges (one of which is education) and a right to be treated equally under the law. Educational policies concerning students' right to privacy and the civil rights of racial, disabled, or non-English-speaking minorities and are based upon the Fourteenth Amendment.

You can learn more about No Child Left Behind at the following Web sites:

http://www.ctredpol.org/fededprograms/newfedroleedfeb2002.htm

http://www.ed.gov/nclb/landing.jhtml

http://www.ruraledu.org/issues/nclb.htm

URLs may change over time. For up-to-date links to relevant Web sites, visit our Companion Web site:

http://education.wadsworth.com/wiseman3e

the ESEA. Federal laws and regulations provide direction and requirements for how these funds are to be used by states and local school districts. When the funds were reauthorized in 2002, ESEA became synonymous with the No Child Left Behind Act, or NCLB. NCLB makes significant and far-reaching changes to ESEA, directing funds to preparation and retention of highly qualified teachers; establishing standards, rigorous curriculum, and regular assessment in reading, mathematics, and science; and to assuring that each student makes adequate yearly progress.

State Authority

The Tenth Amendment places the responsibility for education with the individual states, thus allowing wide variability in how state laws support educational issues. Nonetheless, remarkable conformity exists across the country in how schools are governed and regulated: Each state has compulsory attendance, students attend school for approximately the same amount of time each year (around 180 days), teachers must obtain a license based on similar requirements (i.e., bachelor's degree, successful completion of teacher tests, university coursework), statewide achievement tests are given annually, curriculum standards for subject areas are developed, and student reporting periods are six or nine weeks. State legislatures, the governor, state departments of education, and state boards of education are responsible for representing citizens' views when making educational decisions (Myers & Myers, 1995).

The role of the state in supporting educational initiatives is wide-ranging, but the state generally establishes and interprets educational laws and policies and makes sure schools comply with these rules and regulations. State agencies levy taxes and distribute resulting funds to the schools. School funding, teacher certification, and curriculum are all decided at the state level. State agencies also administer tests, keep records, and provide goals and objectives for students.

Local Authority

Elected officials, mayors, county executives, city councils, township supervisors, and local judges implement laws that govern public and private schools. Many of their decisions influence the types of schools that are established and how they are run. Local school boards and the school superintendents they hire are responsible for the day-to-day operation of schools. They employ teachers, appoint principals, set tax rates, approve budgets, build and maintain school buildings, buy equipment, set school calendars, and negotiate salaries. Even though state and national regulations and policies dictate local school boards' responsibilities, their immediate decisions reflect local concerns and issues and affect local schools, individual teachers, and students. Local policies and actions reflect how citizens of the community want their schools to operate. Many decisions are made at local school board meetings that are open to the public.

▶ *Laws and Decisions That Affect Schools*

Several court cases have had a tremendous impact on schooling in the United States. Federal and district courts commonly make rulings that affect teachers and students, and their decisions are often controversial. Future

© Bob Daemmrich/The Image Works

Many decisions about education are made by the courts and legislative mandates. Recent federal legislation about education involved a great deal of debate and discussion before laws were passed. Other decisions about highly debated issues, such as school prayer and integration, have been argued and ultimately decided in the Supreme Court.

teachers need to be familiar with the following issues and their accompanying court rulings.

Equity

Supreme Court decisions concerning access and equity come from the Fourteenth Amendment, which specifies that "no State shall . . . deny to any person within its jurisdiction the equal protection of the laws." The courts have addressed racial segregation, services for students with special needs, instruction for non-native-speaking students, and school finance equity. Following are several of the most important Supreme Court decisions.

In *Plessy v. Ferguson* (1896), the Supreme Court upheld a state-imposed practice, saying that separate facilities did not violate the Fourteenth Amendment so long as the facilities were equal. In effect, this legalized segregation (Timm, 1996). States were therefore free to build segregated educational systems until the 1954 decision in *Brown v. Board of Education*. Linda Brown, an elementary student, sued the board of education of Topeka, Kansas, alleging that the racially separate school she was attending deprived African American students of equal educational opportunity. The state courts ruled against her, stating that separate but equal facilities assured similar educational opportunities. However, the Supreme Court rejected that argument (and reversed its own 1896 decision) and by doing so issued one of the broadest rulings related to education—that segregated facilities were inherently unequal. The decision undermined the laws based on the "separate but equal" doctrine and established that segregation denies equal protection of the law.

Unfortunately, a Supreme Court ruling alone was not enough to make significant changes in our society, and it wasn't until Congress passed the Civil Rights Act of 1964, which outlawed segregation in our schools, that the interactions between minority and majority populations changed markedly.

English as a Second Language

The 1974 Supreme Court decision in *Lau v. Nichols* quoted from the 1964 Civil Rights Act to require transitional bilingual education for schoolchildren who do not speak English (Fischer, Schimmel, & Kelly, 1998). In the original suit, a group of Chinese American students and their parents claimed that their rights were being violated when they were taught in a language they could not understand, arguing that they were excluded from participating in a program that received federal support. The Supreme Court agreed that when children cannot understand what is being taught and no effort is made to help them learn the language, their rights are violated—and the

Laws and court rulings protect students with language differences who may be at risk in today's fast-paced classrooms. Children who are learning English or have recently arrived from other countries may need individualized assistance to catch up with their classmates.

school district must take affirmative steps as soon as possible to rectify the deficiency.

Students' entitlement to instruction in their first language during the time that they are learning English often creates controversy. Educators continue to disagree about which method is best for teaching English language learners. Some support teaching in English because everyone needs to speak English to bind our country together; others feel that it is the learners' right to receive instruction in their native tongue. Legal processes will not eliminate the debate, but courts will continue to rule on issues of how best to eliminate language barriers and allow students with limited English proficiency full participation in public schools. Although the principal is clear, the debate about specific methods will likely continue as our society grows even more diverse.

New Arrivals

Also covered by the Fourteenth Amendment are issues of public education for children of illegal immigrants. States (particularly Texas and California) and the federal government are in constant debate about using tax money to educate children who are in our country illegally. In 1980, after hearing several other related cases, the District Court of Southern Texas ruled that illegal immigrant children's needs were no different from the needs of any other children and that they were entitled to an education. The court viewed children as innocent bystanders who should not be punished because their parents are in this country illegally. The Supreme Court supported the decision in *Plyler v. Doe* (1982) and asserted that school districts could not deny education to school-age residents whose parents entered the country illegally (Cambron-McCabe, McCarthy, & Thomas, 2004). Despite the Supreme Court ruling, California voters in 1994 approved Proposition 187, which denied free education to anyone living in the state illegally. The state proposition was immediately challenged in court and has yet to be decided.

Religious Freedom

Controversy about the role of religion in schools has gone on since the earliest days of public schooling in the United States. Because religion is so important in the lives of many people, powerful emotions are associated with this issue.

All students can attend schools no matter what their religious preferences, but they are not free to act out their religious beliefs in the classroom nor to impose their actions or beliefs on others. This seems like a simple distinction, but religious ideas and perspectives affect education in many ways. Many disagreements about religious freedom in schools originate from different interpretations of the separation of church and state mandated in the Constitution. The courts are often expected to help determine when religious behavior infringes on individual rights.

Most often the debate concerns the role of prayer, devotionals, and Bible reading during school. The courts have ruled that school-sponsored prayers or Bible reading must be excluded from public schools based on the First Amendment. It is legitimate to study about religion at school, but religious exercise, rituals, and celebrations are against the law. Activities or discussions that approach religious issues and practices from a secular or nonreligious stance are lawful. When the activity or discussion serves a religious purpose, however, it is not in keeping with the legal separation of church and state. Any school-based activity that furthers religion is unconstitutional.

The courts regulated prayer and Bible reading at school nearly forty years ago, but occasional violations occur. The case of *School District of Santa Fe v. Doe* (2000) is a recent example. Using freedom of speech as its basis, the Santa Fe, Texas, school district persisted in conducting student-led prayers over the public address system before football games despite a district court ruling that such prayer before school events violated the Constitutional doctrine of separation of church and state. The Supreme Court agreed to hear the case to determine if student votes indicating widespread student support of the prayer would constitute an exception to the long-established law. In 2000, the Supreme Court ruled that school-sponsored prayers couldn't be part of public school programs where a captive audience of students must listen—whether they care to or not.

In apparent contrast, a 2001 Supreme Court decision reversed a district court decision and found a New York school district guilty of discrimination against a student religious club. The public school, which allowed several extracurricular clubs to meet on school property after hours, had denied the religious club the same rights. The Supreme Court held that the school had established a "limited public forum" wherein freedom of speech must be respected—and from which the school could not bar a club simply because of its religious nature. The No Child Left Behind Act provides an expanded interpretation of what constitute religious expressions and requires assurance from public schools receiving federal funds that they have no policies preventing prayer (McCarthy, Cambron-McCabe, & Thomas, 2004).

Special Needs Students

Based on the Fourteenth Amendment, case law and legislative mandates have made it illegal to exclude children with disabilities from school or to place them improperly in separate educational programs. The most powerful law that protects special needs students is Public L. 94–142, which

FIELD-BASED ACTIVITY

4.1

Select a recent court case that focused on an educational issue. Research the background of the case on the Internet. You will find newspaper articles, court documents, and arguments supporting multiple viewpoints. Read about the origin of the case, how long it took to work its way through the courts, and the final outcome. What impact does the case have on education? How could the ruling of the court case you researched affect you when you are teaching?

INTASC Principle 9

assures free and appropriate education and forbids discrimination against students, no matter what their situation. Originally known as the Education of All Handicapped Children Act, this law is now referred to as IDEA— the Individuals with Disabilities Education Act. In addition, in 1990 Congress passed the Americans with Disabilities Act, or ADA, which prohibits discrimination against people who are disabled. The laws establish that those with qualifying disabilities have additional rights guaranteeing them a free, appropriate education (McCarthy, Cambron-McCabe, & Thomas, 2004). Schools must comply with federal law and meet the needs of all their students or risk losing federal and state funds. Compliance requires the school provide individual education plans (IEPs) for identified students, assessment, and reevaluations and specifies parental rights. This law has been rigorously enforced to provide equal opportunities for all students.

Zero Tolerance

Violent events on school campuses led to the passage of the Gun-Free Schools Act of 1994, which requires school districts to suspend students who bring firearms to school. A zero tolerance policy regarding firearms is a condition of elementary and secondary schools' funding. Many local school districts have adopted broader "zero tolerance" regulations that cover knives and other dangerous weapons. Some schools also apply zero tolerance to drugs, alcohol, and an increasing number of student behaviors (for instance, sexual harassment and hate speech). A recent analysis of zero tolerance policies indicates that it is being applied to younger and younger students and includes activities that happen away from the school campus (for instance, off-campus hazing or parties) (Cambron-McCabe, McCarthy, & Thomas, 2004). Under pressure of these mandates, school officials have applied the very strict rules to unsuspecting students who have brought knives to school to cut brownies or displayed corkscrews during show and tell. The results produced sensationalized press reports ridiculing what appeared to be very harsh punishment for minor infractions. Supporters believe the federal legislation provides teachers and administrators with the backing to remove students from schools when they display bad behavior. Critics feel that the zero tolerance policies are harsh, too far-reaching, and disregard the age and developmental processes of students. Legal questions often arise from application of zero tolerance, and new teachers should therefore know, in detail, how school administrators approach the zero tolerance policy.

Teachers' Rights and Responsibilities

Teachers have the same rights as other citizens, and the "right to privacy" implied in the Fourteenth Amendment protects much of their personal lives. Job discrimination based on age, weight, race, or ethnic origin is illegal. Citizenship, however, can be considered in hiring teachers. Teachers' rights to their own personal or lifestyle preferences are often upheld legally, but teachers are almost never protected against consequences of immoral behavior if the behavior involves students. If a teacher becomes sexually involved with a student or initiates any sexual behavior, the teacher would typically lose the right to teach. If teachers knowingly permit or participate in a student's sexual involvement with others or encourage activities involving alcohol or drugs, they are held accountable. Other rights and responsibilities are not as clear-cut, and courts often must make decisions about the rights of teachers.

When courts must rule on teachers' actions, a major consideration is the likelihood that the conduct negatively affected students or school programs (Strike, 1990). Community standards may also play a role in court decisions. When members of a community believe that certain conduct is immoral, the court ruling may reflect that sentiment. In all cases, court rulings must balance the rights of the teacher against the interests of the school's academic programs as well as community standards.

Academic Freedom and Freedom of Speech

There was a time when teachers were unable to voice their opinions in schools. In 1969, the Supreme Court ruling in *Tinker v. Des Moines* proclaimed that teachers and students retain their First Amendment rights as long as they do not materially and substantially disrupt classes or other school activities. If teachers make false and misleading statements or accusations, however, their freedom of speech is no more protected than anyone else's (Fischer et al., 1998).

Because they are representatives of the school district and the government, teachers do not have total freedom to teach whatever they want. Their manner of presentation, content, and methodology are all controlled. Teachers' classroom expression is governed by *Hazelwood School District v. Kuhlmeier,* which allows school administrators to censor school-sponsored expression or restrict teachers' classroom expression based on legitimate educational concerns. Teachers cannot treat school classrooms as public forums for their personal opinions. Generally, courts rule that teachers' expressions are extensions of the curriculum and can be controlled for educational reasons (McCarthy et al., 2004).

Teachers' rights to teach what they want—their academic freedom—is usually measured against public values. Local school boards do have the right to prohibit the use of certain texts and to control the content of classes—although their reasons for doing so may violate laws about censorship. Teachers cannot refuse to use required texts or to present the established curriculum (Fischer et al., 1998). If there is a disagreement between a teacher and a school board, the school board has the final word (Fischer et al., 1998). The courts usually protect teachers if they use controversial materials that are relevant to instructional goals and are nondisruptive. However, in cases such as *Cary v. Board of Education,* courts are directing that a procedure be in place to review and determine the appropriateness of selected materials before books are approved (Yudorf, Kirp, Levin, & Moran, 2002). As a result, many schools restrict the use of a long list of classroom books and materials.

Child Abuse

Teachers are often the first responsible individuals to realize that children are being harmed or neglected by other adults. The National Child Abuse Prevention and Treatment Act requires teachers to report any known or suspected instance of child abuse. Teachers who fail to report a case of child abuse are legally liable. In fact, any responsible adult who fails to report a suspected case of abuse can be sued. The same law assumes that a teacher will report in good faith and protects teachers from lawsuits if, upon investigation, no abuse is found. A teacher who suspects that a child is abused or neglected should report the situation to the principal or superintendent, who then reports it to either the police or social workers. Be sure you know your school's policies and procedures for reporting suspicious instances.

Unions and Negotiations

In some states, professional associations such as the National Education Association and the American Federation of Teachers help teachers negotiate employment contracts with school boards. A union representative engages in collective bargaining and negotiates with the school board to set salaries and establish certain working conditions for all the teachers in a school district. If negotiations are unsuccessful and teachers are not happy with some aspect of their contracts, they may strike in states where it is legal to do so.

Striking teachers put pressure on the local school board to meet their demands for a new contract by refusing to report to work, leaving students without teachers in classrooms. Twenty-four states prohibit strikes, and the courts often order teachers back into the classrooms. Twelve states impose penalties for strikes, which range from fines to dismissal to, in some cases, imprisonment. Supporters of unions point to increased teachers' salaries and improved working conditions as results of collective bargaining. Critics of unions highlight reduced professionalism and the possible harmful effects on student learning as a result of union-sponsored strikes. For more information about teachers' rights to strike and collective bargaining in individual states, go to http:// www.ecs.org/ecsmain.asp?page=/search/default.asp and search for "Unions/Collective Bargaining."

You can learn more about professional organizations at these Web sites:

National Education Association
http://www.nea.org/

American Federation of Teachers
http://www.aft.org/

URLs may change over time. For up-to-date links to relevant Web sites, visit our Companion Web site:

http://education.wadsworth.com/wiseman3e

Students' Rights and Responsibilities

Just as teachers are guaranteed certain rights by law and have certain responsibilities that are legally prescribed, students also have certain rights and responsibilities. Most important, all children must receive an education and are guaranteed that right by the Constitution and state laws.

In Loco Parentis and Family Rights

When parents place their children in schools, they delegate the supervision and safety of those children to teachers. Teachers have a responsibility and in fact the power to protect and supervise students in their classrooms under a doctrine known as *in loco parentis,* which means "in place of parents." This doctrine provides the state with the right to exercise custodial control over students while they are at school. Accordingly, schools are empowered with the responsibility to protect the interests of the student body and the schools, and schools can be held liable for failing to protect students from school environments where danger is created or enhanced. Schools are also liable if they have been deliberately indifferent and failed to protect students from danger. Generally, schools are held liable if they deliberately ignore potentially harmful situations or fail to act

Concerns about on-campus drugs and violence have required schools to supervise and restrict students' behavior at school. Students' rights must be balanced with the need to assure the safety of the entire student body.

when possible harm can come to students. As students get older, however, the law holds students increasingly more responsible for their own actions.

Searches and Seizures

Many cases related to students' rights are based on the right to be protected against unreasonable searches and seizures (Cambron-McCabe, et. al, 2004). Students' rights are guarded by the Fourth Amendment, "the right of the people to be secure in their persons, houses, papers, and effects, against unreasonable searches and seizures." Well-publicized cases of gun violence in schools and the long-time efforts directed at reducing drugs in schools have resulted in many schools exercising the rights of school officials to search lockers and backpacks. Metal detectors, X-ray machines, drug testing, and alcohol breath tests—all considered ways to search students—are commonplace in some districts. Courts regularly weigh students' rights against safety issues and balance these conflicting issues when making rulings.

Given that drugs and guns are ever more a part of our society, school search-and-seizure cases have increased in recent years. Teachers and administrators can search students' lockers or personal effects if they suspect that students are carrying something illegal or dangerous. The law protects students against unreasonable or arbitrary searches, although searches of school property, such as school lockers, may be viewed differently than searches of students' own backpacks, purses, or other personal items. And because of recent school violence, some states have enacted broad laws that eliminate any privacy related to school lockers. New teachers should ask about the district's policies and practices regarding student privacy.

Freedom of Expression

Legal questions regarding freedom of speech for students often emerge out of the struggle between students' First Amendment rights of freedom of expression and the school district's obligation to provide an orderly environment in which to learn. Students do not lose their freedom of speech when they are in a classroom, but they are subject to some limitations. Schools can impose limits to free speech for legitimate pedagogical reasons. This discretion is increased or limited based on the age of the students, community standards, and other relevant factors.

© 2001 Bill Lisenby

Schools typically control Internet access in instructional settings and restrict use of modern technological tools, such as cell phones, at school.

A great deal of national prominence has been given to the issue of student dress codes at school. Often schools regulate dress with the goal of improving school climate and student self-esteem. At one time, these regulations went unchallenged, but the same Supreme Court decision that supported teachers' freedom of speech also supported students' rights to wear certain clothing unless the presence of the clothing would disrupt or interfere with the teaching–learning environment.

The emergence of the Internet as a teaching tool will, no doubt, spawn new court rulings related to students' rights involving free speech, search and seizure, and plagiarism. On one hand, students should have free access to the information available on the Internet. On the other hand, some form of screening from exposure to inappropriate materials is necessary

FIELD-BASED ACTIVITY

4.2

Observe or take part in a state or local school meeting that focuses on policies established by state or local laws. One of the following activities would allow you to see laws in action and the impact of certain policies on the teaching profession.

- Attend a campaign event, such as a speech or debate, held to provide the public with an opportunity to understand the views of a local political candidate. Listen to what the person says about education. What role does education play in the candidacy? What educational laws and policies does the candidate suggest should be enacted?

- Visit a school board meeting in your local community. Some may televise their meetings on local channels. Who attends the meetings? What decisions do they make? Identify discussions that relate to laws and policies established by state authority or local control.

- Attend an NEA or AFT meeting. Note the laws and policies related to the teaching profession they discuss during the meeting. If there is a strike in the district where you teach, attend any open meetings that may help you to understand why teachers disagree with the local school board.

- If you find no meetings convenient to attend, listen to local public radio or television commentaries. What laws and policies are making news? How does public opinion influence application of laws and policies affecting teachers?

INTASC Principle 10

(Gorski, 2001). Educators must protect their students from pornographic materials, and effective screening software is one way to block access to objectionable sites. Schools also enforce guidelines for copying material from the Internet. Discussing the issue with students is one way to encourage appropriate Internet usage. Many resources are available to help teachers and students with technology, including educational Web sites, such as "50 Great Sites for Kids," and the American Library Association. Students' use of other new communication tools, such as cell phones, are also guided by school policy. No doubt, student use of these communication devices will eventually be tested in court. Be sure you know and acknowledge the regulations of the school where you are observing and teaching.

Ethical Issues for Teachers

Legal responsibilities define the rights and requirements of teachers, but ethical codes also influence the decisions teachers make about students, teaching, and their own behavior. Ethics are the principles of conduct—systems of deciding right and wrong—that govern an individual or a group. They include standards of behavior as well as moral principles and values. Legal and ethical decisions may at times be related, but laws do not typically specify ethical standards for teaching. ("moral" as behavior conforming to accepted prevailing notions, as in the basic moral standards of a community.)

Teaching is considered by many to be primarily an endeavor necessitating considerable teacher reflection on ethical and moral issues (Goodlad, Soder, & Sirotnik, 1990). Teachers, by definition, are in a position of power and responsibility over students in their classrooms, and the exercise of this power and responsibility requires ethical and moral decision making (Fenstermacher, 1990). Each time a teacher assigns a grade, deliberates on a punishment, or intervenes to resolve a student dispute, questions of ethics arise. In addition, teachers are often seen as models of moral and ethical behavior for their students. All teachers lecture students on the importance of fairness and honesty, but what teachers actually do in or outside the classroom to exercise fairness or honesty is more often remembered by students than what they say. For this reason, although recent incidents of alteration of test answers by educators in states that have high-stakes testing may have legal ramifications, the ethical issues they raise and the messages they give to students are even more serious. The following Web site provides a summary of a study about the manipula-

The community may scrutinize teachers' actions, personal values, and goals, given that they serve as role models for their students.

tion of test scores by teachers: http://www.ksg.harvard.edu/press/releases/2003/jacob_study_111703.htm

Reflecting on moral values and ethical issues—what is fair or right or good related to students and teaching—is important for teachers at all stages of their careers.

At times, tensions may exist between a teacher's personal values and goals and those of the community. As a beginning teacher, you may feel that both you and your actions are being scrutinized, particularly during the typical probationary status required of new hires in most districts. This is further confounded because "right" and "legal" are not necessarily synonymous, and the necessity of making on-the-spot decisions does not allow time to consult law experts or books (although doing so would not necessarily resolve every issue). Nevertheless, teachers are governed by ethical and moral mandates as well as written legal ones.

Listing all the situations teachers encounter would be impossible, but some common issues do emerge: The choices teachers make about what content will be emphasized, how students will receive or experience information, and how students will be judged successful in these experiences go beyond technical questions of instructional decision making. For example, most educators agree that using information or information delivery in a manipulative, coercive, or rote manner to indoctrinate students is unethical (Strike, 1990). Instead, educators value enabling students to learn to think and reason using content and to consider opposing arguments. Likewise, evaluation practices that are unfair, inaccurate, or lacking information about how and why the scores were given are generally considered unethical. Teachers are ethically bound to have objective reasons for the assignment of grades, to do their best to minimize bias during the grading process, and to apply a defensible, consistent standard when determining grades. Other ethical concepts that teachers embrace include intellectual freedom and honesty, respect or tolerance for diversity, due process for students in discipline and grading, fairness in punishment, and equity in the allocation of resources such as teacher time and attention (Strike, 1990). The important work of teaching is made more complex by a series of questions and decisions teachers make almost daily. The demands and expectations are great because the job is so important. Take time now to complete the Self-Reflection exercise and to think about what you have learned.

The National Education Association (1975) created a Code of Ethics of the Education Profession to provide standards by which to judge educators' conduct. The code's preamble describes protection of the freedoms of learning and teaching and the guarantee of educational opportunity. The two principles feature guidelines for commitment to the student and to the teaching profession. According to the NEA, ethical behavior related to student learning suggests, among other things, that teachers will not keep students from the pursuit of learning and will not deny access to different points of view. Ethical behaviors related to others in the profession include not making false statements and not assisting a noneducator in the unauthorized practice of teaching. Each principle lists specific behaviors that further illustrate what constitutes ethical behavior for educators. The complete version of the code is available at the NEA Web site listed on page 121.

The code provides rather straightforward guidelines; however, concrete situations in which decisions about ethical and unethical behavior can be extremely complex. In such cases, both new and experienced teachers will make use of all resources available: mentors, administrators, and other advisors.

Some situations, such as when you see signs of child abuse, are straightforward. All states have enacted legislation identifying teachers among the professionals who are required to report suspected abuse. Additionally, most states protect teachers by granting immunity from any liability if reports are made in good faith (McCarthy, Cambron-McCabe &

FIELD-BASED ACTIVITY

4.3

As you observe in your classroom, identify the day-to-day ethical dilemmas a teacher faces. Many of the issues involve interactions with students. Note the struggles that teachers face when grading and evaluating student work, dealing with plagiarism—particularly from the Internet—exhibiting fairness in punishment, and maintaining equity in resources, time, and teacher attention. Share your observations during a small-group discussion among your peers.

INTASC Principle 9

Thomas, 2004). As a result of the pervasiveness of the problem and concern for how teachers handle child abuse, professional development is offered in most schools to help teachers understand their responsibilities.

Other situations are more difficult, such as when a student confides to you that he is worried that his girlfriend may be using drugs. Your first task would be to try to determine the facts as best you can prior to making any decision about informing others. Then, if you determine that the risk of silence on your part is too great to your students, either physically or psychologically, you may have to report the information to a school counselor, nurse, or principal. This option, although risking the loss of trust and further communication from your student, gives first priority to protection of the girl's health. As always, the advice of a mentor, experienced colleague, or other administrator would provide valuable guidance.

In *The Ethics of Teaching*, Strike and Soltis (1998) define ethical issues related to punishment, intellectual freedom, and equal treatment of students. They provide a useful series of case studies designed to elicit reflection and discussion about underlying ethical issues and possible approaches depending on the philosophy and values of those involved. Strike (1990) suggests that consideration of ethical issues may be the best way to prepare teachers for the difficult decisions they may later need to make. Legal and technical prescriptions for classroom behaviors aside, teaching is at heart an ethical and moral activity. In the words of Chris Clark (1990):

The National Education Association code of ethics can be found in its entirety at this Web site:

http://www.nea.org/aboutnea/code.html

You can learn more about one state's Teacher Code of Ethics at the following Web site:

http://www.gapsc.com/Professional Practices/CodeOfEthicsBrochure72403.pdf

URLs may change over time. For up-to-date links to relevant Web sites, visit our Companion Web site:

http://education.wadsworth.com/ wiseman3e

At its core, teaching is a matter of human relationships. Human relationships, whatever else they may be, are moral in character and consequence. After that between parent and child, the most profoundly moral relationship our children experience is that between the teacher and the taught. (p. 27)

The few guidelines for ethical conduct are typically I
Few school districts have explicit ethical codes of co
teaching can best prepare to deal with legal and eth'
aware of laws affecting education, analyzing their ov
the community in which they teach, and reflecti
own and others'—related to the ethical concepts

SELF-REFLECTION

Legal and Ethical Dilemmas

Consider each of these situations and decide whether it is more aptly described as a legal or ethical issue. In some cases, you may check both columns.

	Legal	Ethical
1. A teacher likes to drop by high school parties on the weekend.	_____	_____
2. A girl in your class shows up with bruises on her legs and arms that she tries to hide.	_____	_____
3. You smell alcohol on Johnny's breath when he comes to school.	_____	_____
4. Janie misses school often to take care of her younger siblings.	_____	_____
5. You notice that the lower-level English classes have an overrepresentation of minority students.	_____	_____
6. A group of your students asks you to start each class with a prayer.	_____	_____
7. You plan on having students read *Huckleberry Finn,* and an African American parent objects.	_____	_____
8. Suzy is supposed to be mainstreamed into your class, but the door is not wide enough for her wheelchair.	_____	_____

9. The Tranhs have just moved into your school district, and n_____ _____ speaks Cambodian. _____ _____

10. O_____ _____ that protests the war. _____ _____

11. Yo_____ the fact that o_____ _____ _____ _____
    fa_____ _____

12. Yo_____ _____ _____ _____ _____
    stu_____ _____

13. Yo_____ _____ _____
    lun_____ _____

14. A student turns in a pape_____ _____ook from the Internet as _____ _____
    her own.

Items 2, 4, 6, 7, 8, 9, 10, 11, and 12 have laws that guide a teachers' responses, although they may also be unethical. If you missed any of these, review the discussion on laws in this chapter. The remaining items are ethical in nature and will need to be considered in the context of personal, school, and community values. If you had difficulty identifying legal and ethical issues, you may want to discuss this activity with your classmates.

PORTFOLIO REFLECTIONS AND EXHIBITS

Throughout this chapter you have completed a series of Field-Based Activities. They may serve as the basis for a portfolio representation, you may develop your own portfolio representation, or you may complete the suggested portfolio activities listed here.

Suggested Exhibit 4: Ethics and Legal Concerns

1. Identify one law or policy that may affect you during your teaching. Some specific examples include rulings regarding special or bilingual education or those that deal with school prayer or Bible reading in the classroom. Find the origin of the law or policy. Use the Internet to research your law or topic. Produce a flow chart, diagram, drawing, or written summary that illustrates the political and legal steps that

(continued)

occurred before it affected individual educators. Then indicate on the diagram the possible impact of the law on your own actions in the classroom.

INTASC Principle 9

2. Begin to consider a rationale for your classroom grading or discipline policies. Review the student or teacher handbook from your school that describes these policies. Which aspects of the policies do you feel comfortable enforcing? Which ones would be more difficult for you? Consider any extenuating circumstances that might cause you to question the policy. What does this tell you about your own ethics related to grading? Write a rationale that will serve as a guide when you grade or discipline students. Be sure to consider how your views might be different from those of a teacher from another culture who has had different experiences or education.

INTASC Principle 9

E-Portfolio Entry 4

Identify a recent court case or legal process that focuses on an educational topic. These may include zero tolerance, dress codes, sexual orientation, or student expulsion. Use archives from the Internet to find newspaper articles, editorials, and magazine features about your topic. Develop a chart that identifies all parties involved (i.e., students, teachers, teachers' unions, parents, and so on) and include their roles and views related to the case. Discuss their points of view with your class and determine if each point of view is based on ethical or legal grounds. Develop a chart or visual that represents what you have found.

INTASC Principle 9

ANSWERS TO GUIDING YOUR READING

1. What constitutional rights and responsibilities affect schools?

Four constitutional amendments affect the rights and responsibilities associated with schooling. None of the amendments establish schools; instead, the responsibility for educational processes lies with the states. Other amendments deal with personal rights and responsibilities. In general and with some limits, teachers and students who are involved in our educational settings are assured of the same basic freedoms and rights as any other citizen in our country.

2. What laws govern the teaching profession?

Primarily, state laws govern the teaching profession. They establish and interpret laws and policies and make sure schools comply with rules and regulations. State agencies collect taxes and establish budgets, certify teachers, and develop curriculum and tests. However, the influence of the federal government is more apparent with the passage of such sweeping laws as No Child Left Behind.

3. What are the rights of teachers and students?

Teachers and students have the same rights as other citizens. When teachers' rights are mediated, the likelihood that their conduct negatively affected students or school programs is considered. In serious cases that are being judged by courts, a balance between teachers' rights and schools' interests must be measured. Students are also guaranteed certain rights that are assumed by others in our society. Most important, the Constitution and state laws guarantee all students a free and equal education.

4. What are the important ethical issues related to teaching, and what dilemmas do they present to teachers?

Ethical issues directly related to teaching suggest, among other things, that teachers will not keep their students from learning and will not deny them access to different points of view. Ethical dilemmas often emerge as teachers attempt to be fair to their students, encourage free and exploratory thinking, and protect the rights of students.

 INFOTRAC COLLEGE EDITION EXTENSION

Log onto the InfoTrac College Edition Web site and use it to find out more about issues related to students' and teachers' use of technology, particularly the Internet. Using a keyword search, type in the term "cyber ethics." What are some of the issues? How will you handle them in your classroom?

RELATED READINGS

The following books will provide more information about some of the topics and ideas in this chapter:

Fischer, L., Schimmel, D., & Kelly, C. (1998). *Teachers and the law* (5th ed.) New York: Longman.

> This is a relatively easy-to-read book in a question-and-answer format that provides a comprehensive view of the laws that may affect the classroom teacher. Many examples are provided, and court cases are described in ways that help the reader understand the legal process and its effect on the rights of teachers and students.

Kinchloe, J. L., & Steinberg, S. R. (Eds.). (1992). *Thirteen questions: Reframing education's conversations.* New York: Peter Lang.

> This is a series of philosophical and ethical essays that introduce important issues from differing perspectives. The voices in this book are often critical of existing practices and set out new solutions to some old problems. The chapter authors present information that is often omitted from traditional discussions of educational ethics.

REFERENCES

Epigraph: Schoonmaker, Frances. (2002). *Growing up teaching: From personal knowledge to professional practice* (pp. 53, 55). New York: Columbia University Teachers College.

Cambron-McCabe, N. H., McCarthy, M. M., & Thomas, S. B. (2004). *Public school law: Teachers' and students' rights* (5th ed.). Boston: Pearson.

Clark, C. M. (1990). The teacher and the taught: Moral transactions in the classroom. In J. I. Goodlad, R. Soder, & K. A. Sirotnik (Eds.), *The moral dimensions of teaching* (pp. 251–265). San Francisco: Jossey-Bass.

Fenstermacher, G. D. (1990). Some moral considerations on teaching as a profession. In J. I. Goodlad, R. Soder, & K. A. Sirotnik (Eds.), *The moral dimensions of teaching* (pp. 130–154). San Francisco: Jossey-Bass.

Fischer, L., Schimmel, D., & Kelly, C. (1998). *Teachers and the law* (5th ed.). New York: Longman.

Goodlad, J. I., Soder, R., & Sirotnik, K. A. (Eds.). (1990). *The moral dimensions of teaching.* San Francisco: Jossey-Bass.

Gorski, P. C. (2001). *Multicultural education and the Internet: Intersections and integrations.* New York: McGraw-Hill.

McCarthy, M. M., Cambron-McCabe, N. H., & Thomas, S. B. (2004). *Legal rights of teachers and students.* Boston: Pearson.

Myers, C. B., & Myers, L. K. (1995). *The professional educator: A new introduction to teaching and the schools.* Belmont, CA: Wadsworth.

National Education Association. (1975). *Code of ethics of the education profession.* Washington, DC: Author. [Available online: http://www.nea.org/aboutnea/code.html]

Strike, K. A. (1990). The legal and moral responsibility of teachers. In J. I. Goodlad, R. Soder, & K. A. Sirotnik (Eds.), *The moral dimensions of teaching* (pp. 188–223). San Francisco: Jossey-Bass.

Strike, K. A., & Soltis, J. F. (1998). *The ethics of teaching.* New York: Teachers College Press.

Timm, J. T. (1996). *Four perspectives in multicultural education.* Belmont, CA: Wadsworth.

Yudorf, M. G., Kirp, D. L., Levin, B., & Moran, R. F. (2002). *Education policy and the law* (4th ed.). Belmont, CA: Wadsworth.

5

The Status of Contemporary Students

My own teachers encouraged me and demanded nothing less than excellence. They made me feel smart and I responded. But there was still something wrong with my education. There were lots of smart kids in my elementary school, but they weren't all as economically stable as I was— I came from a working-class family with a father who was a laborer and a mother who was a clerk. I remember one girl in particular; her name was Portia. She was the smartest person I had ever met. She could sum a column of numbers with lightning speed. She could reason beyond her years. But she almost never came to school with her hair combed. Her teeth had not seen a toothbrush in years and she often smelled of urine. I liked her because she was smart and had a great sense of humor. It did not bother me that her house was dark, smelled funny, and had furniture that looked like the kind of stuff people set out curbside to be collected with the trash. I lost track of Portia after elementary school. She did not attend the junior high school where I went to school across town. The last time I saw her was in eleventh grade. Portia was pregnant and had dropped out of school. As smart as I believed I was, I knew I was not as smart as Portia. So why wasn't she on the fast track to college? Why had she been passed over in the academic shuffle?

—Gloria Ladson-Billings, *The Dreamkeepers*

Guiding Your Reading

1. How have family structures changed over the last decade?

2. What impact do culture and language have on classroom contexts?

3. What are some of the major social issues affecting young people's lives?

4. What can future teachers learn from students whose backgrounds differ from their own?

*G*ood teachers relate to their students and place a high priority on maintaining an environment where all students can succeed academically and socially. To accomplish this difficult task, a teacher must not only understand students and accept their differences but also be willing to accept a wide range of ways of looking at the world. Successful teachers understand the impact of family and community experiences, cultural and language diversity, and the changing nature of society.

Effective teachers must have a good understanding of what it is like to be a child or young adult in contemporary society and use that knowledge to react, interact, and respond to their students. Gaining an understanding of students is a complex process that will require an examination of personal beliefs and biases as well as cultural and societal issues.

Families and Communities

The structure of families has changed over the past thirty-five years. In 1965, more than 60 percent of Americans lived in a family unit with a working father and a stay-at-home mother, who provided childcare and managed the house. Today, only 10 percent of families in the United States conform to this traditional structure, and the Internal Revenue Service recognizes thirteen different variations of the family—including dual-career families, single-parent families, and stepfamilies. Although many family issues have remained constant, some characteristics specific to today's families may affect students' educational experiences at any age. Divorce, working parents, and differing lifestyles are all legitimate family organizations for modern-day students.

Divorced and Single Parents

A high divorce rate coupled with nonmarital births has led to a rising number of children living with only one parent. Twenty-eight percent of families with children are headed by one parent, and most single parents are mothers (Annie E. Casey Foundation, 2003). Children are raised by single parents as a result of varied circumstances, but many single-parent homes are the result of divorce. The stress of divorce affects students' responses at school and often results in less-successful school experiences. Additional stresses in single-parent homes are caused by the lower salaries and longer working hours of many single mothers. Some statistics suggest that children of single-parent families have higher dropout rates, lower grades, and poorer attendance than do children who come from two-parent families (Bennett, 1995). However, with support from teachers and parents, students from single-parent homes can be very successful at school. Many young people demonstrate an amazing resiliency that enables them to adjust to a multitude of family difficulties.

© Tony Freeman/PhotoEdit

The number of children who spend time in childcare or after-school programs has increased due to single-parent families and the economic changes that require both parents to work.

Different Family Lifestyles

Stepfamily arrangements are just one example of the myriad family structures children may experience. Almost 20 percent of U.S. families are reconstituted or stepfamilies, which are formed when parents remarry and combine children and families (Sadker & Sadker, 2000). Thirty percent of all children are likely to spend some time in stepfamilies (Bumpass, Raley, & Sweet, 1995). Most children and young people who live in stepfamilies have a host of parents and stepparents, siblings (and perhaps stepsiblings), grandparents, and other relatives—which makes their lives extremely complex.

Other differences in families occur when individuals from different cultures and races marry. Interracial marriages are becoming more common, and cultures may also be mixed within a family through marriage and adoptions. The number of families that fit the traditional one-culture, nuclear family description is decreasing.

Alternative family structures are also becoming more prevalent, including relatives or friends who serve as custodians of children, grandparents or same-sex couples who are raising children, and nonmarried couples living together and raising children. Society is more accepting of this range of family structures, but the curriculum at school may still reflect a narrower view of family life. Teachers can—and should—take an active role in helping all children and young people feel comfortable about their own family structures.

Working Parents

In a majority of families, both mothers and fathers have joined the workforce. In 1970, only 32 percent of mothers of preschoolers worked outside the home, but by 1990, 58 percent were in the workforce. The percentage of working mothers has dropped slightly since 1990 to 55 percent in 2000 and held steady at that number for the next four years (Chaker, 2004). Today, three of four mothers with school-age children are employed, and most of them work full time. In households with two working parents, adequate supervision of children, level of family income, and parental support of school activities (both with time and with money) are some of the concerns that may affect learning.

Working parents are usually away during the day, and work schedules rarely match school hours. Between the time school lets out and the time parents return from work, children may attend day care or spend time with a baby-sitter. Fifty percent of elementary-age children receive nonparental care after school (Plisko, 2000). Teachers, particularly of young children, need to consider that caretakers may be involved in the early afternoon activities of their students and accept that homework or other school-related activities may be supervised by someone other than parents. A teacher who understands the diversity of students' family and home situations may be more understanding of how parents and children respond to school-related activities and the circumstances under which students may have to do homework.

Many children of working parents are left at home alone, unsupervised by any responsible adult, for several hours. According to a recent census report, 50 percent of twelve- to fourteen-year-olds spend seven hours a week home alone, and one out of every ten elementary children spends over four hours a week unsupervised (Belsie, 2000). Some schools implement after-school programs that provide tutoring, snacks, and supervised activities for children of working parents; many schools do not. Being alone and responsible for oneself places stress on latchkey children. Even older children need attention after school: Adolescents who are left unsupervised are more likely to engage in substance abuse, experiment with sex, or have run-ins with the law.

When working parents arrive home in the evenings, children must compete with hectic schedules and work pressures for parental attention. Working parents' busy lives affect their school involvement, and their participation in school-related events is greatly reduced. Unless the workplace supports parental involvement in school activities, working parents may be unable to volunteer at school or to attend school functions.

Communities that once felt a collective responsibility for such children may not offer the support they once did. Modern mobility and the reshuffling of neighborhoods mean reduced stability to residents. However, many churches and other community organizations still play an important role in children's and young people's lives. They often provide after-school, evening, and weekend activities that involve students in worthwhile and meaningful activities. Thoughtful teachers who recognize and build upon the importance of the community in raising children will make classroom lessons and activities more relevant.

Homelessness

One disruptive factor affecting many families is loss of a home or lack of affordable housing. The number of homeless families with children has increased over the past decade (National Coalition for the Homeless, 1999). Forty percent of the nation's homeless are families (U.S. Conference of Mayors, 2001), leaving anywhere from 225,000 to 500,000 of America's children without a home (Kelly, 1993). Homelessness was once considered primarily to be an urban problem, but the rural homeless population is growing—and single mothers and children are the largest group among them (Vissing, 1996). Homeless children exhibit poorer health, more learning problems, and often more behavior problems (Shinn & Weitzman, 1996). Because affordable housing is not always available, families are subjected to much longer stays in homeless shelters—the average stay in New York City is nearly a year (Santos & Ingrassia, 2002). Many children are shuttled from shelter to shelter, remain hungry and tired, and may not be able to provide birth certificates or other records necessary for school attendance. As a result, teachers are recognizing an increased need to address more than the academic needs of their students. Teachers alone cannot respond to all the issues emerging from homelessness. However, they may join a group of professionals—including health care providers, social workers, and juvenile justice workers—who can work together to ensure that students access available social services that will help them and their families in times of crisis. At the very least, teachers should be aware of the services offered to children and young people and know how to refer students to other agencies in their community

Even with all the problems confronting America's children, schools can make a difference. Many schools work with communities and parents to provide a safe, nurturing environment for all students. Effective schools are reaching out into the community to become a center of learning for all members. Parent and community involvement and support in schools contributes to students' successful school achievement. When parents are involved, their children earn higher grades and test scores and stay in school longer. The performance of all students in the school tends to improve when parents are involved in a variety of ways at school. The more the relationship between families and school approaches a comprehensive, well-planned partnership, the higher the student achievement (Berla & Henderson, 1994). Strong community support and involvement is necessary for schools to begin to address the variety of problems and needs facing the children they serve. A comprehensive discussion of parent and family involvement can be found in Chapter 10.

Diversity in Schools

Our schools have not welcomed so many immigrants since the beginning of the twentieth century. Today, one in five students comes from an immigrant family. This cultural diversity has a profound impact on educational needs. Currently, 35 percent of U.S. students are members of a minority group, and by 2040 more than 50 percent of students will be from minority groups (Olson, 2000). More than 150 languages are spoken in schools across the

FIELD-BASED ACTIVITY

5.1

Learn about the neighborhood where the students in your classrooms live. These activities will help you understand more about your students' lives:

- Describe your cultural background and that of your family. Include a description of the community where you grew up.

- Take a walk or drive through your students' neighborhoods. If possible, have a student or parent give you a tour of the neighborhood.

- Attend church or a festival in the area.

- Try to find out where your students spend their weekends, what stores and neighborhood spots they regularly visit, and the identities of heroes and leaders important to their families and neighbors.

- Find out where your students go after school. Who cares for them? What do they do after they leave the school grounds? If they go to an organized activity such as boys' or girls' clubs, church day care, or after-school programs, spend a few afternoons with them.

Compare and contrast the community where you grew up with the one where your students live. Identify cultural and community factors that should be considered by teachers.

INTASC Principles 7, 9, and 10

country, and the number of students identified as having limited fluency in English doubled between 1993 and 2000. Families of Hispanic origin are the largest minority group, and by 2025 nearly one in four students will be a member of that group.

Immigrants come to the United States for economic gain, more personal or political freedom, and an overall better lifestyle. Immigrants from Germany, Italy, Ireland, the United Kingdom, the Soviet Union, Canada, and Sweden are joined by immigrants from Mexico, the Philippines, Korea, China, Taiwan, India, Cuba, and the Middle East. People from all of these regions bring to the United States a wide variety of languages, foods, and religions. Many of these immigrants maintain their own cultural identity, further enriching the American mosaic. Schools serve as an entry into the American society for many children, exposing them to the language and culture of their new country. Most immigrants, especially the first generation, recognize that American schooling is a responsibility and privilege and see it as a way to succeed and give something back to their new homeland.

Today's classrooms include a wide range of cultural, ethnic, and religious diversity, as illustrated by elementary students' self-portraits.

Students' Cultural and Language Diversity

The learning needs of today's diverse students are varied and complex. To best meet the needs of all students, teachers must understand how instruction and learning are influenced by culture and language differences (Pang, 2001). Without this vital knowledge, teachers may unknowingly limit students' potential achievement by prejudicial or ethnocentric practices in the classroom.

Schools need to accommodate great language diversity. The number of students who speak English as their second language has doubled since 1980 (Arends, 2000). Seventeen percent of five- to twenty-four year-olds in the U.S. speak a language other than English at home (Strauss, 2003). Classrooms will include students who speak German, Italian, French, Spanish, Arabic, Vietnamese, Russian, or Tagalog (Fix, Passel, & Sucher, 2003).

In addition to exhibiting language differences, ELL students may know and understand different geography, clothing, holidays, foods, family interactions, religion, and gender roles. Their manner of thinking and problem solving may differ from that of their classmates and teachers.

Within the broad categories of Native Americans, African Americans, Hispanics, and Asian Americans are many diverse cultural groups. For instance, Hispanic children may come from Mexico, Puerto Rico, Cuba, or Kansas City—and each will have a distinct cultural identity. Each student in the classroom may represent not only a different cultural background but also a different level of assimilation into mainstream U.S. culture. Some of these students may resemble (or be) American-born students, whereas others may dress or behave in ways closer to their native cultures.

The differences between school practices and some practices and expectations in diverse families and communities can cause difficulties for some students. For example, the ways in which students are given directions at home or are expected to respond to questions may be different from classroom expectations. Because many schools are still organized to accommodate and reinforce Eurocentric values, beliefs, and behavior, they may increase the disparity between what these children know and can do and what is expected of them at school. The social world of the school may operate by rules different from the rules these children and their families know and use (Bowman, 1994, p. 219). A sensitive teacher will recognize and try to rectify this disparity by honoring each student's cultural background in the process. It seems like a delicate balancing act, but it may be as simple as recognizing that each student is an individual.

Challenges for Teachers

One of the barriers to success that minority students face is the lack of opportunity to interact with teachers like themselves. Even though one-third of the classroom population may be composed of children of minority groups or immigrants, little representation of their background and culture will be seen in the teaching staffs. In the United States, only 13 percent of teachers come from an ethnic or racial minority group. The increasing gap between the cultural backgrounds of teachers and students is critical and likely affects the students' classroom experiences. As long as the teaching profession exhibits such limited diversity, the teachers' culture continues to form the basis for most teaching decisions—even though such traditional methods may not meet the educational needs of students from different cultural backgrounds. This problem is further complicated if students see few role models in the teaching profession that might inspire them to enter the profession in the future.

Teachers, no matter what their ethnicity, are critical to the success of students. Teacher expectations constantly influence classroom interactions and student achievement. Everything in the classroom is filtered through the teacher. Teachers implement the curriculum and select learning strategies for the classroom, drawing on their own background and experiences. Teachers, therefore, must constantly monitor their teaching habits to discern any prejudicial barriers keeping their students from succeeding. In spite of the fact that many teachers lack a frame of reference for dealing with culturally and linguistically different students, they can—and should—recognize and accept the differences in the classroom.

Sensitivity to differences can be represented in something as simple as learning to pronounce names correctly, because learning how to say a student's name shows cultural and personal respect. Classroom environments can be enhanced if the teacher seeks out and presents literature and cultural and linguistic referents that are familiar to students from different cultures. Teachers already know the importance of providing classroom learning opportunities that are responsive to different learning styles: Some students may learn best by working alone, others in cooperative groups, and still others may need more structure, regardless of culture or ethnicity. Finally, teachers may need to spend extra effort to ensure that they give attention to all students in the classroom to help redress any ethnic or racial imbalance depicted in curricular materials.

Of course, many of these suggestions are sound instructional guidelines that are good for all pupils. Teachers may not completely understand the culture of every learner in their classroom, but they can provide a classroom environment wherein all students can learn and have the chance to succeed.

The wide range of cultural differences in the classroom can be used to help all students develop more positive attitudes toward different religions, languages, and ethnicities. Culturally diverse classrooms can serve as a place for everyone to learn about the richness of a multicultural society and to appreciate the vibrant democracy that can emerge from common understandings and acceptance.

FIELD-BASED ACTIVITY 5.2

This exercise can help you identify the range of cultural differences represented in your classroom and compare it with your own experiences. Take a class photo of your students. Locate, or reflect on, a class photo from a classroom that you attended when you were a student of approximately the same age. What similarities do you see? What differences? What experiences have you had that might help you relate to today's students?

INTASC Principle 3

► Societal Changes and Challenges

Students come to school with overwhelming concerns about the world in which they live. They may be unable to concentrate or to see the connection between their world and the world of school. When they leave school at the end of the day, they go home to many different communities with unique challenges and benefits. Students may live in crowded apartment dwellings or large suburban homes. They may live on quiet streets or go to bed hearing the sounds of gunshots in their neighborhood. Students may spend most of the time away from school in front of a television set while others are overly involved in after-school activities such as soccer, music lessons, or dance classes. Some students may live and interact solely with their immediate family; others have opportunities to encounter extended family, church acquaintances, and community members of all ages. Recognizing that students may be dealing with problems or concerns that go beyond the classroom can help teachers meet their educational needs. Teachers who understand the concerns of today's children and young people will be more apt to build classroom contexts that result in student success and empowerment. Poverty, violence, and health care are all important challenges in today's society. Take time now to complete the Self-Reflection exercises and to think about your beliefs.

SELF-REFLECTION

Recognizing Your Beliefs about Poverty

Before you read the section on poverty, consider your beliefs about poor families.

Do you believe that . . .	Yes	No	Not Sure
individuals in poor families do not have jobs?	_____	_____	_____
not many poor families are white?	_____	_____	_____
poverty is mainly an urban problem?	_____	_____	_____
poor children come from single-parent homes?	_____	_____	_____
poor parents do not provide adequate care for their children?	_____	_____	_____

Poverty

Even though the number of children living in poverty has decreased since the high in 1993, the current number is still higher than twenty years ago (Olson, 2000). More children live in poverty than any other group of people in our country. Sixteen percent of school-age children live in households with incomes below the poverty level (Strauss, 2003). Research has shown that children who live in poverty are much more likely to do poorly in academic areas (Olson, 2000). In fact, a poor child is about twice as likely to be a low-achieving student in the classroom. Poverty is also a strong indicator of how well a school with a high number of poor students will perform (McLaren, 1994). Students—even those who are not poor—who attend schools that have a high percentage of students living in poverty are much more likely to be low achievers in school. In fact, a student who is not poor but who attends a poor school is even more likely to be a low achiever than a poor student in the same school (Olson, 2000).

Teachers in today's classrooms may confront poverty in the faces of their students every day, yet most teachers come from a middle-class background with few life experiences to prepare them for the reality of true poverty. Their belief system can be clouded with many myths and misconceptions about living in poverty. Let's examine some of these myths.

Myth #1: Poor families are unemployed and on public assistance. Two-thirds of poor children under age six live in families where one or both parents work (Olson, 2000), and almost one-third of these families include an adult with a full-time job who still cannot earn enough money to raise the family's income above the poverty line. Most poor families earn more money than they receive from welfare (Sherman, 1994). Many family incomes remain below the poverty line, and the number of "working poor" families who earn below the poverty level remains high.

Myth #2: Poverty only exists among minority families. Poverty is color-blind. Child poverty occurs in every race and ethnicity, but the rate of poverty is higher in minorities. African American and Latino children are far more likely to live in poverty than whites. The percentage of poor African American and Latino children is growing, from 47 percent in 1990 to a projected 60 percent by 2015 (Olson, 2000).

Myth #3: Poor children live in big cities. Nearly 60 percent of poor preschool children live in suburban and rural areas. The percentage of children living in poverty is growing much faster in the suburbs than it is in urban or rural locations (Olson, 2000). In addition, poor families and children living in rural areas often also face isolation and other barriers that keep them from getting health care and human support services that are more readily available in the cities.

Myth #4: Poor children come mostly from single-parent homes. Statistics may show that many poor children live in single-parent homes, but almost half of America's poor children and young people live in homes with both parents. If children do live in single-parent homes headed by women, they have a 50 percent chance of living in poverty. Those numbers are even higher among minority children living in single-parent homes headed by women of color (Reed & Saulter, 1990). The average annual income for single-parent homes headed by women is just over $28,000, whereas the average annual income for married couples with children is above $52,000 (U.S. Bureau of the Census, 2001).

Myth #5: Poor children do not have strong family support systems. Just because children are poor does not mean that they do not have people who care about them, and many children from single-parent homes have strong family support systems. Parents and caretakers of poor children want their children to be treated fairly, to succeed in school, and to gain skills that will help them work and play successfully. Many of these parents and caretakers see school as particularly important because it is a way out of poverty, and they support their children's academic growth in any way possible.

Teachers' attitudes about students who live in poverty may be influenced by long-held beliefs, many of which may indeed be myths. Teachers can influence their own expectations and ensure they provide equal access to learning by questioning these long-standing beliefs. Value judgments about students are often based on the teachers' own experiences, which may vary greatly from their students' experiences and values.

Teachers who enter classrooms with preconceived ideas about students' abilities based on income will present an even larger obstacle to poor students. Teachers' beliefs that students from low socioeconomic levels cannot learn as well as their classmates can be translated by the teacher, often unknowingly, into everyday classroom practices. Grouping procedures, questioning strategies, and even curriculum choices are all based on teachers' beliefs about students' capabilities for learning. Expectant voice prompting, less interaction, and differential activities and questions may all subtly communicate unequal treatment. Students internalize these lower expectations into their own self-assessment, and the teacher's beliefs become the students' beliefs as well. Take time now to complete the Self-Reflection exercise and to think about what you have learned.

You may learn more about the impact of poverty on children at:

http://www.childrensdefense.org

URLs may change over time. For up-to-date links to relevant Web sites, visit our Companion Web site:

http://education.wadsworth.com/wiseman3e

Changing Your Beliefs about Poverty

Now that you have read and discussed the section about poor families, review these statements. Did you change your views? If you changed your response, place a check in the last column. What made you change your mind? What are your beliefs now?

Do you believe that . . .	Yes	No	Not Sure	Indicates Changes
individuals in poor families do not have jobs?	_____	_____	_____	_____
not many poor families are white?	_____	_____	_____	_____
poverty is mainly an urban problem?	_____	_____	_____	_____
poor children come from single-parent homes?	_____	_____	_____	_____
poor parents do not provide adequate care for their children?	_____	_____	_____	_____

Review your responses. If you believe you need to develop a greater understanding about the impact of poverty on families and children, select one of the books listed in the Related Readings at the end of the chapter, volunteer in a low-socioeconomic neighborhood near your school, or discuss the issue with your teacher, professor, or classmates.

Violence

Several recent high-profile incidents have caused increased public concern about juvenile violence (Sadker & Sadker, 2000), but, in fact, juvenile violence is on the decline. After dramatic increases in the numbers of serious injuries and deaths related to crime among children during the late 1980s and 1990s, juvenile arrests have dropped to the lowest levels in recent history (U.S. Department of Health and Human Services, 2001). The juvenile arrest rate for murder has fallen over 60 percent, and the arrest rate for other violent crimes dropped by 21 percent. Still, teenagers under the age of eighteen accounted for about 15 percent of violent crime arrests in 2001 (Federal Bureau of Investigation, 2002). Too many children and young

Gang membership is cyclical, and evidence suggests that it is increasing in some environments. The potential for students to join gangs can be reduced by involvement in extra-curricular school activities, such as Boys and Girls Clubs, sports, or church groups that meet their need to belong to a group.

people are killed by gunfire, and hundreds are wounded or experience violent crime in some way.

Disturbing new trends in violent behavior have appeared, however. About one in six middle and high school students say they are bullied, and more than one in twelve report that it happens at least once a week (Nansel et al., 2001). Suicide was the third leading cause of death for young people in 2000, and, every year, as many as 19 percent of high school students seriously consider attempting suicide (Centers for Disease Control and Prevention, 2002).

GANG ACTIVITY People of all ages have a strong need to belong, and gangs are organizations that meet a young person's need to belong to a group. Unlike the benefits associated with some other social organizations, gang life can also lead to crime, drugs, and violence. Gangs, like schools, are in the business of teaching children. Gangs teach role relationships and communication styles, and young people learn the rules of the gang quickly in order to be accepted by their peers. Youth gangs can also meet needs for safety and status (National Crime Prevention Council, 1990). Schools, churches, and family can offer positive alternatives, deterring many children from joining destructive groups.

Most experts agree that gang activity among youth is cyclical. During the early 1990s, gang activity was at a high level, but a decrease in crime in general was also reflected in decreased gang activity. However, during the early 2000s there are indications that gang activity is on the increase again. Gang violence should always be a concern at school, and efforts to care for and attend to disenfranchised youth who are potential gang members should be a focus of school settings. Early intervention with services designed to strengthen family connections is one of the most effective ways to prevent gang violence. While these services are not usually located in the schools, educators should be aware of what churches, Boys and Girls Clubs, and social services have to offer their students.

CHILD ABUSE Another form of violence that can have a profound effect on children is the sad reality of child abuse. Nationally, an estimated 903,000 children were victims of abuse and neglect in 2001 (Child Maltreatment Document, 2001). Classroom teachers are often the first adults to recognize and report abuse, which can be physical, psychological, or sexual. It can be an isolated incident or occur repeatedly over long periods of time. Teachers can take action to avert such abuse. Many incidents of child abuse are reported in the media, but thousands more are reported only by a classroom teacher. Reporting suspected child abuse is a necessary, although difficult, responsibility in the classroom (Fischer, Schimmel, & Kelly, 1999). Teachers may worry that their report will further endanger the child and are often discouraged by the lack of easy solutions to a complex problem. However, silence is complicity—and in many states, it is illegal (see Chapter 4).

You may learn more about violence, children, youth, and young people at:

National Alliance for Safe Schools
http://www.safeschools.org/

National School Safety Center
http://nssc1.org/

National Center for Education Statistics
http://nces.ed.gov/pubsearch/

Eric Clearing House on Urban Education
http://eric-web.tc.columbia.edu/

URLs may change over time. For up-to-date links to relevant Web sites, visit our Companion Web site:

http://education.wadsworth.com/
wiseman3e

Health Care

Many children in the United States do not have access to proper health care. According to the most recent census numbers, 8.4 million children eighteen years of age and under lacked health coverage in 2000 (Maternal and Child Health Bureau, 2000). The strong economy in the late 1990s and the expansion of coverage to low-income children under the State Children's Health Insurance Program contributed to an increase of children receiving health care benefits. Many trends related to children's health services have improved, but other areas are still cause for concern. Many families are still unable to provide private health insurance. Compared with insured children, uninsured children are far less likely to receive medical and dental care and may go without prescription medication or eyeglasses.

The proportion of mothers receiving prenatal care increased steadily during the 1990s; however, racial disparities exist between women who receive early prenatal care. Early childcare varies as well: In 1992, almost half of all two-year-olds had not been fully immunized against preventable childhood diseases (Children's Defense Fund, 1994), and in a 1991 survey, 21 percent of children in the United States had not seen a doctor in the past year (Plante, 1993). Health conditions, just like economic and family situations, strongly influence a student's readiness to learn. Schools can help by providing connections with health professionals that guide families to affordable health care.

The three health care concerns that affect educational achievement are teenage pregnancies (which often cause young mothers to drop out of school entirely), nutritional deficits, and drug abuse.

TEENAGE PREGNANCY At an all-time high in the late 1980s, teen pregnancies have continued to decline during the last decade and the early 2000s. Even so, the number of births by U.S. teenagers remains high. Approximately 1 million teenagers become pregnant every year (Henshaw, 1997); three-fourths of teenage parents are unmarried, and nearly 200,000 are under age eighteen (Ventura, Peters, Martin, & Maurer, 1996). Furthermore, the decline in overall numbers is not consistent across cultural and ethnic groups. Many young parents, usually females, face multiple challenges as they enter adulthood and strive for self-sufficiency. Research shows that the children of teenage parents are more likely to be poor and more likely than other children to have illnesses during childhood, experience more and greater developmental delays, and generally be less successful in school (Stephens, Wolf, & Batten, 1999). Many school programs now offer support to young mothers as they complete their education and go through training to support their children.

An excellent fact sheet, suggestions for ways to prevent teen pregnancy, and help for teenage mothers can be found at the following Web site:

http://www.womenshealthchannel.com/teenpregnancy/index.shtml

URLs may change over time. For up-to-date links to relevant Web sites, visit our Companion Web site:

http://education.wadsworth.com/wiseman3e

NUTRITIONAL DEFICITS Poor nutrition during any period of childhood can have harmful effects on children's cognitive development (Tufts University School of Nutrition Policy, 1993). Nutritional deficits affect students' behavior, school performance, and overall learning development. Even relatively short-term deficiencies can affect a child's behavior. A shortage of iron in the diet, for example, can have a direct impact on the student's attention span and memory. An estimated one-fourth of all low-income children in the United States currently suffer from anemia. Poor children who attend school hungry are often tired and uninterested in school and perform significantly lower on standardized tests than do children who are not hungry. In addition, the combination of lack of physical activity and unhealthy eating patterns produces obesity in children, youth, and adolescents. Nearly 15 percent of young people are overweight, a number that has tripled in the past two decades. Poor nutrition, whether caused by too little food or too much of the wrong foods, can permanently impair emotional interactions, physical growth, brain development, and cognitive functioning. The longer children and adolescents experience any version of poor nutrition, the greater the chance that their social, academic, and physical development will be affected. Free breakfast and lunch programs are now available at many schools for children whose families cannot afford balanced meals. Additionally, educational programs about good nutrition and physical education opportunities will contribute to student's knowledge about good eating habits and healthy lifestyles.

DRUG ABUSE Since 1997, drug use among teenagers has declined. Specific decreases are noted in the use marijuana, some club drugs, cigarettes, and alcohol. Even cigarette use among adolescents declined slightly in the early 2000s. Use of exotic drugs, such as ecstasy, is also on the decline. The only significant increase in drug use among older teens is of crack. In addition, the government survey tracking drug use found that young people's perceived risk and disapproval of experimenting with most drugs, excepting marijuana, had increased (National Institute on Drug Abuse, 2002). The good news about drug use among teenagers is partially attributed to their increased awareness about its dangers.

Adult drug abuse can affect children in different ways, and addictive behavior of significant adults can have serious long-term consequences for children and youth. Pregnant women who abuse alcohol and other drugs put their unborn children at risk. Children may be born developmentally impaired or addicted to substances such as crack and heroin. Children and young people can also experience psychological and physical damage when someone in their homes is addicted to drugs or alcohol. Sleeplessness, depression, neglect, and even abuse may result when adults caring for children are abusing substances.

Studies have indicated that teachers can help identify students from alcoholic or substance abuse homes by watching for particular behavioral problems in the classroom (Edwards & Zander, 1985). For example, children from an alcoholic or substance abuse home may change drastically in personal appearance and health from day to day and exhibit poor attendance and tardiness. They may also exhibit wide ranges of academic performance—one day performing well on academic tasks and the next unable to complete even the simplest assignment. These children may be overly concerned with pleasing adults and are often afraid of parent–teacher interactions. Today many professionals are available to assist teachers when their students are involved with substance abuse. Teachers may help students become aware of the dangers of drug abuse by openly discussing these issues and by offering ways to learn more about the problem. Most schools will have programs and materials available appropriate for all grade levels that include assistance from health professionals or guidance for teachers who present topics related to drug abuse in their classrooms.

Gender

Gender issues have become more open and more complex in all segments of society. For many years educators have held differential expectations for boys and girls (Kohl & Witty, 1996). Differing expectations can lead to varied school experiences that ultimately guide career choices and perpetuate economic differences between men and women. The achievement differences between males and females can be characterized in many ways. Girls will often choose to take fewer science and mathematics classes in school, usually completing only the minimum required for graduation. Girls are also more likely to be found in introductory or lower-level courses than in advanced courses (Pipher, 1994; Tavris, 1992). Most recently, however, evidence showing gender gaps in achievement and systematic disenfranchisement of students of either sex seems to have lessened (ERIC, 2001). Research finds "more similarities than variations in gender differences among racial/ethnic groups" (Coley, 2001. p. 3). Factors such as race and socioeconomic status also appear to interact and impact achievement. When race and socioeconomic factors are considered along with gender, it is notable that African American and Hispanic males lag behind females in many areas of academic achievement.

Attempts should certainly continue to eliminate educational inequities among genders, and it is also apparent that more intensive efforts are needed, particularly with African American and Hispanic males. Students are still making academic choices and displaying achievement in sexually stereotypical ways—ways that could limit advanced study and ultimately career choices. Teachers should be aware and ready to intervene when a preponderance of students in any group, whether ethnic or gender, do not achieve academic success. In many cases, students should be assessed individually so that their strengths and weaknesses can be taken into consideration when making academic decisions—especially if those decisions are atypical.

You may learn more about gender issues at

American Association of University Women
http://www.aauw.org

URLs may change over time. For up-to-date links to relevant Web sites, visit our Companion Web site:

http://education.wadsworth.com/ wiseman3e

Teaching approaches can offset girls' and boys' differing reactions to classroom instruction. "The most valuable resource in a classroom is the teacher's attention. If the teacher is giving more of that valuable resource to one group, it should come as no surprise if that group shows greater educational gains. The only real surprise is that it has taken us so long to see the problem" (Sadker & Sadker, 1986, p. 514).

Learning Disabilities

Students with handicapping conditions and learning impairments are entitled to the same educational opportunities as other students. Special education is individualized instruction designed to meet the needs of students with disabilities (Blackhurst & Burdine, 1993). Public L. 94–142 and the Americans with Disabilities Act (ADA) of 1990 state that people with disabilities should be educated in the least restrictive environment and allowed to live, work, and attend school in settings that provide the greatest possible amount of freedom and contact with people who do not have disabilities. With the support of this legislation, special needs students are no longer being separated from regular students but are included in regular classroom settings and in all the activities of the school. This trend toward inclusion increases demands for schools to create educational programs that meet individual needs. Students who have special education needs are only some of the many students who require carefully designed interventions and support to enhance their learning and life situation (York & Reynolds, 1996, p. 821).

Regular classroom placement of a student with disabilities can have a great impact on the classroom and the teacher. Administrative and family support are important to the successful placement of such students (Villa & Thousand, 1990). Learning specialists can also help ease the transition and provide needed support for the classroom teacher (Margolis & McCabe, 1989). Teachers must be trained in practices and methods that support learning for special education students and must often learn to work together with special education personnel to team-teach classes containing special needs students.

Resiliency of Children

Children, no matter what their background, will have challenges to overcome and adjustments to make. Some must adjust to extremely disruptive events, such as divorce or acts of violence. Others may have to deal with

© Jeff Greenberg/The Image Works

Most children grow up happy. They show a great propensity to overcome hardships and demonstrate resiliency as they adapt to adversity and transform risks. One of the most important factors contributing to young people's resiliency is the support and interest of at least one adult.

their own or family illnesses. Even young people with a stable home life will have some life crises that cause stress in their lives. They may clash with a family member, lose a pet, experience racism, or move from their home. National events such as war, terrorism, or other disruptions can produce anxiety among children.

Children possess qualities that can help them adapt and transform any risk or adversity into a positive experience. When children overcome difficulties and adjust to stress, they are displaying characteristics of resiliency (Bernard van Leer Foundation, 1995). All children have a capacity for resilience that is activated when certain stressful events occur in their lives. Resilient children are able to interact and gain support from others and plan strategies that help them deal with problems. Usually they are self-confident and believe that they can improve their lives. They are hopeful, optimistic, and connected to others (Bernard van Leer Foundation, 1995).

Schools, homes, churches, and the community can foster this resiliency in several ways (Heath & McLaughlin, 1993; Weis & Fine, 1993). The first requirement is that there is at least one person who cares for the child. Positive role models should never be underestimated, and a favorite person can be a confidant and serve as an example for personal identification. A teacher can fill this role in the everyday processes of teaching and learning. Student support systems also provide support to children under stress. The teacher who works to create a caring classroom community will provide students with many options for caring support.

Second, high expectations contribute to resiliency among children (Heath & McLaughlin, 1993; Weis & Fine, 1993). Children and young people develop resiliency if they believe they are worthwhile, and high expectations contribute to their belief in themselves. Schools and teachers are able to communicate high expectations through curriculum that is challenging and meaningful. The learners understand why they are learning and why it is important. A curriculum built on the diversity of learning styles enables each student to depend on his or her strengths and is an important way to foster resiliency. Flexible learning opportunities enable students to meet expectations and perform well in school.

Third, opportunities for participation in activities and involvement with others contribute to resilience in children (Heath & McLaughlin, 1993; Weis & Fine, 1993). Children and young people feel respect and care when they work with others. Ensuring that all students feel they are members of a group and finding ways for all students to contribute to ongoing activities foster traits of resilience. Schools and teachers can help students develop the skills that are needed for them to cope with stress in their lives.

Mission: Teach All Students

One of the fundamental goals of the U.S. education system is to educate all children and adolescents. Despite all our attention toward this goal, disparities in measured opportunities to learn are many times greater in our country than in some other countries (Darling-Hammond & Ancess, 1995). Our schools have traditionally provided good experiences and opportunities for some, but they have delivered greatly different experiences to others—which results in some people consistently having fewer opportunities than others. Many factors contribute to the social dilemma of educational inequity, including differences in school funding, the number of children who live in poverty in a given school district, different levels of excellence in teacher training and teaching, and troubled schools and families. To provide access to academic, social, technical, and general knowledge, educators must strive to provide equity. Equity is not the same as equality. Equality means that all students are treated the same, regardless of the starting point. Equity means that resources are supplied based on need. To meet the goal of educating all children, those children who have more needs will require more resources.

Although some issues related to equity, such as resource equalization, are beyond teachers' influence, classrooms can provide the flexibility, respect, responsiveness, and rigor that encourage students to achieve (Darling-Hammond & Ancess, 1995). Structures that focus on individuals and make the best of their talents, interests, and past experiences can help educators ensure equity for all students.

Teachers in U.S. schools have never before faced classrooms of learners so varied in abilities, language, social class, and race. Yet the schools' responsibility remains the same: Teach all children. Teaching all children—with all their differences—requires teachers to develop an equitable classroom climate where all are valued and all are respected.

Successful teachers who are effective with diverse students are self-reflective about their own attitudes, beliefs, and actions. They constantly work to recognize and eliminate teacher expectations based on race, class, or gender. Effective teachers provide diversity in instructional activities and classroom environment.

Many students come to our classrooms each day with all the indicators associated with failure, with overwhelming problems that threaten to distract them from learning, and yet they succeed and even excel in an academic setting. Students from varied backgrounds and cultures experience few problems with learning within the school context. Within the walls of your classroom, you will meet examples of all of these young people—students with problems to overcome and students who learn easily and quickly. But the mission will be the same: Teach and respect all students.

PORTFOLIO REFLECTIONS AND EXHIBITS

Throughout this chapter you completed a series of Field-Based Activities. They may serve as the basis for a portfolio representation, you may develop your own portfolio representation, or you may complete these suggested portfolio activities.

Suggested Exhibit 5: Determining the Status of the Students You Teach

1. Develop a representation (collage, Venn diagram, computer graphic, picture collection, or written description) contrasting your background with the background of the students in your classroom. Show what is similar and what is different. Illustrate similarities and contrasts between cultures, family structures, neighborhoods, and recreational experiences. Summarize by writing or illustrating how your attitudes have been affected by your past and present experiences. Be sure to include how this knowledge will affect your approach to teaching.

2. Interview one of your students' parents, caretakers, or family members. Ask them about their work, what they like to do in their free time, their own experiences at school, and where their extended families reside. Summarize what you learned from your talk and explain why it is important for teachers to know their students' families.

E-Portfolio Entry 5

Upload pictures of students at your school. Write a summary of what you have learned about their families and communities. Include statistics available from the school about the minority composition, the poverty levels, and the language that the students speak at home.

INTASC Principles 3, 7, and 9

ANSWERS TO GUIDING YOUR READING

1. How have family structures changed over the last decade?

The most striking difference is the increased number of single-family homes. Equally impressive is the number of homes in which both parents are working, leaving many young children in childcare and older children unsupervised. Extended family members or friends are raising children, and a family unit can comprise different cultures or same-gender parents. No matter what the arrangement, children and young people can receive the support they require from all manner of family situations.

2. What impact do culture and language have on classroom contexts?

The expanding diversity of classroom populations affects the language and cultural makeup of almost every school. As a result, teachers are often a different cultural group than at least some and maybe all students, and students can speak a variety of languages. The cultural and language differences offer a diversity of ideas, responses, and reactions in classroom settings and will greatly enrich instructional interactions.

3. What are some of the major social issues affecting young people's lives?

Social issues such as divorce violence, poverty, homelessness, substance abuse, and lack of health care affect students outside and inside the classroom. Teachers can help students cope with challenging social situations by recognizing that students may face events they cannot control, being open to discussing social issues, and understanding when to contact families and social agencies for assistance. Schools provide a place where students can continue to learn, and teachers can make a difference in their lives—no matter what is happening in the world around them.

4. What can future teachers learn from students whose backgrounds differ from their own?

Diversity may bring challenges to teaching, but teachers who accept differences will benefit from being open to students' cultures, learning about their experiences, and mingling in their communities. Classroom diversity can be one of the joys of teaching. One of the most important things teachers can learn from the diversity in their classroom is that students are more alike than different. All students, no matter what their backgrounds and experiences, are capable of achieving when teachers hold high learning expectations and provide relevant opportunities for them to learn.

INFOTRAC COLLEGE EDITION EXTENSION

Log on to the InfoTrac College Edition Web site and use it to find out more about issues related to contemporary students. Choose from the following:

1. Using the keyword search, type in "teaching and cultural differences." Choose an article about cultural differences related to teaching or teacher education that looks interesting to you.

2. Using the subject guide search, type in "poverty." Then choose the View Subdivisions option and select one or more of the following subdivisions: psychological aspects, social aspects, health aspects. Look for articles about families, youth, or children. What do they tell you about the effects of poverty that might influence your teaching?

RELATED READINGS

The following books will provide more information about some of the topics and ideas discussed in this chapter:

Ballenger, C. (1999). *Teaching other people's children: Literacy and learning in a bilingual classroom.* New York: Teachers College Press.

Ms. Ballenger describes her efforts to teach children who do not share her cultural background. She recounts how she listened to and learned from children and how even the time-honored teaching strategy of reading aloud to young children can be challenged in culturally diverse classrooms.

Carger, K. L. (1996). *Of borders and dreams: A Mexican American experience of urban education.* New York: Teachers College Press.

This story of Alejandro, a Mexican American youth growing up in a West Side Chicago neighborhood, describes the struggles and frustrations of bilingual and bicultural children in urban schools. Ms. Carger works with the family to help improve Alejandro's chances in the public school system but finds that even those who understand the system can be frustrated by its bureaucracy.

Kozol, J. (1991). *Savage inequalities: Children in American schools.* New York: HarperCollins.

Kozol, J. (1995). *Amazing grace.* New York: Crown.

Both of Kozol's books are sobering descriptions of poor children's lives. In *Savage Inequalities,* he describes the results of limited resources on several inner-city school districts. *Amazing Grace* describes the day-to-day lives of some of the poorest children in our country. Neither of these books is particularly uplifting, but both present some realities that middle-class Americans need to understand.

Michie, G. (1999). *Holler if you hear me: The education of a teacher and his students.* New York: Teachers College Press.

This compelling book tells the story of what it means to be an urban high school teacher. Told with hope and humor, it provides insights about students whose worlds are different from the teacher's world. Michie also helps us hear the voices of his Latino and African American students by having them tell what they learn as students in urban settings.

REFERENCES

Epigraph: Ladson-Billings, Gloria. (1997). *The dreamkeepers* (pp. 76–77). San Francisco: Jossey-Bass.

Annie E. Casey Foundation (2003). *Kids count: United States profile.* Author [Available online: www.kidscount.org]

Arends, R. (2000). *Learning to teach.* New York: McGraw-Hill.

Belsie, L. (2000, October 31). Ranks of latchkey kids approach 7 million. *Christian Science Monitor,* p. 3, section 1. Retrieved December 2003 from http://search.csmonitor.com/durable/2000.10/31/fp3sl-csm.shtml

Bennett, W. (1995). What to do about the children. *Commentary,* 99(3), 22–28.

Berla, N., & Henderson, A. T. (1994). *A new generation of evidence: The family is critical to student achievement.* Washington, DC: National Committee for Citizens in Education. (Distributed by the center for Law and Education, 1875 Connecticut Avenue, N.W., Suite 510, Washington, DC 20009.)

Bernard van Leer Foundation. (1995). Promoting resilience in children. (*Annual Review* 1995, no. 3). The Hague, Netherlands: Author. (ERIC Document Reproduction Service No. ED 399076)

Blackhurst, A., & Burdine, W. (Eds.). (1993). *An introduction to special education* (3rd ed.). New York: HarperCollins.

Bowman, B. (1994). The challenge of diversity. *Phi Delta Kappan,* 76(3), 218–225.

Bumpass, L. L., Raley, R. K., & Sweet, J. A. (1995). The changing character of stepfamilies: Implications of cohabitation and nonmarital childbearing, *Demography* 32, 425–436.

Centers for Disease Control and Prevention. (2002). Youth risk behavior surveillance—United States, 2001. In CDC Surveillance Summaries, June 28, 2002, MMWR, 51(SS-4), p. 6.

Chaker, A. M. (2004, January 6). Number of working mothers has dropped. *The Detroit News.* Retrieved February 2004 from www.detnews.com/2004/business/0401/06/c03–28171.htm

Child Maltreatment Document. (2001).

Children's Defense Fund. (1994). *CDF report.* Washington, DC: Author.

Coley, R. (2001). Differences in the gender gap: Comparisons across racial/ethnic groups in education and work. Princeton: Educational Testing Services, Policy Information Center. [Available online: http://www.ets.org/research/pic]

Darling-Hammond, L., & Ancess, J. (1995). Democracy and access to education. In R. Soder (Ed.), *Democracy, education, and the schools* (pp. 151–181). San Francisco: Jossey-Bass.

Edwards, D., & Zander, T. (1985, December). Children of alcoholics: Background and strategies for the counselor. *Elementary School Guidance and Counseling,* 20(2), 121–128.

ERIC. (2001). Gender differences in educational achievement within racial and ethnic groups. The Educational Resources Information Center. ED455341. New York: ERIC Clearinghouse on Urban Education. [Available online: http://www.ericfacility.net/databases/ERIC_Digests/ed455341.html]

Federal Bureau of Investigation. (2002). *Crime in the United States, 2001.* Washington, DC: Author, Table 41.

Fischer, L., Schimmel, D., & Kelly, C. (1999). *Teachers and the law.* New York: Longman.

Fix, M. E., Passel, J. S., & Sucher, K. (2003). Trends in nationalization. Washington, DC: The Urban Institute. [Available online: http://www.urban.org]

Goodlad, J. (1990). *Teachers for our nation's schools.* San Francisco: Jossey-Bass.

Heath, S. B., & McLaughlin, M. W. (Eds.). (1993). *Identity and inner-city youth: Beyond ethnicity and gender.* New York: Teachers College Press.

Henshaw, S. K. (1997). Teenage abortion and pregnancy statistics by state, 1992. *Family Planning Perspectives,* 29(3), 115–122.

Hodgkinson, H. (1993). American education: The good, the bad, and the task. *Phi Delta Kappan,* 74(8), 619–623.

Kelly, D. (1993, March 9). A haven for homeless students. *USA Today,* 10.

Kohl, P. L., & Witty, E. P. (1996). Equity challenges. In J. Sikula (Ed.), *Handbook of research on teacher education* (2nd ed., pp. 837–866). New York: Macmillan.

Margolis, H., & McCabe, P. (1989). Easing the adjustment to mainstreaming programs. *Educational Digest,* 55(4), 58–61.

Maternal and Child Health Bureau (2000). *Child health USA.* Washington, DC: U.S. Department of Health and Human Services.

McLaren, P. (1994). *Life in schools: An introduction to critical pedagogy in the foundations of education.* New York: Longman.

Nansel, T. R., Overpeck, M., Pilla, R. S., Ruan, W. J., Simons-Morton, B., & Scheidt, P. (2001). Bullying behaviors among U.S. youth: Prevalence and association with psychological adjustment. *Journal of the American Medical Association,* 285(16), 2094–2100.

National Coalition for the Homeless. (1999). Who is homeless? [*Fact Sheet* #3]. Washington, DC: Author.

National Crime Prevention Council. (1990). *Changing perspectives: Youth as resources.* Washington, DC: Author.

National Institute on Drug Abuse. (2002). High school and youth trends: NIDA InfoFacts. Washington, DC: Author. [Available online: http://www.drugabuse.gov/Infofax/HSYouthtrends.html

Olson, L. (2000, September 27). Children of change. *Education Week,* XX(4), 30–41.

Pang, V. O. (2001). *Multicultural education: A caring-centered, reflective approach.* Boston: McGraw-Hill.

Pipher, M. (1994). *Reviving Ophelia: Saving the selves of adolescent girls.* New York: Ballantine.

Plante, K. L. (1993, February). *The competitiveness and production of tomorrow's workforce: Compelling reasons for investing in healthy children* [Fact sheet prepared for participants in "Children as Capital" corporate health policy retreat]. Washington, DC: American Academy of Pediatrics & Washington Business Group on Health.

Plisko, V. (2000). Commissioners Statement: The condition of education. Washington, DC: National Center for Education Statistics.

Reed, S., & Saulter, R. C. (1990). Children of poverty: The status of 12 million young Americans. *Phi Delta Kappan,* 71(10), K1–K12.

Sadker, M., & Sadker, D. (1986). Sexism in the classroom: From grade school to graduate school. *Phi Delta Kappan,* 67(7), 512–515.

Sadker, M., & Sadker, D. (2000). *Teachers, schools, & society.* New York: McGraw-Hill

Santos, F., & Ingrassia, R. (2002, August 18). Family surge at shelters. *New York Daily News.* [Available online: www.nationalhomeless.org/housing/families article.html]

Sherman, A. (1994). *Wasting America's future: The Children's Defense Fund report on the costs of child poverty.* Boston: Beacon Press.

Shinn, M., & Weitzman, B. (1996). *Homelessness in America: Homeless families are different.* Washington, DC: National Coalition for the Homeless.

Stephens, S. A., Wolf, W. C., & Batten, S. T. (1999). *Improving outcomes for teen parents and their young children by strengthening school-based programs: Challenges, solutions, and policy implications.* Washington, DC: Center for Assessment and Policy Development.

Strauss, V. (2003, October 7). The condition of education: An annual snapshot. *The Washington Post.* Schools & Learning Section A, p. A14.

Tavris, C. (1992). *Mismeasurement of women.* New York: Simon & Schuster.

Tufts University School of Nutrition Policy. (1993). *Statements on the link between nutrition and cognitive development in children.* Boston, MA: Author.

U.S. Bureau of the Census (2001). *Money income in the United States: 2001.* [Available online: www.census.gov]

U.S. Conference of Mayors. (2001). *A status report on hunger and homelessness in America's cities.* Washington, DC: Author.

U.S. Department of Health and Human Services. (2001). *Youth violence: A report of the surgeon general,* pp. 63–67. Washington, DC: Author.

Ventura, S. J., Peters, K. D., Martin, J. A., & Maurer, J. D. (1996). Births and deaths in the United States, 1996. *Monthly Vital Statistics Report,* 46(1), 2. Hyattsville, MD: National Center for Health Statistics.

Villa, R., & Thousand, J. (1990). Administrative supports to promote inclusive schooling. In W. Stainback & J. K. Stainback (Eds.), *Support networks for inclusive schooling: Independent, integrated education* (pp. 201–218). Baltimore: Paul H. Brookes.

Vissing, Y. (1996). *Out of sight, out of mind: Homeless children and families in small town America.* Lexington: University Press of Kentucky.

Weis, L., & Fine, M. (Eds.). (1993). *Beyond silent voices: Class, race, and gender in United States schools.* Albany: State University of New York Press.

York, J., & Reynolds, M. (1996). Special education and inclusion. In J. Sikula (Ed.), *Handbook of research on teacher education* (2nd ed., pp. 820–836). New York: Macmillan.

CHAPTER

6

Classroom Learning Theory

Even though their reading scores don't indicate that they're "smart" in the conventional sense, it's amazing how savvy they are. They are a walking encyclopedia when it comes to pop culture, quoting the lines from their favorite movies verbatim or reciting every lyric from the latest rap CD. But, when I ask them what a dangling modifier is, they say, "Dangle this." Actually, even I hate dangling modifiers.

I think the key is to build on what they already know. I've been trying to pick stories they can relate to and then challenge them to bring the story to life. We just finished reading a story about a kid living in the projects who had to deal with peer pressure and gangs. Some of them admitted that this was the first novel they'd ever read from cover to cover. They loved the book so much, I suggested we make a movie. Since Boys 'n the Hood *is a realistic portrayal of their environment, I thought making a movie would give them the opportunity to emulate John Singleton. When I gave them creative license, they surpassed my expectations. They wrote a script, made scenery, brought in props, and even held the camera. . . . As a reward, I took a handful of them to see the documentary* Hoop Dreams, *because both the book and the movie deal with what it's like to grow up in an urban community.*

—The Freedom Writers with Erin Gruwell, *The Freedom Writers' Diary*

Guiding Your Reading

1. What is the relationship between how humans learn and planning and implementing effective instruction for my students?

2. What do the different theories look like when they are used in a classroom?

3. How can I combine what I know about learning theory so that students learn in meaningful ways?

*Y*ou have probably frequently heard statements such as "teachers are born, not made." The phrase is true to some extent, and it implies that teaching is an art rather than a science. Some teachers do seem to have natural abilities and personality traits that cannot be taught—at least not during the relatively brief period of pre-service teacher education. Thinking of teaching as solely an art implies that people

© 2001 Bill Lisenby

Future teachers are often surprised about the long hours needed to plan lessons and activities and by the effort required to evaluate students' responses and provide feedback.

must be born with the ability to reach and teach children and adolescents, or they will not become good teachers. Does this mean you should abandon your desire to teach if you feel that you do not "instinctively" know what to do when you are working with students? The answer is no.

Fortunately, we know that novice teachers can learn the skills and knowledge that contribute to good teaching, form the scientific basis of the art of teaching, and often differentiate merely good teachers from great ones (Gage, 1984). Expert teachers draw on this knowledge when planning, making decisions, and implementing instruction. Although we cannot directly teach some of the dispositions associated with our notion of good teachers—such as caring, enthusiasm, or empathy—we can provide experiences that can help you develop them. Part of the value of your field-based program lies in the opportunity you have to interact with teachers who possess these qualities.

A large part of the science of teaching is knowledge about the ways humans learn: how we process information, what motivates us to learn, and how learning and motivation change over time and with experience. Understanding how learning takes place helps teachers plan instruction and experiences for students that match their particular needs. Knowledge about how factors such as the type of tasks students perform, interactions with other people, and how attitudes and feelings influence learning enables teachers to reflect about teaching successes and failures. Knowing how previous experiences and learning affect new learning enables us to tailor our instruction for individuals of different ability levels who may come from different cultures or conditions or speak different languages. Although we teach groups in the classroom setting, individuals learn. Understanding how individual differences affect human learning makes us better teachers.

As you continue through your program, you will need more knowledge about human learning to plan and implement instruction, manage groups, and recognize and address individual problems. You may have already taken or plan to take classes in educational psychology, learning theory, or child and adolescent theory. This chapter does not replace those courses, but challenges you to think about teaching decisions in relation to what we know about how students learn.

Typically, experts in teaching and learning have operated in isolation from each other, which makes it difficult to apply or even see the utility of psychological theory for teaching (Alexander & Knight, 1993). Aside from the educational psychology textbooks provided in courses (and often seen by students as unrelated to the real world of classrooms), few teacher education texts draw exclusively on psychological learning theory as a basis for instructional decision making. However, knowledge of learning processes might inform your teaching and provide a basis for observing and analyzing the classes you see in your field-based program. This chapter therefore covers a very limited selection of content. Do not think of this as material you need to memorize, but do use the information to focus your observations and discussions with teachers and your peers. If you are already familiar with the content, seeing the application of it in classrooms will make it more personally meaningful. If much of the content of this chapter is new to you, consider it a framework to help you think about teaching and learning during this course and to introduce you to information you will study in more depth at a later time. The References (at the end of the chapter) lists books and articles that will be valuable as you build your own scientific basis for the art of teaching.

What we know about learning and its relationship to effective teaching cannot be summarized in a single chapter. Many learning theory courses are taught in university classrooms with little contact with schools, students, or teachers. These theories often seem to contradict each other, and you may be left feeling more confused than enlightened. As you read about different approaches to how students learn, think about your own learning experiences. Do you learn some kinds of information best through more direct methods such as lecture or demonstration? Are there other kinds of learning that you have to experience rather than be told?

You have an opportunity through this course to make learning theories meaningful through observation and application. This chapter discusses learning from three perspectives—behavioral, cognitive, and constructivist— that have been useful to educators as they design and implement instruction. No one theory can explain all types of learning in all kinds of situations for every learner. The term "learning" has different meanings for different people and for different tasks. However, reflecting on the various theories

FIELD-BASED ACTIVITY 6.1

Think of a learning experience you have had that was particularly powerful. Be prepared to describe the event to one of your classmates. What did you learn? How did you learn it? What were the conditions (the presence or absence of other people, the amount of time it took)? What made it so effective? Now do the same thing for an experience that was not effective for you. What were you supposed to have learned? Describe the event. List the characteristics of successful and not-so-successful learning experiences. Share the list with your class. Keep these two experiences in mind as you continue to read.

INTASC Principles 2 and 3

while planning or troubleshooting and determining when to apply a particular aspect of a theory becomes part of the art of teaching that you will refine with experience.

▶ *Learning as Behavior*

> At first, Javier was doing well in geometry class. Then he got confused and failed a test. Now Javier has difficulty even completing a quiz because his hands shake so badly he can't hold a pencil. His teacher has decided to give him his next test orally after school.
>
> Students in Ms. Gordon's class receive a construction paper "happy face" every time they move quietly from their reading group into center activities. When they have ten or more happy faces, they can trade them for something in the class "store," such as a sticker or school supplies.
>
> A group of four students completes one of Mrs. Smith's learning centers and carefully puts away all materials. As they are doing this, Mrs. Smith says aloud: "Joe, Amy, Juan, and Alicia all get a scratch 'n' sniff sticker because they have returned their center materials to the proper places."

What do all these scenes have in common? They all contain examples of the application of different types of behavioral learning theory in elementary or secondary classes. Behavioral learning theory has exerted considerable influence on educational practices in the United States for almost half a century. You will recognize many of the applications from your own school experiences and will see others as you observe in classrooms.

Behaviorism is not a single theory; it includes several types of behavioral learning theory and multiple theorists associated with the approach. Many of the distinctions among the different theorists, although important to other theorists and researchers, do not significantly affect the application of the approach in educational settings. For this reason, we will focus on elements that all behavioral theories share and how these common elements apply to the classroom. When differences in theory result in different implications for teaching—as in the differences between observational learning theory and operant conditioning—we highlight and discuss them.

All behavioral perspectives define learning as a lasting change in observable behavior that occurs as a result of experience. Notice that the definition specifies "lasting change." Random or unintentional behaviors do not indicate that learning has taken place. For example, if a student completes a multiple-choice test using a predictable pattern of responses unrelated to the questions (alternating a, b, c, or d for each answer, for example) and gets 25 percent of the answers correct, we cannot say that the student has learned 25 percent of the material.

All behavioral theories also share an emphasis on observable, measurable behavior. A student may know the answers to all the questions on a test but may not respond to the test. Because we have not observed the behaviors (that is, noted the student's correct test answers), we cannot say that learning has occurred. According to strict behaviorists, experience that results in learning comes from interactions with the external environment. Changes due to internal mechanisms, such as those attributed to development, would not constitute learning. From a behavioral perspective, learning occurs when the connection between a stimulus (something in the environment) and the response (a behavior) has been strengthened. Learning is conditioning (recognizing relationships or associations between stimuli) and is dependent on reinforcement (something that strengthens the connection) of the stimulus with the response. All behaviorists share these principles, but they sometimes differ on the type and role of reinforcement in conditioning and the stimuli and responses of interest.

Classical Conditioning

The example of Javier at the beginning of this section is illustrative of a type of behavioral theory known as classical conditioning, first articulated by Ivan Pavlov. A brilliant physician, he won a Nobel Prize based on his work on digestion. However, his observations on the salivation of dogs in the absence of food initiated research that changed the direction of psychology at the time. Pavlov noticed that caretakers of the dogs he used in experiments rang a bell just before distributing their food. The dogs eventually began to salivate in anticipation of food, even when caretakers rang the bell and did not provide food. Pavlov theorized that the food served as a stimulus that naturally prompted a physiological response, in this case salivation. With repeated presentations of the food (unconditioned stimulus) and the bell (conditioned stimulus) together (contiguity of stimuli), the dogs began to associate the ringing of the bell with presentation of food and reacted to the seemingly dissimilar stimulus in the same manner. The unconditioned response of salivation in reaction to food then occurred as a conditioned response of salivation in reaction to the bell. Furthermore, salivation also occurred for sounds that were similar to the ringing of a bell, such as the sound of a tone or buzzer (illustrating the mechanism of generalization). Further research revealed that dogs could be taught to differentiate between similar stimuli (a buzzer or bell) depending on their association with food (known as discrimination). Association of food with a stimulus strengthened the response, and removal of the food from the stimulus resulted in a gradual weakening of the reaction (known as extinction of the behavior).

Although this theory focuses on reflexive behavior (usually emotional and physiological responses to stimuli), it does have some applications to our work with students. Javier's uncontrollable shaking when confronted with his geometry test is explained by this theory. Javier's intense anxiety in response to his first failure on a particular geometry quiz now occurs when he attempts any geometry test. The unconditioned stimulus—in this case, the failure—has become closely related to the conditioned stimulus, the testing situation (including the desk, paper, pencil, and so on). The emotional anxiety that failure elicits, seen in his shaking hands, now occurs in a test-taking situation. The teacher attempts to help him succeed by revising the test-taking situation (that is, giving the test orally) to create a less stressful reaction.

Operant Conditioning

Although classical conditioning has only limited application in the classroom because it deals primarily with involuntary reactions, B. F. Skinner's concept of operant conditioning has widespread application. Operant conditioning provides the framework for many of the basic skill development models, classroom discipline approaches, special education interventions, and computer-assisted instruction models used in schools. Skinner was particularly interested in the application of his theory to education, and he became actively involved in translating his work into practice (see, e.g., Skinner, 1954, 1958, 1968).

Operant conditioning focuses on voluntary behavior used in operating on the environment. From this perspective, the stimulus is something in the environment, and the response is the behavioral reaction. Learning occurs when the connections between the environmental stimulus and the voluntary behavior become strengthened through reinforcement. Reinforcement, defined as any consequence of the voluntary behavior that strengthens, or

Even the complex classroom learning process may be aided by providing tangible reinforcement, such as a cup of dessert, after a task is
completed. Understanding how to use reinforcement is an important
aspect of learning to teach.

increases, the behavioral response to the stimulus, is contingent on performance of the behavior. Whereas other behaviorists waited for animals
to learn through exploration, using the theory passively to explain behavior
(e.g., Thorndike, 1913), Skinner actively manipulated the environment to
obtain specific kinds of learning. Through the basic mechanisms of positive
reinforcement, negative reinforcement, extinction, and punishment, he ex-
perimented with increasing or decreasing behaviors (Skinner, 1963, 1969).

POSITIVE REINFORCEMENT Positive reinforcement means receiving something desired as a consequence of operating in some way on the environment (that is, behaving in a particular manner). The behavior increases
because the reinforcement is contingent on performance of the behavior.
Skinner's research on cats and pigeons indicated that this mechanism is
perhaps the most effective way of increasing desired behavior. The keys to
effective positive reinforcement include consideration of the degree of
desirability of the reinforcer, or its potency, as well as issues of satiation,
or "too much of a good thing." Although primary reinforcers (such as food,

water, shelter, physical comfort, and affection) are powerful motivators, they may not always have the desired outcome or may not be feasible in instructional settings. Food works best when people or animals are hungry, for example, but withholding food to increase the potency of the reinforcer presents ethical problems in a school setting. Similarly, chocolate may be a child's favorite food, but children may soon tire of a steady diet of chocolate, reducing its potency as a reinforcer.

Secondary reinforcers are objects, gestures, or events that acquire the status of a primary reinforcer through association with that reinforcer. In classrooms, teachers use some primary reinforcements (such as candy, snacks, or hugs), but they most often use secondary reinforcers (such as praise or grades). To make sure that a reinforcer is desirable to students and to guard against satiation, teachers also may use systems that enable students to choose their own rewards. Teachers reward students for desired behavior with objects, or tokens, that appear to have little or no value but that can be "traded" by the student for a variety of desirable objects or experiences. The example of Ms. Gordon and the construction paper "happy faces" illustrates this type of system, called a token economy, using positive reinforcers.

NEGATIVE REINFORCEMENT Negative reinforcement, another mechanism to increase behaviors, involves removing something undesired. The removal of something unpleasant or unwanted, such as electric shock, is contingent on performance of desired behaviors, such as pushing a lever. An animal subjected to electric shock will push a lever as frequently as needed to avoid the shock. Likewise, an American history teacher might promise a class that if students do their homework all week they won't have any homework over the weekend. Students who view weekend homework as something to be avoided will do homework during the week. As with positive reinforcement, student perceptions of the degree of unpleasantness of objects or experiences determine the effectiveness of the negative reinforcer. Students who enjoy doing homework or students who never do homework anyway will not respond as desired. Another difficulty with this approach lies in reinforcing the notion that something like homework, which research indicates results in increased learning for students (Wang, Haertel, & Walberg, 1993), is something students should avoid. Teachers should carefully consider the unintended consequences of negative reinforcement.

A variation of negative reinforcement called the Premack principle (Premack, 1965) has been particularly useful in classrooms. In this approach, students agree to do a less-desired behavior so that they will also be able to do a more-desired one. For example, a band instructor may

FIELD-BASED ACTIVITY

6.3

What kinds of reinforcers do you see teachers using? Ask your teacher how she or he uses reinforcement in the classroom. How do students respond? Share in your discussions what you are seeing and compare the different methods of positive or negative reinforcement used in your school.

INTASC Principle 2

tell students that if they do a good job playing one of the classical tunes they are learning they can also play a modern one of their choice.

Positive and negative reinforcement increase behaviors, but Skinner determined that other mechanisms decrease behavior. Extinction, or reinforcement removal, eventually extinguishes behavior. For example, students who shout out answers to questions rather than raising their hand eventually should stop shouting out if the teacher does not acknowledge the contributions. However, the classroom is more complex than the laboratory, and students may continue to shout out if classmates provide reinforcement by acknowledging the answers or by noticing the aggressive behavior. Although the teacher has removed reinforcement, other students provide reinforcement. Ignoring the inappropriate behavior, enlisting the cooperation of the class in also doing so, and providing positive reinforcement when students raise their hand may all be needed to modify the unwanted behavior.

PUNISHMENT Punishment, in the form of painful or undesirable consequences, also decreases behavior. Punishment can be of two types: presentation punishment, which involves receiving something not desired, or removal punishment, which consists of removing something desired. Teachers or administrators who administer corporal punishment are engaging in presentation punishment. A secondary teacher who refuses to allow a student to attend a sixth-period pep rally because the student arrived late for class three days in a row is using removal punishment. An elementary teacher might place a misbehaving student in time-out, removing the student from participation with the rest of the class, as removal punishment. The premise for time-out is that the student sees participation in class as a desirable event and will decrease the incidents that result in the time-out.

Negative reinforcement may be confused with punishment; the important difference lies in the consequences of the particular action. Both negative reinforcement and presentation punishment involve an undesirable object or event. However, their aims are different: negative reinforcement encourages a particular behavior; presentation punishment discourages a particular behavior. Negative reinforcement encourages students to perform in a certain way to remove or avoid something undesirable. Reinforcement depends on performance of certain behaviors. Conversely, presentation punishment discourages certain behavior by providing a negative consequence. If the student behaves in a certain way, something unpleasant happens as a result.

Removal punishment differs from both negative reinforcement and presentation punishment because it involves loss of a desirable object or experience. However, teachers may have difficulty determining or controlling something that is desirable to students. One particular kind of removal punishment, response cost, works in conjunction with a positive reinforcement system to remove previously awarded reinforcers when behavior is inappropriate. Using the example of Ms. Gordon's class, students might have to forfeit a "happy face" each time they fail to properly return materials. (We might recognize this approach when we lose money—that is, pay fines—for traffic violations or overdue library books.)

Although some kinds of punishment can decrease undesirable behaviors, the side effects of punishment often make it less than effective for teachers. Punishment does not deal with the reasons or desires associated with misbehavior and may only suppress the behavior for as long as the punishment is in place. Students may expend more effort to avoid getting caught than in behaving appropriately and may continue to engage in negative behaviors when the teacher is not looking. Even if students want to engage in appropriate behavior, punishment rarely provides any indication of what students should do or why the behavior is inappropriate, and it may cause resentment, particularly when physical punishment is used, which leads to further problems. The form of punishment used also may have unintended consequences. Giving extra schoolwork as punishment conveys that schoolwork is undesirable. This may reduce certain kinds of negative behavior, but it will not increase the kinds of positive behavior encouraged in most classes.

Schedules of Reinforcement

Certain patterns or schedules of reinforcement are more effective for some purposes than for others. Reinforcement schedules can be either continuous, which means that a desired response receives reinforcement every time it occurs, or intermittent, which involves reinforcement of desired responses periodically. Continuous-reinforcement schedules are most effective for encouraging development of new skills or knowledge. For example, an algebra teacher may demonstrate the steps needed to solve simultaneous equations and have students work with her. After each step, the teacher praises students liberally for correctly executing the step with her. This gives students feedback (that is, continuous reinforcement) about their performance and strengthens correct performance at an early stage of skill learning. Using this method, the danger of strengthening incorrect performance is reduced because the task has been broken down into small parts, and students receive feedback about performance on each part before continuing to the next part.

When students have advanced somewhat in their skill development, however, an intermittent schedule becomes more effective. Two types of intermittent schedules exist: ratio and interval.

Ratio-intermittent schedules depend on the number of times a response occurs and can be either fixed or variable, as follows:

Fixed-ratio schedules provide reinforcement after a certain number of desired responses. For example, our algebra teacher might announce to the class that as soon as students have correctly done five problems in a row they can start on their homework assignment, with the possibility of finishing it by the end of class.

Variable-ratio schedules also rely on a certain number of correct responses prior to reinforcement, but that number varies in unpredictable ways. In this schedule, students might have to finish only two problems on some days prior to beginning homework, five on others, or the entire set on others. The intent of the teacher would be to keep them working steadily because they never know how many problems they will have to complete before they can start their homework. The teacher guides them through the assignments, directing them to complete problems one at a time.

Intermittent-interval schedules are time- rather than number-dependent and can also be either fixed or interval, as follows:

Fixed-interval schedule. That same algebra teacher might announce that all worksheets will be taken up on Friday each week for a grade, setting a fixed time-dependent interval for reinforcement. The danger inherent in this schedule is that students will wait until just prior to the time for reinforcement to do their work. Teachers, if they are not aware of the consequences of employing fixed-interval reinforcement schedules (or even not aware that that is what they are using), may complain that students "wait until the last minute to do their work." Students, however, are responding in a manner consistent with the reinforcement schedule the teacher has chosen. To obtain different responses, another type of schedule should be used.

Variable-interval schedule. This is also time-dependent, but reinforcement occurs at varying, rather than fixed, intervals. The teacher using this schedule would take up worksheets for a grade at random times during the week. If the grade on these assignments is important to students, then students will keep up with daily work, not knowing when the teacher may choose to grade them. If the teacher wants students to spread their effort out evenly over a period of time rather than waiting until just prior to reinforcement, a variable-interval schedule is more effective. In general, variable-reinforcement schedules, in particular variable-ratio schedules, are more effective at sustaining student effort over a long period of time.

Understanding and being able to use reinforcement schedules provides teachers with a means of managing individual and class behavior (see Chapter 7). Teachers can also use four processes associated with operant conditioning—shaping, chaining, cueing, and fading—to understand how students acquire complex skills and to design instruction to help them learn skills.

Shaping. This is a means of reinforcing successive approximations of a desired behavior until students can produce the behavior. For example, if a teacher wants students to write a paragraph, the teacher might initially reward students for simply taking out paper and pencil. As students move closer to mastering the target behavior, the teacher eliminates rewards for the approximate behaviors.

Chaining involves integrating the component skills of a complex skill or task. Behavioral theory dictates that complex behaviors be broken down into their component parts so that each part can be taught and reinforced. To shape behavior, teachers must first understand the smaller steps or component skills that make up a more complex behavior and then break the task down for students. However, to accomplish integrated performance of the behavior rather than performance of a series of component skills, the components must ultimately be linked. A common mistake in classrooms is the conviction that, if we teach the subcomponents to students, they will automatically be able to integrate them.

Cueing and fading also play important roles in teaching and learning complex skills.

Cueing. Skinner found that pigeons could learn when to perform behaviors by discriminating certain cues in the environment. Reinforcement occurred in the presence of some cues but not others. For example, Skinner's pigeons "danced" in the presence of some kinds of light sources but not in others. Similarly, a red light at an intersection cues us to put on the brakes; a green light cues us to press the gas pedal. Likewise, students in classrooms are cued to appropriate behavior by teachers' direct statements ("Remember, no talking while another student is reading"), physical presence or movements (walking up and down the aisles during seatwork to cue students to work on assignments), nonverbal expressions (frowns or raised eyebrows), or other signals (flipping the lights on and off to signal a change of activities). Although teachers often use cues purposively, they are sometimes unaware of the cues they give or the way students interpret them. For example, a teacher may want students to engage in deep processing of the text they are reading but may not give them adequate time to do so. The amount of time given becomes a cue that students use to judge whether they should read at a surface level or for deeper meaning (Knight, 1990; Knight, Waxman, & Pedrone, 1989).

Fading. This is one way to help students to become independent learners. If students perform academically only in the presence of certain teacher-controlled cues, they will not perform when the teacher is no longer present. Therefore, the teacher needs to gradually withdraw the controlling cues (that is, allow them to fade) while continuing to reinforce the behavior. For example, a teacher might cue students to engage in interactive discussion of readings by standing in front of the whole group and asking thought-provoking questions. She could then gradually diminish her presence as the cue by having other students take over the role of "teacher" (see, e.g., Palincsar & Brown, 1984).

Observational Learning

Operant conditioning has provided teachers with an understanding of many classroom behaviors and with mechanisms for changing student behaviors. Nevertheless, the theory fails to account for learning in the absence of direct experience. We know that some students learn behaviors that were not directly reinforced. Bandura (1982) proposes a variant of conditioning wherein students learn new behaviors or continue to perform existing behaviors through vicarious conditioning. They watch others and observe the consequences of their behavior. The example of Ms. Smith using a token economy and awarding scratch 'n' sniff stickers to a group of students is an attempt to obtain similar behavior by others in the classroom. The four students receive positive reinforcement from the teacher. The remaining students have observed this and are likely to perform similarly if they also have hopes of obtaining stickers.

Depending on the status of the model and the conditions of reinforcement, modeling serves to (1) focus attention on behavior or aspects of behavior, (2) change inhibitions that observers might have about performing certain behaviors, and (3) arouse emotions. Students may learn from models directly by attempting to imitate a model's behavior, as when a kindergarten student makes a "B" sound after the teacher demonstrates the sound. Students may also learn in less direct ways. Symbolic modeling refers to imitating behaviors displayed by fictional characters in books, movies, or television. Such behaviors range from dressing like a rock star to imitating a wrestling stunt. Students may also develop behaviors by synthesis, or combination, of parts of observed behaviors. For example, teens may combine movements they have seen two different rock stars use to create a new dance step. Abstract modeling is even more complex and involves extraction of rules or patterns from observing different examples. For example, by observing the speech patterns of the teacher or the models on tape, students taking Spanish may learn that adjectives usually follow nouns.

For observational learning to happen, however, certain characteristics must be present (see, e.g., Schunk, 2000). Students must relate or feel some degree of similarity to the model and must perceive that they are capable of performing the behaviors. For example, misbehavior of a well-liked classmate that goes unchallenged in the classroom may result in similar incidents of misbehavior by others in the class. Likewise, rewards for desired behavior to one classmate may result in an increase in the same kind of behavior by other students. However, a person must feel capable of performing the behavior. A short person might relate to Michael Jordan and observe the accolades that he receives for his dunking the basketball. Nevertheless, the person who is five feet three inches tall, with no hope of growing taller, might not perceive that he or she is capable of ever performing a slam dunk and therefore might not play basketball.

Several processes determine the success of modeling as a classroom strategy. Observers first must observe the desired behavior and retain it in memory so they can subsequently perform it. Then they must reproduce the behavior. Finally, they must be motivated to perform the behavior. Motivation, in this case, is the reinforcement received by the model for performance. If the observer does not view the reinforcement as desirable, motivation to perform will be low. For example, middle school students may not view a teacher's public praise of a fellow student's assistance with chores in the classroom as desirable. For this reason, they would not assist the teacher for fear of receiving similar (embarrassing) praise. Look at the following example and try to identify the processes involved in observational learning:

A ninth-grade English teacher passes out graded essay exams. She then places one of the answers copied onto a transparency on the overhead projector. She says: "Look at the answer one of your classmates wrote [no name appears on the example]. I gave this an A grade. Let's look at it together and see why. First notice the thesis sentence . . ."

What does the teacher do to enable her students to learn from the example? How does she focus attention? What reinforcement does she provide? Would students likely be motivated to reproduce this behavior? Why or why not?

Applying Behavioral Theory in the Classroom

Behavioral learning theory has had considerable impact on the strategies teachers use in classrooms because it provides tools for planning for instruction, teaching skills and knowledge, managing student behavior, and assessing the effectiveness of teachers' classroom behaviors. Planning tools include guidelines for formulating behavioral objectives that explicitly describe the observable, measurable behavior targeted, the conditions under which this behavior will be performed, and the criteria by which success will be judged. In addition, behavioral theory contributes procedures for task analysis to aid teachers in breaking down tasks into sequential, component skills that they can teach using shaping and chaining processes. The creation of token economies, use of the Premack principle, and adherence to appropriate reinforcement schedules, all described above, enable teachers to strengthen desired behaviors.

Rosenshine's Direct Instruction Model

The teaching model presented in Figure 6.1 has been used extensively to evaluate both students and teachers. The model's teaching functions are consistent with behavioral learning theory. Using behavioral theory to assess the effects of instruction helps teachers improve their own teaching and assist others in improvement. The focus on observation and measurement of observable behaviors has resulted in behavior checklists or observation instruments that can be used by teachers in their own classrooms or in the classrooms of their peers (see, e.g., Good & Brophy, 1999). The use of instruments that simply record behavior, without providing an inference or judgment, provide objective

You may learn more about direct instruction at:

http://www.parentscoalition.org/resources /fact-sheets/directinstruction.htm

URLs may change over time. For up-to-date links to relevant Web sites, visit our Companion Web site:

http://education.wadsworth.com/ wiseman3e

FIGURE 6.1   **Teaching Functions**

1. Daily Review and Checking Homework

Check homework (routines for students to check each other's papers).

Reteach when necessary.

Review relevant past learning (may include questioning).

Review prerequisite skills (if applicable).

2. Presentation

Provide short statement of objectives.

Provide overview and structuring.

Proceed in small steps but at a rapid pace.

Intersperse questions during demonstration.

Highlight main points.

Provide sufficient illustrations and concrete examples.

Provide demonstrations and models.

Give detailed and redundant instructions and examples.

3. Guided Practice

Practice with teacher guidance.

Question students and require overt practice.

Check for understanding (CFU) by evaluating student responses.

Provide additional explanation, process feedback, or repeat explanation.

Provide response and receive feedback to all students.

Ensure that all students participate.

Provide prompts during guided practice (where appropriate).

Encourage sufficient practice.

Continue guided practice until students achieve a success rate of about 80 percent.

4. Correctives and Feedback

Follow firm responses with another question or short acknowledgment of correctness (e.g., "That's right").

Follow hesitant correct answers with process feedback (e.g., "Yes, Linda, that's right because . . .").

Provide practice based on student need.

Monitor students for systematic errors.

Obtain a substantive response to each question.

Include sustaining feedback to correct (i.e., simplify the question or give clues).

Explain or review steps.

Reteach the last steps.

Elicit improved responses when the first one is incorrect.

Continue guided practice and corrections until students meet the objectives of the lesson.

Provide praise in moderation (specific praise is more effective than general praise).

5. Independent Practice (Seatwork)

Allow time for sufficient practice.

Provide opportunities for practice directly relevant to skills/content taught.

Practice until responses are firm, quick, and automatic (reaching a 95 percent correct rate during independent practice).

Inform students that seatwork will be checked.

Hold students accountable for seatwork.

Actively supervise students, when possible.

6. Weekly and Monthly Reviews

Review previously learned material.

Provide opportunities for review in homework.

Administer frequent tests.

Reteach material missed in tests.

SOURCE: Adapted from Rosenshine, B., & Stevens, R. (1986). Teaching functions. In M. C. Wittrock (Ed.), *Handbook of research on teaching* (3rd ed., pp. 376–391). New York: Macmillan. Reprinted by permission of the Gale Group.

data about students as well as nonthreatening data about teacher behaviors. Teachers can use the data in assessments of their own practice, in teacher research, in peer coaching, or to identify and resolve instructional and managerial problems in the classroom. The Interactive Seating Chart in Figure 6.2 is one example of an instrument designed to provide teachers with information about teacher and student behavior.

Learning as Cognition

Mr. Garcia is teaching the concept of density to his science students. He provides groups of students with several types of clear liquids (e.g., water, alcohol) and a bucket of ice cubes. He asks students to drop ice cubes in each of the liquids, record what happens, and discuss their findings in groups. Many students are surprised to find that the ice cubes float in some liquids but sink in others. The next day he engages the entire class in a discussion of their findings and elicits their theories concerning the experiment.

Ms. Lee teaches secondary economics. Prior to beginning a series of lectures on international trade, she describes the different kinds of bartering for playthings that might take place among children at a playground and relates this to some of the concepts they will encounter in her lectures.

Mr. James is teaching his fifth-grade students about the Civil War. He puts a chart on the overhead projector that has Political Beliefs, Social Beliefs, and Economic Beliefs as column headings, and Northern Leaders and Southern Leaders as row headings. He assigns groups of students to gather information about each of the cells in the chart and to fill them in. During the discussion following the group work, they look for similarities and differences in the two groups and predict how that might affect the struggle. Mr. James also encourages the class to change the chart to better capture the information they have gathered.

What do all these examples have in common? Each vignette provides an example of a different type of cognitive theory (i.e., traditional or cognitive information processing) about how people learn. Like behavioral theory, cognitive theory consists of many different approaches. However, they all share certain underlying principles that make them look somewhat alike when they are applied to classroom instruction. In addition, they all differ from behavioral theory in ways that are evident in classroom applications. As was done for behavioral learning theories, this section will review only a few of the many cognitive learning theories that might help you make decisions about instruction. It will then discuss how these theories are similar and different from one another and how they are different from

FIGURE 6.2   **Interactive Seating Chart**

Use this chart to record student and teacher interactions in the classroom. First familiarize yourself with the codes for behaviors listed at the top of the chart. Then make a seating chart for students in a class you plan to observe. Using the codes provided, record next to the names of students the type of interaction each has with the teacher as it occurs.

? Asks a direct question	+ Praises or supports responses	✓ Social comment
? Asks an open-ended question	C Corrects a response	* Student-initiated comment
✓ Checks for understanding	G Corrects & guides response	– Reprimands behavior

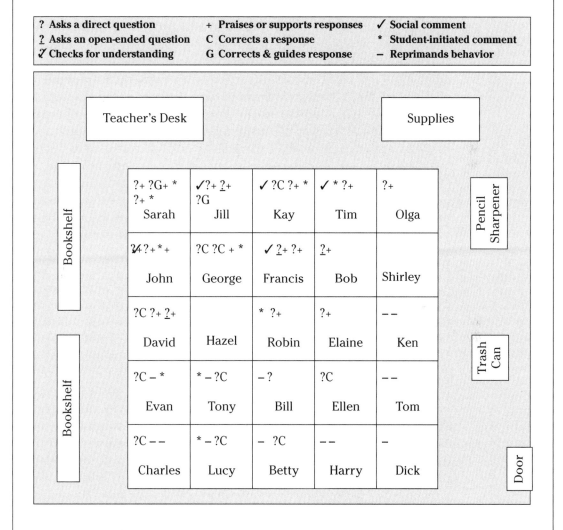

SOURCE: Knight, S. L., & Stallings, J. A. (2001). *Learning to teach in inner city schools training manual.* College Station: Texas A&M University, College of Education.

behavioral learning theories in their application. Then we will provide a rationale for using both in the classroom, depending on the kinds of student outcomes you want.

Comparing Behavioral and Cognitive Approaches

The common features of behavioral learning theory discussed above all emphasize observable, measurable behavior and the importance of reinforcement to strengthen desired behaviors. From a behavioral perspective, teachers need to break tasks, skills, and knowledge into smaller components and teach and reinforce performance of component behaviors. Repetition or practice of these component skills is a key feature of most of the models drawing on behavioral theory. In many ways, the learner remains passive, reacting to the environment in ways that respond to the reinforcement received. Behaviorists see knowledge as learned patterns of associations and define learning as acquiring new associations. Applications derived from this theory will be particularly helpful in creating basic classroom management procedures, teaching basic skills and knowledge, and teaching psychomotor skills. The teacher's role consists of arranging the environment and circumstances so that students make the desired associations. Because motivation depends on external reinforcement for behavior, external rewards such as food, money, and grades are important.

Cognitive learning theories view the learning process from a very different perspective (see, e.g., Bransford, Brown, & Cocking, 2000). They focus on covert activities of the mind rather than on overt, observable behaviors. The learner actively tries to understand what is going on in the environment rather than passively respond to associations between stimuli and responses. Cognitivists define knowledge as organized sets of mental structures and procedures; learning is the change in these mental structures brought about through mental reasoning. Students do not merely receive information—they construct knowledge by incorporating new information into existing knowledge. This may require them to add on to existing knowledge, to change the existing knowledge, or to change the new knowledge in some way. (This may sound familiar to those of you who have studied child development; Piaget's conceptions of assimilation and accommodation describe these processes.) Misconceptions often occur when students alter incoming information to fit with what they already know. This misconception may remain or be altered by new knowledge. Applications from this theory emphasize the active role of the learner in exploring the environment and tend to focus on learning complex skills and knowledge. The role of the teacher is to provide students with opportunities to explore their environment and facilitate this discovery. Because motivation springs from the learners' need to make sense of their world, intrinsic rewards are important in this theory. Successful problem solving, accounting for phenomena that are contrary to expectations, and accomplishment of tasks would all elicit such rewards. Mr. Garcia's experiment with the ice cubes and the liquids should be intrinsically motivating to students because they observe a puzzling situation that they cannot initially explain.

Traditional Cognitive Theory

Traditional cognitive learning theory has often been associated with discovery learning, but discovery is not as important as making learning meaningful. Jerome Bruner and David Ausubel, two cognitivists who have had considerable influence on elementary and secondary classrooms, disagree about how meaningful learning occurs. They do, however, concur that the emphasis should be on meaningful understanding of the substance of material rather than on verbatim recall. They both accentuate the importance of seeing relationships among ideas, learning generalizable concepts and principles, and organizing information both in written and oral text as well as in the mind of the learner.

Experienced teachers learn how to use numerous teaching and learning strategies and will select activities that motivate their students and meet individual needs.

Jerome Bruner (1966) advocates student discovery of concepts and principles through experiences in which the student observes specific instances of the concept or principle. He suggests that students engage in more meaningful learning when it is accomplished inductively—that is, learners will reason from the specific (the floating or sinking ice cubes) to the general (frozen water is less dense than A and more dense than B). The way Mr. Garcia "teaches" density to his science students is an example of discovery learning in which students inductively discover scientific principles through exploration of specific instances.

David Ausubel (1968) advocates presentation of information to students in a deductive manner, often referred to as reception learning. In other words, students should be able to infer specific instances from a general principle or rule presented by a teacher during lectures or text. To make learning meaningful, one must enable students to connect new information with what they already know rather than merely have them memorize information. He claims that discovery learning and reception learning will be meaningful only if students have the ability to connect the new learning to something they already know. Without specific attention to meaning, either form of learning could be "rote."

For example, have you ever participated in a science lab experiment in which you were able to fill in the blanks of the lab sheet but had absolutely no idea what you were supposed to have "discovered"? Discovery learning can require a great deal of time and effort and often results in mere rote learning or the discovery of incorrect principles. To overcome this problem, Ausubel suggests incorporating advance organizers in lectures or texts to enable students to make connections during the more efficient reception learning.

Advance organizers present information at a higher level of abstraction than will be utilized later, so that subsequent concepts can be incorporated into the more general concepts presented in the organizer. In the vignette above, Ms. Lee used the playground analogy as an advance organizer for the less familiar concepts to be introduced in her international trade lecture. The organizer uses language that is easy for learners to understand. In the work of Ausubel, advance organizers generally take the form of shorter, more abstract readings or oral summaries prior to a lecture or reading, but other research has supported the use of concrete models, analogies, examples, organizing principles or rules, and discussion of primary themes (Mayer, 1983). Graphic organizers such as Venn diagrams, wherein two overlapping circles illustrate common features, or webbing, in which circles connected by lines illustrate relationships, may achieve the same objectives.

Cognitive Information Processing Theory

One of the most useful approaches to learning is also one of the most recent. Based on cognitive theory but with several elements compatible with behavioral theory (including an attempt to make covert processes overt so they can be observed and measured), cognitive information processing (CIP) theory uses the computer as its model for how humans process information. CIP theorists (several theories exist, but will be treated in this section as one) are interested in how humans acquire, store, and retrieve information. This examination of mental structures and processes has implications for the design of effective instruction and may help us better understand instructional failures as well.

At first, this theory characterized the human mind as selective in the type of information acquired and stored (Klatzky, 1980). Although this theory has been replaced with other, more current theories, the implications for instruction remain similar. Data from our environment enters our sensory register (SR) through our various senses. However, due to the sheer volume of environmental data, we understandably must screen and reduce these data. Teachers can help ensure that students focus on desired information by providing visual and verbal cues that some information is more important than other information. Cues such as "Listen carefully to the following because . . ." or underlining or highlighting important information on overheads or on the board help focus attention. Inconsistent events also attract our attention because we tend to try to make sense of our world. Mr. Garcia's ice cube experiment would direct student attention to the behavior of ice cubes in liquids because they behave in a manner inconsistent with our typical experience with ice in water.

Despite their utility, external cues are not sufficient to focus attention. What we attend to in the environment is influenced by our previous experiences as well as by the context of the situation. The tendency for humans to try to make new information meaningful may result in different perceptions of the same environmental stimuli by different people or revisions of what they hear or see in order to make the information more compatible with what they already know. For example, I observed a group of kindergarten students learning the pledge of allegiance in a Houston, Texas, classroom. The teacher recited the pledge slowly, phrase by phrase, emphasizing key words. The young students immediately repeated what she said. When they came to the part that says "with liberty and justice for all," one young girl loudly recited "with liberty and Joske's for all." At that time, Joske's was a large department store in Houston. Although "justice" was not a familiar term, the idea that everyone should have a Joske's seemed perfectly reasonable to this little girl, and that is what she thought she heard!

Teachers call attention to important information and focus student attention in many ways. Here are some categories that provide a framework for thinking about strategies that focus attention.

Verbal statements
Visual displays
Demonstrations
Unusual or puzzling events

Thought-provoking questions
Verbal or visual emphasis
Use of student names

As you visit classrooms, look for examples of the ways teachers focus attention and list as many as you can under the category headings. Which ones seem to be most effective?

INTASC Principles 5 and 6

This tendency to perceive information in a personally meaningful way means that we cannot assume that each student perceives messages, information, or experiences in the same way. Knowing our students' backgrounds and previous experiences in an area, consciously creating a context that will bring out related experiences or information, and continually checking student perceptions will help students learn and perhaps prevent development of misconceptions. However, directing students' attention to important information and determining whether their perceptions of information are consistent with the teacher's intent is only part of the process.

Data selected for attention in the SR are transferred to short-term memory (STM), also referred to as working memory or consciousness. This is the site of conscious thought and processing of data. STM has a limited capacity of seven plus or minus two "chunks" of information (Miller, 1956). These chunks will be lost within thirty seconds unless they are rehearsed (repeated over and over, as we might do when we have looked up a telephone number and need to remember it long enough to get to a phone and dial it) or transferred into long-term memory (LTM) for later retrieval. Long-term memory has, for all practical purposes, an unlimited storage capacity. One of the teachers' goals, then, is to enable students to retain important information in STM long enough to be able to process and transfer it to LTM. To do this, the teacher must focus students' attention on appropriate information in their environment, provide information in a way that does not overload the capacity of STM, and facilitate students' acquisition of strategies that aid in processing information for storage.

Understanding how to help students overcome some of the limitations of STM related to the amount of information that can be processed is important for teachers. A chunk of information refers to a meaningful piece of information. For example, the numbers 1, 4, 9, and 2, considered separately, would constitute four chunks of information. However, considering them together as a date that has meaning to us, such as 1492, would constitute only one chunk of information. It is easy to remember numbers—or any smaller pieces of information—when they are organized into meaningful chunks.

Students who do not possess strategies for organizing information in meaningful ways or for making connections between new and existing information can be taught to do so with a resulting increase in memory capacity and problem solving (Bransford, Brown, & Cocking, 2000). Teachers can model strategy use for students as well as teach strategies explicitly to students. Knowledge about students' existing strategies and the strategies most successful for a given task enable teachers to integrate strategy instruction into specific content areas. Figure 6.3 provides a list of the kinds of strategies students may use to facilitate learning and problem solving.

Both lack of strategies and the way information is presented may have a negative impact on student learning. Because of the limitations of STM, students may not be able to handle all of the information presented at one time. For example, consider this dilemma and try to explain it in terms of information processing theory:

> A math teacher complains, "I stood there for fifteen minutes and explained the procedure for dividing fractions until my throat hurt from talking! I know fractions are hard for fifth-graders—and it took a long time for me to describe the process—but this morning they came in and it was as if they hadn't even been there—or had only been there for part of the time! They just have no initiative! I just don't get it—what do I have to do to get them to pay attention?"

This math teacher was frustrated because she thought the students were not listening. In reality, she may have overloaded their working memory and caused an STM bottleneck that prevented them from being able to retain the information long enough to transfer it to LTM. The students also may not have had strategies to organize this incoming information, and the teacher may not have provided the material in an organized fashion or in a way consistent with STM capacity.

Another way of overcoming limitations of STM is to make some of the operations that are typically carried out in STM automatic or externally supported so they do not take up limited processing space. For example, students working on math word problems may not have enough processing capability to understand the problem and also determine and implement appropriate algorithms or strategies to solve the problem if they also must perform certain computations (e.g., addition, subtraction, multiplication) simultaneously. For students who have not yet mastered these basic

FIGURE 6.3 **Sample Learning Strategies**

Reading Comprehension

Looking up unknown words in the dictionary/glossary

Guessing at the meaning of unknown words by examining the context of the sentence

Stopping and rereading when a passage is difficult to understand

Asking yourself questions about the passage

Predicting what will come next in a passage

Summarizing passages/portions of text when reading for extended periods of time

Main Idea

Searching for and identifying the main idea of a lecture or passage

Determining what is the main idea of a passage or assignment

Mathematical/Science Problem Solving

Defining the problem (stating a clear idea of the concepts involved)

Selecting important information in the problem

Mentally representing the problem (e.g., drawing a diagram)

Applying appropriate heuristics

Working backward

Working forward

Solving a simpler problem within the problem

Relating to a similar problem

Using trial and error

Applying appropriate algorithms

Knowledge Acquisition

Mentally linking new material to previously learned material

Using visualization techniques to help remember new material

Using mnemonic devices

Summarizing information mentally to self

Teaching information to someone else

Keeping up with reading and assignments so that new information is gained gradually

Asking questions during class

Attention/Concentration

Studying in an area that is free of external distractions

Clearing the desk of unneeded items while working or studying

Refocusing when your mind drifts during a lecture or while studying/reading

Maintaining your focus while completing a task

Motivation

Reminding yourself of the importance of completing a task

Looking for something interesting in assignments/tasks

Rewarding yourself after successfully completing a task

Study Skills

Having a designated place in which to study

Taking notes during a lecture

Reviewing notes as soon as possible after a lecture

Using underlining, note-taking, highlighting, outlining, concept mapping during studying/reading

Skimming over material or readings before a lecture is given

Time Management

Beginning an assignment soon after it is assigned

Keeping a systematic record of tasks that need to be completed

Being aware of which tasks need to be completed first

Being aware of how long tasks will take to complete

Test-Taking

Brainstorming possible questions that might appear on a test

Underlining key words in a test question

Crossing out possible incorrect answers to a multiple-choice question

Marking difficult items and returning to them after attempting other items

---

SOURCE: Adapted from Knight, S., & Boudah, D. (1998). *Teacher research training manual.* College Station: Texas A&M University.

skills, external supports such as calculators or computers may free up processing capability so that higher-order tasks such as solving word problems can be accomplished concurrently with acquisition of basic skills.

The manner in which information is transferred, or encoded, into LTM is important because it will affect how we retrieve it. The more connections that exist among pieces of information, the more likely we will successfully retrieve what we need. Encoding is the process of forming internal mental representations, or schema, by making connections in LTM between new information and existing information. As described earlier, meaningfulness is one of the characteristics of learning considered desirable by cognitive learning theorists. Meaningfulness, from an information processing perspective, refers to the number of connections between ideas in LTM. Therefore, increasing connections among ideas or pieces of information serves two purposes: We have a more complex, or meaningful, representation of information, and we are more likely to be able to retrieve relevant information when we need it because we have increased the number of means of access.

The information within a schema may be differently arranged depending on the learners' prior experiences. Culture and language histories, unique environmental contexts and experiences, interactions with various adults, and individual abilities are some of the many influences on schema. Humans construct knowledge in ways that are uniquely theirs. Although students in classrooms may be taught the same basic concepts, all children will not learn exactly the same thing, in the same sequence, or in the same way.

A very simple interaction can illustrate how a young child becomes an active participant in learning and predicts, confirms, or integrates new information. A young child looks out the window and sees something flying through the sky. Using prior knowledge available in established schema, the child points to the airplane and predicts by saying, "Bird, bird!" The mother, standing close by, reacts to the prediction by saying, "It looks like a bird doesn't it, but hear the noise; that is an airplane." The child is unable to confirm the original prediction but has modified his or her schema to include flying objects that are not birds but that are noisy and called airplanes. The existing schema is modified, and a new category of flying objects is added.

Applying Cognitive Theory in the Classroom

Given the manner in which we process information, the teacher's goal in the classroom is to facilitate construction of meaningful representations by arranging instruction so that students make appropriate connections and increase the number of connections between old and new information. To do this, we need to ensure that students actively process information rather than merely memorize material. The notion of active student involvement in processing information differentiates behavioral from cognitive approaches. Although few behaviorists would deny the need for active engagement in academic tasks (see, e.g., Brophy & Good, 1986; Good & Brophy, 1999), the nature of that engagement is different from a CIP perspective and may not always be visible to external observers. To actively engage students mentally, the teacher can employ strategies that prevent mere rote association or memorization of information: Asking questions or having students ask questions that cue students to think about connections or to analyze examples or applications, asking students to paraphrase content, giving them opportunities for problem solving, having students write about what they are learning, and engaging them in hands-on activities as often as possible are ways to initiate active involvement and discourage rote memorization. We cannot view their thinking processes, but we can see the products of their thinking.

In addition to providing opportunities for active mental processing of content, teachers can also use (and teach students to use) strategies for organizing information in ways that expose possible connections between existing pieces of information and between prior and new knowledge. Strategies for organizing information into patterns or categories can be used by teachers to present information in a way that makes connections clear and by students to make sense of material from lectures or text. For example, providing graphic organizers that show relationships among concepts, such as concept maps, flow charts, graphs, diagrams, and tables, may help students see connections that might otherwise be missed.

The example of Mr. James teaching his class about the Civil War uses several teaching strategies compatible with cognitive approaches. Mr. James actively involves students in using a chart to discover patterns and relationships. He provides some initial structure, but students are responsible for seeking information rather than passively receiving it. Because Mr. James gives students the initial structure for the categories, he reduces the difficulty of the organizing task that their age and prior knowledge might have made too difficult. The partial assistance he provides, which will be gradually removed or reduced as students gain competency in the use of graphic organizers, is referred to as scaffolding. Just as scaffolds are used to support the erection of a building and then removed as sections of the building are completed, assistance provided to students can be reduced when no longer needed. In addition to providing scaffolding, the teacher systematically addresses both the content of the activity and the process used to organize information in the following discussion. Engaging students in a discussion about how the categories of the chart might be revised to better fit the information they collected will encourage students to explore and develop their own organizational strategies.

Actively engaging students in processing information and using and teaching organizational strategies may facilitate meaningful connections, but other teaching strategies may also be necessary to consciously increase the number of connections within existing knowledge frameworks and between new and old knowledge. Teachers may need to help students make connections by explicitly pointing out differences and similarities. For example, a second-grade teacher may need to show a series of examples of problems that require subtraction without regrouping and a series of problems that show subtraction with regrouping and make the differences explicit. Teachers can also use and have students use analogies that show the similarities in dissimilar objects or ideas. Strategies to create meaning where none exists initially for the student may also be necessary at times. The use of verbal mnemonics (using an acronym such as HOMES to remember the Great Lakes) or imagery (associating words or ideas with familiar places that are easily recalled) can aid both encoding and later retrieval of information that students want to remember.

From an information processing perspective, perhaps one of the most important tasks of the teacher is to provide students with the means to improve their own learning. "Metacognition" is the conscious awareness of how we process information, our effectiveness in doing so, and the means for improving effectiveness when needed. As with strategy use, teachers can have a direct impact on students' metacognitive abilities. "Thinking out loud" for students while demonstrating procedures or solving problems, including modeling difficulties encountered while doing so, provides students with a model for strategy use as well as diagnosis and repair of errors in thinking. Having students think out loud while they are performing tasks or solving problems, either with you or with a peer, makes thinking processes public and available for discussion. Figure 6.4 provides a protocol for using this technique. Often the students themselves will become aware of the effectiveness of specific strategies as they are engaged in thinking aloud. Asking students to explain how they arrived at an answer or if they can provide an alternate way of arriving at a similar or different answer emphasizes the importance of the process used to arrive at answers and provides additional models of thinking. Metacognitive awareness provides a valuable first step toward enabling students to become independent learners. Certainly, the sheer volume of information available today makes efficient and effective information processing a priority for our schools.

One current popular instructional approach that relies heavily on information processing theory combined with neuropsychological research

FIGURE 6.4 **Think-Aloud Protocol**

Phase I General Instructions

Say "I'm going to ask you to solve some problems about [social studies, science, reading, math]. You can solve these problems any way you like. In fact, I'm really not even interested in whether you get the right answers. But I am interested in what you do when you read passages, answer questions, or solve the problems—the strategies you use. For this reason, I'm going to ask you to talk aloud as much as you can while you work. I'm going to turn on the tape recorder when you begin in order to help me remember what you are saying [optional]. OK?"

"You won't have to do anything special. Just work like you normally would. Some students tell me that they "mumble to themselves" when they're reading or solving problems. If that's what you do, then all you'll have to do today is mumble a little louder. In any case, try to talk constantly when you're not reading silently. Say what you're thinking and doing even if it doesn't make sense."

Phase II Problem Solution and Student "Think-Aloud"

Read the instructions to the student and ask him/her to begin. Turn on tape recorder [optional]. Say as little as possible, being careful to use only neutral, nondirective phrases. Use only the following prompts:
"Can you say what you're thinking?"
"That's very clear."
"Please tell me what you are writing."
"Mmm."
"OK."
"I see."
Continue this until the student has answered the questions following the passage.

Phase III Debriefing

Even if the student talked continually, there may be many unclear points in the protocol. Ask the following clarifying questions after the student has finished:
"Could you summarize for me how you got your answer?"
"Can you say some more about it?"
"Can you explain to me what you were thinking when you [asked yourself that question, got that picture in your mind, made those notes, etc.]?"
"Is there anything else you can think of?"

SOURCE: Knight, S., & Boudah, D. (1998). *Teacher research training manual.* College Station: Texas A&M University.

about how the brain functions is "brain-based" learning and teaching (Jensen, 1998). The approach familiarizes teachers with the anatomy of the brain and the biological processes that underlie learning. Although the biological research in this area does not provide direct implications for the classroom, proponents of brain-based teaching and learning suggest that these studies guide us in ways we can arrange the environment so that we stimulate the processing and growth of students' brains and brain cells. They highlight the importance of stimulation, novelty, and active mental involvement in classroom activities. Successful teaching from this perspective incorporates the information processing strategies discussed above (strategies for gaining attention, making learning meaningful through connection of prior and new information and experiences, and overcoming limitations of short-term memory).

www You can learn more about brain-based teaching at the following Web site:

http://faculty.washington.edu

URLs may change over time. For up-to-date links to relevant Web sites, visit our Companion Web site:

http://education.wadsworth.com/wiseman3e

Current Trends

In the past decade, cognitive theory has replaced behavioral approaches as the dominant theory directing the development and implementation of new instructional models and strategies. Both traditional (that is, behavioral) and information processing cognitive approaches provide students with opportunities to acquire meaningful knowledge and to develop higher-order skills, such as problem solving and reading comprehension. In addition, information processing theory has focused attention on the importance of understanding students' prior knowledge, the strategies they use to process information, and the way they approach and solve complex problems. Information processing theory has also emphasized the importance of "thinking about our own thinking" and provided the tools to make our own as well as our students' intellectual processes more visible and more effective.

Learning as Constructivism

A third approach to learning theory that holds promise for classroom instruction, but lacks the strong research base that the previous two approaches offer, focuses on the role of social interaction in learning (see, e.g., Von Glaserfield, 1997). Compatible with cognitive approaches that emphasize the active, constructive nature of learning and development of meaningful connections, social constructivist approaches focus on the role of peers and adults in the construction of knowledge. This theory suggests that cognitive abilities are acquired through interactions with others, particularly through assistance provided by others that enables us to accomplish tasks that we may not be able to do on our own. As the learner actively transacts, interprets, and interacts with the environment and with other people, understandings and knowledge from the learner's background begin to guide the learning process (Strickland, 1995). A great deal of learning occurs in social contexts, and learners' relationships with others serve a vital function in communication. How people interact, what comments they provide, and how they view the world become part of learning. The Voice of a Preservice Teacher box on the next page presents one teacher's view of a classroom that takes a constructive approach to learning and instruction.

The work of Vygotsky (1962, 1978) has been particularly influential in the development of constructivist theory (see, e.g., Lee & Smagorinsky, 2000). From this perspective, students learn best when provided with tasks that are within their zone of proximal development. This zone encompasses behaviors that the student cannot yet perform alone but can accomplish given assistance. Peers, teachers, or other adults who are more competent provide prompts and assistance as needed in the course of interacting toward accomplishment of a meaningful task. This concept is similar to the notion of scaffolding (discussed earlier in relation to cognitive information processing theory).

Apprenticeship models best reflect the type of instruction consistent with a Vygotskian approach to learning. Apprenticeships have long been common means of learning and acquiring skills in medical schools, doctoral institutions preparing future professors, and trades such as carpentry or tailoring. Students learn by interacting and working with those skilled in the profession or trade, and they learn in an authentic context, such as a hospital or factory, as opposed to a simulation of the context. Although this is possible only to a limited extent in elementary or secondary schools, the challenge is to create an environment as similar to the real world as possible so that tasks are tied to real-world situations.

The work of several theorists who have studied the elements of successful apprenticeships may facilitate transfer of the apprenticeship model to school settings (Collins, Brown, & Newman, 1989; Rogoff, 1990). Students need to have opportunities to observe skilled peers and adults model the skill—in other words, while the mentors are engaged in the skill or learning to be acquired. Students need to perceive that the mentor's engagement in the task is actually connected to real-world settings rather than to artificial tasks performed only in schools and classrooms. Beyond

Voice of a Preservice Teacher

I entered the empty classroom while the students were at lunch. The classroom looked as though some catastrophe had occurred and everyone had made a mad dash for the exit—collecting and dropping valuable and unvaluable items along the way. The desks were in disarray. I couldn't quite determine whether they were arranged or disarranged that way. No desktop was visible. Books stacked on books, stacked on paper, game pieces and other indescribable objects covered each desk as well as much of the floor. Five birds filled the air with song and the sounds of birdseed dropping to the floor. A ship's sail, made from a bedsheet, hung from the ceiling, a wooden plank stretched from one desk to another, and a wicker basket lid resting on a desk looked as though it might be used for a helm. What a mess, I thought to myself. How could children possibly learn among all of this?

And then the children came in, filling the room with third-grade talk. Mostly I heard, "Mr. Landmann, Mr. Landmann" as they asked question after question. The class began with the activity of rewriting the script of The Tempest. *Each child had been assigned a character to portray in a video of the play at a later date. Children simply began calling out their invented script lines and asking questions such as, "Will the audience know what a sprite is?" Then someone said, "Ariel should say, 'Father, don't get so overheated.'" I was surprised at their maturity, cooperation, and wonderful ideas. They conducted themselves much like a team of writers might behave working on a movie script or Broadway play. Mr. Landmann's position was that of coordinator and editor, reminding the students of time restraints and prop limitations. Again, I was dumbfounded and very impressed.*

Two words describe best the characteristics of successful learning—autonomy and interaction. The children were involved. They—not the teacher—were the creators of almost every activity that took place. Mr. Landmann had only to initiate and then the students took over the responsibility to make it work.

I wonder if I'll be a teacher like Mr. Landmann. One who is open to all kinds of possibilities for teaching and learning. One who raises expectations and limits for teaching and learning and who provides opportunities for children to excel beyond what the curriculum expects of them. I hope to teach lessons that require students to discuss and interact with each other so that talking and listening is not considered disruptive chatter but reflective thinking.

Teachers who plan instructional strategies that meet the needs of their students will encourage positive responses to classroom activities.

this, the skilled adults or peers need to provide coaching in the form of direct instruction and feedback. In addition to coaching, students need opportunities to practice and to receive appropriate assistance as they practice. Information processing theory labels this activity scaffolding, but Rogoff refers to it as guided participation and stresses the importance of the skilled mentor's assessing the demands of the task in relation to the skills of the apprentice and structuring tasks so that apprentices constantly increase their skill level. Mentors encourage apprentices to reflect on their performance in comparison with experts and peers and may require apprentices to articulate what they are doing as a means of testing their knowledge. This practice should not be limited to mere imitation, however, but should provide opportunities for apprentices to explore new ways of approaching and accomplishing tasks.

www

You can learn more about Vygotsky and metacognition at:

http://www.massey.ac.nz/

http://www.oise.utoronto.ca/

URLs may change over time. For up-to-date links to relevant Web sites, visit our Companion Web site:

http://education.wadsworth.com/wiseman3e

Putting It All Together: Using Behavioral, Cognitive, and Constructivist Theories

The three theories discussed in this section define learning from three very different perspectives, and the skilled classroom teacher will find value in the use of all three, depending on the needs of the students in the classroom and the kind of learning outcomes desired.

Behavioral theory provides ways to manage classroom behaviors and to teach basic intellectual and motor skills. Instructional strategies based on this theory are particularly helpful with younger students, students with learning or behavioral disorders, and students of low ability.

Cognitive theory promotes student acquisition of dispositions and skills associated with complex tasks or tasks that have multiple solution paths or right answers. Information processing theory also enables us to understand and assess students' cognitive processing so that we can encourage more effective processes and ultimately transfer control of the learning process to the student.

Constructivist theory suggests ways we can take advantage of the social nature of the classroom to provide meaningful experiences for students that are more likely to transfer to the world outside of the classroom.

SELF-REFLECTION

Matching Learning Goals and Learning Theory

Following is a list of learning goals appropriate for different classroom settings. Check the learning theory that seems most appropriate to accomplish each goal.

	THEORY		
Learning Goals	Behavioral	Cognitive	Constructivist
1. The first-grade students will learn the beginning consonant sound "B."	_____	_____	_____
2. High school students will work with business-people in the community to learn business-based technology applications.	_____	_____	_____

Learning Goals	THEORY		
	Behavioral	Cognitive	Constructivist
3. The fifth-grade students will graphically illustrate concepts about the American Revolutionary War.	_____	_____	_____
4. Students will use strategies to improve reading comprehension, such as predicting outcomes, self-questioning, and summarizing.	_____	_____	_____
5. When the bell rings, middle school students will quickly be seated and begin work on their warm-up exercises.	_____	_____	_____
6. Preservice teachers will develop advance organizers for a science unit they will teach to secondary students.	_____	_____	_____
7. The junior English students will design a children's book and share it with nursery school students at the local Head Start program.	_____	_____	_____
8. Physical education students will be able to jog a mile in less than fifteen minutes.	_____	_____	_____
9. Second-grade students will be able to edit their own stories for publication in the class anthology after working with a fourth-grade writing partner.	_____	_____	_____

Do you have three checks in each column? Be sure that you matched the goal with the learning theory that would provide the most appropriate instructional approach.

If you had any difficulty matching the goal and the learning theory, go back over the chapter, discuss your responses with a peer, or read some additional information about learning theories.

Answers: Behaviorist theory is best applied to goals 1, 5, and 8. Cognitive theory is best applied to goals 3, 4, and 6. Constructivist theory best matches goals 2, 7, and 9.

PORTFOLIO REFLECTIONS AND EXHIBITS

Throughout this chapter you completed a series of Field-Based Activities. The activities may serve as the basis for a portfolio representation, or you may develop your own exhibit or complete one of the suggested portfolio activities listed here:

1. Use the Interactive Seating Chart (see Figure 6.2) while observing in a classroom. Analyze your findings and ask the classroom teacher to comment on it. How were your analyses similar and different? Would you revise your interpretation in any way after talking with the classroom teacher? If this were your class, what would you do based on the data obtained? Include your data and a summary of your analysis with the teacher's comments in your portfolio.

2. Discuss problems of classroom management or motivation with one of the teachers in your school. Together, select a target behavior of a student (or students) that needs changing. Define the behavior clearly. Choose a period of time during which the behavior is likely to occur and keep a baseline record of the behavior by making a note each time the behavior occurs during that time period. Share your data with the teacher and discuss possible cues or reinforcements that contribute to the behavior. Include in your portfolio the data, a summary of your interpretation of the data, and possible ways to extinguish the negative behavior or strengthen a positive behavior.

3. Conduct a think-aloud interview with a student to determine what strategies the student is using to approach and solve a complex task. Choose a task requiring higher-level thinking typical of the content area and age group of the student you plan to interview (i.e., math word problem, science experiment, summary of a reading). Interview the student, transcribe the tape of the interview, and analyze the kinds of strategies the student uses in relation to his or her success on the task provided. Figure 6.4 may help you identify some of the strategies used.

E-Portfolio Entry 6

Enter the data from your classroom observations into an Excel program (or other spreadsheet software). Create a graphic that shows what you observed. Underneath the graphic, write a few sentences about what you've learned from your classroom observations.

INTASC Principles 1, 4, and 6

ANSWERS TO GUIDING YOUR READING

1. What is the relationship between how humans learn and planning and implementing effective instruction for students?

Learning theory forms the basis for instructional decision making. Understanding the three major theories (such as behavioral, cognitive, and constructivist) provides a way for teachers to understand how to encourage particular behaviors, responses, and interactions. Knowledge about how students learn will help teachers plan effective instruction. Three basic learning theories form the foundation for teaching and learning, and skilled teachers will find value in using aspects of all three, depending on the needs of the students in the classroom.

2. What do the different theories look like when they are used in a classroom?

Teaching behaviors representing behaviorist, cognitive, and constructivist theories will look different when used in a classroom. Behavior theory applied in the classroom can be recognized when teachers use behavioral objectives, task analysis, token economies, the Premack principle, and reinforcement schedules. When cognitive theory is applied to classroom settings, students are engaged in asking and responding to questions, problem solving, and hands-on learning. Constructivist theories are being used when students learn from skilled peers and adults who are modeling a skill.

3. How can I combine what I know about learning theory so that students learn in meaningful ways?

Using different theories of learning while planning for instruction and determining when to apply particular aspects of a theory become part of the decision making associated with teaching. Behavior theory provides ways to manage classroom behaviors and teach basic intellectual and motor skills. Cognitive theory suggests ways of helping students deal with complex tasks or tasks with multiple solutions. And constructivist theory helps students transfer classroom learning to the world outside the classroom. An effective teacher will use instructional strategies grounded in all three theories depending on the goals and objectives of the instructional processes.

INFOTRAC COLLEGE EDITION EXTENSION

Log on to the InfoTrac College Edition Web site and use a keyword search to find an article about how learning theory relates to you. Type in "learning theory and preservice teacher."

Alternatively, look for more information about constructivism and how it is defined. Using a keyword search, type in "constructivist and teaching" or "constructivist and classroom" and read about applications of constructivist approaches.

RELATED READINGS

The following books will provide more information about some of the topics and ideas discussed in this chapter:

Brooks, J. G. (1993). *The case for constructivist classrooms.* Alexandria, VA: American Association of Curriculum Development.

This book describes activities and teaching principles in which a constructivist theory is applied to classroom contexts. In addition to some focus on research and inquiry, Brooks provides good examples of how constructivist learning theory translates to teacher practice.

Costa, A. L. (2001). *Developing minds: A resource book for teaching thinking* (3rd ed.). Alexandria, VA: Association for Curriculum Supervision and Curriculum Development.

Developing Minds explores how we are beginning to understand better how the brain learns, use technology in the classroom, and focus on assessment of student achievement. This book illustrates the characteristics of effective and creative thinkers and problem solvers by examining classrooms and schools that are more thoughtful places.

Freiberg, H. J., & Brophy, J. E. (Eds.). (1999). *Beyond behaviorism: Changing the classroom management paradigm.* Upper Saddle River, N.J: Pearson, Allyn & Bacon.

Many educators are looking for alternatives to the paradigm of behaviorism that is currently so prevalent in the American classroom. This edited volume includes chapters by many leaders in the classroom management field and examines the philosophical underpinnings of behaviorism and shows why the change is needed.

Gagnon, G., & Collay, M. (2000). *Designing for learning : Six elements in constructivist classrooms.* San Francisco: Corwin Press.

This book builds on the pioneering work of Piaget and Vygotsky to describe constructivist classrooms. If is full of examples about how to organize groups, build bridges, ask questions, arrange exhibits, and invite reflection—all constructivist teaching/learning designs.

Sousa, D. (2001). *How the brain learns.* Thousand Oaks, CA: Corwin Press.

Sousa reviews research on brain function and explains the applicability of information processing theory to the classroom. Worksheets and activities enable teachers to apply the research directly to their own classrooms.

Sprenger, M. (1999). *Learning and memory: The brain in action.* Alexandria, VA: American Association of Curriculum Development.

Sprenger, who is a classroom teacher, summarizes the neurological research on brain functioning and offers practical suggestions for applying it to the classroom.

Wolfe, P. (2001). *Brain matters: Translating research into classroom practice.* Alexandria, VA: American Association of Curriculum Development.

Similar to the book by Sprenger, this publication reviews brain structure and functions, discusses the information processing model, and offers ways that teachers can match instruction with brain functions.

REFERENCES

Epigraph: The Freedom Writers with E. Gruwell. (1999). *The freedom writers' diary: How a teacher and 150 teens used writing to change themselves and the world around them.* New York: Main Street Books.

Alexander, P. A., & Knight, S. L. (1993). Dimensions of the interplay between teaching and learning. *Educational Forum,* 57(3), 232–245.

Ausubel, D. P. (1968). *Educational psychology: A cognitive view.* New York: Holt, Rinehart & Winston.

Bandura, A. (1982). Self-efficacy mechanism in human agency. *American Psychologists,* 37, 122–148.

Bransford, J., Brown, A., & Cocking, R. (2000). *How people learn.* Washington, DC: National Academy Press.

Brophy, J. E., & Good, T. L. (1986). Teacher behavior and student achievement. In M. C. Wittrock (Ed.), *Handbook of research on teaching* (3rd ed., pp. 328–375). New York: Macmillan.

Bruner, J. (1966). *Toward a theory of instruction.* Cambridge, MA: Harvard University Press.

Collins, A., Brown, J., & Newman, S. (1989). Cognitive apprenticeship: Teaching the craft of reading, writing, and mathematics. In L. Resnick (Ed.), *Knowing, learning, and instruction: Essays in honor of Robert Glaser* (pp. 453–494). Hillsdale, NJ: Erlbaum.

Gage, N. (1984). *Hard gains in the soft sciences: The case of pedagogy.* Bloomington, IN: Phi Delta Kappa.

Good, T., & Brophy, J. (1999). *Looking in classrooms* (8th ed.). New York: Longman.

Jensen, E. (1998). *Teaching with the brain in mind.* Alexandria, VA: Association for Supervision and Curriculum Development.

Klatzky, R. L. (1980). *Human memory: Structures and processes* (2nd ed.). San Francisco: W. H. Freeman.

Knight, S. (1990). The effect of cognitive strategy instruction on elementary students' reading outcomes. In S. McCormick & J. Zuttell (Eds.), *National reading conference yearbook* (Vol. 38, pp. 241–251). Chicago: National Reading Conference.

Knight, S., & Boudah, D. (1998). Participatory research and development for the improvement of teaching and learning. Paper presented at the annual meeting of the Southwest Educational Research Association, Austin, TX.

Knight, S. L., & Stallings, J. A. (2001). *Learning to teach in inner city schools training manual.* College Station: Texas A&M University, College of Education.

Knight, S., Waxman, H. C., & Pedrone, R. N. (1989). Examining the relationship between classroom instruction and elementary students' cognitive strategies in social studies. *Journal of Educational Research, 82*(5), 270–276.

Lee, C., & Smagorinsky, P. (2000). *Vygotskian perspectives on literacy research.* Cambridge: Cambridge University Press.

Mayer, R. E. (1983). *Thinking, problem solving, and cognition.* San Francisco: W. H. Freeman.

Miller, G. A. (1956). The magical number seven, plus or minus two: Some limits on our capacity for processing information. *Psychological Review, 63,* 81–97.

Palincsar, A. S., & Brown, A. L. (1984). Reciprocal teaching of comprehension-fostering and monitoring activities. *Cognition and Instruction, 1,* 117–175.

Premack, D. (1965). Reinforcement theory. In D. Levine (Ed.), *Nebraska symposium on motivation* (Vol. 13). Lincoln: University of Nebraska Press.

Rogoff, B. (1990). *Apprenticeship in thinking: Cognitive development in social context.* New York: Oxford University Press.

Schunk, D. (2000). *Learning theories: An education perspective.* Upper Saddle River, NJ: Prentice-Hall.

Skinner, B. F. (1954). *Science of learning, art of teaching.* Harvard Educational Review, 24, 86–97.

Skinner, B. F. (1958). Teaching machine. *Science, 128,* 969–977.

Skinner, B. F. (1963). *Science and human behavior.* New York: Macmillan.

Skinner, B. F. (1968). *Technology of teaching.* New York: Appleton Century Cross.

Skinner, B. F. (1969). *Contingencies of reinforcement: A theoretical analysis.* New York: Appleton Century Cross.

Strickland, K. (1995). *Literacy not labels: Celebrating students' strengths through whole language.* Portsmouth, NH: Boynton/Cook.

Thorndike, E. L. (1913). *Educational psychology: The original nature of man* (Vol. 1). New York: Teachers College Press.

Von Glaserfield, E. (1997). Amplification of a constructivist perspective. *Issues in Education,* 3, 203–210.

Vygotsky, L. (1962). *Thought and language.* Cambridge, MA: MIT.

Vygotsky, L. (1978). *Mind and society.* Cambridge, MA: Harvard University.

Wang, M., Haertel, G., & Walberg, H. (1993). Toward a knowledge base for school learning. *Review of Educational Research,* 63(3), 249–294.

7

Successful Classroom Environments

Kay seems to be everywhere at once during children's work periods. Today is typical. I've charted her movement during a 20-minute period at times only to find my field notes a tangled maze of lines and time notations. Typically, she interacts with each group and with each child before a period is over, fields questions from around the room, and is alert to potential problems or interruptions. It is a rare work period when she does not get to every child at least once, spending anywhere from a few seconds to several minutes with groups, focusing on each individual through comments, gestures, or eye contact. She positions herself at eye level when she speaks to a child, either by squatting down next to the table or leaning over. More often than not, she is questioning rather than giving directions.

When it is time to go to the rug for meeting, Kay asks for attention. Her voice reaches the far corners of the room—she could have been on stage, she has a voice that carries. She asks the children to take their supplies to the "back rug," giving them a specific place to put them—she says this keeps them from bombarding her with things to put away and gives them ownership of the classroom. . . .

. . . the usual pattern for discipline is through the curriculum. Kay pulls children to the rug to give directions rather than talking with them as they are at their desks. She focuses them on learning tasks and encourages them to settle the problems they have in working together before she intervenes. She uses language like "you need" and "these are the choices." Her directions are concrete and sequential. Kay's classes are always lively, and she has a high tolerance for noise if the children are on task.

—Frances Schoonmaker, *Growing Up Teaching*

Guiding Your Reading

1. What factors must be considered when establishing effective learning environments?

2. How do a teacher's personal views affect learning environments?

3. How does a teacher encourage student involvement and positive behavior?

4. What are ways that students can be grouped for maximum instructional effectiveness?

*E*stablishing effective learning environments is a demanding task. The most successful teachers fashion environments where all learners have the potential to succeed. For everyone to benefit from educational opportunities, competent teachers must orchestrate many factors and make multiple decisions. Components of instruction—in addition to managing twenty or thirty students single-handedly—include managing materials, scheduling activities, moving from activity to activity, and managing behavior. Management approaches and decisions reflect one's beliefs about learning, student development, and the roles of teachers and students. Classroom management also reflects the personalities of the teacher and the students who are in the classroom.

Although knowledge about successful strategies is expanding, classroom management is a major concern of both beginning and experienced teachers. Some techniques will emerge from experience, but you can learn a great deal by observing veteran teachers who maintain effective and well-ordered classrooms, by acknowledging your own beliefs about power and control, by participating in field experiences that provide opportunities for you to plan and manage instruction, and by reflecting on your perceptions and experiences.

Careful planning encourages and motivates students and helps avoid behavior and discipline problems. Planning and organization should result in predictable classroom procedures, a comfortable environment, and realistic teacher expectations. Teachers who plan and organize daily routines and schedules based on the needs of their students, the nature of the learning process, and the desire to provide motivating instructional strategies and materials are more likely to have successful classrooms. This chapter presents several aspects of classroom environment, organization, and instructional planning.

▶ Establishing a Personal Management Style

A teacher can select from a wide range of management styles. When you think about your own education, you may remember some teachers who were extremely strict and enforced rules and regulations and others who were very warm, interactive, and flexible. One teacher might have encouraged a great deal of drill and memory work, whereas another teacher focused on exploration, multiple responses, and active participation in interpreting and solving problems. Some teachers avoid controversial issues, choosing to focus their students on teacher-selected topics. Other teachers cover a wide range of issues, encourage debates and ambiguity, discuss current topics, and capitalize on students' curiosity. Almost all of these approaches can be successful with most students and in some situations.

A healthy learning environment means that students will learn designated content, misconduct is diminished, and worthwhile academic activities occur (Brophy, 1988). Effective classrooms do not emerge by chance. Classroom environments that work require personal reflection about teachers' roles, an understanding of what works in classroom organizations, a

© Photodisc

Effective teachers coordinate and balance a complex set of learning processes, interpersonal relationships, individual differences, and instructional strategies to establish a successful learning environment for their students.

Describe the learning environments in the school setting where you are currently working. Are they structured, highly defined classrooms where teachers deliver traditional lectures and make assignments that are graded and returned? Or are they more relaxed, in that there are discussions, small-group activities, and student-directed lessons? Which of these provides a more comfortable learning environment for you? Develop a list of descriptors that make you the most comfortable, keep you interested, and help you learn most effectively.

INTASC Principles 3 and 4

view of the relationship between management and instructional decisions, and the ability to use multiple methods while organizing classroom components of classroom organization.

How a teacher establishes a positive classroom climate is a central issue in learning to be a teacher. Authority is most effective when based on respect and caring for students. Classrooms require structure and rules designed to produce situations in which all students feel safe and look forward to academic success. Care and control in the classroom can be blended, and the combination of these two important elements empowers students and clarifies their roles. In addition, classroom interactions can demonstrate and teach caring, communication skills, and democratic principles (Ames, 1992; Noddings, 1995). A balanced approach to classroom management includes respectful treatment and avoids producing situations in which students feel alienated and disenfranchised.

Factors Influencing Classroom Environment

Many factors must be considered when a teacher is setting up the classroom for instruction. Teachers implement some factors, and others exist independent of teachers' actions. Your beliefs about your students and your philosophy of teaching will certainly affect how you establish classroom procedures. Outside influences will affect the learning environment in numerous ways. Recognizing the various influences on classroom environments is important, even though teachers are not always able to control all of them. This section examines the context that teachers must consider when creating classroom learning environments. (Chapters 3 and 5 provide an in-depth review of societal conditions that affect classrooms.)

Home and Social Contexts

Some student behavior and attitudes originate outside the school environment. Violence, gangs, drugs, poverty, and homelessness affect some students directly and others in more subtle ways. Traditionally associated with inner-city schools, these influences are increasingly evident in small cities, rural communities, and suburbs. Children are exposed to tough situations at younger and younger ages. Although the status of children is improving in many ways, one may still encounter gang activity among fourth-grade students, alcohol abuse among eleven- and twelve-year-olds, and pregnancy among young teenagers.

Family life exerts a strong influence on students' school behaviors and responses. Students may live in nontraditional family structures: Aunts, uncles, grandparents, or older brothers and sisters may be the heads of some households. Students' homes may be headed by single or divorced parents or by two parents who both work, so parents are not always present to oversee their children. After school, some students let themselves into an empty, unsupervised home. Almost all families care and want the best for their children, but changing family structures have stressed the educational system. Schools assume more responsibility for teaching lessons once taught by parents and for providing after-school care and other support systems.

Probably no other circumstance affects children and their learning as much as poverty and the resulting conditions. Poverty inevitably affects students' health and well-being. Children from poor families may not receive the nutrition or medical care necessary to maintain good health. They may come to school hungry or sick—certainly at a disadvantage for learning. Poverty reduces the resources that a family can provide for its members, so that experiences taken for granted by middle-class parents—vacations, visits to zoos and museums, attendance at cultural events—may be beyond the reach of poor students. Even more dramatic is that schools located in low-income areas may lack resources available to schools in affluent areas. Poor schools do not have the textbooks, computers, or wide variety of class offerings found in wealthier schools. So, in one way or another, poverty makes a substantial difference in the school experiences of some children.

Of course, many students and their families overcome great odds to succeed—usually where a strong community, family support system, and role models encourage students to value their school experiences. In fact, students from all economic groups can lack the support they need to deal with societal issues, and teachers are usually well aware of their plight. Students make decisions each day about their response to society, and schools can play a role in these decisions: Positive, well-managed classrooms and school environments have been connected to prevention of delinquency, teen pregnancy, and drug abuse (Dryfoos, 1990). Child-friendly schools have been suggested as possible mediators of risk factors that often lead to failure in school (Bennett, 1998). Effective teaching and learning processes can enhance student self-understanding, self-evaluation, and self-control (McCaslin & Good, 1992). In order to learn, students must feel confident to attempt tasks, problem solve, ask and answer questions, and receive feedback from teachers and their peers. Participating in classroom activities can be a daunting task. An effective learning environment provides students with a sense of community, opportunities to develop interpersonal communication and conflict management skills, and motivation to take the risks necessary for learning.

Students' Characteristics and Needs

Students may differ in developmental levels, culture, experience, gender, language, and intellectual and physical abilities. These differences provide both the joys and the frustrations of teaching.

AGE In classroom management, one of the first considerations is the age and maturity of students. Older students, for example, may be much more sensitive to issues of power and control and may need more chances to see and practice choice and negotiation (Glasser, 1988). Younger children will need more opportunities to learn how to make good decisions. The nature and complexity of the content presentation also change as children gain more academic experiences. Most teachers focus on a particular age—primary or high school, for example—study the behavior, and become experts about learning abilities of children at that age.

BACKGROUND Also consider students' cultural and experiential backgrounds when developing instructional and management methods (Kuykendall, 1992). The diversity in today's classrooms may require teachers to use multiple ways of interacting. Teachers bear the responsibility for how teacher behavior is interpreted and internalized by students who come from different backgrounds and have different experiences than their teachers (Dana, 1992). (See Chapter 5, in the section "Diversity in Schools.")

Understanding individual learning needs of students will assist the teacher in planning a wide range of instructional activities that encourage academic achievement for all students.

LANGUAGE Teachers continue to have increased chances to hear different languages in their classrooms. All children who come to school speaking languages other than English are not the same and will possess different levels of fluency and literacy. Bilingual and bicultural education is designed to meet the needs of students who do not speak English. Instructional programs require the application of many and varied teaching skills to help students make the transition to English, maintain support for continued growth in the native language, and provide intense study in English language. Ideally, bicultural, bilingual programs help build students' pride in native culture while preparing them for success in English-speaking schools and society.

Some differences in classroom experiences are caused by how teachers respond to student diversity. Interactions between teachers and students create students' lifelong beliefs about their own capabilities. These experiences are hugely affected by how teachers set up and manage the classrooms where diverse groups are learning.

SPECIAL NEEDS Specific management skills are required for students with special intellectual and physical needs, including gifted and talented stu-

Voice of a Teacher

There has been so much written about how teachers treat girls and boys differently, and I worry that I am not conscious enough of what I do in the classroom. I try to call on everyone equally. I use girls and women as examples during my teaching. I also try to select literature that shows women in strong roles. But it's hard to do this all the time. Textbooks aren't always helpful. Media, television, and newspapers don't always provide female role models. When I make an explicit attempt to be gender-conscious, I find it takes additional time to add examples, watch my own behavior, and rethink my actions. I am not sure that I am gender-conscious in everything I do. It's easy to forget this concern when things are moving quickly in the classroom.

dents, special education students, and students with behavior disorders. With the passage of Public L. 94–142, special education students were given the right to receive public education in the least restrictive environment. Originally, the law was interpreted to provide special teachers, classrooms, and conditions for students who might have special needs. This practice isolated students from their peers, and the label "special" often reduced teacher expectations about their performance. A more recent approach, often referred to as inclusion, is to include special students in regular classrooms, mainstreaming them with other children and providing additional support (such as modified inclusion or special teachers) to help them succeed in classrooms with their peers. Students participate in specialized and limited environments only when their needs cannot be met in regular classrooms. This approach can put a great deal of pressure on regular classroom teachers, who will need to plan and implement many types of instruction for a diversity of student characteristics, including those with handicaps or gifts.

You may learn more about Public Law 94–142 at the following Web sites:

http://www.ridgewater.mnscu.edu/

http://www.scn.org/~bk269/94-142.html

URLs may change over time. For up-to-date links to relevant Web sites, visit our Companion Web site:

http://education.wadsworth.com/wiseman3e

Expectations of Teachers and Learners

Researchers have demonstrated that the expectations about what it means to be a teacher and a student in a particular classroom are defined within the first few days of school (Fernie, Kantor, & Klein, 1990). However, classroom expectations reflect more than the immediate interactions between students and teachers.

TEACHER EXPECTATIONS Teachers' expectations of students' achievement exert powerful influences on classroom behavior (Good & Brophy, 1999). Expectations—whether about a group or an individual—affect what is taught, how it is taught, and the attitudes of both teacher and learners. Student success in learning particular content is greatly affected by teacher expectations. Indeed, expectations can override teacher effectiveness as well as student abilities. When teachers hold low expectations for the learning achievement of some students, the most advanced teaching strategies are sure to be ineffective (Bartolome, 1994).

Teacher behaviors and school practices that reflect a belief that minority or poor students will not succeed in school create lower expectations for poor or minority students. For many years, there has been a discrepancy between the achievements of some minority students and white students (Jeneks & Phillips, 1998), evidenced by the high percentage of minority students in low-ability and remedial groups versus the mostly white middle-class membership in gifted programs. Some prejudices, perceptions, and misunderstandings can be overcome in classrooms where activities are well planned and highly organized. Teachers can counter the problem of low expectations by providing learning environments that facilitate successful teaching of students who typically do not succeed in schools.

The most effective contexts leading to optimum student achievement are classrooms where all students feel valued, respected, and capable of succeeding despite their differences (Olsen & Mullen, 1990). Building effective classroom organization means understanding that children have different interests, learning styles, and abilities and will require different considerations during instructional planning. Understanding these potential differences and using that knowledge to organize instruction can improve the learning environment for all students.

STUDENT EXPECTATIONS Students, like teachers, come to the learning context with expectations, beliefs, and attitudes that enhance or reduce their cognitive, physical, linguistic, and problem-solving abilities. They gain ideas of what should happen in a classroom from their friends, family, and from television and other media. Parents' attitudes toward education affect students' views of what should happen in classrooms. As students proceed through school, their own life experiences teach them what they should expect from school and what teachers' expectations of student behavior and academic achievement might be. Both student and teacher expectations can influence the curriculum, the organization, and the everyday events in a classroom.

The School Context

School contexts have a substantial impact on classroom processes. The climate, organizational structures, decision-making procedures, and types of professional support available will play a role in teachers' personal approaches to classroom management. Schools in which teachers work collaboratively and have developed a common vision of success will be able to offer support and establish healthy classroom contexts. When a sense of belonging exists for all students, an overall positive environment can thrive. Some secondary schools are experimenting with variable schedules to provide extended periods of time with one adult and one group of peers so students have time to develop healthy relationships. Good quality of life within a school is an essential part of a healthy learning environment.

Instructional Tasks

Management procedures are most effective when tailored to instructional methods. What is being taught and how it is being taught will affect your decisions about classroom management and organization. Some information might be best delivered through direct instruction by the teachers, whereas other information may be learned effectively through discussion or independent reading. Using a variety of instructional tasks will ensure that differences in learning preferences will be taken into account, but this variation can also require different management techniques. When teachers move away from lecture and presentation methods and rely on more interactive, small-group discussion practices, managing the classroom becomes more complex (McCaslin & Good, 1992). You will need to consider varied management methods to facilitate varied instructional methods, such as whole language approaches or cooperative learning techniques. The use of nontraditional instructional methods will require teachers to help students be successful when working with groups, sharing ideas, debating issues, and providing peer assistance. (Chapter 8 contains much more information about designing instructional processes.)

▶ Developing Effective Classrooms

Fundamental components of successful classroom management can be fostered by teachers and have a positive impact on the classroom environment, including recognizing effective teaching behaviors, creating positive interpersonal relationships, and enhancing on-task behaviors.

Recognizing Effective Teaching Behaviors

What does a good teacher do? What behaviors do they display? Classic educational research describes the behaviors of teachers who are most successful during traditional teacher-centered whole class instruction (Brophy & Evertson, 1976; Doyle, 1986; Emmer, Evertson, & Anderson, 1980). Although teacher behaviors have not been studied as much in more interactive, student-centered classrooms, these three proactive behaviors, identified in early research, seem to make sense in most settings (Jones, 1996):

© Stephanie Knight

An effective learning environment requires teachers' attention to many factors including student relationships, on-task behaviors, student organization, time, and materials.

AWARENESS The teacher actions most associated with effective teaching include an explicit awareness of what is going on in the classroom, or "withitness" (Kounin, 1970). Most good teachers know their students, understand interactions, and can usually predict behavior and responses from their students. Teachers who are "with it" know when students are not attending to instruction or when they are upset or happy and can redirect classroom activities to take advantage of or defuse classroom attitudes. A change of pace or activity can be made at a critical time if a teacher maintains close contact with what is going on in the classroom.

TRANSITION PLANNING Good teachers also plan smooth transitions between activities. They understand that procedures for moving from one activity to another should be clearly understood by students. They introduce specific routines to change activities and to move from small-group to large-group instruction. If rules for transitions are clearly articulated, students do not lose valuable time when making instructional transitions, and disruptive behavior is avoided.

FAIRNESS Good teachers find ways to hold students accountable for assignments and classroom activities. Teachers should expect assignments and activities to be completed in thoughtful and productive ways and should provide feedback when students respond or provide a product. The feedback should be appropriate, and students should understand how and when feedback will occur. Effective teachers apply rules and enforce expectations in a consistent and fair manner that students can predict in any situation (Savage, 1999).

Each of these behaviors makes very good sense in any type of instructional setting. They have become the mainstay of expected teacher behaviors, although some educators encourage more consideration of instructional objectives and methods in defining good teacher behaviors (Jones, 1996). For example, the importance of "withitness" might decline if a teacher uses a great deal of small-group or independent work where student problem solving is not as controlled as in traditional classrooms. Teachers may not control each aspect of problem solving and learning, and the smoothness of transitions may be interrupted when students are developing their own learning processes. A more modern approach is therefore to allow instructional goals to guide the classroom management techniques instead of imposing specific teacher behaviors before the instructional outcomes are identified.

Creating Positive Interpersonal Relationships

Roles and relationships of learners and teachers must be considered when planning for instruction (Green, Kantor, & Rogers, 1990). The relationships between teachers and students are dynamic and change with each new class or when a new learning strategy is introduced (Zaharlick & Green, 1991).

TEACHER–STUDENT RELATIONSHIPS Interacting with young people is one of the major reasons to become a teacher, but these same interactions can also be the greatest source of frustration and stress to teachers. Teachers report that much of the stress associated with their work comes from managing student behavior (Jones, 1996). Teachers deal with a wide range of students, including students with special needs—academic, social, personal, and emotional characteristics that require extra attention and can cause unpredictable results during class interactions—which can make it more difficult to plan and manage instruction.

The quality of interactions between teachers and students affects students as well as teachers. Since the 1960s, educators have known that positive relationships between teachers and students can improve academic behavior. Students do care about what their teachers think about them. When students believe that their teachers care about and respect them, they are more positive and have higher academic achievement (Phelan, Davidson, & Cao, 1992).

Students more at risk of failure in school need more support from teachers than do students who are more successful (Wehlage et al., 1989). At-risk students need to feel that they belong in the classroom and that their teachers care about them. Several educators have made this point regarding the relationships between teachers and minority students. Comer (1988) wrote that "no matter how good the administration, teachers, curriculum, or equipment; no matter how long the school day or year; and no matter how much homework is assigned, if students do not attach and bond to the people and program of the school, less adequate learning will take place" (p. 46). Most important, teachers should realize the importance of expressing a sense of optimism that all students can learn (Wehlage et al., 1989).

Teacher feedback to students about their work plays an important role in positive learning environments. Clear and specific feedback that is immediate, focuses on students' performance and effort, and avoids comparisons with others is most effective. When grades and test scores produce environments where comparisons are made and success and failure is numerically calculated, it may be difficult to promote a cooperative (as opposed to a competitive) environment. Standardized test-driven settings described in Chapter 3 are becoming increasingly popular, and teachers must develop positive feedback strategies that focus on individual progress and achievement over time.

PEER RELATIONSHIPS More effective classrooms result when the students get along and can work together. A classroom personality develops from the combination of students in the classroom. Classrooms offer an opportunity for prolonged contact with peers, and interactions serve more than an educational role in students' development: They contribute to social roles, adult personality patterns, and future peer associations. Instructional strategies requiring students to accomplish tasks cooperatively and in small-group settings make positive peer relationships even more important.

Some research has shown that students' achievement increases when they are accepted by their classmates, and students work together to establish norms related to how they perform and respond in the classroom (Jones, 1996). Teaching students to interact and collaborate more with each other may ultimately enhance classroom behavior, increase school achievement, contribute to positive learning environments, and develop important life skills (Jones, 1996). Attention to student relationships and developing a culture of cooperation encourages behavior skills that are valued in society and the workplace.

Conflicts among students are inevitable. They are a natural part of personal relationships. Some schools have adopted conflict management approaches to help students manage and negotiate disagreements. Students are taught to recognize differing perspectives and feelings, explain reasons underlying the differences, reverse their views of conflicts, invent options, and agree upon a solution (Johnson & Johnson, 1995). Often conflict resolution techniques are embedded in existing curriculum and practiced during real classroom conflicts.

FIELD-BASED ACTIVITY 7.2

Observe in the classroom setting and determine what types of behavior students display when off-task. What are they doing when not paying attention to their teacher or when they quit working on the classroom assignment? Are they reading, talking to each other, or distracted in other ways? Complete the chart in Table 7.1. Compare your findings in a class discussion and define task-oriented behavior. Are you tolerant or intolerant when students do not do what the teacher expects? What does this tell you about your view of teaching and authority?

INTASC Principles 5 and 6

TABLE 7.1	Off-Task Behaviors	
Behaviors	**Descriptors**	**Observation Notes**
Chatting	Student is talking with others.	
Disruptive Behavior	Students are making noises, teasing others, roaming around the classroom.	
Personal Needs	Students are sharpening pencils, being excused to go to the bathroom, getting a drink of water.	
Uninvolved	Students obviously are not listening or taking part in classroom activities, and are daydreaming, staring.	
Waiting	Students are standing in line, raising their hands, waiting on teacher.	
Sleeping	Students have their heads on their desks, eyes closed.	
Other Behaviors		

Successful Learning Environments

Effective teachers establish environments that maximize the time that a student is on task or actively engaged in learning. On-task behavior is directly related to a student's classroom behavior and academic success. Instructional components that lead to on-task behavior describe well-managed classrooms. To plan instruction that achieves the most on-task behavior, teachers must motivate students, provide support for success, communicate high expectations, offer flexibility and variation, present relevant and meaningful activities, encourage cognitive engagement, and provide appropriate feedback. Following are details about these methods of establishing a well-managed classroom, where students are on task and learning.

MOTIVATE The ability to motivate, to engage students in learning, is a crucial element for establishing a positive learning environment. Children are born with the motivation to learn (Wlodkowski & Jaynes, 1990). The curiosity of infants, toddlers, and preschool children who ask questions, experiment, and acquire new information is a joy to watch. Too often, formal educational practices suppress the spontaneous joy of learning evident with younger children. By the time students reach high school, their motivation to succeed in school may be diminished by negative attitudes toward school, social expectations, and other nonschool agendas. Competition for a student's attention, approaches to learning which are rigid and do not vary, constant evaluation, and grading are a few of the factors that may reduce motivation about school learning.

The motivation to learn must become a habit, a routine, and a priority in young people's lives that contributes favorably to learning in school (Wlodkowski & Jaynes, 1990). Many school factors—including the nature of the task, responsibility, rewards, use of groups, evaluation, testing, and teacher expectations—affect motivation (Mahler & Anderson, 1993). Culture, family, school, organizational structures, and individual personality all come to bear on learners' motivational levels. Despite so many outside influences, motivation to learn can be taught and encouraged. A good teacher increases the potential for academic motivation to learn in various ways.

PROVIDE SUPPORT FOR SUCCESS Students will work to accomplish learning tasks if a support system helps them avoid frustration and confusion. Teachers supply this support by making tasks manageable, providing models for accomplishing tasks, and being sure that students understand explanations and processes (Blumenfeld, Puro, & Mergendoller, 1992). Small-group collaboration and opportunities to share learning provide additional support for learning demanding material. Scaffolding—initially giving a great deal of help and facilitative encouragement and gradually requiring students to do more and more on their own—is another useful way to provide support during learning activities.

Successful teachers make sure that their students can take part in the learning activities. When introducing a particular routine or strategy, the teacher ensures that everyone knows how to participate and what is required for success. Even students at the secondary level must be taught some instructional procedures: For example, if the teacher is using a particular cooperative learning technique and students are taking on roles such as leader, timer, and question poser, students should be taught what is expected of each role.

COMMUNICATE HIGH EXPECTATIONS Teachers' expectations and student motivation are linked. Teachers and students must believe that success is possible, that tasks are reasonable, and that all students can do the work. Students are willing to attempt difficult tasks if it is clear that those around them believe they can succeed. All students should be expected to do their best, and no exceptions should be made because of gender or culture. Teachers and students should share the belief that all students can and will achieve, no matter what their gender, ethnic, or linguistic background.

PROVIDE FOR FLEXIBILITY AND VARIATION Having available a multitude of tasks at appropriate levels of difficulty enhances motivation. Students who are able to select their mode and method of learning in various situations will be more motivated to focus on their learning tasks. Some tasks must be completed by all students, and at times the teacher will select the focus. But when it is appropriate for students to learn different information or in different ways, consider giving them choices. If students are allowed to select from a range of tasks, they will come closer to selecting the activities that are most motivating to them. The tasks should be challenging but realistic and should provide choices for learning in different ways.

Ability grouping and other comparative and competitive approaches can have a negative impact on motivation. Whenever possible, good teachers minimize processes that compare students or require them to compete against each other. The practices associated with comparison and competition can send the message that not everyone is expected to succeed in the same way. Teachers who use flexible grouping techniques based on achievement of specific skills or knowledge (as opposed to grouping by ability, for example) treat their students as if they all can learn. Several types of arrangements are described in the section "Flexible Grouping" below.

PLAN RELEVANT AND MEANINGFUL ACTIVITIES A most important contribution to the motivation of student learning is how much students value and are interested in the material. Connections to students' lives and opportunities to transfer their knowledge and strategies to new learning situations will motivate their learning.

Such relevant learning activities produce the active and personal engagement that demonstrates motivation. Individual contributions, discussions, and sharing of life experiences are simple ways to make learning relevant. Focusing on topics that students find interesting, such as current events, popular culture, and media, will also increase the relevance of learning activities. Sometimes the teacher must help make connections to develop interest and relevance—for example, presenting a Shakespearean plot as an analogy for a contemporary problem.

EMPHASIZE COGNITIVE ENGAGEMENT Students must be encouraged to answer questions and complete assignments and, as a result of their work, receive feedback (Blumenfeld et al., 1992). Cognitive engagement is encouraged when students synthesize, represent, demonstrate, and apply their knowledge in a variety of ways. Success is defined as more than coming up with one right answer; it should involve manipulating the information, considering multiple answers, and sharing predictions and hypotheses.

PROVIDE FEEDBACK To motivate continued learning, students need to know when a learning component ends and how to assess the impact of the activity on their own personal learning (Brophy, 1988; Lepper, 1983). The more learner goal-setting and self-monitoring you can implement, the more motivated students will be. Students should be held accountable for learning and understanding material, not just for getting the answers correct or making good grades. The frequency and form of teacher feedback both play an important part in the classroom motivational process (Good & Brophy, 1999).

Clearly, the teacher is key in motivating students. In addition to using all the techniques described, teachers motivate students by being enthusiastic learners themselves. Providing a good example for motivated learning is one of the most successful techniques teachers can use. Students want to know what activities and abilities interest adults. Reading, for example, is very easy to model. Sharing information and personal reading can be a powerful lesson in motivation to read and learn. When teachers share their excitement about learning new information, students are intrigued and interested. When teachers demonstrate that learning is important, motivating, and relevant, students will become increasingly self-motivated to be active learners. One way for teachers to demonstrate their enthusiasm for learning is to involve students in collaborative learning. Working and learning together is an excellent way to involve students in the learning process.

Organizing Students, Time, and Materials

Schools should provide a predictable structure for students that remains responsive to student's needs. Effective teachers who are willing to incorporate their students' desires, interests, and concerns into the daily routine and who demonstrate flexibility with daily plans and routines will better meet the needs of their students. Personal events, such as neighborhood or family emergencies or crises within their peer groups, affect students' interest and attention. Worldwide events such as wars, national disasters, and presidential elections have an impact on the classroom. Sometimes teachers may abandon regular routines and refocus instruction to recognize relevant and current student interests. Generally, however, students should know what to expect from classroom instructional routines.

Organizing Students

The way a teacher organizes a classroom full of students should be based on the goals of instruction, the desired nature of interaction, and the responses required during lessons. Small groups, large groups, or individual student arrangements are all viable grouping procedures depending on the instructional objectives.

GROUPING LEARNERS Students can be grouped in many different ways during instruction. Distinctive classroom mixtures will require a variety of arrangements because the way individuals work together will require various organizational patterns. The key to arranging and managing the classroom is to be flexible and to experiment with different groupings to find the best one for the students, the activities, and the materials involved.

Students can benefit from this variety: They will produce different reactions when interacting with small groups of peers, peer pairings, or large groups. Small-group arrangements may ensure that all students will have an opportunity to take part in discussions. Not all learners will volunteer in large-group settings, and small groups can encourage a great deal of interaction. Large-group work can provide a good opportunity to hear many ideas or to summarize learning and new knowledge. Large groups can present a wider range of ideas and solutions than small groups. Small groups may be more manageable than whole classes and can be assigned special projects. Any or all of these can be used in the course of a school day.

Although a teacher can use most any method for making group assignments, the teacher should avoid any organization that labels the learner. It is much more beneficial and positive to organize the class based on student and instructional needs. Following are several options:

ABILITY GROUPING Grouping by ability or special talents is a controversial issue. Placing students into groups according to their abilities, usually measured by some form of standardized testing, is designed to reduce the wide range of differences among students so that more effective instruction can be provided. Recently, however, ability grouping has come under intense scrutiny and is no longer viewed as the optimum method of organizing students for instruction. Although some benefit may be seen for high-

Instructional goals and activity selection may require small- or large-group management skills. Students' interactions and responses will vary based on the instructional grouping.

ability students, ability grouping presents problems for low-ability students (Garmon, Nystrand, Berends, & LePore, 1995). More specifically, here are several detrimental practices associated with ability grouping:

1. Ability grouping labels students. Often the placement of students in groups will affect their perception of their learning abilities for years to come. The results of grouping have been shown to be long-lasting; most adults can remember which group they were in during their school experiences.

2. The groups remain constant through several years of schooling. Students seldom move from one group to another.

3. Instruction varies among groups. Instruction directed at students identified with less ability is usually more focused on simple tasks, less reading and problem solving, and more rote learning. Many of these differences in instruction only maintain the differences in school performance.

4. Members of minority groups and poor children have been overrepresented in low-ability groups for years. Students whose language, experiences, and culture are different seem to be at risk on achievement tests. Ability groups reflect this discrepancy.

Teachers may have reason to establish ability groups to help students learn a particular skill or strategy, but once the strategy has been learned the group should be disbanded.

FLEXIBLE GROUPING One way to arrange the class in small, manageable groups is to establish flexible grouping practices (Good & Brophy, 1999). Membership in a flexible group terminates when the reason for establishing the group is accomplished. Small groups can be set up for long periods of time (a grading term, semester, or even the entire school year) or may be set up for short-term projects or objectives. The goals and objectives of the small groups should be explicitly delineated and understood by the students (and of course by the teacher), and follow-up activities should be carefully described and monitored. Several types of small flexible groups can contribute to successful learning environments, as follows:

1. Special project groups can work on activities that accompany instruction. A teacher may arrange students in groups to conduct lab experiments, read similar content, or interview other students in the school about a particular topic. Small flexible groups can be assembled to complete problems or work on other skills.

2. Interest groups can be arranged to enable groups of students to read, discuss, and complete activities based on common interests. Interest groups provide students with more opportunity to make decisions about classroom activities. For example, some students may group together because they are all interested in science fiction. However, they may read different books and share their stories or identify common elements of the genre they are reading. Another interest group could be formed to study poetry and songs. They might all share poetry orally or write their own poetry as a result of their common interest.

3. Research groups—established to locate, organize, and report information—are particularly appropriate for instruction in content areas. Before research groups set out to work on their own, they should be taught the research skills that will be needed. The teacher can demonstrate many of these skills in whole class settings before placing students in small groups.

4. Instructional groups are formed when more than one student could benefit from teacher-led instruction. For example, a group of learners who are having difficulty with long division could meet together to receive extra instruction. These groups are disbanded when all group members understand the strategy, skill, or concept.

5. Brainstorming and categorizing groups are usually short-lived and are established to begin reading, discussing, or writing. Students are placed in small groups to list everything they know about a concept or a topic or to design questions they would like to answer during study.

6. Expert groups may be formed and assigned a topic on which they are supposed to become "experts." After studying and researching, the group becomes a resource for the rest of the class. Expert groups may be required to do the research, be familiar with a particular portion of the text, or perfect some skill that can be taught to others in the class.

COOPERATIVE GROUPING Cooperative learning describes a certain type of student grouping arrangement that could be used in conjunction with the six flexible grouping options described above. Figure 7.1 outlines one way to use cooperative group work in the classroom. The teacher plans activities from any content area and sets common goals by assigning responsibilities for learning within the group. In most cases, four or five students form a cooperative group that works together to solve a problem or complete a task. Individual evaluation may be included as in Slavin's (1987) cooperative grouping approaches. However, individual competition is downplayed, and the work of the entire group is recognized for evaluation. The entire team is responsible for motivating all in the group to complete their tasks. Cooperative learning has been set up in many ways; following are basic guidelines for introducing the instructional strategy:

1. Clarify rules and procedures before implementing the procedures. After a teacher decides what is to be accomplished cooperatively, demonstration and instruction should accompany the task so that students are assured of success. Students should be explicitly aware of the goals and intentions of cooperative groups. Sample rules for the procedure might include the following:

   Know your responsibilities.

   Understand one another's roles.

   Help others who need help.

   Do your part and contribute to group activities.

   Use rules for disagreements and discussions.

   Ask the teacher for help only as a last resort.

2. Organize the groups. Most cooperative learning activities arrange the class in groups of three to six students. Each student is assigned a specific role. The individual is responsible for that role, and his or

| FIGURE 7.1 | **Sample Cooperative Learning Lesson** |

Task: Each group will compare two reading selections. The teacher will have discussed methods of comparison in advance.

Group Responsibilities

1. Be sure that all group members have a copy of the two reading selections.

2. Involve each group member.

3. Assign roles and responsibilities.

4. Use the format provided by the teacher.

5. Share group work with the rest of the class.

6. Evaluate group performance after completion.

Individual Responsibilities

1. Read the selections to be compared.

2. Contribute to the summaries of the two texts.

3. Contribute at least two ways the stories are alike.

4. Help the entire group complete the format provided by the teacher.

5. Help the group contribute information to the whole class activity.

Evaluation (by the teacher)

1. Review the small-group summaries.

2. Evaluate group skills in making decisions, achieving goals, and helping each other.

3. Evaluate each small group's contribution to the class summary.

her contribution is necessary to complete the tasks successfully. Some of the tasks that might be assigned include:

Encourager

Observer

Materials monitor (makes sure all students have materials)

Recorder (writes responses from group members during group activities)

Reporter (reports responses from group members during large-group discussions)

3. Clarify purpose. Describe the goals for the activity and describe the task that is to be completed. Cooperative learning groups can accomplish reading activities, discussion or problem-solving activities, research activities, or any other work that is logical for more than one person to do.

4. Explain and demonstrate procedures. Students must be clear about the procedures and logistics of the group work. Plan some time to teach students what will happen in small groups. The small-group activity can be introduced through whole class discussion, role-playing, or demonstration. Some of the skills students may need to learn to work in cooperative groups include making space for people, communication skills, elimination of put-downs, taking turns, and active listening (Hill & Hill, 1991). Students may need time to practice these skills before working together in cooperative groups.

5. Observe student interactions. Cooperative learning teaches students how to be independent and to interact with others, but it requires careful monitoring by the teacher. During activities, the teacher moves from group to group, noting problems, suggesting solutions to any potential conflicts, and generally guiding activities. Even though students are held responsible for their own learning, the teacher is still involved actively in students' work.

You may learn more about cooperative learning at the following Web sites:

http://www.cde.ca.gov/iasa/cooplrng2.html

http://www.ericfacility.net/databases/ERIC_Digests/ed370881.html

http://www.memphis-schools.k12.tn.us/

URLs may change over time. For up-to-date links to relevant Web sites, visit our Companion Web site:

http://education.wadsworth.com/wiseman3e

WHOLE CLASS INSTRUCTION Working with the entire class may not be the best arrangement for all types of instruction, but some activities can be very successful if the whole class is involved. Discussions, enrichment activities, concept introduction, reading aloud, and direct instruction and skills and procedures can be accomplished with the whole class. It is useful for several reasons:

1. *Whole class instruction is efficient.* Presenting the information to the entire class at one time can free the teacher to provide more attention to individuals and smaller groups who may need more intense and repetitive instruction. Whole class instruction can be more economical when presenting some strategies and information. It is an excellent way to present routines, discuss new approaches, and respond to information. Small-group work can follow whole class instruction and focus on different aspects of the main theme of instruction.

2. *Whole class instruction provides students with time to interact with those of differing abilities and opinions.* Whole class approaches avoid labeling or focusing on special abilities and offer an opportunity for a wide range of interests and abilities to be recognized. Students at all levels of ability can participate easily in whole class sharing and instruction, thus feeling that they are a part of the class. Even if all students do not participate in discussions, they can learn a great deal by listening.

3. *Whole class activities contribute to establishing a classroom community.* Students who share and interact with each other build common experiences, languages, stories, and procedures. This is a time when all students in the class can share their ideas and understand others' perspectives. It is a time to get to know each other.

Almost any type of activity that can be accomplished in small groups can be done in whole classes and vice versa. The activities for the entire class should offer something for everyone. In-depth discussions or strategy instruction that applies to only a few students should be saved for small groups.

TEACHER–STUDENT CONFERENCES Conferences are an instructional strategy that can be used to encourage, monitor, evaluate, and guide students. Conferences can be conducted for individual students, small groups, or whole classes. The teacher is responsible for planning and organizing the structure normally used in each situation.

Conferences are individual or small-group meetings wherein teachers and students discuss a wide array of academic issues. The teacher has a different role during conferences: Although the structure for what happens during the conference is provided by the teacher, the activities are guided by students who are responsible for establishing the topic or focusing on strategies. Students should do most of the talking during a conference; the teacher's role is to listen and support students during the learning process.

While others in the class work independently, a teacher provides one-on-one attention to this student. Student–teacher conferences allow teachers to evaluate student learning and help them with specific learning needs.

These discussions provide teachers with information that can help and guide student learning.

Conferences may be regularly scheduled with students or can be initiated by the teacher or student. The main objective is to provide students with an opportunity to discuss their individual learning with the teacher. Conferences have been used extensively in teaching reading and writing (Wiseman, 1992), but they could be adapted for use across the curriculum. Conferences have four parts: sharing, questioning, interacting, and guiding (Pappas, Kiefer, & Levstik, 1990):

1. *Sharing.* Conferences can begin by having students share what they have been learning or accomplishing in class. If students have been keeping journals or other written records of class work, they can be encouraged to share some examples of their work with the teacher.

2. *Questioning.* The teacher listens to the student and asks questions about what the student is sharing. If the teacher is meeting with more than one student, the other students are also invited to ask questions.

3. *Interacting.* The conference includes opportunities to share new information, read orally, provide examples of learning, or share favorite or interesting issues. During the conference, the teacher notes and records discussion topics and examples for later reference.

4. *Guiding.* The teacher and the students discuss future plans for learning. Students can identify what else they need to learn, and the teacher can guide them to the next steps. At the conclusion of a conference, students know their next step in relation to the learning activity.

A conference can be used at any grade level to encourage independent learning and to respond individually to students. Once students learn the logistics of a conference, they can conduct conferences with each other.

Peer conferences give students an opportunity to share their learning and may be effective at the secondary as well as elementary levels. Conferences can be arranged and encouraged by the teacher or may occur spontaneously when a collegial atmosphere is established in the classroom. In a classroom that values the learning of individuals, it is not unusual to have student-initiated conferences. Often, informal conferences between students mirror the components of teacher-led conferences (Graves, 1994).

STUDENT PAIRS Student pairs can support instructional organization in numerous ways: to accomplish a goal, clarify an instructional objective, or tutor each other in a particular strategy. Students will need to hear their teachers and peers' responses to their own work to develop ways to respond to each other. They need to have guidance in how to respond to the work and ideas of classmates, and this requires teaching and demonstration.

FIELD-BASED ACTIVITY 7.3

Use the descriptions in your text to produce a list of different ways of grouping students. Invite some of the teachers or student teachers from your school into your classroom to talk about how they organize their students for instruction. Share the list with them and ask them what grouping arrangements they have used. What classroom management concerns do they feel these different kinds of grouping arrangements present? What do they see as the pros and cons of different grouping procedures?

INTASC Principles 4 and 5

Highly capable students can work on their own. A student's ability to engage in independent study is often dependent upon a teacher's skill in organizing lessons and providing motivation.

Students can be paired to accomplish a specific goal. Teachers can pair students to provide each with practice in a particular strategy. Sometimes students can explain a new idea more clearly to their peers than a teacher can. One adaptation of student pairs is cross-age tutoring, wherein older students tutor younger students and thus provide teachers with some help and younger students with individual attention. For example, a ninth-grade English teacher and an eleventh-grade English teacher might design activities that feature juniors working one-on-one with ninth-graders to produce stories or book reviews.

INDIVIDUAL, INDEPENDENT ACTIVITY Many times, students will work independently. Daily plans will include projects and assignments for students to complete on their own without direct teacher supervision. While students are working independently, the teacher can meet with small groups and individuals. Individual activity must be planned carefully because of the potential for off-task behavior.

Organizing Time

Scheduling requires consideration of many activities and school structures. The school day may be divided in different ways depending on the grade level, teaching arrangements, and overall school schedule. At any grade level, the school day is full of activities that limit instructional time: Class pictures must be taken, assemblies must be attended, and guest speakers heard. A teacher will make many decisions about how the remaining time is organized. Even though the school's master schedule influences how a teacher organizes classroom time, the amount of available time and the nature of the learning activity will also be major considerations for a teacher who is planning daily activities (Epanchin, Townsend, & Stoddard, 1994).

The modular scheduling concept, which establishes specific amounts of time for instructional blocks, has existed in secondary schools for many years. Usually it is set up around forty- to sixty-minute blocks (we are all familiar with science period, math period, and band period). These time blocks remain constant regardless of learning requirements or learning demands. Some schools, however, are experimenting with other methods.

One of the difficulties of teaching in high school is covering content in regimented time blocks. Some content may require longer periods of attention; other content requires less. Some subjects can be best taught in short time blocks, and other learning might be most effective in longer in-depth sessions. One of the innovations in high school scheduling is to vary course durations, providing longer time periods for some courses and teaching two or more subjects together in others. For example, history may be taught in a ninety-minute block on alternating days, and English and social studies or science and math may be taught in two- or three-hour blocks.

Scheduling for elementary schools is usually more flexible because there are no predetermined subject periods, but teachers who plan elementary instruction must make allowances for interruptions from "pull-out" classes or other special classes. Students may leave the classroom for physical education, music, art, library, and special classes. Elementary teachers also work with special teachers in English as a second language, bilingual, or special education to plan for times when students with special needs are scheduled in multiple programs. Making transitions and guiding students through many interruptions can be particularly problematic.

An important element in scheduling the day for elementary students or the week for secondary students is that they learn a predictable schedule. Students want to know what to expect in their classes. At times they can be flexible, but overall predictability helps them feel in control and understand what is expected during the school day. Most elementary and secondary schedules viewed in the context of an entire week will include time for the following activities:

1. *Whole class activities.* The teacher should plan for time when the entire class works together on specific activities. At this time, the teacher focuses class work and organizes the day, class period, or week. Whole class instruction time can be used to teach new strategies, discuss new information, talk about the behavior that is expected of each student, lecture, read aloud, have students read, or have discussions of general or topical interest.

2. *Independent work time.* There are scheduled times when students will work on their own, making independent selections of reading material, working lab problems, or writing responses to assignments. Even very young students will have some daily independent work time: Some can be assigned in response to assignments or discussions introduced during whole class activities. Independent work time may occur for the entire class or for part of the class working independently while the teacher works with small groups. The rules for independent work should be established early, and everyone should be aware of how this time is conducted.

3. *Discussion or sharing time.* Discussion provides opportunities to talk about what students have read and written in their independent work. Sharing time provides opportunities to discuss books, share personal writing, check lab problems, reteach, and evaluate the effectiveness of instruction. Sharing time may be different from class focus time, when teachers implement specific plans and objectives, because it may be guided by what the students wish to discuss or share.

Organizing Materials

Classroom materials are diverse and supplied by different parties. Schools usually provide basic textbooks, some selected lab materials, and access to multimedia. Teachers may contribute some of their own books, references, and media equipment. Students also may provide materials they have written and designed to classroom instructional processes.

BASALS AND TEXTBOOKS Instructional organization traditionally relies on textbooks, which are provided in most classrooms. One common example is the graded series of textbooks (also called basals) that are used for teaching elementary reading. Textbooks exist for almost all content areas at the elementary and secondary level. In addition to reading texts, social studies, science, mathematics, English and other textbooks provide the major source of instructional reading material. Most lesson structures include before-reading, during-reading, and after-reading activities and discussions. The before-reading activities provide background information, develop vocabulary, and establish purpose and learning objectives. Skills instruction can be part of the introductory activities or part of the conclusion of a lesson. The skills emphasized in the introductory phase are subject-related. For example, social studies might focus on globe and map skills, and science might focus on laboratory skills. Teachers are given guidance through lesson plans suggesting discussions and activities that reinforce, reteach, or enrich the concepts and enable teachers to evaluate what students have learned.

Almost all states have approved textbooks and basal readers that school districts can select for use. These approved texts usually reflect the statewide curriculum and cover the objectives and goals identified by the state. The school districts select their texts from the state-adopted list.

Textbooks can play an important role in the instructional process as one source of material for teachers. Textbook publishers provide teacher's editions that have many suggestions for instruction as well as specific lesson plans for particular units, concepts, and supplemental materials. For example, a school using a social studies series might also purchase maps, globes, and atlases created to support the textbook. A science series publisher might offer lab manuals, microscopes, and charts for sale along with the texts themselves.

The suggested plans accompanying the textbooks can be used as a framework for instruction. Suggestions can give teachers ideas about where to start their instruction, show how to introduce and augment discussions of topics, serve as surveys to begin the study of a concept, and establish initial concepts about a topic before students begin a self-directed study. It is not unusual to see a single textbook adopted and used in classrooms as the sole source of information on a subject. This total reliance on basal readers and textbooks means that the books control what is taught, how it is taught, and in what order instruction is presented to students. This total dependence may not be desirable for several reasons:

- Learners may have differential prior knowledge and interest in the topic.

- Students may need different levels of motivation to encourage their interest in a topic, and textbooks do not always present material in an interesting way.

- Students with reading problems or language difficulties will benefit from having course content presented in a variety of ways.

- Using a variety of materials for classroom, including Internet documents and current periodicals, assures that students are learning up-to-date information.

These concerns demonstrate that textbooks alone are not adequate for teaching most subjects. Students are more likely to read and learn if a large variety of printed and other media is available. Effective use of textbooks suggests that teachers should use their knowledge of the content, the student, and instructional methods to select a variety of materials to support the instructional approaches used in the classroom.

CHILDREN'S AND YOUNG ADULT LITERATURE Teachers of elementary, middle, and high schools can take advantage of the wide range of children's and young adult literature available to teach almost any subject. Literature, both fiction and nonfiction, provides an excellent resource in planning instruction. Students can learn concepts, facts, and ideas from both expository and narrative literature. Literature can be used to build knowledge, motivation, and interest in a range of topics. Supplementing textbooks with literature increases opportunities to read about, write about, and discuss many different subjects.

NEWSPAPERS, MAGAZINES, AND OTHER CURRENT PERIODICALS Current periodicals will sometimes have the most up-to-date information about topics being presented in the classroom. Options for older students include popular periodicals, newspapers, or special-interest magazines. *Weekly Reader* and *Scholastic Magazine,* written for young people, are two periodicals found in many classrooms. Use of magazines and periodicals enriches the classroom and ensures that a wide range of interests, cultures, and perspectives are represented during instruction.

COMPUTERS AND MULTIMEDIA Teachers have increasing opportunities to use computers and other multimedia technology in their classrooms. CD-ROMs, email, and the Internet greatly expand the resources available. Teachers can find new instructional approaches, access teaching units, and identify resources from all over the world. Students can use the technology to complete research projects, communicate with others, identify sources for further contact, and present projects in varied ways. Only the teachers' and students' imaginations will limit the ways that this technology contributes to classroom planning—especially given the fast pace at which technology continues to emerge.

Much information can be provided in print, film, and recordings, and teachers find many effective ways to use tapes, CDs, television, movies, and VCRs in instruction. These common technological tools enrich units of study or reading assignments and meet the needs of visual and aural learners.

Physical Arrangement

The physical arrangement of classrooms should support routines, grouping, and instructional activities. Arrangements will vary according to the amount of space, equipment, and furniture available. The room's size, space, and shape are relatively constant, but teachers can arrange the furniture and equipment to emphasize group work, individual work, or whole class discussions. Secondary teachers who share classrooms with other teachers and teachers not assigned a specific classroom need to discuss how they can best arrange rooms to support different needs and approaches. Classrooms should invite effective movement from small groups to individual work to whole class sharing. Materials should be easily available to students. Some teachers will need a classroom with movable desks, chairs, and tables so that the room arrangements can be changed for certain activities. In general, a room should provide a large space for whole class instruction and sharing, a smaller area for small-group work, display and bookshelves, and individual work spaces. If possible, quiet spaces for individuals should be provided during learning opportunities.

The most effective classroom reflects a teacher's philosophy and the students' work. The physical arrangement of the classroom, materials, and equipment all make a statement about the philosophy of instruction. Classrooms can be arranged to say "Let's read, talk, and write about what interests us." Classroom arrangements may also suggest a student-centered focus and a challenge to try things. Circular arrangements or round tables stimulate interactions. The arrangement of the classroom can reflect different instructional approaches and different student needs. Teachers will recognize what arrangements are most advantageous to their teaching style over time and with some trial and error.

FIELD-BASED ACTIVITY

7.4

Sketch the layout of the classroom where you are assigned. During classroom observations, watch carefully to see what student behavior is encouraged by the physical arrangement of the room. Watch what students do as they walk into the classroom and prepare for the day's activities. Watch how the arrangement of the room contributes to the instructional processes in the room. Share your observations in class and associate particular types of classroom learning and interactions with specific classroom physical arrangements. Can you identify a link?

INTASC Principle 5

 ## Discipline

Experienced teachers who create well-managed classrooms will avoid a great many conflicts and have significantly fewer classroom disruptions. Even so, students occasionally bring problems to school, and even the most effective teachers will be confronted with unproductive student behavior that requires intervention (Brophy, 1996). Discipline is the process of helping students manage their unproductive behavior and responsibility (Armstrong, Savage, & Henson, 2002). Disciplining students for disruptive behavior should be part of a continuous plan that is explicit to the teacher and students. Skills necessary for teachers during disciplining procedures are the ability to listen, knowledge of conflict-resolution techniques, the ability to work with teams of professionals who can focus on the disruptive behavior of a particular student, and the knowledge to develop and carry out management and discipline plans.

The most important aspect of attending to disruptive behavior is to return the classroom to a constructive atmosphere. Regaining control of the classroom quickly and avoiding involvement of more students than necessary is top priority following any type of disruptive behavior or confrontation. Several strategies are important for the teacher in these situations:

1. Try not to create unreasonable requirements or overreact to disruptive incidents. Teachers may contribute to the crisis by exerting too much control or power, responding in a prejudicial or grudging manner, or not attending to students' behaviors (Seeman, 1988). Teachers should examine their own contributions to disruptive situations.

2. Analyze the underlying cause of the behavior by clarifying what behaviors are of concern, determining what is wrong with the behavior,

identifying what behaviors are desired, and suggesting a plan to correct the condition (Charles, 1996).

3. Be honest about your feelings. If you are upset, disappointed, or angry, explain that to students. They will be the first to know if you are trying to mask your feelings. They will respect you for your honesty and realize that you have emotions and reactions similar to theirs.

4. Be consistent and follow through with what you have said you will do. When rules of discipline are established, it is crucial that the teacher follow through with those processes. Behavior that is unacceptable one day should remain unacceptable another day. Threats should be avoided; they will only encourage student challenges.

5. Above all, be fair with your students. If you have made a mistake, applied rules indiscriminately, or have implemented actions that are not working or were not fair in the first place, apologize to your students. They will respect you for your honesty and openness.

When student misbehavior is serious and teachers' efforts fail to result in appropriate behavior, more severe strategies are needed. Usually, this occurs with collaborative consultation between classroom teachers and other educational resource staff. Consequences may involve corporal punishment and suspension from school in states where it is allowed. Punishment by itself will not teach desirable behavior and its impact is rather limited—therefore it should never be considered routine. Be sure you know your school's policies toward any type of severe punishment and disciplinary practices. Punishment will be most effective when combined with other classroom management strategies. (See Chapter 6 for a discussion of the negative consequences of punishment.)

Most educators believe the use of force does little to encourage compliance with rules or to promote good behavior, because punishment may have unintended consequences that make it an undesirable option. Suspension from school is another severe response for violation of school rules. Except in cases in which students are dangerous to themselves or others, school suspension should be discouraged (Pinnell, 1985). In cases of corporal punishment and suspension, student behavior is controlled by outside forces and the student is not developing and internalizing self-controls. Some schools provide in-school suspension centers, which remove students from the classroom but enable them to continue their studies. Take time now to complete the Self-Reflection exercise and to think about what you have learned.

What Matters?

Think about what you value most in classrooms. Then rank order the following values from 1 (most value) to 12 (least value). (One space has been left blank for you to add any descriptor that you value that is not included in this list.)

_____ Quiet   _____ Equality

_____ Laughter   _____ Fairness

_____ Respect   _____ Self-direction

_____ Orderliness   _____ Caring

_____ Creativity   _____ Competition

_____ Freedom   _____ _____

Now look at your top three choices. What does this say about the rules you will enforce and the behaviors you will encourage in your own classroom? For example, if you chose quiet, orderliness, and respect as your top three values, you might not feel comfortable implementing activities that require considerable student movement and interactions. If you selected creativity, freedom, and self-direction, you might be more comfortable with high levels of student interaction and student-led activities.

Voice of a Teacher

Keeping a classroom on-task and involved is a complicated task. It's hard to explain to someone else about your own classroom discipline because it is such a personal thing. I have developed a discipline system that reflects my personality, experience, and philosophy. Students contribute to the organization in a classroom too. The makeup of the class makes a big difference in how I manage instruction and keep order and discipline. Some years my discipline is much easier to establish than others.

I believe that management and discipline are closely related. I have found that good organization helps reduce the discipline problems in my classrooms. When my students understand what is expected of them, know what work they need to finish, and how I will respond to them . . . most of them will work in class. They really want to be actively engaged—they like to interact with each other while engaged in interesting, meaningful activities.

(continued)

Don't get me wrong. There are times my students don't go along with my planning. They may not be motivated to learn what I am trying to teach. Or they may need a great deal of structure to get them into the learning mode. Kids do need limits. I have to establish limits, rules, and follow through— do what I say I will do.

Another important aspect of classroom management and discipline is to figure out how you can show respect for your students. I try and listen to what they say and listen carefully to what they are telling me. I try to see the movies they see and read what they are reading. I can't always understand or enjoy their music—but I try. When I show that I know about some of these things, my students are really impressed. They know that I am interested in what they are doing.

I worried more about classroom management and discipline when I started teaching than I did any other thing. It didn't matter how much anyone talked to me about it—it's hard to know how to juggle all the aspects of classroom discipline and management—it is mostly learned while you are in front of a classroom. And each teacher will have his or her own individual way of approaching classroom organization. If I were to give a new teacher advice, I would suggest that the teacher read as much as possible and then approach his or her first classroom with the idea that it will be organized, well planned, and respectful. And then I would tell new teachers to remember that classroom management and discipline will get easier with experience.

Classroom Environments and Decision Making

The management of a classroom requires a teacher to make numerous decisions in a fast-paced, complex environment. Decisions range from the physical organization of desks and tables to intense personal interactions during teacher–student confrontations. Decisions about organizing and planning for instruction can seem overwhelming for beginning teachers, and they often must draw on numerous support systems to help with the task.

A new teacher's own experiences play an important role in how he or she organizes a classroom. How you were taught during your schooling will influence how you organize your classroom. In addition, what you observed during your teacher preparation process will help you make decisions about your own classroom. But experience is not the only way to learn about classroom environments. Knowledge about classroom organization can also be accessed through reading professional books and journals. The topic of effective classroom environments has received a great deal of attention from thoughtful and experienced educators, and their insights will help a beginning teacher make informed decisions. Given the complexities of classrooms, the many needs of students, and the growing knowledge about good classroom management techniques, new teachers will experience great challenges as well as find much support as they establish their own classrooms.

PORTFOLIO REFLECTIONS AND EXHIBITS

Choose one of the Field-Based Activities suggested in the text, develop an exhibit that represents what you have learned during the readings and discussions accompanying this chapter, or complete the suggested portfolio exhibit listed here. Your response to the activities or your exhibit may become part of your teaching portfolio.

Suggested Exhibit 7: My Emerging View of Classroom Management

1. Review your responses to each of the Field-Based Activities in this chapter. Compile your personal list of the descriptors that emerged after each of the activities. Summarize in writing what your responses to each of the activities had in common. Identify the descriptors that were mentioned with each of the activities.

2. Represent your responses to classroom management and organization in some explicit and descriptive way. Use a graphic, such as a continuum, a computer program, a drawing, an essay, or a collage, to describe how you see yourself as a classroom manager. Will you be flexible, traditional, creative, structured, or eclectic? Describe your thoughts about classroom environments. Be prepared to share your representation with your classmates.

E-Portfolio Entry 7

Review the description you produced in Field-Based Activity 7.1. Locate Web sites that would help you implement your ideal classroom management approach. Add the list of Web sites to your portfolio files.

INTASC Principles 5 and 6

ANSWERS TO GUIDING YOUR READING

1. What factors must be considered when establishing effective learning environments?

   Many factors must be considered when a teacher is setting up the classroom for instruction. Some factors—such as home and school contexts, students' characteristics and needs, and teachers' and learners' expectations—cannot be controlled, but are important factors to consider when planning for instruction. The nature of the school context itself affects the classroom learning environment. The aspects that teachers can control—teachers' own behaviors, expectations, and interactions and classroom management and organization—are crucial factors contributing to an effective learning environment.

2. How do a teacher's personal views affect learning environments?

   Teachers' beliefs, expectations, and attitudes about classroom life are conveyed when teachers interact and teach students. Expectations affect what is taught and how it is taught. Students react positively in learning situations in which there is a belief they can achieve at a high level. Teachers who hold high expectations of students will most likely have a positive effect on classroom learning environments.

3. How does a teacher encourage student involvement and positive behavior?

   Teachers who plan relevant lessons, interact well with students, hold high expectations, and attend to many aspects of classroom management will encourage student involvement and positive behavior. Attention to student and teacher–student relationships and building a culture of classroom cooperation encourages student involvement in learning activities. Successful teachers make sure that their students can take part in the learning activities, exhibit on-task behaviors, and experience success when involved in learning activities

4. What are ways that students can be grouped for maximum instructional effectiveness?

   A variety of small and large student groups contribute to instructional effectiveness. Students work alone, in small groups, and as an entire class. The group arrangement depends upon the activities and goals the teacher has established for learning. It is most beneficial and positive to group students based on instructional needs.

INFOTRAC COLLEGE EDITION EXTENSION

Log on to the InfoTrac College Edition Web site. Choose an educational journal and a topic from the chapter and find articles of interest to you. Here are some suggestions to get you started:

1. Using the PowerTrac search, choose journal from the index and type in "Educational Leadership." Then choose subject from the index, and type in "classroom management." Your search expression should look like this: Jn Educational Leadership and su classroom management.

2. Do the same search for the Instructor journal.

RELATED READINGS

The following books will provide more information about some of the topics and ideas discussed in this chapter:

Collins, M., & Tamarkin, C. (1990). *Marva Collins' way: Returning to excellence in education.* New York: Putnam.

Marva Collins, a successful Chicago teacher, presents some inspiring ideas about establishing a successful classroom environment. She talks about how she motivates children who might normally be unsuccessful in our schools.

Esquith, R. (2003). *There are no shortcuts.* New York: Pantheon.

An award-winning teacher talks about the challenges and joys of working with hard-to-teach students. He tells his students that "learning isn't easy and there are no shortcuts." Esquith intersperses critiques of educational institutions with his account.

Gruwell, E., and the Freedom Writers (1999). *The Freedom Writers Diary.* New York Doubleday.

A young high school English teacher develops an innovative approach to interest her "unteachable, at-risk" students. Focusing on racism and using the English curriculum, she develops classroom activities that help her students comprehend the impact of intolerance and misunderstanding. Her students helped her write this book, which was based on five years of diary entries.

REFERENCES

Epigraph: Schoonmaker, Frances. Growing up teaching: *From personal knowledge to professional practice* (pp. 88–89). New York: Teachers College Press.

Ames, C. (1992). Classrooms: Goals, structures and student motivation. *Journal of Educational Psychology,* 83(3), 261–271.

Armstrong, D. G., Savage, T. V., & Henson, K. (2002). *Teaching in the secondary school: An introduction* (5th ed.). Upper Saddle River, NJ: Merrill Prentice Hall.

Bamburg, J. (1994). Raising expectations to improve student learning. Oak Brook, IL: North Central Regional Educational Laboratory. (ED 378 290).

Bartolome, L. (1994). Beyond the methods fetish, toward a humanizing pedagogy. *Harvard Educational Review,* 64(2), 173–194.

Bennett, W. (1998). A nation still at risk. *Policy Review,* 90, 23–29.

Blumenfeld, P. C., Puro, P., & Mergendoller, J. R. (1992). Translating motivation into thoughtfulness. In H. H. Marshall (Ed.), *Redefining student learning* (pp. 112–125). Norwood, NJ: Ablex.

Brophy, J. (1988). Educating teachers about managing classrooms and students. *Teaching and Teacher Education,* 4(1), 1–18.

Brophy, J. (1996). *Teaching problem students.* New York: Guilford.

Brophy, J., & Evertson, C. (1976). *Learning from teaching: A developmental perspective.* Boston: Allyn & Bacon.

Charles, C. M. (1996). *Building classroom discipline* (5th ed.). New York: Longman.

Comer, J. (1988). Educating poor minority children. *Scientific American,* 359(5), 42–48.

Dana, N. (1992). Towards preparing the monocultural teacher for the multicultural classroom. Paper presented at the 72nd annual meeting of the Association of Teacher Educators, Orlando. (ERIC Document Reproduction Service No. ED 350 272)

Doyle, W. (1986). Classroom organization and management. In M. Wittrock (Ed.), *Handbook of research on teaching* (3rd ed., pp. 392–431). New York: Macmillan.

Dryfoos, J. (1990). *Adolescents at risk: Prevalence and prevention.* New York: Oxford University Press.

Emmer, E., Evertson, C., & Anderson, L. (1980). Effective classroom management at the beginning of the school year. *Elementary School Journal,* 80(5), 219–231.

Epanchin, B. C., Townsend, B., & Stoddard, K. (1994). *Constructive classroom management: Strategies for creating positive learning environments.* Pacific Grove, CA: Brooks/Cole.

Fernie, D., Kantor, R., & Klein, E. (1990). School culture and peer culture influences on adult and child roles in a preschool classroom. Unpublished paper presented at AERA, Boston.

Garmon, A., Nystrand, M., Berends, M., & LePore, P. (1995). An organizational analysis of the effects of ability grouping. *American Educational Research Journal,* 32, 687–715.

Good, T., & Brophy, J. (1999). *Looking in classrooms* (8th ed.). New York: Longman.

Glasser, W. (1988). On students' needs and team learning: A conversation with William Glasser. *Educational Leadership,* 45(6), 38–45.

Graves, D. (1994). *A fresh look at writing.* Portsmouth, NH: Heinemann.

Green, J. L., Kantor, R. M., & Rogers, T. (1990). Exploring the complexity of language and learning in classroom contexts. In B. Jones & L. Idol (Eds.), *Educational values and cognitive instruction: Implications for reform* (Vol. II, pp. 400–422). Hillsdale, NJ: Erlbaum.

Hill, S., & Hill, T. (1991). *The collaborative classroom: A guide to cooperative learning.* Portsmouth, NH: Heinemann.

Jeneks, C., & Phillips, M. (Eds.). (1998). *The black–white test score gap.* Washington, DC: Brookings Institute.

Johnson, D., & Johnson, R. (1995). *Reducing school violence through conflict resolution.* Alexandria, VA: Association for Supervision and Curriculum Development.

Jones, V. (1996). Classroom management. In J. Sikula (Ed.), *Handbook of research on teacher education* (pp. 503–524). New York: Macmillan.

Kounin, J. (1970). *Discipline and group management in classrooms.* New York: Holt, Rinehart, and Winston.

Kuykendall, C. (1992). *From rage to hope: Strategies for reclaiming black and Hispanic students.* Bloomington, IN: National Educational Service.

Lepper, M. R. (1983). Extrinsic reward and intrinsic motivation. In J. Levine & M. Wang (Eds.), *Teacher and student perceptions: Implications for learning* (pp. 212–232). Hillsdale, NJ: Erlbaum.

Mahler, M., & Anderson, E. (1993). Reinventing schools for early adolescents: Emphasizing task goals. *Elementary School Journal, 93,* 593–610.

McCaslin, M., & Good, T. (1992). Compliant cognition: The misalliance of management and instructional goals in current school reform. *Educational Researcher, 21*(3), 4–17.

Noddings, N. (1995). *Philosophy of education (Dimensions of Philosophy Series).* Boulder, CO: Westview Press.

Olsen, L., & Mullen, N. (1990). *Embracing diversity: Teachers' voices from California's classrooms.* San Francisco: California Tomorrow Project.

Omotani, B. J., & Omotani, L. (1996). Expect the best: How your teachers can help all children learn. *The Executive Educator, 18*(8), 27, 31.

Pappas, C. C., Kiefer, B. K., & Levstik, L. S. (1990). *An integrated language perspective in the elementary school: Theory into action.* New York: Longman.

Phelan, P., Davidson, A., & Cao, H. (1992). Speaking up: Students' perspectives on school. *Phi Delta Kappan, 73*(9), 795–804.

Pinnell, G. S. (1985). The "catch-22" of school discipline policy making. *Theory into Practice, 24,* 289.

Savage, T. (1999). *Developing self-control through classroom management and discipline* (2nd ed.). Boston: Allyn & Bacon.

Seeman, H. (1988). *Preventing classroom discipline problems.* Lancaster, PA: Technomic.

Slavin, R. E. (1987). Ability grouping and student achievement in elementary schools: A best evidence synthesis. *Review of Educational Research, 57*(3), 293–336.

Wehlage, G., Rutter, R., Smith, G., Lesko, N., & Fernandez, R. (1989). *Reducing the risk: Schools as communities of support.* London: Falmer Press.

Wiseman, D. L. (1992). *Learning to read with literature.* Boston: Allyn & Bacon.

Wlodkowski, R. J., & Jaynes, J. H. (1990). *Eager to learn: Helping children become motivated and love learning.* San Francisco: Jossey-Bass.

Zaharlick, A., & Green, J. L. (1991). Ethnographic research. In J. Flood, J. Jensen, D. Lapp, & J. Squire (Eds.), *Handbook of research on teaching the English language* (pp. 205–225). New York: Macmillan.

Lessons in Today's Classrooms

Someone has to raise the bar, and that person is the teacher. If fifth-grade students are reading at a first-grade level, placing first grade books in front of them will never help them catch up with the students across town who not only are in higher-achieving classrooms but have parents and tutors helping them every step of the way. Someone has to tell children if they are behind, and lay out a plan of attack to help them catch up. If this means staying after school or taking extra hours sitting with the child and reading, so be it. There are no excuses. Students new to the country or living with economic hardship are just as capable of becoming top students as their more privileged peers in other parts of the city. However, they will never get there if the teacher doesn't believe this. Children need and deserve our belief in their ability to improve skills. I constantly encourage my students to reach their highest. Not a day goes by that I don't tell them that I'm not smarter than they are, only more experienced. I try and inspire them by reminding them of where they once were and how assignments that were once difficult have become easier due to their willingness to practice their skills with discipline. They have confidence because I build it in them.

If we want our students to explore new worlds, we must demand they make the journey . . .

—Rafe Esquith, *There Are No Shortcuts*

*T*eachers make decisions every day. Decisions about what they should teach. Decisions about what materials they should use. Decisions about how to encourage learning in the classroom. Clarke and Peterson (1986) report that teachers make a decision on how to best affect student learning about every two minutes in the classroom. Many factors contribute to a teacher's planning process.

Approaches to Classroom Instruction

Describing all the different concepts, definitions, models, and approaches used to explain how teachers plan, organize, and implement their instruction would take several volumes. This chapter will instead examine two general categories, teacher-centered approaches and student-centered approaches, which provide a good overview of the choices available to teachers.

Teacher-Centered Approaches

Teacher-centered approaches hold the teacher responsible for all classroom activity. The teacher identifies topics of study, conceptualizes the goals, establishes the sequence of learning activities, presents the materials, and develops assessment procedures. The teacher explicitly identifies outcomes and controls and determines instruction. A common type of teacher-centered approach is direct instruction, during which the teacher relies on

a structured process to direct students' thinking and participation. Instructional activities include whole group review, instructional input, and guided and independent practice. The teacher constantly checks for understanding and relies on drill and practice activities.

Direct instruction presents learning in small structured steps, requiring practice and structured feedback to make sure the student is learning. The teacher plays a major role: presenting material, guiding students, and providing students with extensive practice routines. This approach is especially useful when students are required to learn and master well-defined concepts and skills such as mathematics computations. Direct instruction uses many of the mechanisms of behavioral learning theory: classical and operant conditioning, reinforcement, and observational learning (see Chapter 6).

Student-Centered Approaches

Student-centered approaches to instruction require a great deal of student participation and interaction between teacher and students and among students. Although the teacher facilitates and structures learning, students have a lot of responsibility and are delegated a portion of the authority during learning activities. The focus of instructional strategies is on cooperation and class cohesiveness.

Student-centered approaches are also known as indirect methods because the teacher is involved less directly—teachers shift from their traditional roles as information providers into a more facilitative, supportive role. This approach emphasizes teaching students how to learn through peer and teacher interactions. Because students are involved in setting their own goals, they develop and share multiple opinions, question ideas and positions, and refer to multiple sources. Students may be asked to contribute personal experiences that offer information and clarify issues. Learning strategies are focused on the scientific or discovery method: gathering facts, hypothesizing, testing solutions, and revising solutions.

What Is Your Teaching Orientation?

1. You are planning a lesson to teach fifth-graders fractions. You prefer to:

    a. present fraction facts on the overhead followed by practice worksheets.

    b. have students use manipulatives to depict fractions.

2. You are planning a lesson to introduce Shakespeare to high school students. You prefer to:

    a. have students take turns reading out loud, followed by class discussion.

    b. have students divide into small groups, read the selection together, and then rewrite it in language familiar to them.

3. You are planning a lesson to teach how to calculate area to middle school students. You prefer to:

    a. read the text together and have students work problems on the board.

    b. have groups of students measure the classroom for new carpet and compare their answers.

4. You are planning a lesson to teach interrogatives in your Spanish class. You prefer to:

    a. present the rules and then use drill and practice exercises to reinforce your lesson.

    b. divide into teams and play the game Twenty Questions.

5. You are teaching a lesson on cell structure in biology class. You prefer to:

    a. use the diagrams in the textbook to illustrate the structures.

    b. have students use technology to develop graphics that demonstrate cell structure.

6. You are planning to teach students how to predict outcomes while reading. You prefer to:

    a. use the questions embedded in the reading selection.

    b. initially model predicting outcomes while reading the passage and then have students assume the role of teacher and predict outcomes while reading aloud.

Look at your responses. If most of your responses were "a," you are probably more comfortable with a teacher-centered approach. However, if you chose "b" most often, you probably prefer a student-centered classroom. If your responses were mixed, determine any patterns in your preferences. For example, did you prefer teacher-centered activities for older students, or do you believe particular activities seem to be better-suited for one or the other approach?

Student-centered approaches appear to improve students' attitudes toward learning, increase motivation, develop social skills, and perhaps encourage higher-level thinking skills. Critics of student-centered approaches maintain that basic skills learning is less emphasized in a total student-centered approach.

Establishing Goals for the Classroom

Teachers use goals and objectives to select the topics and activities for the day. Goals statements define what students are expected to learn and guide teachers' instructional planning. Objectives, or learning intentions, are measurable and state what learners should be able to do as a result of a lesson or series of lessons. These help teachers reach their goals. Ideally, the teacher will manipulate all the classroom materials, methods, and climate to successfully attain stated goals and objectives. Effective teachers not only understand the importance of establishing goals and how they fit into the larger framework of the total curriculum but also make sure students understand them as well.

District, state, and national educational guidelines influence a teacher's academic goals. According to Tyler (1974), goals establish priorities for what students learn and should be based on subject mastery, student needs

Instructional approaches should include opportunities to learn in a variety of ways. Depending on the demands of the curriculum, students may benefit from student-centered or teacher-directed learning experiences.

and interests, societal concerns, community priorities, instructional theory, and research. Essential content for each grade level and learning objectives for each subject are outlined by standards set outside the classroom. Standardized testing requirements also affect the curriculum content, given that teachers are accountable for student achievement or mastery of test objectives.

State and National Goals

In recent years, several national teacher organizations—including the National Council of Teachers of Mathematics, the National Council for the Social Studies, the National Council for Improving Science Education, and the National Council of Teachers of English—adopted curriculum frameworks designed to develop learners who can think independently in real-world situations. These frameworks shift the focus away from curriculum based on isolated skills and memorization of basic facts to more complex thinking and problem solving (Falk, 2000).

State educational guidelines contribute to individual teachers' goal-setting processes. State-mandated tests are typically required at specific

You can learn more about national goals at:

http://www.odedodea.edu/2001_ strategic_plan/research_study/goal.html

http://www.ed.gov/legislation/ESEA/Guidance /app-c.html

Address: Department of Defense Education Activity (DoDEA), 4040 North Fairfax St., Arlington, VA 22203–1635

URLs may change over time. For up-to-date links to relevant Web sites, visit our Companion Web site:

http://education.wadsworth.com/wiseman3e

grade levels, and pressure to perform well can be intense. Figure 8.1 is a sample of instructional targets that help teachers prepare their students in mathematics for the Texas Assessment of Knowledge and Skills. Fourth-grade teachers in Texas, who know that they and their schools will be held accountable for their students' achievement in these areas, study these state guidelines and incorporate them into their curriculum to ensure students understand the material to be tested. Check the Web site of your state educational agency or other state educational resources to determine whether your state has guidelines that you must incorporate into your lessons.

FIGURE 8.1 **Example of TAKS Objectives and TEKS Student Expectations**

GRADE 4 TAKS Mathematics, Objective 1

Objective 1: The student will demonstrate an understanding of numbers, operations, and quantitative reasoning.

4.1 Number, operation, and quantitative reasoning. The student uses place value to represent whole numbers and decimals. The student is expected to

   (A) use place value to read, write, compare, and order whole numbers through the millions place.

4.2 Number, operation, and quantitative reasoning. The student describes and compares fractional parts of whole objects or sets of objects. The student is expected to

   (A) generate equivalent fractions using [concrete and] pictorial models;

   (B) model fraction quantities greater than one using [concrete materials and] pictures;

   (C) compare and order fractions using [concrete and] pictorial models; and

   (D) relate decimals to fractions that name tenths and hundredths using models.

(continued)

4.3 Number, operation, and quantitative reasoning. The student adds and subtracts to solve meaningful problems involving whole numbers and decimals. The student is expected to

(A) use addition and subtraction to solve problems involving whole numbers; and

(B) add and subtract decimals to the hundredths place using [concrete and] pictorial models.

4.4 Number, operation, and quantitative reasoning. The student multiplies and divides to solve meaningful problems involving whole numbers. The student is expected to

(A) model factors and products using arrays and area models;

(B) represent multiplication and division situations in picture, word, and number form;

(C) recall and apply multiplication facts through 12 x12

(D) use multiplication to solve problems involving two-digit numbers; and

(E) use division to solve problems involving one-digit divisors.

4.5 Number, operation, and quantitative reasoning. The student estimates to determine reasonable results. The student is expected to

(A) round whole numbers to the nearest ten, hundred, or thousand to approximate reasonable results in problem situations; and

(B) estimate a product or quotient beyond basic facts.

OBJECTIVE 1—FOR YOUR INFORMATION

At fourth grade, students should be able to

- Sequence numbers or the words associated with numbers (for example, listing the names of children in order from greatest to the least based on their height);

- Work with comparisons using pictorial models, word phrases (is less than, is equal to, etc.), or symbols (<, >, =);

- Solve problems with fractions or decimals representing whole numbers, numbers greater than one, or numbers less than one;

- Use pictorial representations to determine a missing factor;

- Work with problems and choose among answers that have information expressed in numbers or ranges of numbers; and

- Round numbers before performing any computations when estimating. Students may need to use compatible numbers.

SOURCE: Texas Education Agency. (2002). *Texas assessment of knowledge and skills: Information booklet* (p.11–12). Austin: Texas Education Agency: Student Assessment Division.

School districts also develop curriculum guides for teachers to use in planning. These guides often incorporate national and state standards and may be organized into subject matter units of study or around specific disciplines. School districts may also adopt special units of study, such as dental care or AIDS awareness, that teachers are required to teach at certain grade levels.

Assessing Curriculum Needs

Successful teachers serve as translators between the written curriculum and the needs of the students, constantly striving to define the written curriculum in a comprehensible, meaningful way for students. Bringing a written curriculum and preset curriculum goals to life in a real classroom, with a wide range of students operating at various levels of achievement, requires constant problem-solving and critical thinking skills based on several assessments of the students' needs.

At the beginning of any curriculum unit is the assessment of need, which can be defined at several different levels. Subject matter and grade level needs are defined by the state and district curriculum guidelines, but interest and ability needs of students must also be considered. Teachers use their knowledge of child and adolescent development; understanding of their students' backgrounds; interactions with students, parents, and community members; and a variety of classroom evaluation procedures to learn about individual needs of their students. As teachers and students interact during the year, teachers become more familiar with the capabilities of their students.

Long-range planning decisions often occur before the semester or year begins. Teachers decide on broad topic areas or upcoming units of study based on what they want students to be able to do at the completion of the unit. Teachers estimate the time needed to accomplish their learning goals and plan a calendar for the year, knowing it will change constantly as students' interests and academic needs demand.

One technique for assessing what elementary and secondary students already understand and what they want to learn about a topic is filling out a K-W-L chart (Carr & Ogle, 1987). The K column represents what students already know about a topic—underscoring the need to link prior knowledge with new information (as discussed in Chapter 6). Students can work individually, in small groups, or with a whole class to discuss and record information they already know about the topic. Students then record or dictate the information to the teacher to complete the K column. The W column lists what students want to know about a topic. Questions are generated individually and in small groups and then reported to the class for recording and categorizing. This information can help teachers increase student motivation by making class topics interesting and relevant to students, because they have assisted in goal-setting for their own learning. The last column on the K-W-L chart is for recording new learnings—what students learn about the topic. The K-W-L chart therefore serves as a guide throughout the unit or lesson. Questions asked before the lesson are answered and crossed off the list as new learning occurs. New questions are added to the list, which may lead to extensions of a unit or topic. As a summary for learning, the last column is filled in after students have completed the activities. This chart therefore not only guides discussions; it is also an excellent way to informally evaluate what students have learned.

After looking at goals set outside the classroom and at the learning needs of the students, teachers continue the individual planning process by reflecting on past experience. Based on their own previous experience with a grade or subject, teachers establish short- and long-range goals. Retaining successful practices and redefining activities or processes that were unsuccessful, they learn to adopt high expectations and to recognize unrealistic goals.

Short-range planning occurs every day in a variety of ways as teachers assess learning needs on a weekly or even an hour-by-hour basis. Short-range plans are constantly changing. For example, a math concept may prove to be more difficult than expected, and the lesson for the next period

FIELD-BASED ACTIVITY

8.2

Fill in a K-W-L chart, like the one shown below, for your own learning. Complete the first two columns now before you teach your lesson. Use the information you gained in Field-Based Activity 8.1 to help you generate ideas for your first two columns. Discuss your charts in small groups and then compile lists with the whole class. Fill in the last column after you have taught the lesson. Ask yourself these questions: What do I already know about planning and teaching a lesson? What do I want to know? What have I learned?

Topic: Planning and Teaching a Lesson

K	W	L
What I know . . .	What I want to know . . .	What I learned . . .

INTASC Principle 1 and 4

or for the next day may need to be adjusted. A writing activity may require more time than planned, and the activity may be extended into several additional upcoming class periods. Students may become very interested in a current event in the news, and the social studies unit may be modified to include this new topic of interest.

Creating, Selecting, and Adapting Resources

When students actively participate in acquiring new knowledge and are allowed to take some responsibility for their own learning, teachers must seek out many materials and resources to support the variety of classroom activities. They can supplement textbooks with age-appropriate literature, reference materials, current periodicals, audiovisual aids, and computer software related to the topic. Needed materials can, however, be just as individual as the learning taking place in each classroom. Mr. Landmann, the third-grade teacher we met in Chapter 6, is constantly seeking out costumes and props suitable to portray the major characters in history so that when the third-graders present their research in a living history museum at the end of each six weeks they are properly attired. As a part of her unit on insects, one first-grade teacher worked to find live silkworms so that her students could observe them growing, spinning a cocoon, and eventually hatching into moths.

FIELD-BASED ACTIVITY

8.3

Schedule a teacher planning conference. Discuss these questions with your teacher before beginning to plan your lesson and record the answers:

- What subject will I be teaching?
- Are there district and state guidelines for this subject?
- How will my lesson fit into a larger unit of study?
- What time constraints will I have? How long should my lesson last?
- What resources are available?
- What should the student be able to do on completion of the lesson?

INTASC Principles 1, 2, 4, and 8

▶ Using Technology

In most modern classrooms, technology is an extension of the teacher's lesson plan, and students' thinking processes can be enhanced by using new technologies (Jonassen, Peck, & Wilson, 1999). "Student motivation, attention and enthusiasm increase with technology in the classroom. Through technology, students become active participants, who are encouraged to creatively problem solve, explore and expand their horizons beyond the classroom" (Franzee & Rudnitski, 1996, p. 310). Following are some technological tools that allow students to actively participate in their own learning and to construct new meaning.

Multimedia presentations. Multimedia presentations integrate sight, sound, and interactivity to convey a message. New technologies available on multimedia software are engaging students in new ways. Multimedia presentations now may include text, pictures, sound, video, and animation. Multimedia can also include record-based data, numeric

© Stephanie Knight

Technological innovations emerge at a rapid pace, requiring continuous learning on the part of the teacher and the students. Many students have access to computers at home and come to school with strong technological expertise. A resourceful teacher can maintain equity of access and enhance classroom learning using computers and multimedia tools in a variety of ways.

data, and just about any form of communication (Jonassen, Peck, & Wilson, 1999). Such presentations can help students make learning meaningful and personal (Wilson, 1991)—the personal connections required for learning to occur (Hawkins & Collins, 1992). Commercially or teacher-prepared multimedia presentations can be used in interactive ways, with students selecting the path of their own learning and moving through the material in ways that are individually meaningful to each student. Jonassen (1986) suggests that this nonlinear presentation of material is similar to the way the brain stores information naturally and can encourage students to find relationships among the pieces of information presented. Students can also create their own presentations on the computer, manipulating new learnings into a creative presentation. These presentations provide a sense of ownership about producing a physical product as evidence of their understanding (Bruder, 1991).

Telecommunications. With a computer, modem, and a phone line, classrooms are able to interact with the world. Students and teachers can take advantage of electronic mail, listservs, electronic bulletin boards, chat rooms, and videoconferencing. With Internet access, learners can communicate with other classrooms in different locations, contact experts in a field of study, and access resources in libraries around the world. Electronic communication can occur synchronously or not, making it possible to hold conversations over days and weeks. Email is asynchronous, or delayed, communication. Chat rooms can carry on synchronous conversations where several people are online at the same time. New tools are becoming available almost daily, making telecommunications more and more viable for all classrooms and providing expanded instructional options.

Instructional games and simulations. Games and simulations can provide practice, remediation, and enrichment for students in the classroom. Lessons introduced in a whole class setting can be expanded into individual or small-group practice in an instructional game provided by computer software. Some simulations are appropriate for use in a discovery lesson, enabling students to discover concepts and information first through their interaction with the computer, leading to later discussion and further instruction by the teacher.

Visualization and modeling. Technology allows students to experience phenomena in new ways. For example, computer simulations can show students how a disease spreads throughout a country, the evolution of plants, or the three-dimensional structure of an earthquake fault. Instructional simulations can use animation, video, and virtual reality. Visual simulations help students learn the basics about a particular model or concept. Students can build their own simulations or models to demonstrate what they have learned.

Computer-assisted instruction (CAI). One of the first ways computers entered the classroom was through computer-assisted instruction, which provides tutoring and practice with instant assessment and feedback capabilities. Drill and practice activities are not seen as the most innovative use of technology (Jonassen, 2000), nevertheless, they are still used in some educational settings. Students are presented with new material, and the computer assesses student responses and can provide immediate reteaching based on those responses. The level of difficulty is adjusted automatically by the computer so instruction is individualized to meet each learner's needs.

One issue raised by technology-based instruction is how to provide equal access to all students. Most schools in affluent areas have no problem providing students with technology such as access to the Internet, but poorer schools may lack the most basic equipment—such as computers (Wepner, Valmont, & Thurlow, 2000). In an effort to provide all students with access to technology, the federal government passed the Telecommunications Act of 1996, which established the University Service Fund Education Rate (E-Rate) to support educational use of the Internet. Schools and libraries can apply for government help to underwrite the cost of supplying Internet connections and hardware.

Creating Relevant Curricula

Today's curriculum is often a sequential, skill-oriented continuum using direct teacher instruction, because many educators believe that students must master a fundamental set of basic skills before they move on to more complicated, higher-level thinking activities. Mathematical concepts are often taught as discrete skills, such as how to multiply a two-digit number or solve simple algebraic equations. Individual language arts skills might include how to decode a word with a consonant blend, divide words into syllables, or use correct capitalization in a sentence. Skills typically are isolated and practiced until students are able to demonstrate understanding. This kind of instructional approach does provide benefits (see "Learning as Behavior" in Chapter 6): A list of sequential skills helps teachers diagnose learning weaknesses so they can design a specific plan of remediation to address student needs. This diagnosis and remediation cycle allows for frequent feedback, rapid pacing, and repeated opportunities for practice. Teachers are able to assess students' achievement easily and to make adjustments as needed.

Even though test results can improve in this scenario, studies have found that this skills approach, which is more repetitive and less challenging, provides fewer opportunities for students to learn higher-order skills (Allington & McGill-Franzen, 1989). A skills-based curriculum can keep traditionally low-achieving children from progressing to more challenging, meaningful activities and often results in a program that fails to encourage problem solving, reading comprehension, or meaningful writing activities (Knapp et al., 1995). Students in such an environment often have difficulty connecting the skills practiced in isolation with integrated, more meaningful tasks. Those students who already find school alien to their personal experience see little reason for completing isolated skill activities and end up falling further behind because they must master basic steps before they can move on to more challenging, and interesting, activities. By underestimating what students are capable of accomplishing, teachers might postpone more interesting work and deny students a chance to apply the skills they have been taught (Knapp et al., 1995; Knapp & Shields, 1990).

In contrast, some schools are looking at the strengths students bring with them to school rather than at the deficiencies. Learners from poor and affluent backgrounds alike come to school with important skills and knowledge about the world around them—including sophisticated language abilities and numerical concepts. Instruction in advanced skills enables students to integrate prior learning into the process of knowledge acquisition and helps students build on existing basic academic skills. Instead of looking at what children do not know, a curriculum based on integrated skills acknowledges what students already know (Means & Knapp, 1991).

Integrating Basic Skills

MATHEMATICS In mathematics, schools can offer a more challenging curriculum by emphasizing mathematical concepts along with computational skills. Students at all levels need frequent opportunities to apply mathematical concepts to real-life problems so they can form the connections that help them draw on their own experiences. Students may then be involved in solving complex, meaningful problems about issues they consider important. Computational skills can be embedded in the more global task of problem solving, enabling students to see the big concepts rather than spending the majority of their school time memorizing isolated and unconnected facts. Students learn basic mathematical skills as they are needed, connecting the skill with a meaningful purpose for learning the skill.

Reading

The No Child Left Behind legislation prescribes a Reading First Curriculum specifying five major components and recommends that states include them in early reading instruction. The five—phonemic awareness, phonics, fluency, vocabulary, and text comprehension—were identified by a panel established by the federal government to study reading. The reading panel's recommendations for instruction were based on an extensive review of reading research completed in the last thirty years. However, in addition to ensuring that students possess the basic reading skills, reading instruction should focus on gaining meaning—that is, giving students a purpose for using skills within the context of a story. Age-appropriate literature and reading material reflecting a diversity of backgrounds and cultures are integral to the reading program. Within such a reading curriculum, students are often encouraged to select their own reading material, increasing interest and building on prior experience. Teachers, and sometimes whole schools, implement a time of sustained silent reading, wherein students choose their own books and read silently for a set amount of time each day. At the secondary level, teachers can incorporate approaches to reading for knowledge in specific content areas that continue to build comprehension skills.

 The following Web site will provide you more information about Reading First:

http://www.ed.gov/programs/readingfirst/index.html

URLs may change over time. For up-to-date links to relevant Web sites, visit our Companion Web site:

http://education.wadsworth.com/wiseman3e

WRITING A strong curriculum for writing draws on the experiences and knowledge of students, with less emphasis placed on the mechanics of writing such as spelling, punctuation, and grammar and more emphasis placed on the process of writing. Students brainstorm for writing ideas using past experiences, write several drafts with input from teachers and peers, apply mechanical skills to revisions, and then produce a final piece of writing to share with others. Stories of experience, community, and family are shared in the classroom, and all students have the opportunity to bring their out-of-school experiences and culture into the classroom through shared writing. Students consistently reflect on their own lives through autobiography and story. Written biographies of community elders or other influential adults in the community can also bridge the gap between home and school. Writing skills, formerly taught in isolation, are taught as a necessary part of the process and as the need for understanding arises. Students are able to see the purpose of learning the skill when it is embedded in the writing process.

VERBAL SKILLS A strong curriculum for all students also emphasizes verbal communication, with constant dialogue as the central form of communicating knowledge. Teachers are no longer solely responsible for transmitting knowledge to a passive student: Students must be engaged in the learning process as half of a two-way communication.

Just as skills are no longer viewed as isolated pieces within subject areas, individual subjects are also viewed as pieces of a larger integrated curriculum. Reading, writing, and mathematics are all combined across the curriculum. Readers comment on literature with written responses. Writers seek examples of style and tone through reading a variety of authors. Mathematicians write out answers to complicated problems in narrative form. Verbal communication is also important, and students are encouraged to talk about their solutions with teachers and other students in a variety of formats.

> **www** If you wish to learn more about how teachers are creating relevant cirricula, you may do so at:
>
> **http://www.teachnet.com**
>
> URLs may change over time. For up-to-date links to relevant Web sites, visit our Companion Web site:
>
> **http://education.wadsworth.com/ wiseman3e**

Integrated Instruction

Integrated instruction has several definitions. First, it can refer to how teachers approach skills instruction. Integrated curriculum embeds basic skills instruction into processes that demonstrate real uses of the skill. For example, elementary students learn the skills by using phonics and addition facts during reading activities and mathematic computations. The skills may be the focus of instruction during the initial presentation to the students, but their relevance to learning and understanding how to comprehend reading material or how the addition facts relate to mathematic computations is a formal overall goal of instruction. Secondary teachers may embed skills and facts in identified themes and issues such as communication or conservation (Clarke & Agne, 1996). Drill and practice of basic facts is used in integrated curriculum, but the skills learned are repeated and linked in the total process. Learning skills related to specific subject areas is more meaningful and relevant when integrated into real uses.

Second, integrated instruction can mean overlapping the learning of different subject areas. At times, different subjects are easily integrated for more meaningful instruction. For example, when studying a particular country in social studies, students can read literature presenting characters from the country's culture, use mathematic skills to graph population or determine distances on a map, look at art and listen to music of that specific culture, and review the types of animal and plant life associated with the country's geographic area—thus bringing many subjects together in one unit of study. Integration becomes more difficult when attempting to work across more than two or three content areas or when teachers are departmentalized based on subject areas. Elementary teachers do this quite easily because they are usually responsible for more than one subject. Integrated instruction is somewhat more difficult for middle school and secondary teachers, because they must work together across content areas. Middle school and secondary teachers who are content specialists (i.e., English, mathematics, or science teachers) are trained to teach in one area and may feel that some of their content is lost when integration occurs. Also, some teachers and administrators may discourage integration of content areas for fear that all topics included in statewide tests would not be covered. However, participating in cross-content planning teams can help bridge traditional barriers between content areas.

Linking Disciplines

Many teachers may prefer an integrated curriculum that links the disciplines throughout the day. As students get older and move into the more discipline-structured environment of secondary schools, integrated instruction becomes more difficult. Teachers who want to integrate subjects across disciplines often have to locate a willing partner in another discipline, and even then they face the further difficulty, when schedules cannot be coordinated, of not sharing the same students. Some secondary schools arrange their schedules to encourage cross-disciplinary teaching by scheduling classes such as math and science together in two- or three-hour blocks. The shared blocks of time for two different subject areas provide opportunities for students and teachers to work together across the disciplines. Some university education programs have integrated mathematics and science methods courses to set examples for future teachers.

Learners must continually search for connections between new learning and familiar concepts to make sense of the new information. An integrated curriculum makes it easier for students to see patterns and connections between disciplines. When they learn ways to connect and organize new information, students are able to understand the content more deeply and are then able to transfer this new information to other areas (Franzee & Rudnitski, 1996). "Because the learner is constantly searching for connections on many levels, educators need to orchestrate the experience from

Relevant and challenging curriculum motivates students, establishes a
purpose for learning, utilizes a variety of teaching and learning approaches,
and provides students with opportunities to talk to each other about
what they are learning.

which learners extract understanding. They must do more than simply
provide information or force the memorization of isolated facts and skills"
(Caine & Caine, 1994, p. 5).

For many years, research has shown that the majority of teachers in
the United States, especially in secondary education, are still following the
prescribed written recipe of the textbooks with little deviation—students
read the chapters and answer the questions (Goodlad, 1984; Sizer, 1984).
However, some teachers are breaking new ground, developing curriculum
that is student-centered and organized to help students make connections
between subjects. Recent research has shown that such integrated techniques involving students in problem solving and critical thinking can lead
to greater achievement and more meaningful learning (Aschlbacher, 1991).

Teachers who use an integrated approach often build classroom activities around problem solving and projects that incorporate higher levels of
thinking (Jacobs, 1989). As students work to apply and demonstrate their
knowledge, effective teachers begin to give students a greater voice in the
curriculum, and the roles of teacher and student begin to change (Franzee
& Rudnitski, 1996). Teachers who use a thematic or integrated approach to
curriculum believe not only that subjects should be interrelated but also

that students should be part of the goal-setting process. The teacher is no longer seen as the source of all knowledge in the classroom, directing all activities and learning, but rather as a guide and a resource for students as they need assistance in getting meaning from the curriculum.

Thematic Teaching

Thematic teaching is an effective strategy for helping students make connections between disciplines. Units of study may last only a week in the lower grades when students stay in the same classroom the whole day or six weeks or longer in upper grades. These units integrate learning objectives from many different subject areas under one thematic umbrella and are often selected from students' interests, a piece of literature, seasonal topics, or other material. Classroom space is designed with collaboration in mind. Students are expected to be active participants, and classroom areas are provided to encourage reading, writing, listening, and speaking. Secondary teachers may make a special effort to seek out colleagues who will collaboratively plan and participate in integrated thematic units across content areas. For example, English, history, art, and music teachers may collaborate on a Shakespearean unit focusing on appropriate literature, history, art, and music associated with a specific play.

Teaching for Multiple Intelligences

Many teachers have found Howard Gardner's (1983, 1991, 2000) theory of multiple intelligences useful when they are making decisions about content and activities for students in their classes. Gardner's theory identifies at least eight separate kinds of abilities or intelligences in which people may excel, and more may exist. The eight intelligences discussed by Gardner are linguistic or verbal, musical, spatial, logical-mathematical, bodily-kinesthetic, interpersonal (an understanding of others), intrapersonal (an understanding of self), and naturalist (recognition of animal and plant species). Gardner bases his theory on several sources of evidence, including research that suggests that different abilities may be located in different parts of the brain. Some individuals are extremely gifted in several areas, but are known for specific talents. For example, Michael Jordan, an extremely talented basketball player whose on-court behaviors indicated expert control of his body and movement, is an example of someone with a highly developed bodily-kinesthetic intelligence, whereas the charismatic Oprah Winfrey demonstrates strong interpersonal intelligence among her many other talents. When students do not possess the linguistic talents needed for success in school settings, their talents are often ignored. Some students with nonacademic talents fail to receive any reinforcement for them in schools and may become underachievers when their unique ways of thinking and learning are not recognized. The idea of multiple intelligences suggests that artists, musicians, naturalists, designers, dancers, therapists, entrepreneurs, and others who show gifts should be given equal attention in learning situations. Gardner reminds teachers that the human capacity for problem solving may occur in different areas. Gardner's theory has been particularly popular in schools, but other theorists such as Robert Sternberg (1985, 1990) also offer approaches featuring more than one definition of intelligence that can be used to enrich classroom instruction.

One advantage of applying a theory of multiple intelligences in classrooms is that we begin to think about students in terms of abilities other than those traditionally emphasized. Students can gain recognition for their ability to play musical instruments or to choreograph dances in a school play. The child who is constantly drawing elaborate sketches of battle scenes or comic book characters may be viewed in terms of his or her spatial intelligence and encouraged to develop these abilities. Students who assume leadership or facilitative roles in extracurricular activities may have well-developed interpersonal intelligence that can be utilized and rewarded in classroom settings as well. When teachers look for multiple intelligences rather than relying solely on the traditional definition, they increase the opportunities for student success in educational settings.

Emotional intelligence—a person's ability to monitor one's own and others' emotions—has recently received attention (Goleman, 1997). Very closely related to Gardner's personal intelligence, emotional intelligence is related to skills such as recognizing feelings, managing emotions, empathy, communication, cooperation, and resolving conflict. Emotional intelligence is related to leadership development, cooperating with others, and provides a framework for understanding a large set of social, interpersonal skills.

Another advantage of thinking about multiple intelligences is that it expands teaching strategies beyond the linguistic and logical ones traditionally used in classrooms. Although Gardner (1995) cautions against approaches that try to rigidly match instructional strategies to individual intelligences, increasing the variety of instructional strategies to represent eight ways of teaching results in a more interesting, creative classroom. Teachers can go beyond lecture and seatwork to include music, drama, creative movement, and art in their repertoire of activities. At the elementary level, classroom centers devoted to storytelling, nature, or building can nurture various intelligences. At the secondary level, the use of portfolios with examples of artistic productions, musical recitals, collaborative projects, and self-assessments provide outlets and encouragement for different intelligences.

Including Diversity

Equity and diversity should be included in every curriculum area, not just in special units of study (Banks, 1995). A two-week unit on African American leaders or on women's issues, although better than no mention at all, leads students to believe these issues are outside the mainstream of the normal curriculum. Every unit taught can have a story of a different culture in it. Examples that reflect the history of all groups should be integrated throughout the curriculum, not set apart as a special event to be studied in isolation at a special time of the year.

The materials a teacher selects for the classroom affect the success of all students. Diversity in the classroom should be reflected in the diversity of curriculum materials. Texts and other materials should reflect a variety of cultural backgrounds and be free of stereotypical language and characters.

Textbooks are often criticized for presenting history from a single majority viewpoint. For example, the stories of Thanksgiving and Christopher Columbus have long represented the European perspective on these events. As classrooms become more diverse, so must the perspectives of historical events. Textbooks also often use stereotypical images and language that can be nonrepresentative of students' background and culture.

Classroom libraries need to have a variety of multicultural books. No one book can represent one subject or one culture perfectly. Within each multicultural group are many different experiences and personalities. Although books may show some similarities among people of all colors, they should not depict all characters as talking and acting the same, regardless of color. Culture brings individual, distinct differences to characters and stories. Books also need to reflect changing times. Folktales from a particular culture can provide information on values and traditions of a group of people, but current stories from a variety of cultural backgrounds are also needed to tell the full story of how a culture has evolved.

Teachers will also consider academic diversity when planning for instruction. Students who have special learning needs require additional attention. An individual education program (IEP) is a long-range plan that is required by law to ensure educational opportunity for students with disabilities. The goal of the IEP is to involve classroom teachers, special education teachers, counselors, parents, and students, who all provide input for developing an accurate and relevant description of a student's strengths and weaknesses in many settings. Knowledge about the student is then used to develop an educational program that is tailored to the student's needs. Actual details of the IEPs are included in the teacher's daily and short-range plans. The IEP guides teachers as they establish classroom learning goals for exceptional students who may have unique needs.

IEPs are developed for a wide range of disabilities, including severe reading problems; sight and hearing impairment; and physical, emotional and mental limitations. It is reviewed annually and modified as students progress.

Effective teachers are familiar with the cultural background of students in their classrooms. Such knowledge helps teachers learn to accept and respect students for their differences, realizing differences are strengths rather than deficiencies. Teachers learn to appreciate the variety of backgrounds and experiences that students bring with them. Each person in the classroom, including the teacher, contributes a unique perspective. Each person has something to offer to the learning community. Good teachers encourage positive self-esteem when they recognize, validate, and respect each individual student's unique cultural background, making connections constantly with students' out-of-school experiences and cultures.

Instructional Guidelines

The content of the curriculum and the materials used to convey concepts are critical to the success of all students, but individual teachers bring their own personalities into the classroom as they seek out the best strategies for teaching the content. The selection of equitable instructional strategies is an important teaching responsibility. Following are several guidelines to help in this selection process:

- *Maximize time on-task.* Engage students in learning activities for the majority of the academic time. To accomplish this, teachers have to spend time planning and preparing learning activities before the instructional time. All necessary materials must be ready and organized for easy distribution so that students can begin work quickly with all the materials they need. Establish routines to make transition times move quickly and efficiently. The focus of the classroom and the majority of the time should be spent on meaningful learning activities.

- *Model thinking strategies aloud.* Effective teachers constantly model powerful thinking strategies—talking through their thought process as they explain solutions and responses. Every step of the learning task is modeled carefully to ensure success for all students. Students are routinely expected to follow the teacher's example and are often asked to "think aloud" so that others can learn the process of solving problems. (Chapter 6 includes an example of a think-aloud protocol.)

- *Encourage multiple ways of solving problems.* Effective teachers encourage students to come up with creative ways of approaching problems.

The process of how students reach a solution is at least as important as finding the correct answer. Teachers encourage students to use their own background and knowledge of the world to reach solutions unique to them. Problems must, therefore, be centered in the real world and applicable to the age group and interest of students.

■ *Make dialogue an integral part of the teaching process.* Effective teachers make dialogue the central means for teaching and learning. Students are engaged in discussion about their learning, not only with the teacher but with each other, and are constantly called on to explain or justify their responses to others. Throughout the process, student language is not devalued.

■ *Use cooperative learning activities in the classroom.* Cooperative learning is a way of promoting respect, understanding, and positive relations in a diverse classroom by encouraging students to work together in small groups to maximize their own learning and that of their peers (Johnson, Johnson, & Holubec, 1984). Cooperative tasks can encourage teamwork, intercultural understanding, and positive interactions when group members realize that they must combine their talents and abilities to complete the required task. Leadership responsibilities are shared, and students learn to help each other succeed.

Lesson Planning

An experienced teacher's lesson plans are usually little more than a written outline to follow. The lesson plan may describe the instructional goal, the behavioral objective, the activity, and the materials needed, but these plans usually serve as a means for teachers to organize their thoughts. Much more planning occurs in the teacher's mind than is ever written on the lesson plan.

For preservice teachers observing in an experienced teacher's classroom, this internalized decision making can be deceiving. Because extensive lesson plans are not written down in detail, some may think little planning was done prior to the lesson. When teachers are beginning to learn how to plan, clearly written lesson plans provide a necessary reminder of the thought processes that experienced teachers may have internalized through many years of practice.

Teachers often experiment with several different formats for lesson plans until they find one that works well with their particular style of instruction. Most lesson plans have some basic components in common as they guide a teacher through planning and teaching these important components of a lesson:

- *Objectives.* The learning outcome described in an objective is what students should be able to do on completion of the lesson. The language of the objective must be specific enough so that the learning can be measured and student outcome is observable. However, the often rigidly stated behavior objectives of the 1970s fit better with cognitive objectives. Objectives help teachers answer important questions about student learning. Were students able to achieve the objective? How did they demonstrate their understanding?

- *Motivation/introduction.* Starting a lesson and gaining the attention of the learner is a critical, and often overlooked, part of teaching a lesson. Each lesson should begin with an instructional focus that prepares the learner for active engagement in the lesson and should be designed to arouse curiosity and interest. Depending on the readiness of the learners and on the learning environment, this activity can be as simple as leading the class in a review of a previous lesson on insects or as complicated as a dramatic retelling in costume of the Gettysburg Address. Student motivation must be taken into account when planning a successful opening, and all students must be actively engaged in the lesson from the very beginning. In classrooms with young learners, this may mean physically moving students to a location in the room where they can focus on instruction. The introduction is also the time to inform students, in vocabulary suitable to the age group, about the objective of the lesson and what they will be required to do at the completion of the lesson to demonstrate understanding.

- *Teaching activities.* The direct instruction segment of the lesson is the time to help students recall past learning. Previously learned information can be recalled from experiences outside of school or from the lesson the previous day, but the connection to past learning is critical. The actual teaching portion of the lesson can take many forms. A teacher can guide a whole class in a discussion of new concepts, or students can work together in small groups to discover new learnings. Whatever the format, careful planning is necessary to ensure maximum time on-task.

- *Student activities.* Students need the opportunity to interact with new concepts and learning materials independent of the teacher. Student activities provide necessary practice for students to achieve the objective. Activities can involve everything from independent seatwork or lab activities to creative writing and art demonstrations.

Teachers monitor and provide feedback as students practice and interact with the materials.

- *Closure/evaluation.* At the close of the lesson, a teacher restates the learning objectives, summarizes the activities, and provides opportunities for students to demonstrate mastery of the objective. The closure of the lesson should have a direct relationship to the objective and the desired outcome. This component is one of the most difficult for beginning teachers because they often are unable to gauge how much time is needed for the other facets of instruction.

- *Classroom management concerns.* Effective teachers provide a positive learning environment in the classroom where students feel safe from physical and emotional abuse—a classroom climate free of intimidation, insult, and criticism. Talking about respecting others is not enough. The environment of the classroom must encourage students to display responsible behavior and discourage abusive and disrespectful behavior. Effective teachers do not assume that students come to school with strong interpersonal and social skills. They teach these important life skills along with the academic subjects. Planning for classroom management concerns should be part of the lesson planning process. How should students move from one activity to another to ensure little wasted time? Which students might have difficulty working together? Where in the lesson might potential problems develop?

You may learn more about creating lesson plans at:

http://www.ericsp.org/

URLs may change over time. For up-to-date links to relevant Web sites, visit our Companion Web site:

http://education.wadsworth.com/wiseman3e

▶ *Evaluation and Assessment*

Structured evaluations, anecdotal records, interviews and interest inventories, and student self-evaluations are all traditional ways that teachers can stay informed about their students' learning. A more recent trend in assessment and evaluation is the portfolio system. Traditionally used by artists, actors, and models to demonstrate their work and potential, portfolios allow students to demonstrate their work and potential by collecting samples, examples, and responses to chronicle their learning, growth, and development. A portfolio is a collection of materials indicating an individual's thinking, problem-solving abilities, attitudes, beliefs, and knowledge acquisition. Portfolios are more than collections of responses to class assignments; they include self-reflections, summaries of work, and descriptions of students' work.

The lesson plan in Figure 8.2 was completed by a preservice teacher as part of a thematic unit on ecology and habitats for first-graders. Notice how carefully she planned out each part of her lesson—estimating the time needed for each part of the lesson, writing notes to herself on questions and content information, and anticipating possible classroom management concerns before they occurred. Evaluation of the lesson focused on student performance and was linked closely to the objective. Although the formal lesson plan does not show it, the teacher's reflection on what worked and what could be improved in each lesson component is an important part of informal evaluation of instruction.

FIGURE 8.2   Sample Lesson Plan

Week One, Day One
General Introduction, First Grade

OBJECTIVE (WHAT STUDENTS SHOULD BE ABLE TO DO AFTER COMPLETING THE LESSON):

- The students will be able to define the terms "ecology" and "habitat" in their own words.

MATERIALS NEEDED (ALL THE RESOURCES NEEDED TO TEACH THE LESSON):

- Word cards (ecology and habitat)

- *Professor Noah's Spaceship* by Brian Wildsmith

WHAT I WANT TO ACCOMPLISH (PERSONAL TEACHING GOAL FOR THIS LESSON):

- I want the students to have a basic understanding of the terms "ecology" and "habitat" because the rest of the unit will build on these terms.

FOCUS AREA (IF SOMEONE WERE OBSERVING THIS LESSON, I WOULD WANT THEM TO HELP ME BY CONCENTRATING ON THE FOLLOWING . . .):

- Are the students on-task? Have I organized the discussion to ensure everyone the opportunity to participate?

(continued)

Sample Lesson Plan (continued)

Brief Outline of Lesson and Times (step-by-step description):

MOTIVATION/INTRODUCTION: 2–3 MIN.

- Show printed vocabulary word cards and ask students to predict their pronunciation and meaning. Record predictions.

TEACHING PROCEDURES AND STUDENT ACTIVITY: 5–8 MIN.

1. Show and pronounce the first word (ecology) and have students tell what they may already know about the word.

Once prior knowledge is activated, then add to definitions to provide a clear understanding. Ecology is the relationship between an organism and its environment. Different animals live in all different parts of the world and do different things to survive in their environments. The way humans treat these different places affects the health of the animals who live there. What are some things that people may do to prevent animals from being able to live in a certain place anymore? (pollute, litter, cut down trees, destroy environment)

2. Repeat step one with the word "habitat." 5–8 minutes

Explain that the different parts of the world where animals live and grow are called habitats. As humans, we need a special kind of habitat. What are some of the different things humans need to live and grow? Name them (food, shelter, clothing). What kind of habitat do we need? Could we live in the forest or desert? Because all animals are different and need different things to live and grow, all habitats are different. Think about all the different kinds of animals and where they live. Can anyone name some habitats? (desert, forest, swamp, rain forest)

3. Share book with students. 10–12 min.

Today I am going to share a book with you about animals that live in a forest as their habitat. They live there happily until something happens to their habitat. Listen while I read the book aloud and then we will talk about it.

4. Ask higher-level thinking questions. 5–8 min.

- What part of the story could really happen? Could not really happen?
- Are the animals in our world in danger? Why or why not? Share pictures of panda bears and black rhinos.
- How can we help solve this problem?

5. Share information on chart tablet with students. 8–10 min.

Have one student read a part of this summary information and then discuss what the student has read. Have the class read this part chorally. Continue this process until all the information is shared.

CLOSURE/EVALUATION (HOW DO STUDENTS DEMONSTRATE NEW LEARNING?): 5–8 MIN.

Return to the predictions of the meaning for "habitat" and "ecology" and have students decide what predictions were correct. Each student will then write or dictate a simple definition of each new vocabulary word in their own words.

CLASSROOM MANAGEMENT CONCERNS (WHERE CAN PROBLEMS BE ANTICIPATED AND PLANNED FOR?):

- Have all materials ready to share.
- Have brainstorming chart paper available.
- Watch the transition to and from floor—plan for orderly transition.
- Enforce good listening skills—raising hands.

Becoming a Reflective Teacher

Teachers who are effective in classes with a wide range of student differences are self-reflective about their own attitudes, beliefs, and actions. They constantly work to recognize and eliminate teacher expectations based on race, class, and gender and are continually asking questions at the completion of each lesson, looking for the strengths and weaknesses that will have an impact on future improvements. Here are some questions you can ask yourself after teaching your lesson:

- What was the most effective part of the lesson? The least effective?
- What were students most enthusiastic about and why?
- If you had the opportunity to teach this lesson again, what would you do the same? What would you do differently?
- Were there any surprises, and how did you handle them?

Using the following sample lesson plan or one provided to you by your instructor, plan a lesson that you will teach in your field-based placement.

LESSON PLAN OUTLINE

   I. Objective

   II. Materials needed

   III. What I want to accomplish

   IV. Focus area

   V. Procedure

      a. Motivation/introduction

      b. Teaching procedures and student activities

      c. Closure/evaluation

   VI. Evaluation and assessment

   VII. Classroom management concerns

INTASC Principles 2, 3, 4, 5, 6, and 7

Reflecting on Learning

Successful teachers maintain high expectations for all students, and the influence of teacher expectations on student achievement is strong (Good & Brophy, 1999). Teachers' attitudes about students and resulting actions can help or hurt student performance. Teachers can perpetuate self-fulfilling prophecies in ways that influence their students' beliefs about themselves. Teachers' interactions with students reflect their expectations about performance. Eventually, students conform to these expectations, and teachers' beliefs become reality. Teachers can also influence student achievement by sustaining effects. In this case, a teacher expects a certain academic performance from a student because of past experience and fails to see any change in that pattern even when student behavior actually changes. Teachers translate their expectations in a variety of ways. Low-achieving students are often located farther away from the teacher in the classroom and receive less time to respond to a teacher's questions, less attention, fewer opportunities to answer questions, and less feedback on responses. Self-reflection and careful monitoring of classroom response patterns can help teachers see when lowered expectations are keeping students from higher academic achievement.

It has long been apparent that teachers must become "kid-watchers" and continually work to get to know each individual learner in a crowded classroom of diverse students (Goodman, 1977). "Kid-watching" is crucial during our current phase of accountability. Not only must teachers understand students' formal test achievement, but they also assess student behaviors and performance in less-formal ways during daily interactions. Anecdotal records are notes teachers keep as they observe students' learning. These can be brief notes kept in a notebook or on index cards. Teachers might also record reflections in their lesson plan books about the success of a particular lesson and suggestions for future improvements. One teacher keeps a pad of sticky notes on her seating chart. As she walks around the room observing students, she records the information she observes on the note for that particular student. Later the notes are placed in the child's portfolio.

Anecdotal records readjust teachers' visions of who and where students are and sharpen teachers' insights into how students travel along the paths to learning. Observing children closely as they learn helps teachers understand individual and idiosyncratic child-based standards of growth, accomplishment, and failure (Mathews, 1992).

Peer coaching is defined as "the assistance that one teacher provides another in the development of teaching skills, strategies, or techniques" (Strother, 1989, p. 824). Teachers in peer coaching situations can observe in each other's classrooms, work together on classroom research, study current practices as part of a study team, or just work together to solve common problems. Peers—not supervisors or evaluators—work together to learn more about teaching and learning (Gottesman, 2004). Peer coaching is a form of direct assistance that helps teachers improve instruction: "The process is intended to examine the efficacy of the teacher's practices, not the teacher's competence" (Nolan, Hawkes, & Francis, 1993, p. 53). Peer coaching is a supportive, not evaluative, process that encourages professional, not social, interactions in a school and has a teacher-specified focus (Gottesman, 2004; Robbins, 1991).

Peer coaching requires training and preparation time to be effective. Teachers who will work together are identified and a structure for observation must be agreed on. The two teachers who are working together meet prior to the agreed-on observation time to identify concerns and a focus for the upcoming observation. One inviting teacher asked a peer coach to "map" her movements around the room when she taught to see if she was unintentionally ignoring any students. The observing teacher watched the lesson and drew lines on a seating chart to show the movement of the teacher around the room. Each time the teacher stopped, the observer marked an **X** on the chart. The observation chart was left with the inviting teacher so she could reach her own conclusions. The resulting observation report was clear—a table of students in the front was not receiving the same teacher attention as the rest of the class. In a conference after class, the inviting teacher and the observing teacher discussed possible ways to alleviate the problem and then discussed further areas for focused observation. (Figure 6.2 on page 177 is another observation instrument that teachers can use to help each other improve instruction.)

The Dynamics of Instructional Organization

Teaching lessons and delivery of instruction include long-term, deliberate planning as well as numerous fast-paced daily decisions. Effective teachers establish goals and make plans for an entire year, semester, or week. These plans serve as maps for daily instruction. Not all factors can be taken into account during long-term planning, so effective teachers question their instructional process as they teach, making changes based on how their students respond to what is presented.

Personal philosophy, beliefs, and recognition of students' needs result in unique approaches to day-to-day instruction. A great deal of what a teacher believes about students and teaching will be reflected in the lesson plans. Day-to-day lesson plans are one way that a creative teacher expresses individuality. The decision making associated with planning lessons is a dynamic and ever-changing process that keeps teaching alive and vibrant.

PORTFOLIO REFLECTIONS AND EXHIBITS

Suggested Exhibit 8: Lesson Planning

Your lesson and personal reflection can be added to your teaching portfolio. There are several ways to illustrate your lesson planning and implementation in the portfolio. Possible representations include the following:

- A lesson plan that you designed
- Samples of student work
- Feedback from your university or classroom supervisor
- Pictures of your students participating in the lesson

- Handouts, games, or other supplementary aids you developed to go with your lesson

- Audio and/or video tapes

To complete the representation of your lesson planning, include a self-evaluation and personal reflection about what you learned from presenting your lesson. What went well? What goals do you have for yourself the next time you have an opportunity to plan and teach a lesson? The lesson that you prepared and taught during your introductory class will serve as a benchmark to help you see how you continue to grow throughout your university preparation.

E-Portfolio Entry 8

Develop a technology-based, illustrated representation of the lesson plan you developed and delivered. Include the plan and any handouts you prepared, scan student responses and pictures of your students as thy participated in the lesson. Finally, write a short self-evaluation of your lesson.

INTASC Principles 2, 3, 4, 5, 6, 7, 8 and 9

ANSWERS TO GUIDING YOUR READING

1. How do teachers decide what to teach?

   Teachers use district, state, and national educational goals to guide decisions about what to teach. Other sources that help teachers make instructional decisions include the state and local curriculum and the sequence of textbooks. Finally, teachers take into account the needs and interests of students when making instructional decisions.

2. What instructional resources are available to teachers?

   Teachers seek out materials and resources to support a variety of classroom learning experiences. Textbooks, children- and adolescent-level literature, reference materials, current periodicals, audiovisual aids, computer software, and the Internet are all resources that can be used for instructional planning and lesson delivery.

3. How can teachers use technology in the classroom?

   Modern technology is a tool that can extend teachers' lesson plans in every subject. Through technology, teachers can encourage their students to creatively solve problems, expand their horizons, and explore beyond the classroom. Furthermore, technology is a communication tool that links students to those outside the classroom and helps them make contacts not possible in the past.

4. How is integrated instruction different from discipline-based instruction?

Integrated instruction can be described in two ways. First, teachers can integrate instruction when they embed basic skills instruction (i.e., mathematics computations or grammar) into processes that demonstrate real uses of the skill. In other words, students would learn grammar by writing and learning the skills as they are used in their own work. Integration is also used to describe when two subjects, such as social studies and art, are taught together in themed lessons or units and students learn skills associated with both areas. In contrast, discipline-based instruction occurs when teaching and learning focuses on one subject and deals with topics specific only to that topic.

5. How do teachers plan for individual lessons?

Lesson plans usually follow a structured outline whose several basic components guide a teacher through planning and teaching. The components may include objectives, introductions, teaching activities, student activities, and classroom management concerns. Several lesson plan outlines are available, and most teachers find one that adapts best to their manner of teaching.

6. How can teachers evaluate the success of their teaching?

A teacher's success is judged by how well students learn. Informal and formal evaluations, anecdotal records, and student self-evaluations provide evidence about teachers' successes. Additionally, teachers ask certain questions or discuss and write about the content following a lesson to monitor what their students have learned. Effective teachers also examine their teaching by considering what was successful and changing what they do when necessary. Reflection about one's teaching helps teachers continue to learn and improve their teaching skills.

INFOTRAC COLLEGE EDITION EXTENSION

Log on to the InfoTrac College Edition Web site. To learn more about instructional planning in your content area, pair the term "lesson planning" with a specific content area such as social studies or mathematics and type in a search term similar to the following: lesson planning and mathematics.

Or, if you are interested in finding out how to plan so that you encourage multiple intelligences in your classroom, type in the following: lesson planning and multiple intelligences.

RELATED READINGS

The following books will provide more information about some of the topics and ideas discussed in this chapter:

Armstrong, T. (1994). *Multiple intelligences in the classroom.* Alexandria, VA: Association for Supervision and Curriculum Development.

Armstrong provides an overview of Gardner's theory and gives concrete suggestions to teachers for implementing the multiple intelligences approach in classrooms.

Ladson-Billings, G. (1994). *The dreamkeepers: Successful teachers of African American children.* San Francisco: Jossey-Bass.

This book examines successful teaching and learning strategies used by African American teachers, who tell their own stories in the text. As a result, we are able to envision intellectually rigorous and culturally relevant classrooms. This book will teach you important lessons about teaching all children.

Schaafsma, D. (1993). *Eating on the street: Teaching literacy in a multicultural society.* Pittsburgh: University of Pittsburgh Press.

You will learn about cultural differences and how they can affect instruction as you read this account of seven teachers who guided fifth-, sixth-, and seventh-graders to explore, interpret, and write about their community.

Sternberg, R., & Grigorenko, E. (2000). *Teaching for successful intelligence.* Arlington Heights, IL: Skylights.

This easy-to-read book includes specific lessons and units for building successful intelligence abilities.

REFERENCES

Epigraph: Esquith, Rafe. *There are no shortcuts* (p. 54). New York: Pantheon.

Allington, R., & McGill-Franzen, A. (1989). School response to reading failure: Chapter 1 and special education students in grades 2, 4, and 8. *Elementary School Journal, 89,* 529–542.

Aschlbacher, P. R. (1991). Humanitas: A thematic curriculum. *Educational Leadership, 49*(2), 9–16.

Banks, J. A. (1995). Multicultural education: Historical development, dimensions, and practice. In J. A. Banks & C. M. Banks (Eds.), *Handbook on research in multicultural education* (pp. 3–42). New York: Macmillan.

Bruder, I. (1991). Guide to multimedia: How it changes the way we teach and learn. *Electronic Learning, 11*(1), 22–26.

Caine, R. M., & Caine, G. (1994). *Making connections: Teaching and the human brain.* Palo Alto, CA: Addison-Wesley.

Carr, E., & Ogle, D. (1987). K-W-L plus: A strategy for comprehension and summarization. *Journal of Reading, 30*(7), 626–631.

Clarke, C., & Peterson, P. (1986). Teachers' thought processes. In M. R. Whitrock (Ed.), *Handbook of research on teaching* (3rd ed., pp. 255–296). New York: Macmillan.

Clarke, J. H., & Agne, R. M. (Eds.). (1996). *Interdisciplinary high school teaching: Strategies for integrated learning.* Boston: Allyn & Bacon.

Falk, B. (2000). *The heart of the matter: Using standards and assessment to learn.* Portsmouth, NH: Heinemann.

Franzee, B., & Rudnitski, R. (1996). *Integrated teaching methods: Theory, classroom applications, and field-based connections.* Albany, NY: Delmar.

Gardner, H. (1983). *Frames of mind: The theory of multiple intelligences.* New York: Basic Books.

Gardner, H. (1991). *The unschooled mind: How children think and how schools should teach.* New York: Basic Books.

Gardner, H. (1995). Reflection on multiple intelligences: Myths and messages. *Phi Delta Kappan, 77,* 200–210.

Gardner, H. (2000). *Intelligence reframed: Multiple intelligence for the 21st century.* New York: Basic Books

Goleman, D. (1997). *Emotional intelligence.* New York: Bantam.

Good, T., & Brophy, J. (1999). *Looking in classrooms* (8th ed.). New York: Longman.

Goodlad, J. I. (1984). *A place called school.* New York: McGraw-Hill.

Goodman, Y. (1977). Kid watching: An alternative to testing. *Elementary Principal, 57,* 41–45.

Gottesman, B. (2004). *Peer coaching for educators.* Lanham, MD: Scarecrow.

Hawkins, J., & Collins, A. (1992). Design-experiments for infusing technology into learning. *Educational Technology, 33*(6), 26–31.

Jacobs, H. H. (1989). *Interdisciplinary curriculum: Design, development, and implementation.* Alexandria, VA: Association for Supervision and Curriculum Development.

Johnson, D. W., Johnson, R. T., & Holubec, R. (1984). *Circles of learning: Coopera-tion in the classroom.* Alexandria, VA: Association for Supervision and Curriculum Development.

Jonassen, D. (1986). Hypertext principles for text and courseware design. *Educational Psychologist,* 21, 269–292.

Jonassen, D. H. (2000). *Computers as mindtools for schools.* Upper Saddle River, NJ: Merrill.

Jonassen, D. H., Peck, K. L., & Wilson, B. G. (1999). *Learning with technology: A constructivist perspective.* Upper Saddle River, NJ: Merrill.

Knapp, M., & Shields, P. (1990). Reconceiving academic instruction for the children of poverty. *Phi Delta Kappan,* 71(10), 753–758.

Knapp, M. S., Shields, P., & Turnball, B. (1995). Academic challenge in high-poverty classrooms. *Phi Delta Kappan,* 76(10), 770–776.

Mathews, C. (1992). An alternative portfolio: Gathering one child's literacies. In D. Graves & B. Sunstein (Eds.), *Portfolio portraits* (pp. 158–170). Portsmouth, NH: Heinemann.

Means, B., & Knapp, M. (1991). Cognitive approaches to teaching advanced skills to educationally disadvantaged students. *Phi Delta Kappan,* 72(4), 282–289.

Nolan, J., Hawkes, B., & Francis, P. (1993). Case studies: Windows onto clinical supervision. *Educational Leadership,* 51(2), 52–56.

Robbins, P. (1991). *How to plan and implement a peer coaching program.* Alexandria, VA: Association for Supervision and Curriculum Development.

Sizer, T. (1984). *Horace's compromise: The dilemma of the American high school.* Boston: Houghton Mifflin.

Sternberg, R. (1985). *Beyond IQ: A triarchic theory of human intelligence.* New York: Cambridge University Press.

Sternberg, R. (1990). *Metaphors of mind: Conceptions of the nature of intelligence.* New York: Cambridge University Press.

Strother, D. (1989). Peer coaching for teachers: Opening classroom doors. *Phi Delta Kappan,* 70(10), 824–827.

Tyler, R. W. (1974). Considerations in selecting objectives. In D. A. Payne (Ed.), *Curriculum evaluation: Commentaries on purpose, process, product.* Lexington, MA: D. C. Heath.

Wepner, S. B., Valmont, W. J., & Thurlow, R. (2000). *Linking literacy and technology: A guide for K-8 classrooms.* Newark, DE: International Reading Association.

Wilson, K. (1991). New tools for new learning opportunities. *Technology and Learning,* 11(7), 12–13.

9

School Contexts, Organization, and Leadership

Alphonse Laudato, the principal, arrived first in the morning and did not leave until long after most teachers went home. During the day, Al roamed the hallways, a short man in an oxford shirt with a clip-on necktie and, though in his forties, very trim. He had gone to college to play baseball and football he said, and had drifted into education. He looked like an athlete. He rarely stayed still.

Al belonged to Kelly School, and Kelly School belonged to Al. He once said, "I'm responsible for every teacher who walks in this door. Not that I'm in charge of everybody, the only one in charge, but I'm responsible. Come in, talk, and I'll decide if we're going to do it."...

On really important matters, he usually did what was best for the students. Somehow he always seemed to find the money for new books or materials or field trips. She [Chris, a teacher at Kelly School] thought Kelly's classes remained small partly because of Al's clever budgeting. She gathered that Al sometimes fell out of favor on Suffolk Street, school administration head-quarters, but she thought it significant that during the first crucial year of desegregation, Suffolk Street had sent Al to Kelly to soothe the white parents who had demanded proof that their children would be safe down in the Flats. Al, with a great deal of help from the chief secretary, Lil, kept the school running smoothly. The office of the Director of Bilingual Education for the city was situated in Al's school. At least once a year Al would pick a fight with that department over some small administrative matter. The director insisted though, that he could easily forgive Al because of the way Al ran Kelly School.

—Tracy Kidder, *Among Schoolchildren*

Guiding Your Reading

1. What are some of the characteristics of schools in urban, suburban, and rural settings?

2. How are schools organized?

3. What leaders take responsibility for schools?

4. What are some of the ways that teachers demonstrate leadership?

5. How can preservice teachers demonstrate leadership?

*W*hen you begin your formal training to become a teacher, you will probably focus primarily on the twenty-five children facing you in an elementary classroom or the one hundred to two hundred students that cycle through a secondary teacher's classroom in one day. Your attention to the classroom is not unusual. Beginning teachers are typically most concerned about lesson plans, materials, and the classroom management techniques that will help them get through the day-to-day teaching process. They attend to their own classroom, planning for instruction and interacting with their students. Although understanding the basics necessary to run a classroom is vital, there is much more to being a teacher than what happens inside the classroom. Many other tasks and people contribute to teaching and learning. Interactions within an organizational structure and with the leaders of schools are important aspects of day-to-day teaching routines and activities. Teachers are part of a large, complex organization requiring numerous professional interactions.

The nature of teachers' professional interactions will be greatly influenced by the context of the school. The community and neighborhood where the school is located, the grade level of the classrooms, and even the arrangement of the school will make a difference in teachers' responsibilities and roles. The characteristics of city, suburban, and rural locations will interact with the grade level arrangements and contribute to the educational context.

School leadership plays an important role in teachers' work and establishes the context of any school. Educational leaders have a great deal of responsibility, not only to the students but also to teachers, the community, and even governmental bodies. Educational leaders are responsible for establishing the vision, goals, and accountability systems for schools. The traditional requirements of school leaders such as superintendents, principals, and supervisors can be carried out in different ways depending on contexts, philosophies, and personal styles. The role of an educational leader is expanding and changing to meet the needs of increased student diversity in today's schools. Recently, school leadership has been expanded to encompass roles that many teachers play (Lambert, 1998).

One advantage of becoming a teacher in a field-based setting is that it provides immediate exposure to the whole context of a school and a school district. Preservice teachers in school–university partnerships who are formulating their professional identity will learn that teaching is not an autonomous job with teachers and learners working behind classroom doors. They will learn about the organizational structures, leadership roles, and the multiple responsibilities of teachers that are routine in today's educational settings.

▶ Community Contexts

The location of schools and the size of the community affect teachers' day-to-day working conditions and environments. Small districts may serve fewer than five hundred students, whereas large metropolitan districts such as New York City, Los Angeles, or Chicago educate thousands of children. Smaller schools, such as Snook, Texas, or Genoa, Illinois, may have only one superintendent and a single building for an entire Pre K-12 school. Large districts like New York City have multiple superintendents, school boards, and administrators, and hundreds of buildings to maintain. Schools across our nation have different organizational, administrative, and leadership systems, but all work with children and families who have diverse experiences, talents, and concerns. Urban, suburban, and rural schools develop educational contexts that reflect the values and expectations of the surrounding communities. Providing the best educational environments, meeting the challenges of a diverse society, and using available resources to their maximum benefit become the focus for the staff of any school, no matter where it is located. Size, contexts, poverty, student diversity, and community identity are all distinguishing characteristics of schools.

Urban Schools

Because all schools interact with their environment, the problems faced by urban areas are also present in schools (Forsyth & Tallerico, 1993). Cities are often described as being in crisis. Instances of crime, deteriorating school

Schools are located in many different environments. Their locations— whether in cities, towns, suburbs, or rural settings—provide different educational challenges and rewards.

facilities, and teacher burnout are common in portrayals of urban schools. Actually, reports about conditions in urban schools are somewhat ambivalent, presenting both negative and positive views of what it is like to be a student in a large city school.

On the negative side, the schools in our large cities have been associated with crisis for many years, and the statistics depicting their failures are often overwhelming. Urban schools are perceived as being plagued with insurmountable problems, often failing the students who attend. Cities across the country regularly report dismal academic results (Rist, 2000). In 1990, only 10 percent of the tenth-graders in Chicago were able to read; graduating seniors in New Orleans were reading at levels lower than 80 percent of the graduating seniors anywhere else in the United States; and over half of Houston's elementary students were repeating grades because of unsatisfactory progress (Englert, 1993). Urban schools are also faced with extraordinary challenges. Students in urban schools are more than twice as likely to be assigned to special education classes and to live in poverty. They are also far more likely to have difficulty speaking English, to drop out of school, and to change schools more often (Plisko, 2003). Not only are the problems complex, they are long-term. With the exception of a few cities, an overwhelming amount of evidence suggests that conditions in many urban schools have worsened in the last twenty-five years (Englert, 1993; Ouchi, 2003; Rist, 2000). Historically, test scores of urban students have been lower than those of suburban students, and students in city schools have continued to achieve at levels lower than those in suburban and rural schools (Ornstein & Levine, 1989). Some cities report dropout rates as high as 70 percent among some student demographics (National Center for Education Statistics, 2001).

On the positive side, during the past decade, urban schools have focused on improving student achievement and have achieved some degree of success. Nevertheless, issues of diversity, economic conditions, and teacher quality continue to present major challenges for large school districts. One indisputable fact about teaching in urban schools is that a richness and variety of diverse cultures and ethnicities are present. Minorities make up a large share of city dwellers, and the numbers continue to increase. In the one hundred largest U.S. school districts, 69 percent of students are minorities, compared with 39 percent in other school districts—making urban school populations more ethnically and culturally diverse (National Center for Education Statistics, 2001). Urban-dwelling minorities represent a mix of racial and ethnic groups, with no single group dominating. The makeup of urban school students is constantly changing. The percentage of African American students in central cities has been fairly constant for more than twenty years, but the number of Hispanic students has more than doubled. Furthermore, new immigration from Middle Eastern and Asian countries continues to increase the cultural and linguistic challenges for urban schools (Crosby, 1999). Increased heterogeneity of the city populations has an impact on educational strategies and human relationships, making it crucial for teachers and school administrators to welcome and understand cultural and ethnic diversity.

The diversity in city schools is exacerbated by the great range of socioeconomic statuses among students' families, notably an especially high number of children from economically disadvantaged families. In fact, poverty is a fundamental issue in the crisis status of educational and other social institutions in cities (see Chapter 5). Over half of students in the largest cities in the United States are eligible for free and reduced lunch (National Center for Education Statistics, 2001), so urban schools face the challenge of educating many students who live in poverty. Poverty affects all aspects of students' lives, and educators often find themselves dealing with issues such as health, social services, and housing to help provide the basics for their students. Transportation and housing become major issues in urban students' lives. Children and young people who live in the city tend to have more health-related problems than young people in other areas. All the characteristics that poverty inflicts on families can affect the education of city children.

Teachers often find themselves struggling with the inequities present in city schools. In addition to (and partly because of) the tasks emerging from diversity and economic challenges, city schools have difficulty identifying and retaining qualified teachers, especially minority teachers. Most students in urban schools will be from racial and/or linguistic "minority" groups, but teachers continue to be mostly white, female, and monolingual (Pang & Gibson, 2001). This is particularly evident in subjects such as science and math. Salaries are not as high as they might be in suburban schools and, because of the contextual and environmental conditions (e.g., no supplies, buildings in disrepair, dangerous locations), city teachers combat high turnover and morale problems. "But it is the intensity of working for and caring about students in urban schools that makes effective urban teachers different from their counterparts in the suburbs" (Gordon, 1999, p. 304). The political, demographic, and economic diversity combined with the scarce resources of most urban school districts make it difficult to maintain the same learning standards as those in better-equipped, well-funded schools in other settings (Urban Institute, 1995). Urban teachers must understand their students and deal with tough situations in a caring manner, all the while focusing on student achievement and high learning standards.

Despite the grim picture, many examples of effective urban schools exist (Casserly, 2004). Cities have long been identified with educational innovation and reform and, as a result, have been the source of miraculous and confirming success stories of improving school conditions. Houston, Seattle, and Chicago report recent improvements in conditions at their schools and increases in student achievement as measured by standardized tests. Houston, for example, reported that 85 percent of their eighth-graders passed the Stanford 9 achievement text (up from only a 50 percent passing rate in 1994) (Ouchi, 2003).

Teachers also cite the benefits of teaching in city schools: The diversity of inner cities offers a richness and tolerance for a wider range of behavior. More community support and attention to educational quality increase the political power and special interest group activity that provide support for educational issues. Large cities also offer more economic, cultural, financial, religious, and noneducational resources to educational institutions.

One of the most hopeful signs that urban schools can meet the numerous demands of the setting is that educators are now promoting smaller and more personal schools (Pipho, 1995). Supported in part by grants from the Bill and Melinda Gates Foundation, New York City has pioneered by opening smaller high schools whose attendance ranges from 110 to 600 students. The Gates's small schools project provided financial support and guidance for the creation of ten new small high schools and for breaking five existing high schools into smaller units. These schools are characterized by a great deal of interaction among parents, teachers, and students, and these small, creative learning environments offer some hope for success. Los Angeles is also considering breaking up its large high schools into smaller schools.

In a separate but similar trend, some inner-city school districts, such as Philadelphia, have attempted to establish contracts with private companies to set up plans and programs to improve educational systems. Privatization of schools was a popular idea a few years ago and is still a trend to watch closely.

Even though urban school teaching has been identified as one of the most stressful career choices (Farris, 1996), many teachers feel that the rewards are great. Teachers who are socially oriented look forward to the challenges of inner-city schools. Curriculum is designed to encourage diversity of all kinds and to enable students to examine the social realities of their world and bring the richness of the urban setting into the classroom.

You may learn more about urban school settings at the following Web sites:

http://eric-web.tc.columbia.edu/

http://www.cgcs.org/

URLs may change over time. For up-to-date links to relevant Web sites, visit our Companion Web site:

http://education.wadsworth.com/wiseman3e

Private schools also play an important role in the education of city students, and many new teachers choose to begin their careers in schools supported by churches or other nonpublic resources. Whether they work in public or private schools, teachers who succeed in inner-city schools experience challenges and rewards not as evident in other settings, and these educators have a fierce commitment to urban school reform.

Suburban Schools

Suburban school districts are typically located outside of large cities. In many cases, urban dwellers have left the city and relocated to leave the problems associated with inner-city settings. Traditionally viewed as a middle-class white environment, more middle-class and affluent minority families have been moving to the suburbs, particularly those outside the largest metropolitan areas (Population Reference Bureau, 1999). Rising incomes among African American families and other minorities have also enabled them to move to suburban settings where parents believe their

Voice of a Teacher

I teach at an urban middle school located in a neighborhood that is rich in African American history. More recently it has also been the home of Hispanics and other immigrants from all over the world. It is a wonderful neighborhood with a great deal of character that matches the culturally diverse people that work and live in the area. For years, the area was home to many minorities who were able to buy and rent affordable housing in the area. Now, the lovely Victorian brownstone homes are being bought by young professionals who can walk downtown to work. The new residents are remodeling the homes, and new restaurants and shops are appearing along the streets. Most recently a large condo filled with urban flats was built in the middle of the neighborhood. And of course, the inevitable green logo of that popular coffeehouse chain has appeared on the corner. The gentrification of the neighborhood has greatly affected the neighborhood where my school is located. I am concerned that many of my students' families will not be able to afford to live here much longer.

So far, the neighborhood changes have yet to change the makeup of my classroom. I am the only one in my classroom that is not black or Hispanic. The neighborhood where my students have spent most of their lives is a rough place to grow up. However, my students have had rich experiences that enliven classroom discussions and writings. I find hidden talents as they tell me stories, dramatize their lives, and share their dreams. My students have taught me a great deal. They are vibrant kids that care a great deal about their families, friends, and community. I wake up every morning knowing that I am blessed to teach the kids of this city and neighborhood. I wouldn't change my job for the world.

children will have access to better schools (Richard, 2000). The new residents of suburban settings join the established middle-class families that have lived there for years, making suburban schools more diverse than they have been in the past.

The concentration of middle-class, working professionals in suburbs results in the perception of more affluent neighborhoods and a school population coming from two-parent families, a mother in the home, and parents with more time and resources to spend with their children. But in reality, suburban schools vary in their makeup and approach to education.

The number of students living in poverty and the severity of other social problems may not be as great or as concentrated as in urban settings, but they are still present in suburban contexts. Some neighborhoods include low-income housing, whereas others are upscale and affluent, creating a great contrast between school settings in suburban areas.

Shuttered businesses and families living in poverty are evident in some older established suburban neighborhoods, but more often rapid, sprawling growth is changing the nature of living in suburbia. Even the definition of suburbia is changing. Once considered to have strong links to a large city, new suburban developments are not as economically dependent on nearby cities, and many of these areas are developing as unique communities.

Suburban students face many of the challenges of the inner city, but in addition, they may face problems associated with working families. A high percentage of single or married working parents leave for work before their children go to school, and these parents arrive home long after school is out. In many households, students either are in childcare facilities or are latchkey children. Many schools offer before- and after-school programs so that students are not unattended when parents are out of the home. On the other hand, older students who do not take part in extracurricular activities, volunteer, work part-time, or participate in church or other outside-of-school organizations have very little supervision after school.

Because suburban parents have higher incomes, the tax base provides resources and tax support not available to inner-city schools. Suburban schools are able to build and repair physical facilities, equip their schools with up-to-date technology, and pay their teachers well. Suburban schools usually have substantial flexibility in their curriculum and offer courses that prepare students for postsecondary educational opportunities. Furthermore, they can generally offer a wider range of extracurricular activities to accompany basic coursework.

Suburban teachers and administrators are more highly educated and better paid than their counterparts in urban and rural settings. Suburban schools are the settings where most beginning teachers imagine themselves teaching. Teachers experience different challenges in suburban schools than do teachers in urban or rural schools. Parents and students expect a great deal from their schools, and parents are vocal if they do not feel their children are getting the education they deserve. Suburban families focus on test scores and entrance into college, and teachers must have the same expectations.

Suburbs must come to grips with dramatic changes in their communities and schools in the near future (Richard, 2000). School enrollment is growing rapidly, making it difficult for schools to meet the demands on their buildings, budgets, and teachers. The most far-reaching change in the future of suburban schools remains the increasing diversity of socio-economic, racial, ethnic, and age groups that accompanies fast population growth. Suburban schools already experience increasing diversity as Americans of different ethnicities purchase homes and move to new developments outside the city. Many suburban locations are becoming more international as immigrants bypass the cities and settle in the nearby communities. The changing nature of suburban communities will certainly affect the educational context where teachers work and live.

Rural Schools

The U.S. government defines rural areas as nonmetropolitan communities with fewer than 2,500 inhabitants or fewer than 1,000 inhabitants per square mile (Herzog & Pittman, 1995). Since the 1800s, the flow of the U.S. population has been from rural locations to urban and suburban communities. Nevertheless, numerous small rural school districts still exist. Nationally, 27 percent of all school districts are small and rural, and just under 20 percent of elementary and secondary students are educated in rural settings (U.S. Department of Education, 2004). Rural schools have different challenges. Schools serving a ski resort in Colorado do not face the same issues as one located on an island off the coast of Maine or in a small town near a pineapple field in Hawaii.

Rural communities are changing as farming and other agriculture-related occupations continue to evolve. Large farming operations, fast food, and nationally based retailers have all affected the economy of rural America. Many families have remained in the same community for decades, but family mobility is becoming more and more evident due to the lack of jobs, availability of low-rent housing, and the lower living expenses in rural areas. Children of long-term farm community residents move to the city to find work, and new families who wish to take advantage of the lower living expenses in rural areas move into houses next to long-time residents. A thirty-year decline in job opportunities has forced many students in rural schools to seek training that will take them away from their homes to work in more populated areas. Simultaneously, the declining population rates in rural areas now seem to be reversing. In the 1990s the population of rural areas grew at the same rate or faster than other areas of the nation, and many communities experienced a rebirth of sorts (Huang, 1999). Population growth requires that new businesses and services are available, thus contributing to the local economy. Many rural schools have benefited from the improved financial conditions and from the steady income growth that comes from new jobs and resources resulting from increasing population.

Rural communities offer a great deal of diversity and share many of the problems that urban and suburban schools have, although on a smaller scale. Problems of violence and crime are evident in small towns, but not at the same level as in more populated areas. Poverty is traditionally associated with inner-city settings, but a great amount of poverty is also located in rural areas—particularly in Appalachia and other locations in the South. Even though poverty has been somewhat alleviated by recent economic growth, more than one-quarter of rural residents live just above the poverty line (Huang, 1999). Other than central cities, rural areas have the highest rate of poverty in our country (Dewees, 1999). Such a large proportion of families having marginal income status has a great impact on rural schools' present and future. As a result, rural schools are typically smaller and poorer than nonrural schools (Herzog & Pittman, 1995). Rural school districts may have difficulty raising the resources needed to finance education, maintain existing schools, and build new facilities for growing school enrollments. Just as in city schools, poverty affects students' ability to learn, and educators are often involved in finding social services and support for low-income families.

Some of the positive stereotypes of rural communities, such as close connections with community and family, a slower pace of life, and close contact with agriculture and nature, suggest strengths associated with small community contexts. Schools are often the center of community life, with school activities such as Friday night football and basketball games the focus of the week's events (Farris, 1996). A sense of community, small businesses, and small settlements of people where everyone knows and watches out for one another are also positive aspects of rural contexts. A close-knit family feeling characterizes schools in rural areas, even though students and parents may be critical of the facilities and resources (Herzog & Pittman, 1995).

Rural settings are facing great challenges from the same socioeconomic issues that affect both urban and suburban areas. Rural populations are predicted to continue growing at a faster rate than populations in other settings, and diversity will likely increase in some areas. South Texas, Arizona, New Mexico, and California already host large immigrant populations (Huang, 1999). By far the largest number of immigrants settling in these western rural environments are Mexican, but other immigrant populations are also increasing in other rural areas. Rural schools that teach large numbers of immigrants must somehow determine how to increase their spending and include appropriate instruction for these concentrated immigrant populations.

Certain other characteristics are associated with rural schools. Historically, vocational and agriculture programs have been important in rural schools, but the decline in jobs associated with these professions has changed the look of rural education. Rural students have higher graduation rates than urban students, but fewer students from rural contexts attend postsecondary schools (DeYoung & Lawrence, 1995). Community colleges are becoming important options for rural students to pursue educational opportunities beyond high school.

One unique rural educational issue is the ambivalence of parents regarding educational experiences that prepare their children for work in cities and large urban areas. Rural young people who are educated tend to leave their community to find work (DeYoung & Lawrence, 1995). Older community members believe rural life is preferable to urban life, and they feel that education takes young people away from the rural contexts. This belief may cause rural voters to reject referendums that would provide money and resources for rural schools.

Teachers and administrators in rural areas tend to be less experienced and lower paid than their counterparts in metropolitan areas (Herzog & Pittman, 1995), and rural schools often have difficulty attracting teachers. The slower lifestyle of rural communities and the isolation from cultural and recreational centers discourage beginning teachers from looking for jobs in small towns. Rural schools may not always be able to provide the range of courses offered in larger schools because they lack certified teachers for advance placement courses in foreign language or higher-level math and sciences. Rural teachers may therefore need to teach a wider range of courses than they would in larger school districts. They often have more opportunities to assist with extracurricular activities such as coaching, cheerleading, or debate teams. Many rural areas are holding out hope that new technologies will provide new ways to offer courses not currently available.

 You may learn more about rural school settings at the following Web sites:

http://www.nces.ed.gov/surveys/ruraled/

http://www.ruralchallengepolicy.org

URLs may change over time. For up-to-date links to relevant Web sites, visit our Companion Web site:

http://education.wadsworth.com/wiseman3e

Teachers often choose to teach in rural schools because they find it easier to become part of the community and to interact with the families of their students. They also enjoy teaching a wider range of courses and having opportunities to become involved in leadership and school activities. Rural schools provide exciting challenges and offer teachers a career choice that is shaped by the small community context.

FIELD-BASED ACTIVITY

9.1

Identify some of the salient characteristics of your school. Where is it located? How does its location affect its context? Does your school have unique problems because of its location? Do the characteristics of your school match descriptions of urban, suburban, or rural locations described in this chapter?

INTASC Principle 3

Organizational Contexts

Traditionally, school organization was rather simple. Most schools were divided into elementary, junior high, and secondary schools. Usually kindergarten through sixth-grade classes were grouped together in elementary schools, grades seven and eight made up the junior highs, and ninth through twelfth grades were identified as high school. Innovations and new understandings have increased the options for and acceptance of several different school organization patterns. There is no longer a "standard" arrangement for grade levels in elementary and secondary schools. Grade level arrangements are often determined by students' requirements, physical space needs, community traditions, and administrative decisions.

Preschools

The growing acceptance of the importance of early education and the need for childcare have resulted in the emergence of educational programs for three-, four-, and five-year-old children (Bowman, Donovan, & Burns, 2000). Preschool education today certainly means more than childcare. Many preschool programs provide very young children with stimulating experiences and opportunities to develop language skills and other important concepts. Early childhood programs usually focus on language and on social, emotional, and physical development, providing young children with a strong foundation for school learning. Even though preschool curriculum is flexible and includes time for play, reading aloud, naps, nutrition, and social interaction, important support for the developing young child is of the utmost importance.

One well-known successful early childhood education program is Head Start, a government-subsidized preschool program begun in the

1960s. Head Start was designed to provide preschool experiences that would help children from low-income families succeed when they entered school. Its success generated a great deal of support from parents and lawmakers, and the program evolved into an educational organization that supports the families of young children and collaborates with other service providers and community programs. Recently, federal funds have been directed toward major initiatives such as No Child Left Behind, and funding for Head Start has been reallocated to other educational programs for young children. Most likely, Head Start will be restructured in the near future.

Early childhood programs vary in quality, content, organization, and relationship to public schools. They may be offered at a school or may be located in another community-based setting. Schools, particularly those in low-economic-status communities, can obtain government funds to establish preschool programs within the school.

Preschool programs may be combined with day care so that children experience structured learning. Many children attend private, church, or Montessori programs that provide them with such experiences during their preschool years. The curriculum is very flexible, as are the requirements for educators who work with very young children. Requirements for preschool teachers differ from state to state, and some states do not require teachers to meet the same certification requirements as kindergarten, elementary, middle, and high school teachers.

If you want to know more about programs for young children or check the status of federal programs such as Head Start, these Web sites will provide additional information:

http://www.ed.gov/offices/OERI/ECI/

http://www.naeyc.org

URLs may change over time. For up-to-date links to relevant Web sites, visit our Companion Web site:

http://education.wadsworth.com/wiseman3e

Elementary Schools

Elementary schools play an important role in the learning and development of young children from ages five to twelve. Most elementary schools are organized by grade level, and the classrooms are self-contained, with one teacher planning and delivering instruction for all subjects. Most early elementary school experiences are devoted to reading, writing, spelling, and mathematics, with smaller amounts of time designated for social studies, science, art, and music. In states with well-developed accountability systems and standardized tests, schools increasingly focus on basic skills before moving on to other subjects. They may departmentalize, focusing on single-subject classes in the upper grades and hiring special teachers for certain subjects such as art, music, or physical education.

Traditionally, elementary schools included kindergarten through sixth grade, but it is not unusual to see any number of grade arrangements in elementary schools today. Primary school arrangements may include preschool, kindergarten, and first and second grades in one building and the intermediate grades three to five in another building. Arrangements may be based on space and other special needs of the school. Elementary schools have a full range of special education services and bilingual programs and may include programs for gifted and talented students. Preschool programs, middle school arrangements, and programs for at-risk students have expanded the complexity and offerings at elementary schools, and extra space or special configurations may require the district to arrange grade levels in unique ways. For example, schools may move the fifth- and sixth-grade students to share buildings with seventh- and eighth-grade students to make room for early childhood students in an elementary school building.

Elementary teachers are trained to understand the developmental needs of children and must complete a series of certification requirements before taking a position in a school district. The instructional roles and

© Eastcott-Momatiuk/The Image Works

Elementary, middle, and secondary school organizational structures separate students of differing ages. Some schools provide opportunities for different ages to work together. High school or middle school students can be involved with younger students in various ways benefiting all involved.

requirements of elementary teachers differ from school to school. Teachers may be rather isolated, working with the students in their classroom without many interactions with others, or they may be part of a teaching team that plans and teaches together. The working conditions, arrangements, and requirements for elementary teachers vary widely and offer a future teacher many choices.

Intermediate Grades and Middle Schools

The educational needs of older elementary children may be taken care of in several ways. Intermediate grade children may be part of an elementary school organization or attend a middle or junior high school. The more than five thousand middle schools and junior high schools in our country educate preadolescents, ages eleven to fifteen (Lewis, 1993). Intermediate grades and middle schools focus on children as young as ten or eleven and as old as fourteen or fifteen.

The term "middle school" refers to a school for adolescents only, and it provides a transition between the elementary and high school experiences. Middle school is often associated with junior high schools and the terms may be interchanged, but in some cases there is a distinctive approach to the middle school experience. Middle school educational philosophy recognizes that the rapid physical and emotional growth during the early teens requires a unique approach. A junior high school model more typically resembles a high school structure, with a strong emphasis on individual subject presentation. The most common organization for middle schools is grades six through eight (Kellough & Kellough, 1999).

Middle-level education philosophy incorporates instructional practices that meet the special needs of adolescents. Team teaching, common teacher planning time, and thematic teaching are all characteristics of middle school teaching. Middle school incorporates elementary teaching methods to instruct specific content area material, preparing students for the subject-focused instruction of junior high and high school. Most middle schools are departmentalized but encourage interrelationships and connections across subjects in an interdisciplinary manner. The focus on content becomes greater with each successive middle school grade level.

You can learn more about middle school education at this Web site:

http://www.nmasa.org/

URLs may change over time. For up-to-date links to relevant Web sites, visit our Companion Web site:

http://education.wadsworth.com/wiseman3e

Children establish lifelong interests and develop their self-concepts during the middle school years. For this reason, exploration and encouragement are important. Middle school educational approaches attempt to reduce the competition in coursework and extracurricular activities so that adolescents will take opportunities to try activities regardless of their skill level. Making sure that all children feel a part of their educational experience is an important goal of middle school educators. Focusing on inclusiveness, middle school cheerleading teams may have as many as seventy-five members, and everyone who wishes can be a member of the basketball team. The great emotional and physical changes of young adolescents provide teachers with many challenges. Teachers at the middle school level must be highly student-oriented and enjoy the special challenges of adolescents who are straddling childhood and teenage years.

Junior High and High Schools

The focus of junior high and high schools is on general subjects, college preparatory curriculum, and vocational training. Students usually have a wide variety of course offering options available. Junior highs may serve the same age group as middle schools and can include any combination of grades seven through nine. Junior highs, which typically do not offer the interdisciplinary approach of middle schools, are set up more like high schools and focus on individual subject areas. High schools commonly include grades nine through twelve, but some include only grades ten through twelve. Concerns about the transition to high school have prompted many districts to create campuses or wings within existing high schools specifically for first-year students. Some districts also offer magnet high schools, which emphasize a particular area of study such as science or the arts.

High school students have many social pressures and must make decisions that will affect the rest of their lives. Growing independence from adults and strong peer relationships are the focus of adolescent emotional development. Behaviors and attitudes related to smoking, drinking, dating, and driving are established during this time. High school students also begin to develop interests and abilities that will influence their future career paths and lifestyles. Students can legally drop out of high school at age sixteen, and the dropout rate is a particularly troublesome issue for most high schools.

High schools have encountered great criticism for not meeting the needs of older teenagers. Recently, because of the perennial low test scores of many high school students, there has been a great

www To learn more about the Bill and Melinda Gates small school project, go to the following Web site:

http://www.essentialschools.org/pub/ces_docs/about/org/gates_pr.html

URLs may change over time. For up-to-date links to relevant Web sites, visit our Companion Web site:

http://education.wadsworth.com/wiseman3e

deal of pressure to change teaching and learning processes in high schools. Reform efforts focus on reduction in class size, more interaction between high school students and teachers, and a curriculum that is more relevant to issues and problems that teenagers face outside of school. The Bill and Melinda Gates small school project is an example.

High school teachers are trained as subject matter and educational specialists and usually major in a content area such as math, biology, or English. Their certification typically allows them to teach grades seven through twelve, but this may vary from state to state. Junior high and high school teachers are much more focused on the subject matter than are their elementary and middle school colleagues, and they may teach five or six daily classes in a specific content area.

An example of some of the resources available for secondary teachers can be reviewed at this Web site:

http://7-12educators.about.com/

URLs may change over time. For up-to-date links to relevant Web sites, visit our Companion Web site:

http://education.wadsworth.com/wiseman3e

Leadership in Today's Schools

In the past, definitions of school leadership implied that only administrators such as principals and superintendents were leaders in a school setting. More recently, school reforms and changing views have redefined leadership roles as much more complex, requiring collaboration and contributions from multiple viewpoints. Districts and schools that embrace this more collaborative view of leadership have expanded the definition to encompass teachers, staff members, parents, and the entire education community in decision making (Neuman & Simmons, 2000). This view of leadership directly affects teachers' roles, and in many schools teachers are required to participate in various decision-making processes about teaching, learning, and policy making. Although traditional administrative roles are still present in most schools, educational leadership in many instances has become the job of the entire education community.

State Policymakers

State have the major responsibility for establishing and funding schools, and many leadership issues begin at the state level. Although states may have different requirements, boards or individuals who are appointed or elected establish educational goals and guide the state's educational process.

STATE GOVERNMENTS State governments have a great deal of influence on the educational opportunities available in individual districts. The state is responsible for the funding patterns that support its schools, and governors are often seen as leaders in educational reform efforts. Several presidents (including former President Clinton, when he was governor of Arkansas, and President G. W. Bush, when he was governor of Texas) were viewed as strong educational supporters and gained political attention through their work in education.

Policies associated with No Child Left Behind have been federally mandated, but the states continue to exert a great deal of control over the schools (see Chapter 4). They may develop and require competency tests for both students and teachers, establish teacher certification regulations, develop state-adopted curriculum and textbook selection processes, set school year schedules, oversee special needs accommodations, and make rulings about many aspects of school life.

In most cases, the state has a direct impact on teachers and on what happens in individual classrooms. This is particularly obvious in states that emphasize mandated achievement tests. Most states develop standardized tests, establish test schedules, score and tabulate results, and respond to district performance on tests by recognizing successful school achievement based on testing.

STATE EDUCATIONAL AGENCIES AND SCHOOL BOARDS State agencies and school boards have official authority over schools, particularly in areas of high school requirements, student achievement testing, curriculum guidelines, teacher certification, and professional development of teachers (Myers & Myers, 1995). State agencies are made up of professional educators who establish state guidelines and implement the policies of the state legislature and school boards. Their duties include ensuring that schools comply with state requirements, maintaining high standards for students, and conducting research that informs the public about schooling. The state agency also assists local school districts in interpreting new laws passed by the legislature.

Some states have both a state educational agency and a state school board, and the two entities usually work closely with one another. State school boards are most often composed of elected citizens or those appointed by the governor. They meet regularly to discuss school policy, review curriculum, and select state-adopted textbooks. In several states, the school boards accredit the teacher preparation programs and encourage the professional development of experienced teachers. School boards may also grant waivers to schools, enabling them to try innovations not covered by existing standards.

Voice of a School Board Member

When I won my election to the school board, I expected to help make decisions about textbooks, high school schedules, and budgets. I never thought that being a member of the school board in a small city would result in any kind of notoriety, but I soon found otherwise. About two years after I first became a member, the school board was asked to approve the name of a new elementary school after a famous state hero. Even though the historical figure was well-loved in the state, he was a slave owner. I had very strong feelings against naming the school after him, believing that it would be offensive to some of the parents and children who attended the school. Instead, I favored using the opportunity to recognize a well-known female African American educator. I expressed my opinion openly at a school board meeting. I was not prepared for the reaction. Members of the board immediately became involved in a heated discussion. Once the nightly news and local newspaper reported the school board disagreement, the community immediately became embroiled in the discussion. It wasn't long before the state and national news agencies picked up the story. Imagine my surprise when the New York Times *printed a story about the school-naming incident. I was interviewed by television and radio commentators. In the end the school was named for the female educator. Serving on the school board does not always require that individuals stand up for their beliefs at the risk of causing long-term community controversy, but there is always the chance that might happen.*

Teachers should be aware of the policies established by state agencies and school boards, because they can have a direct influence on important issues such as what and how teachers teach, when they teach, and how they and their students are evaluated.

Local Policymakers and Administrators

States make broad decisions about policy, curriculum, testing, and other issues related to education, but local school boards and administrators enforce and interpret these policies. In this way, local educational governance such as school boards, unions, and districtwide leadership directly affect the day-to-day working conditions and environments in schools.

LOCAL SCHOOL BOARDS The local school board is a group of elected citizens who oversee the total process of schooling in the community. Depending on the state and the community, the school board may have a great deal of responsibility for leadership and advocacy for the educational process for young people (Cohen, 1990). It contributes to the development of long-range goals, attracts and retains high-quality personnel, and ensures that resources are directed to students with the greatest need. It oversees the implementation of goals and policies and checks to make sure objectives are being accomplished.

A typical school board meeting addresses citizen and parental concerns as well as teacher and staff issues, approves building plans and budgets, and supports and suggests local educational efforts. Controversial issues such as sex education, role of prayer in schools, and censorship are often considered by the school board. The school board attempts to build policy consensus in school districts with factions and pluralistic differences. One of their big jobs is to interview, identify, evaluate, and supervise the superintendent. As a result, the superintendent's role can be greatly affected by the district's school board.

School board meetings offer a good example of the democratic process. Board members discuss and make decisions about issues that are reflections of societal concern. School boards that are attuned to their constituency listen to citizens and are influenced by what they hear. The most positive outcomes occur when decisions and solutions represent multiple constituencies in the community. Their decisions are usually made quietly and without a great deal of fanfare, but sometimes the entire community gets involved. Controversial issues can produce television cameras at board meetings, newspaper reporters at the schools, and citizens' debates in newspapers.

This Web site provides additional information about the role of school boards in educational settings:

http:www.nsbf.org

URLs may change over time. For up-to-date links to relevant Web sites, visit our Companion Web site:

http://education.wadsworth.com/wiseman3e

SUPERINTENDENTS AND THE CENTRAL OFFICE The superintendent is the chief executive of an entire school system. As in most leadership and administrative jobs, the superintendent's role reflects the personality of the individual. Approaches to the demands of the job vary dramatically. A superintendent may be visible in school hallways, drop in at community gatherings, or appear regularly in local newspaper articles. The accessibility of the superintendent depends on the individual's administrative style, but the superintendent's influence is felt in all aspects of schooling in a community. The superintendent is usually the point person for the community in regard to educational issues and is responsible for the public view of the school. The community holds him or her responsible for establishing and maintaining a shared vision that reflects community values. In addition, the superintendent is responsible for overseeing the budget, conducting bond elections that raise money for the schools, working with the school boards, meeting state and local directives, and supervising and working closely with principals, curriculum directors, and other administrators in the district.

The amount of contact between teachers and superintendents will depend on the school setting. New teachers in a large city will probably seldom see their superintendent, whereas a small-town superintendent may know most of the teachers by name. Some large-school superintendents make it a point to walk the halls of their schools so that teachers are familiar with them and feel free to talk to them. The principal may serve as a liaison between the school and the superintendent and, in all but the very large districts, the superintendent and the principals probably will know each other very well and have a strong working relationship.

A superintendent's office may be referred to as the central office or central administration. The central office is the hub of the entire district operation. Central offices in large cities may be housed in multiple buildings, but in small school districts, the superintendent and support staff are often located in one of the school buildings. In most cases, a physical complex is devoted to the administrative aspects of a school district. Central office administrators include curriculum directors, special program coordinators, teacher appraisal specialists, and personnel officers. Professionals in the central office assist schools and monitor compliance with state and federal requirements. One group of educators who may support teachers at either the district level or on the school campus are the supervisors or curriculum directors. Assigned to oversee the instruction of a particular content or specialty area, these specialists operate at the district level or are assigned to a specific school. Schools also employ early childhood,

FIELD-BASED ACTIVITY

9.2

Tour a district's central office. Arrange to have someone who works in the office explain what they do. Think about how a new teacher would depend on the support and resources offered by the office.

Note: Smaller school districts may not have a central office. Find out how the services typically provided by the central office are offered in smaller districts.

INTASC Principle 10

special education, gifted and talented, and English as a second language supervisors who may be housed in the central office, visit school campuses regularly, establish professional development activities in their particular area, engage in problem solving with a teacher who is experiencing difficulty, or develop classroom innovations.

SUPERVISORS AND CURRICULUM DIRECTORS Teachers encounter district supervisors and curriculum directors during professional development sessions and curriculum planning projects. Professional development sessions may be conducted after school, during the week or so before school starts, or for longer periods of time during the summer. These sessions are usually planned by supervisors and directors to introduce a new teaching approach or to work on instructional areas targeted by school goals and objectives (such as improving math scores on state achievement tests). Central office curriculum directors are responsible for guiding the development of new curriculum. They often bring representatives from individual schools together as a work group to design new guidelines for teaching and learning. Supervisors and curriculum directors are often outstanding teachers who have demonstrated a great deal of curriculum and instruction understanding, hold an advanced graduate degree, and also possess leadership skills to offer needed guidance and direction. They can be a great help to new teachers and will often be available to observe instruction and make suggestions for improvement. Some large school districts hire a supervisor for new teachers, and his or her job is to support beginning teachers during their first year.

School Building Administration and Leadership

Teachers work for and with many people—students, parents, school boards, communities—but principals and building-level administrators develop a very close working relationship with teachers. Principals are the most immediate supervisors of teachers and serve an important leadership function in any school. The principal's role has been identified as the primary factor contributing to excellence in public schools, regardless of the ethnic or socioeconomic factors of the school community (Zigarelli, 1996). The principal's main job is to oversee the day-to-day operations of the school campus, but he or she often performs a variety of other functions and extends leadership opportunities to others.

A review of a principal's day reveals the variety of activities that are a part of his or her job. The principal may arrive at the school before teachers. This may be the only quiet time he or she has in the day to go over budgets, write memos to the central office, or establish a schedule for the

In addition to providing leadership for schools, principals play many roles during the school day. Charismatic principals are often recognized for creative and successful leadership.

next school year. When teachers begin arriving for their day, they often stop to talk with the principal about a student, an encounter with a parent in the grocery store the night before, or their progress on curriculum development. On other mornings, teachers might want to talk about conflicts between two teachers, ordering more paper, or requesting a substitute teacher for a personal day of leave. As the early morning continues, the principal's office begins to fill with children arriving at school. Parents may stop by the office with compliments, complaints, requests, or greetings for the principal. As more children begin to arrive, the principal walks the halls greeting the children. He or she may stop to visit with students, interacting and commenting on their concerns. Once the bell rings and the school day starts, the principal divides the time between attending meetings at the central office, dealing with parental phone calls, meeting with local community groups, writing reports for state requirements, balancing the budget, ordering supplies, and meeting with small groups of teachers. At lunch, he or she may make an attempt to be present in the lunchroom or appear at the bus stop or on the playground during recess. As the school day continues, the principal may be called to fix the heat, help with a sick child, monitor a group of children while a teacher returns an important phone call, or talk to a parent. After the children leave, the principal may meet with teachers, conduct staff meetings, attend extracurricular activities associated with the school, or have an hour or two of paperwork to finish before the day is over. In the evening, the principal may attend school board meetings or other activities associated with the school.

Principals in secondary schools may have daily schedules similar to the one just described, but with some differences. Their day starts early and ends late, but they may be working on larger budgets, ordering supplies for larger groups of teachers, and working more closely with professionals from central administration. Secondary principals also work with assistant principals who supervise teachers and deal with individual student concerns. Supervisors and teacher team leaders take a great deal of responsibility for developing and implementing curriculum, but it is the principal's job to establish the vision, facilitate communication, and make sure standards are being met in all subject areas. Principals in larger schools may not have the same close, working relationship with teachers common in smaller schools, but they can be found supporting and attending sports events, concerts, drama productions, and other events that are part of the school's extracurricular activities.

Principals differ widely in the way they perceive their role (Leithwood, 1992; Riehl, 2000). Personal philosophies, personalities, idiosyncrasies and habits, administrative styles, personal interactions, and beliefs about student development all contribute to the uniqueness of leadership style. Some principals may be very reserved, whereas others are accessible and easy to approach. A supportive principal will remove obstacles, provide material and emotional support, manage details, share in the professional comradeship, and help establish the goals for the school (Sergiovanni, 2000). Principals have many tasks, but some—such as required teacher observations, curriculum leadership, and mentoring—are particularly important to new teachers or preservice teachers. Just like teachers, principals have professional standards to guide their practices. The ISLLC Standards for School Leaders, produced by a consortium of states and major organizations in 1996, attempts to define and describe the important knowledge, dispositions, and performances necessary for successful principals. Let's examine a few of these important roles.

ESTABLISHING VISION Principals are responsible for maintaining the school vision and for implementing the practical steps to accomplish educational goals and objectives. They help establish a "clear vision of short- and long-range goals for the school" (Sergiovanni, 1992, p. 7). A school's context and character reflect the goals and objectives established through the principal's facilitation. Not only must a principal have a clear vision of the school, but he or she must also communicate that vision to staff, parents, students, and community members. They must be extremely knowledgeable about teaching and learning and be able to effectively motivate and inspire their staff members. Perhaps most important, they must put the interests of students above all else, even when politics threaten to intervene. The recent impact of testing on teaching is one example in which principals must balance the focus on test results with what is best for teachers and students. It is a difficult balance to maintain.

In one elementary school, the principal was the leader in recognizing the richness that accompanies the large number of international students in attendance at his school. The school hallways, curriculum, extracurricular activities, and pride became rooted in a focus on internationalism. The teachers and staff welcomed children from around the world and the school became known for its diversity. All the teachers in the school accepted the responsibility of preparing new teachers and became involved in a complex school–university partnership. The goals of internationalism and teacher education established a unique culture that influenced every teacher in the school.

The most important goal of any school is the success of all students, teachers, and professionals in the school. The achievement and happiness of students comes first in establishing a vision for the school, but principals must also have high expectations for teachers and themselves. A principal's way of administrating and leading can have a great impact on the potential success of all who work and learn in the school. Successful principals have figured out how to balance their focus among teachers, children, and the community.

MANAGING THE SCHOOL Principals are crucial contributors to schools and the way they operate. They manage the budget, oversee equipment purchases, hire teachers, and establish school schedules. Although they may distribute their managerial responsibilities to other professionals in the school, principals are ultimately responsible for administration. Schools with a large number of students may hire assistant principals to be responsible for scheduling, student conduct, curriculum development, or other issues related to the complex process of school leadership. But when there is a problem to be solved, an issue to discuss, or teaching/learning expectations to uphold, the principal must administer and guide the process—always using a knowledge of learning, teaching, and student development to inform management decisions.

MAINTAINING HIGH STANDARDS FOR INSTRUCTION The principal plays an important role in implementing and maintaining effective instructional programs within a school (Fullan, 1991; Hansen & Smith, 1989). The principal's beliefs about students' abilities to learn and teachers' ability to teach affect long-range and everyday teaching and learning processes (Greenfield, 1991). The principal is actively involved in decision making about instruction and must attend to instructional objectives as well as instruction strategies. The principal is also responsible for collecting information and using data in a manner that keeps everyone in the school well informed about the performance of teachers and students.

Principals have a great influence on the work of teachers. The way principals interpret what teachers do is of primary importance to those teachers, and they must involve teachers in developing the priorities and policies for the school they share. Two examples of their direct impact on a teacher's career are instructional assessment and professional development activities. Consider that principals are responsible for observing and assessing teachers' classroom instructional behaviors. They provide feedback on teachers' instruction, interactions with children, and classroom procedures. They are responsible for providing ongoing professional development for teachers at their school. Effective principals work hard to build up staff capacities so that they can take on some of the leadership in a school (Sergiovanni, 2000). They keep in touch with beginning teachers and provide support and advice for them. The principalship is a demanding and important role and one that influences each new teacher's professional development.

FACILITATING SHARED DECISION MAKING One impact of the reform movement of the last ten years is to involve as many people as possible in local school decision making. Shared decision making, sometimes referred to as site-based management, reflects a less centralized approach to school leadership and requires a great deal of collaboration and trust (Midgely & Wood, 1993). Collaborative decision making means many things and takes many forms, depending on the people involved. It usually means placing as much decision-making authority as possible with the teachers, counselors, parents, and other professionals at individual school buildings (Myers & Myers, 1995). A team of decision makers typically includes the principal, teachers, other school staff, community representatives, and parents who work together to make decisions. These leadership teams can have an impact on who is employed at a school, what curriculum is implemented, and what textbooks are purchased.

One of the most common issues that arise with a site-based decision-making process is the sharing of power by those who have traditional leadership roles. Superintendents and principals must make dramatic shifts in their ideas about leadership to support shared leadership processes. Likewise, parents and others may not be familiar with decision-making respon-

FIELD-BASED ACTIVITY

9.3

Ask a principal or an assistant principal to talk with you about some of the events or activities that occur during the work day. As the principal talks, try to determine which of the duties described in the text take most of the principal's time. Create a chart or graph that illustrates the principal's responsibilities.

INTASC Principle 10

sibilities and may not possess the skills and time required to make good decisions about the school. Many districts are still experimenting with this concept, and as you begin your career you may see many levels of success with this process.

A school–university partnership usually illustrates a shared decision-making process. In most cases, a leadership team makes decisions about the teacher education process. School administrators, teachers, and university faculty make decisions for the students in the teacher education program.

Teachers as Leaders

Teacher leadership has been implemented in traditional roles such as department heads, textbook selection committees, and union representatives, but these traditional roles are limited compared with the leadership opportunities that are emerging. "Teachers who become leaders experience personal and professional satisfaction, a reduction in isolation, a sense of instrumentality, and new learnings—all of which spill over to their teaching" (Barth, 2001, p. 443). Teachers in leadership roles can choose textbooks and instructional materials, design professional development and inservice programs, define school budgets, evaluate teacher performance, and even select new teachers and new administrators for their school. More innovative involvement in teacher leadership can come about as a result of participation in teacher-as-researcher or action research projects, in which teachers collect data to answer questions about their own teaching or instructional practices.

Teachers have a great deal of insight about and responsibility for decisions about teaching and can play an important role in providing instructional leadership. Instructional leadership focuses on decisions related to students and their learning and is guided by high expectations of students and teachers and an emphasis on instruction (Heck, Larsen, & Marcoulides, 1990). Instructional leaders also use the results of students' achievement,

FIELD-BASED ACTIVITY

9.4

Attend at least one team meeting or professional development session. Note the roles of the teachers that work at your school. Using the list provided here as a guide, determine which skills were most apparent.

group process	running meetings	visioning
enabling	advocacy	facilitation
conflict management	goal-setting	listening
budgeting	action research	network building
honoring dissenters	collaboration	consensus building
giving away power	cultural sensitivity	feedback

INTASC Principles 9 and 10

strengths, and challenges to make decisions about instruction. For example, in the role of instructional leaders, teachers may identify the writing process as an area that needs strengthening in their school. They may recognize this need as a result of their students' test scores or because other teachers have expressed a desire to become more knowledgeable in this area. The teacher leaders may arrange for a consultant to come to the school and work with small groups of teachers, present model lessons in classrooms, and expose teachers to innovative methods for teaching writing. The consultant and the teacher leaders might provide opportunities for teachers to participate in process writing workshops during the summer and work with groups of teachers to develop lesson plans for the coming year. As they implement their plans, they continue to monitor their students' writing development through test scores and the authentic assessment of portfolios.

Teachers can exercise their leadership talents in several ways. Teachers demonstrate instructional leadership when they become involved in planning and delivering professional development activities for the continuing education of their colleagues. Successful teachers can share their favorite strategies and innovative techniques with other teachers. When teachers plan, design, and deliver learning plans or activities for their school's professional development, the activities and processes they plan reflect concerns and interests of their colleagues and are more meaningful.

Teacher leaders can also facilitate the organization and management of their schools. Schools with more than one or two teachers at each grade level or within content areas usually have team leaders who are responsible for communication, announcements, decision making, and planning. The principal or their fellow teachers appoint team leaders. This small-

Sharing among teachers is an important aspect of professional practice. Working together offers teachers support and collegiality, and provides an opportunity for individual teachers to serve in leadership roles.

group arrangement facilitates participation in decision making and provides a greater opportunity for all teachers to express their opinions. "When teachers lead, principals extend their own capacity, students enjoy a democratic community of learners, and schools benefit from better decisions" (Barth, 2001, p. 445).

The number of opportunities for teacher leadership is increasing and requires the modern teacher to consider a wider range of tasks related to the profession. Individuals who work in a shared leadership manner must possess strong personal and interpersonal skills (Barth, 2001). They must recognize and appreciate the ideas of their colleagues and patiently hear everyone's ideas and solutions. It is not easy to assume new roles. Teachers who are in these roles must know how to deal with change, persuasion, and conflicts. But most of all, teachers who take on new roles must learn how to use their time differently. Even with help, it is difficult not to feel stressed as the roles of teachers expand and change (Wasley, 1991).

Experienced teachers seldom view themselves as leaders (Bellon & Beaudry, 1992; Wasley, 1991). It is, however, becoming an increasingly important part of a teacher's career. Schools offer a growing number of opportunities and situations in which teachers can become leaders. You

Voice of a Teacher

I love teaching elementary children and have never regretted my decision to become a teacher. I would have been perfectly satisfied to teach third-graders for the rest of my life, not knowing that anything else was possible, but thanks to the Professional Development School program, I have experienced types of teaching that were never dreamed of by the previous teachers in my family.

Recently, I applied for and received a position as a co-teacher for a math methods course that was made available by the Professional Development School program. I wanted to teach this course because I knew that math was a weak area for me and I wanted to challenge myself as a teacher. I've been surprised by the changes I felt as a result.

Teaching this course and working with college students, has helped me to acquire more information. I am a learner as well as a teacher. I feel more pride in what I do, which causes me to perceive myself differently. My role as a teacher has changed and expanded. I feel that my colleagues' perceptions of me have changed also, which increases my self-esteem. Whether these feelings are real or imagined on my part, the result remains the same. My teaching has improved.

It's a wonderful change of pace to work with college students. I feel the same joys when they succeed or learn a new concept that I do with my elementary students. The difference is the level of learning. We can deal with concepts and discuss topics that are far above my third-grade students. One of my favorite aspects of this class is when they come to me to discuss a problem or an idea that they have for a lesson. Many of their ideas are creative, and they are so enthusiastic about teaching that it's contagious. I've always felt that I touch the future when I work with my eight-year-old students, but now I also touch the future of all those children my college students will teach. What a phenomenal responsibility!

Teaching this math methods course and participating in the Professional Development School program has opened up a whole new world for me. It satisfies that part of me that needs to be different in a family of teachers and also that part of me that needs to teach. Someone called me a teacher leader the other day. I was really surprised to hear that term used to describe what I do. I think of myself as a teacher and never consider how I provide leadership in my field. It may be difficult to separate teaching and leadership skills.

may have many chances to exercise your instructional leadership capabilities throughout your career. Take time now to complete the Self-Reflection exercise on page 314 and to think about what you have learned.

Preservice Teacher Leadership

Preservice teachers rarely consider leadership opportunities during their training and in fact may be unconcerned about leadership roles because they view such roles as the responsibility of superintendents, principals, and experienced teachers. Recognizing leadership responsibilities, taking part in activities that encourage leadership, and understanding the challenges of leadership in today's schools should be components of the preservice teachers' experiences.

Recognizing that leadership is part of the teacher's role is the first step to becoming a teacher leader. Teaching and leading are not necessarily separate processes. Several defining elements and skills are common to both teaching and leading. Day-to-day classroom routines require leadership skills. A teacher constantly assesses situations, develops strategies, and implements plans that solve problems. "Passion, meaning, and purpose" are the foundation for both leadership and teaching (Bolman & Deal, 1994, p. 3). "As a person learns to be a good teacher, he or she also learns to be a good leader" (Gardner, 1989, p. 18). Classroom interactions also require leadership skills. Teachers use skills related to problem solving, persuasion, and conflict resolution when interacting with children and young people. In addition, teaching and learning situations provide numerous opportunities for achieving goals set for yourself and for helping students achieve their goals.

Preservice training offers methods, concepts, and ideas to help you develop into a successful classroom leader. You may find opportunities to exercise your leadership skills within your university training processes. Whole class and small-group activities offer future teachers an opportunity to work with others and learn collaborative processes. Many future teachers take part in summer jobs, community or church activities, or volunteer efforts that require them to help make decisions and guide others.

Although it is easy to understand the connections between leadership and teaching, it is not always easy to recognize the more subtle aspects of leadership that exist in schools. Understanding the roles and differing perspectives of all those involved in the educational process and finding ways to exercise your own leadership capabilities can provide insights into the complexity of leadership in our schools.

Leadership Paths

Read these statements about leadership, and circle the answer that reflects your view.

1. As a teacher, I expect to take part in making decisions about my school.   Yes   No

2. My principal will establish the vision and mission for my school.   Yes   No

3. It is not my role to question decisions my principal makes.   Yes   No

4. The central office, superintendent, and curriculum directors should establish the direction of my school.   Yes   No

5. It is important for teachers to collaborate and make decisions about school improvement.   Yes   No

6. If my school's test scores fall, the central office should set goals and objectives for my school.   Yes   No

7. It is the teacher's responsibility to understand and take into account parental goals and objectives.   Yes   No

8. Teachers should involve students in determining their needs based on results of standardized and in-class assessments.   Yes   No

9. New teachers need to understand how to collaborate with others.   Yes   No

10. Experts from the central office should determine the professional development needs for teachers.   Yes   No

Tally the number of yes responses you gave to items 1, 5, 7, 8, and 9. This gives you an indication of where you are on the path to shared leadership. Then tally the number of yes responses you gave to items 2, 3, 4, 6, and 10. This tally represents your traditional leadership. Now compare the two. Are you farther along on the shared or traditional path to leadership? Is this the path you want to take? If so, what kinds of questions would you ask principals when you are interviewing for teaching positions?

PORTFOLIO REFLECTIONS AND EXHIBITS

Prepare a portfolio exhibit. Adapt one of the Field-Based Activities completed in this chapter, create your own exhibit, or complete suggested Portfolio Exhibit 9 to represent the learnings and understandings you developed in this chapter.

Suggested Exhibit 9: School Leadership

Your portfolio representation for this chapter should include

1. A summary of the Field-Based Activities you completed for this chapter.

2. The selection and explanation of the activity that was most important to your learning.

3. A graphic (a web or some other relational graphic) to illustrate all the different types of leadership teachers can demonstrate. Use the text or other readings to support your observations. Describe each leadership role and some of the effects of teacher leadership. Note which leadership roles can be developed during your preservice experience.

E-Portfolio Entry 9

Display the organization graphic you produced using technology tools. Use clip art, graphics, or programs such as Inspiration to illustrate teacher leadership.

INTASC Principles 9 and 10

ANSWERS TO GUIDING YOUR READING

1. What are some of the characteristics of schools in urban, suburban, and rural settings?

Some characteristics of schools vary dramatically in urban, suburban and rural settings. Size of the physical facilities, number of students, grade arrangements, organizational structures, and leadership processes reflect unique needs of the communities where schools are located. All schools share common characteristics that come from a focus on educational goals and working with children, adolescents, and families who are culturally, economically, and experientially diverse.

2. How are schools organized?

There is no standard arrangement of grade levels in elementary and secondary schools. Grade level arrangements are often determined by physical space needs, community traditions, and administrative decisions. School organizations provide a configuration of grade levels that meets the needs of preschool, elementary, intermediate, and high school students and satisfies administrative needs for physical space. When all is taken into consideration, the grade level arrangements vary greatly in each school district.

3. What leaders take responsibility for schools?

Patterns of school leadership are varied. Traditional administrative roles are still present in most schools, where superintendents and principals hold the major responsibilities for leading faculty and other professional staff. Some districts and schools have changed the definition of leadership to encompass teachers, staff members, parents, and the entire education community in decision making. In most cases, the responsibility for leadership in schools is a collaborative effort involving many stakeholders.

4. What are some of the ways that teachers demonstrate leadership?

Teachers develop leadership skills as they guide their students in daily learning activities. Teachers traditionally demonstrate leadership by participating in textbook selection committees, as union representatives, and as department chairs. Roles related to mentoring, team leadership, curriculum development, school–university partnerships, and staff development sessions provide additional opportunities for leadership. Innovative involvement in teacher leadership can come about as a result of participation in teacher-as-research projects in which teachers collect data to answer questions about instructional practices.

5. How can preservice teachers demonstrate leadership?

Preservice teachers can learn about leadership as they learn to teach. Many leadership skills are needed when responding to classroom situations. Collaborative activities required in university coursework also provide opportunities to work with others. Many future teachers take part in university leadership opportunities, summer jobs, community or church activities, or volunteer efforts that require demonstration of leadership abilities.

INFOTRAC COLLEGE EDITION EXTENSION

Log on to the InfoTrac College Edition Web site and choose one of the following searches to expand your knowledge about school organization and leadership.

1. Using the PowerTrac option (choose the author index and the keyword index and type in the descriptors), find the work of educational researchers who have written about school organization and leadership. You may use someone mentioned in the chapter or try the following:

   au Michael Fullan and ke organization

   au Linda Lambert and ke leadership

2. The *Phi Delta Kappan* journal often has articles about school leadership. Using the PowerTrac option and the search term below, discover the kinds of articles about leadership the journal has featured recently:

   jn Phi Delta Kappan and ke leadership

RELATED READINGS

The following books will provide more information about some of the topics and ideas discussed in this chapter:

McIntyre, D. J., & O'Hair, M. J. (1996). *The reflective roles of the classroom teacher.* Belmont, CA: Wadsworth.

This book presents the many roles of the teacher and encourages each teacher to develop those capacities. Leadership is one teacher's role, which is described in realistic classroom scenes.

Sergiovanni, T. J. (1992). *Moral leadership: Getting to the heart of school improvement.* San Francisco: Jossey-Bass.

The author presents school leaders who understand that attending to "people" will create more effective and successful schools.

REFERENCES

Epigraph: Kidder, Tracy. *Among Schoolchildren* (pp. 44, 46). New York: Avon.

Barth, R. (2001). Teacher leader. *Phi Delta Kappan,* 82(6), 443–449.

Bellon, T., & Beaudry, J. (1992, April). Teachers' perceptions of their leadership roles in site-based decision making. Paper presented at the annual meeting of the American Educational Research Association, San Francisco.

Bolman, L. G., & Deal, T. E. (Eds.). (1994). *Becoming a teacher leader: From isolation to collaboration.* Thousand Oaks, CA: Corwin Press.

Bowman, B., Donovan, M. S., & Burns, M. S. (Eds.). (2000). *Eager to learn: Educating our preschoolers.* Committee on Early Childhood, Pedagogy, National Research Council. Washington, DC: National Academy Press.

Casserly, M. (2004). What the nation didn't hear about urban NAEP. *Urban Education* 13(1), 5. Retrieved February 2004 from http://www.cgcs.org/urban educator/2004/jan_vol_13_no_1_5/jan_vol_13_no_1_5.html

Cohen, M. (1990). Key issues confronting state policy makers. In R. F. Elmore (Ed.), *Restructuring schools: The next generation of educational reform* (pp. 251–288). San Francisco: Jossey-Bass.

Crosby, E. A. (1999). Urban schools: Forced to fail. *Phi Delta Kappan,* 81(4), 298–303.

Dewees, S. (December, 1999). Improving rural school facilities for teaching and learning. Eric Digest; ERIC Clearinghouse on Rural Education and Small Schools. [Available online: http://www.ael.org/eric/digests/edorc998.htm.]

DeYoung, A. J., & Lawrence, B. K. (1995). On hoosiers, yankees, and mountaineers. *Phi Delta Kappan,* 77(2), 105–112.

Englert, R. M. (1993). Understanding the urban context and conditions of practice of school administration. In P. Forsyth & M. Tallerico (Eds.), *City schools: Leading the way.* Newbury Park, CA: Sage.

Farris, P. J. (1996). *Teaching, bearing the torch.* Dubuque, IA: Brown & Benchmark.

Forsyth, P. B., & Tallerico, M. (Eds.). (1993). *City schools: Leading the way.* Newbury Park, CA: Corwin.

Fullan, M. G. (1991). *The new meaning of educational change.* New York: Teachers College Press.

Gardner, J. (1989). *On leadership.* New York: Free Press.

Gordon, G. L. (1999). Teacher talent and urban schools. *Phi Delta Kappan,* 81(4), 304–307.

Greenfield, W. D. (1991). The micropolitics of leadership in an urban elementary school. Paper presented at the annual meeting of the American Educational Research Association, Chicago.

Hahn, A., Danzberger, J., & Lefkowitz, B. (1987). *Dropouts in America: Enough is known for action.* Washington, DC: Institute for Educational Leadership.

Hansen, J. M., & Smith, R. (1989). Building-based instructional improvement: The principal as an instructional leader. *National Association of Secondary School Principals Bulletin,* 73(518), 10–16.

Heck, R. H., Larsen, T. J., & Marcoulides, G. A. (1990). Instructional leadership and school achievement: Validation of a causal model. Educational Administration Quarterly, 26(2), 94–125.

Herzog, M. J. R., & Pittman, R. B. (1995). Home, family, and community: Ingredients in the rural education equation. *Phi Delta Kappan,* 77(2), 113–118.

Huang, G. G. (1999). Sociodemographic changes: Promises and problems for rural education. ERIC Clearinghouse on Rural Education and Small Schools. Office of Educational Research and Improvement, U.S. Department of Education ED-99-CO-0027. [Available online: http://www.ael.org/eric/digests/edorc987.htm.]

Kellough, R. D., & Kellough, N. G. (1999). *Middle school teaching: A guide to methods and resources* (3rd ed.). Upper Saddle River, NJ: Merrill.

Lambert, L. (1998). How to build leadership capacity. *Educational Leadership,* 55(7), 17–19.

Leithwood, K. A. (1992). The principal's role in teacher development. In M. Fullan & A. Hargreaves (Eds.), *Teacher development and educational change* (pp. 86–103). London: Falmer Press.

Lewis, A. C. (1993). *Changing the odds: Middle school reform in progress, 1991–1993.* New York: The Edna McConnell Clark Foundation.

Midgely, C., & Wood, S. (1993). Beyond site-based management: Empowering teachers to reform schools. *Phi Delta Kappan,* 75(2), 187–194.

Myers, C. B., & Myers, L. K. (1995). *The professional educator.* Belmont, CA: Wadsworth.

National Center for Education Statistics. (2001) *Drop out rates in the United States: 2000.* Washington, DC: Author. Retrieved February 19, 2004, from http://nces.ed.gov/pubs2002/droppub_2001/

Neuman, M., & Simmons, W. (2000). Leadership for student learning. *Phi Delta Kappan,* 82(1), 9–12.

Ornstein, A. C., & Levine, D. U. (1989). Social class, race and school achievement: Problems and prospects. *Journal of Teacher Education,* 40(5), 17–23.

Ouchi, W. G. (2003). Making schools work: A revolutionary plan to get your children the education they need. New York: Simon & Schuster.

Pang, V. O., & Gibson, R. (2001). Concepts of democracy and citizenship: Views of African American teachers. *The Social Studies,* 92, 260–266.

Plisko, V. (2000). *Commissioners Statement: The condition of education.* Washington, DC: National Center for Education Statistics.

Pipho, C. (1995). Urban school problems and solutions. *Phi Delta Kappan,* 77(2), 102–103.

Population Reference Bureau. (1999). America's racial and ethnic minorities. *Population Bulletin,* no. 54, p. 3. [Available online: http://www.prb.org/pubs/population_bulletin/bu54-3/part5.htm.]

Richard, A. (2000). Remodeling suburbia. *Education Week,* XX(7), 1, 28–36.

Riehl, C. (2000). The principal's role in creating inclusive schools for diverse students: A review of normative, empirical, and critical literature on the practice of educational administration. *Review of Educational Research,* 70(1), 55–82.

Rist, R. C. (2000). Student social class and teacher expectations: The self-fulfilling prophecy in ghetto education. *Harvard Educational Review* 70(3), 257–265.

Sergiovanni, T. J. (1992). *Moral leadership: Getting to the heart of school improvement.* San Francisco: Jossey-Bass.

Sergiovanni, T. J. (2000). *The principalship: A reflective practice perspective.* Boston: Allyn & Bacon.

Urban Institute. (1995). Improving student performance in the inner city. *Policy and Research Report.* [Available online: www.urban.org/periodcl/prr26_1b.htm.]

U.S. Department of Education. (1999–2000). *National Center for Education Statistics, Common Core of Data, Local Education Agency Universe Survey.* Washington, DC: Author.

Wasley, P. A. (1991). *Teachers who lead: The rhetoric of reform and the realities of practice.* New York: Teachers College Press.

Zigarelli, M. A. (1996). An empirical test of conclusions from effective schools research. *Journal of Educational Research,* 90(2), 103–110.

Families and Communities

Listening to the family is the only way to get the full picture of the child, an understanding of how what we do at school might fit or not fit into what is likely to happen at home. Since children are educated four-fifths of their waking lives outside of school, families are, in the end, primarily responsible for the education of their children. When school people ignore this, they are undercutting the effectiveness of both school and home.

But even after we get through the school and family introductions and establish the principle of collaboration, it isn't smooth sailing. The family is still endlessly negotiating how to translate the differences between school and home in a context fraught with judgments of the highest order—is this teacher or school good enough, competent enough, well intentioned enough, or smart enough to count on? For elementary school teachers there are twenty to thirty different such families every year who are passing judgment on them—and whose support the teachers' success depends on. (The numbers are far higher in high school, but teachers are probably less aware of such judgments since they see so many students—well over a hundred—each semester.) And to make matters worse, even in those cases where choice is open, it's not so easy to just drive out and try another school or teacher, as you might with an auto mechanic. Teacher and family are pretty much stuck with each other—at least for a year.

—Deborah Meier, *In Schools We Trust*

Guiding Your Reading

1. What are the school's and the teacher's roles in encouraging collaboration with parents and others?

2. How can multiple partners help students, and what are the benefits of collaborative educational efforts?

3. How can beginning teachers involve others to improve the success of students?

A teacher's work typically occurs in a single classroom characterized by daily lessons and learning activities. As you have seen in this course and as you observe in the schools, schooling goes far beyond the walls of classrooms and school buildings. When school is a collaborative endeavor, successful practices evolve from the team effort of many potential partners. Not all partners are educators—but partners from noneducational settings can create an expanded educational context. "When schools, families, and community groups work together to support learning, children tend to do better in school, stay in school longer, and like school more" (Southwest Educational Developmental Laboratory, 2002).

Working with multiple partners may make the educational process more complex, but student success and achievement increases with additional partners. Depending on their roles, partners support teachers' daily work in different ways. Perhaps the most obvious, but also the most important, partnership is between school and family. Students, teachers, and schools all benefit when parents or other caretakers show an interest in their child's education. Other potential partners include professionals who work regularly with children and parents, health and human service professionals, businesspeople, community members, and university or other educational partners.

A teacher who is aware of the importance of home, community, agency, and business involvement will plan and encourage activities that naturally involve partners. Some traditional partnerships, such as parents and schools, are expected; other collaborations, such as those between social workers and teachers, are less common but also beneficial. This chapter discusses the importance of collaboration and support in young people's school achievement and suggests benefits, barriers, methods, and techniques that encourage the involvement of parents, community, business, and health and human service professionals.

The task of collaborating with educational partners to develop innovative approaches to common problems is difficult. It takes time, commitment, and effective interpersonal skills. Connections to groups outside the school contribute to an expanded support system for students and to the increased likelihood that they will succeed.

▶ *Families as Partners in Education*

Parents, family members, and others who provide the primary care to students make important contributions to the students' educational process. During the past decade, the federal government has advocated family involvement. Federal educational goals from the 1980s and 1990s put a great deal of responsibility on parent partners in educational activities, stating that "by the year 2000, every school will promote partnerships that will increase parental involvement and participation in promoting the social, emotional, and academic growth of children" (U.S. Department of Education, 1994, p. 2). This emphasis has persisted through the presidential terms of Reagan, G. H. Bush, Clinton, and G. W. Bush, indicating that the notion of parents as partners in the educational process is not a fad. The No Child Left Behind policies are based on the assumption that increased parental involvement in many aspects of schooling is an important goal. As a result of this legislation, parents in low-performing schools may transfer their children to a better-performing school. Parents must also be informed if their childrens' teachers do not meet the requirements necessary to be considered a high-quality teacher.

Evidence supports the importance of parent and family participation. When parents are involved in schools, students are more likely to succeed, attend school regularly, earn better grades, graduate, and go to college (Southwest Educational Developmental Laboratory, 2002). Parental involvement in school results in clear gains in student achievement (Henderson & Berla, 1994). Involved parents have children with more positive attitudes about school and higher aspirations for the future (Epstein, 1993, 1995).

Parental and family involvement results in achievement gains and improved attitudes toward education for the following reasons (Scott-Jones, 1988): Parents and primary caregivers are children's first teachers and have worked with their children for five or six years before teachers become involved. Parents know their children and continue to have a powerful influence on their attitudes and learning. Of course, adult support does not provide the same positive influence in all situations. Parental attitudes can vary

Parental involvement in school activities has the potential to improve the school environment and student achievement. Successful schools provide numerous ways for parents to take part in their children's education.

from helpful to intimidating to indifference or to open hostility. Understanding parents and caregivers helps teachers establish appropriate partnerships that will support their students' academic endeavors.

Family involvement tends to decline as children get older. For the most part, parents of elementary-age children control the environment and resources available to their children and have a great influence on children through the decisions and choices they make. Families continue to influence young people even as they begin to exercise their own independence in middle and high school, although this influence is not as obvious and direct (Hollifield, 1994). The changing relationship between families and their older children requires adjustments in parents' and teachers' expectations as students take on more responsibility for decision making.

The common decline in parental involvement at middle and high school can be avoided if parents and teachers consider and plan for the changing needs of students. All students, no matter what level, want their families to understand and be more knowledgeable about school (Epstein, 1995). When children are young, they are usually delighted to see parents and other family members at school. As students get older, they can take responsibility for engaging their family in school activities and communicating with them about homework and school decisions. In middle and high school, parental and family involvement may not be as explicit as it was in earlier years and may take different forms, but it remains equally important.

Teachers often perceive minority parents as less involved in their children's education. Many factors such as bad experiences in school, traditional deference to institutions, inability to speak English, and other social/cultural patterns contribute to the perception of lower involvement by minority parents. All parents need to feel comfortable in the school setting before collaborating with educators. Without fail, parents and caretakers from all groups will respond favorably when they become aware of the need, are treated with respect, and are provided strategies to help their children at home.

Teachers, family members, and students all benefit when parental involvement is successful (Spaulding, 1996). As family members and educators interact with each other, more understanding and acceptance develop among all involved. Parents' observations provide teachers with insights into the lives of students and give a different perspective on school behaviors. Sharing information about the child's situation at home or at school supports successful learning and more effective classroom interactions and planning. Likewise, when families understand what is occurring at school, they can support students and become involved in school activities. Parents and family members involved in school activities recognize that teachers understand their children and know about their backgrounds, including any special circumstances in their history. Teacher expectations of students are often affected by adult family members' involvement in school activities. Adults who work closely with the schools almost always perceive that teachers believe each child will succeed in school (Spaulding, 1996).

In addition to providing teachers with information about students, family members can become involved by visiting, volunteering, or working on projects at the school. The school can receive additional support from parents and family members when they contribute extra hands, additional ideas, untapped resources, and different perspectives to ongoing school activities. The presence of family members in the school and classrooms also means that community values are represented in the school. Family involvement in schools is one way to take advantage of a diversity of cultures and have the diversity represented in hallways, committee meetings, and school functions. At the same time, family involvement sends a signal to children and young people that learning and schools are important to the community and to the significant people in their families.

FIELD-BASED ACTIVITY

10.1

Write a short narrative about your memory of your own family members' involvement with your schools. What did they do? When did they come to school? Were they interested in and involved with your school experiences? Did their involvement change as you entered middle school and high school? If possible, contact your parents or other family members to determine what they remember about their involvement in your education. Share these stories with your peers.

INTASC Principles 9 and 10

Characteristics of Family Involvement

Rioux and Berla (1994) and Flaxman and Inger (1992) point out that family involvement can take many forms. Some activities take place at school, such as parent attendance at school events or participation in parent–teacher organizations. Others take place at home when parents help with daily homework activities. No matter what form the involvement takes, certain elements characterize programs that are successful. Schools with successful family involvement programs share the basic assumption that collaboration with others benefits students from elementary grades through high school. These schools encourage and nurture involvement and collaboration.

Parent involvement is more likely to occur in some groups even when schools make a concentrated effort to involve all families (Sheldon, 2003). Children from low-income and minority families have the most to gain from parental involvement in the schools. Family participation in the education of these students enhances their achievement (Henderson & Berla, 1994). Despite this outcome, most collaborative programs have primarily attracted white, middle-class, English-speaking family members. Parents and other family members from all socioeconomic levels, but particularly from low-income and minority groups, may be intimidated by interactions with school personnel and be afraid the problems their child is encountering in school will ultimately be blamed on their inability to raise the child properly. In this manner, a child's difficulty in school can add to an already-stressful home situation, leaving parents feeling like failures (Comer, 1994). In addition, some parents may relate school to their own past learning problems or bad experiences with school personnel.

Factors That Encourage Family Involvement

Parental involvement in schools sometimes depends on the ages and needs of the children. Family members may have every intention of being a partner with teachers, and for some this comes naturally. Other family members may need to be encouraged and instructed on what will help their children and their teachers. Family involvement can be encouraged by the district or school administration or by individual teachers. More than any other strategy the school may employ, the teachers' interactions and encouragement build successful relationships between homes and schools. Teachers and schools can foster positive involvement by employing the following strategies (Epstein, 1993; Fredericks & Rasinski, 1990):

FULFILLMENT OF BASIC NEEDS Families can supply the basic needs for their children. A secure home that provides food, clothing, shelter, and school supplies contributes a great deal to school success. Teachers may take this obligation for granted, but some families struggle to meet even basic requirements. Teachers may need to obtain help in meeting student needs from other professionals, social workers, community health professionals, or others. When it appears that families are having a difficult time providing basic needs to their children, teachers can be catalysts for involving other professionals who can help the families.

HOME–SCHOOL COMMUNICATION Family involvement is encouraged when effective communication is established between home and school. Teachers and schools assume a great deal of responsibility for creating lines of communication to parents. Positive communication helps family members learn about the nature of the school and the daily routines. When family members do not respond to school queries, teachers and administrators should investigate the reasons for communication failures and apply problem-solving strategies to encourage parental response.

RECOGNITION OF FAMILY DIFFERENCES Families demonstrate a wide range of comfort with school involvement. Many parents and family members assume that they will become involved in ongoing school activities. They visit classrooms, attend school plays, volunteer for specific jobs, and participate in instructional activities or as guest speakers. Mothers, fathers, and other family members become involved through organized volunteer programs, which encourage individuals outside the school to become involved in school activities. Some family members may become familiar with the school and know the names of many children in the school. Other family members are more hesitant because they do not know how to become involved, need a great deal of encouragement to participate, or perceive that they lack the resources or time for involvement.

HOME-BASED INVOLVEMENT Teachers may need to change their own definitions of family involvement. Involvement does not always mean that family members are visible at the school and participate in every opportunity available. Another way that busy family members can demonstrate their support of schools and the learning process is to participate in instruction at home. Well-planned, home-based activities provide a way for working parents and other family members to stay connected with school activities. Homework assignments provide one means for this, but a creative teacher might use television watching, Internet research, and reading together as part of a comprehensive plan to encourage students and family members to work together on school-related activities. Many teachers also encourage parents to just talk to their child at home about school activities, homework, and classroom events as a way to establish a system of accountability and to express caring and engagement in the child's education.

SCHOOLWIDE GOALS AND OBJECTIVES Schools that effectively involve parents have school goals and plan for regular parental involvement. Teachers might provide individual opportunities in single classrooms, but when family involvement is an overall school goal and accompanies a larger plan for increasing and maintaining parental involvement, the plan has more chances to be successful and long-term. Successful schools foster parental involvement in goal-setting and encourage parents to participate in school governance.

MULTIPLE METHODS OF INVOLVEMENT Schools should offer parents several ways to get involved. When families have such options, they can select ways to work with their schools that best suit their comfort, work schedule, talents, and abilities. Activities, meetings, and parent–teacher conferences should be planned at different times of the day so that working parents can arrange schedules and care for their younger children. Different family values, abilities, and schedules should be considered when teachers and schools plan home–school connections. Providing interpreters for multilingual family members is another way to create a comfortable and welcoming environment.

RECOGNITION Everyone likes to be recognized for contributing in a positive way. Family members who are recognized for their involvement in schools and classrooms respond positively and enthusiastically. Positive reinforcement can result in parents who view their participation as a valued and recognized contribution to the child's academic career.

CHILDREN AS RECRUITERS Most parents will respond to their children's requests, particularly if children register a great deal of excitement and enthusiasm about their parents' involvement in school.

INCLUSION OF ALL SIGNIFICANT ADULTS Parental involvement can include other family or community members. Brothers and sisters, aunts and uncles, grandparents, regular caretakers, and good friends can all take part in classroom events. Families take many different forms and do not always reflect traditional mother-father-children units. Parental involvement activities should be flexible enough to include all definitions of families.

COLLABORATION AMONG FAMILIES Involved families can work to recruit other families to participate in the classroom. Once family members understand routines in the schools, they can take over the training of new classroom volunteers. When a teacher forms teams of regular classroom supporters, these helpers can explain to other parents how to read aloud, how to help children with their math, and how to help in other learning tasks.

CHILDCARE PROVISIONS One way to encourage family involvement is to provide childcare for young children who are not yet in school. This encourages greater participation by family members who are caretakers to young children and assures that everyone who wishes to be involved in the school has the opportunity to do so. Childcare supported by volunteers or paid for by parent groups increases the chances that parents of young children can be involved in school activities.

In addition to the strategies described here, some schools use other techniques to make parents feel welcome. Employing volunteers from the community to serve as greeters of school visitors is one way to make parents feel more welcome. One school in Washington hired a parent to greet all visitors to the school. She was a member of the neighborhood, and almost all the parents recognized her and felt comfortable walking into the school when she was there to greet them. This particular greeter did not stay a stranger to anyone, and even people who had never visited the school before were greeted with a big hug and a warm hello. Everyone felt welcome at the school, and the school became a gathering point for the community.

Schools can develop a family-friendly attitude by providing physical space for families. Some schools provide a room for parents to gather. The family room becomes the hub of involvement activities and provides a community meeting place, a training center for parent and family education, and a place for families to meet their children. When schools provide a comfortable place for family members, it signifies a concrete commitment to the importance of partnerships in students' learning and school

FIELD-BASED ACTIVITY

10.2

Talk to students in your classrooms about how they feel when members of their family visit the school or volunteer to work on school activities. Begin a list of tips and guidelines that reflect what students, family members, and teachers relate to your class about family involvement.

INTASC Principle 10

success. At the very least, the routine for parents and family members who visit the school should be readily recognizable so that they feel a part of the school instead of feeling left out.

Family Involvement in Elementary and Secondary Schools

Most family involvement techniques are appropriate for elementary school. Educators unfortunately have less experience using the family-centered approach with older students. Although family involvement is most common in the elementary years, communication with schools continues to be a high priority at the secondary level and has many positive results and benefits. Practices associated with family involvement need to be reconstructed when adapting to middle school and high school. By the time students are in middle school, visits by parents must be carefully planned to support students who are generally pulling away from their parents and focusing on relationships with their peers. A parent's appearance in the hallway can cause extreme embarrassment, but a parent's absence at a sports event can be terribly upsetting. Middle school children like to know that their parents help plan behind the scenes and support them at home, but they do not necessarily want their parents' involvement to be obvious. By high school age, students' attitude toward parental involvement continues this pattern: Older children want their parents to work with them to gain information, discuss important topics brought up at school, and help them make decisions about careers and college. High school students are usually comfortable having their parents attend a seminar on career choices or a band concert. However, they may feel very uncomfortable having parents show up during the school day to observe in their classrooms. Many high schools plan open-house events, which encourage high school students and their parents to go through the daily schedule together so that parents can have a better understanding of their children's school day.

CLASSROOM VISITS One way to encourage parental involvement at the elementary level is to invite parents to visit the classroom. Having their parents or other adult acquaintances in the classroom to read, tutor, or help with a bulletin board can be exciting and comforting. The classroom should be open to parents, and each parent should feel comfortable visiting during instruction. Classroom visits can be arranged in different ways and for differing purposes.

Observation of classroom instruction is the minimum level of parental activity in the classroom. A teacher may have a set time when family members are welcome to visit to observe specific teaching and learning activities. Visits that incur no obligation other than observing in a friendly, welcoming classroom encourage involvement by family members in other activities throughout the school year.

Classroom visits help familiarize family members with classroom routines and procedures. One of the simplest things for visitors to do when they visit elementary classrooms is to share favorite stories or reading material. Family members can be included in daily read-aloud sessions and can share their favorite books. Tutoring in math, helping with writing, or working with individuals and small groups can all be accomplished during parent visits to the classroom.

Classroom visits with older students might not occur as regularly and might only involve very special occasions, such as a performance or guest speaker. Some secondary teachers invite parents to talk to classes about their jobs or special areas of expertise related to course content. Classroom visits in middle school and high school are best planned and organized with a great deal of student input.

FAMILY MEMBERS AS VOLUNTEERS The roles that parent volunteers can assume are endless. Many schools have parent volunteer programs that are regular support systems for school involvement. Family members may be responsible for an ongoing, specific job associated with school routines. They may assist in elementary classrooms by listening to children read aloud, working as scribes for children, or helping children learn math facts. Family members can help in secondary schools by accompanying groups on field trips, selling tickets at sports events, and tutoring children who might be having trouble in content areas. In some schools, parents are morning greeters as the older children arrive at school, and they also walk the halls during class changes. The presence of family members provides teachers and administrators with needed assistance, and the practice has noticeably decreased rowdiness and negative behavior.

SCHOOL CONFERENCES Teachers and family members discuss individual children during school conferences. Conferences are one way for teachers to measure the level of involvement of parents. Teachers get frustrated when family members do not appear, and they assume that families do not care for their own children when they fail to respond to school invitations. Ladson-Billings (1994) provides some insights about parental response from another perspective:

> One of the persistent complaints among today's teachers is that parents are not involved enough in the schools. Teachers lament the fact that more and more children come from households where both parents work. One statistic suggests that 75 percent of parents never visit their children's schools. I don't recall my parents going out of their way to come to school. Perhaps once a year they came for a conference or a student performance, but neither my mother nor my father was very visible. They were too busy working. They expected me to do what the teacher told me to do. However, if my teachers needed my parents for something, all they had to do was call. (pp. 39–40)

Teachers would do well to remember that family members' perceptions may be very different from their own and that parents may have numerous reasons not to respond to invitations to conferences and involvement.

Many school districts require conferences with parents or other family members to communicate how students are doing at school. Unfortunately, most conferences occur as a result of students doing poorly at school.

One important role of the teacher is to communicate to parents and caretakers. Meetings between parents and teachers should occur often enough so that both are comfortable talking and working together to provide the best educational environment possible.

Because of this, family members often feel very insecure when they are scheduled to discuss their child's work with a teacher. If teachers also arrange contacts with family members to talk about positive events and behaviors, conferences will not be dreaded. Most family members enjoy talking about their children, and conferences give them an opportunity to discuss progress, strengths, and potential problems. Conferences to produce long-term goals (i.e., Individual Education Plans) are required by law and in most cases are an excellent way to involve parents in the children's education. Conferences provide information to both parents and teachers, making their respective jobs somewhat easier.

When family members arrive at school, the conference atmosphere should be comfortable and relaxed. It is good to have something concrete to discuss during the first moments of the conference. Work samples, writing folders, records of progress in content areas, and portfolios can guide the discussions, providing samples of work and anecdotes of classroom activity. Conferences provide an opportunity to interpret tests and help parents and others understand the results. Teachers alleviate many fears by discussing students' classroom responses and behaviors. This in turn encourages parents to provide information about home behavior that may help teachers better understand their students.

Telephone conferences and home visits provide an important opportunity for parents to talk to a teacher in a more comfortable, less threatening environment. These types of contacts are most reasonable for working family members who cannot visit the school during the day.

The Center of Families, Communities, Schools, and Children's Learning can help you identify effective parent–school partnerships. You can learn about the five types of parental involvement at:

http://npin.org

The Parent Teacher Association Web site has good ideas to encourage parent involvement:

http://pta.org

URLs may change over time. For up-to-date links to relevant Web sites, visit our Companion Web site:

http://education.wadsworth.com/wiseman3e

Many levels of involvement can be expected from families, but the ultimate goal is to gain family commitment to the importance of active home–school cooperation. Parents, family members, and teachers should plan together for home–school involvement and work together to implement these plans (Rutherford & Billig, 1995). Very few programs of family involvement ever achieve this level of cooperation, and, once achieved, it is very difficult to maintain. Even so, a high level of parental involvement should be the goal and desired outcome of each effort.

Challenges of Family Involvement

Family involvement in school activities makes sense, but it is not always as simple as it sounds. Parents and other family members do not always feel comfortable in schools, and educators often dismiss their views as unimportant to the educational task (Ayers, 1993). Certain attitudes and situations can interfere with interactions between parents and teachers. Sometimes school has a particular emotional impact on parents and family members. For example, parents may have experienced school failure themselves and feel uneasy when asked to become involved with their children's classroom activities (Wilson & Wilson, 1994). If parents have not finished school, do not speak English, or feel inferior to the teacher and other school personnel, they may find it extremely difficult to be in the school setting and feel comfortable with their children's teacher. Parents' discomfort can increase if they do not understand what they are to do or if they feel they have nothing to offer in the school setting.

Parents and family members can also feel uncomfortable talking about their parenting skills, particularly if they are having difficulty providing some of the basic needs for their children. Family members may be embarrassed that they cannot provide school supplies or pay for school lunches. When students are exhibiting behavior problems or are not progressing in their schoolwork, parents may feel responsible. Teachers need to understand that caretakers may be very worried about their children but may not understand how to respond to the children's actions and behaviors that are causing concerns in school. If family members believe schools are being judgmental, they may avoid contact or view teachers' queries about their children's progress as attacks on their own competence as parents (Hamilton & Osborne, 1994).

Sometimes communication difficulties between the home and school create serious family and school discontinuities, discouraging parent–school linkages that could provide support systems for students with limited English proficiency (Chiang, 1994). Immigrant parents who work long hours, encounter linguistic and cultural barriers, and lack familiarity with the U.S. educational system often avoid coming to schools and talking to teachers. Parents need to understand what to do and how to collaborate with the teacher to help their children succeed at school (Flores, Cousin, & Diaz, 1991). Unless parents, families, teachers, and administrators work together to build a supportive learning environment, students will not receive all the benefits available to them.

Transportation, time, energy, and childcare needs are all barriers that may prevent parents from participating in school activities. These barriers are particularly troublesome for low-income families who have few resources

Volunteer to work in an activity or project that includes parents and other family members. In an elementary school, it might be decorating the school for a carnival or family night. In a middle or high school, it might be working in a concession stand during a sports event or chaperoning a dance on Friday night. Share some things you learned about parents and families with your classmates.

INTASC Principle 10

and less-flexible job schedules (Hamilton & Osborne, 1994). At the same time, low-income families are in particular need of support and interactions that contribute to their children's education. A good education is one way they can help their children have successful adult lives.

Teachers may contribute to noninvolvement of families by not understanding how to include them in the education of their children. Teachers may not have the skills or the experience to recognize the benefits of working with parents and families. Many teacher education programs do not emphasize working with families. Teachers may feel uncomfortable talking with families, and this may be more problematic for new teachers. School policies should explicitly emphasize the benefits of family involvement and encourage outside involvement of other caring adults. Otherwise, a teacher who has many tasks to complete may feel that parental involvement is just another intrusion that represents yet another time-consuming task. Research demonstrates that students' achievement and attitude about school can be heavily influenced by parental involvement, so it makes sense to find ways to include parents as partners.

Teachers' Roles

Working with parents requires good interpersonal skills and, when conducted with respect, interactions with families will be successful in establishing the contact necessary for helping children do their best. The National Board for Professional Teaching Standards (1994), which seeks to create common standards for teachers throughout the United States, states in Proposition 5 that "highly accomplished teachers work to create positive relationships with families as they participate in the education of their children." Teachers need to develop skills and understandings to foster collaborative relationships between school and family. Basic interpersonal skills of communication and respect go a long way in establishing school–family relationships. However, at times, conversations with family members may involve difficult issues. Parents respond positively to reinforcement of their attempts to increase their child's well-being. Teachers who attempt to understand parents' actions will increase the number of positive interactions with parents and will enhance parents' and family members' perceptions of their own abilities. Teachers should be honest and direct when talking to parents, praising children and their efforts with sincerity.

One way to ensure that all voices are heard is to institute a school-based governance team with representatives from school and family groups. Together, this team, guided by the school principal, works to develop a school plan that includes strategies for a positive school climate and academic goals for all students. When a positive, inviting school climate is the goal of all participants, parent involvement can be built in as an integral and necessary activity (Comer, 1994). When the entire school supports and encourages parental involvement, it becomes easier for each individual teacher to work with parents in productive ways.

Community Involvement

Education should be everybody's business—"a common enterprise in which all adults of the community unite to protect, nurture, guide, and educate the young" (Hindle, 1993, p. 34). The community as a whole influences the way children feel about themselves, their attitudes toward education, and student success in schools (Engein, 2003). Explicit connections between schools and communities will affect children.

> When the community is engaged with the school, resources and benefits flow both ways. Community partners provide on-site supports and opportunities for students, their families and their neighbors. In turn, the school maintains an active presence as a community hub, providing opportunities for family involvement, tapping into the community as a resource for learning and serving as a center for community problem solving (Coalition for Community Schools, 2003).

Role models from all aspects of life demonstrate the importance of learning and the value of an education. If students see that everyone around them cares about what and how they do in school, it can boost their self-confidence, attitude, and achievement.

Accomplished teachers understand their school's community and use it as a powerful resource for learning by taking advantage of the many opportunities for enrichment and exploration. The community serves as a learning and resource lab for developing tolerance and civic responsibility and for understanding about human differences. Experienced teachers will find activities and events in the community (especially those important to students) and use them as starting points for discussions and as foundations for curriculum and classroom lessons.

To effectively use available resources, teachers must first understand the community and how the environment affects the students and the school. The community's context, culture, and personality contribute to the fabric of its schools. The ethnic, religious, and cultural diversity; the economic and business settings; and the religious and historical values are all important parts of the school. Using that knowledge to build classroom projects, activities, and lessons provides a solid context for good teaching and learning.

Many valuable resources are offered by individuals in the community. Alliances with community organizations, such as churches, women's clubs, the NAACP, and fraternal groups, can bring people and resources into the schools. Volunteers from these organizations may serve as mentors, tutors, or resources for lessons on specific cultural groups. More important, they can give key advice on curriculum content. Senior citizens, parents, businesspeople, and local organizations can also enhance and supplement teaching and learning activities: They can visit classrooms, tutor students, provide emotional support, and participate in governance and administrative activities. They can volunteer in the school and support school sports, music, and theater by attending events.

Incorporating the community into school activities produces citizens who understand and are supportive of schools and encourages good public relations between education professionals and community members. Informed and supportive citizens influence decisions in the schools by voting on school issues, participating on school boards, and supporting education experiences with their own work and leisure time. When schools include and consider the community in educational endeavors, they receive needed support in times of bond elections and other efforts that require resources to improve educational environments. Citizens who are familiar with the students and the local school support the efforts of educators. When schools lose the support of their citizens, schools suffer economically and cannot generate the resources they need for continued growth and progress. Successful schools require more than the economic resources from their communities. A community that believes that its school is important to everyone's well-being conveys that message to teachers and students, thus improving the chances of success for everyone involved.

Partnerships between schools and communities can also help solve some of our most difficult social problems. Communities and schools work together to curb violence, drug abuse, teen pregnancies, and other tough problems. Many effective community collaborations result in improved educational programs, changes in school climate, and an increase in family support systems (Epstein, 1995).

Communities include families and children and also businesses, community services, health and human social services, institutions of higher education, city government, juvenile workers, and others. Educational experiences are enhanced when people from other community settings become involved in the welfare and education of young people. Communities that encourage their agencies and institutions to assist children and families are capable of building an effective support system that has great potential to enrich educational experiences. To develop a truly educated person, school efforts must go far beyond the classroom. Without the help of people outside the classroom, even the best teachers will have difficulty educating their students.

Business Partners

The collaboration between business and education, focused on helping schools succeed, is developed in several different ways (Hindle, 1993). Businesses and public schools often collaborate to offer special programs to particular schools or to sponsor students for career exploration. Sometimes a three-way partnership is formed among businesses, universities, and public schools. Business–education collaborations are almost always created under the belief that a broad-based alliance among many sectors of the community is necessary to provide the best schools possible. Here are some ways that business can support education:

- *Resources.* Businesses can provide resources beyond the basic expectations of school support (Hindle, 1993). They may provide money and equipment to support special programs, such as summer tutoring, field trips, or college/career exploration. Technology-based businesses have regularly supported school programs that feature technology. Computer companies have provided computers, scientific companies have donated lab equipment, and other companies have even stocked school libraries.

- *Special programs.* Business supports supplementary programs that enhance students' educational experiences (Hindle, 1993). Special programs encouraging students' interest in math and science are one focus of business-oriented programs. Business-sponsored programs may occur in the summer, on Saturdays, or after normal school hours. Activities are planned to give students opportunities to serve as junior interns, office helpers, or lab assistants. Businesspeople who develop mentoring relationships with individual students have a great influence on student attitudes about schools and career.

- *Expertise.* Businesspeople also offer their expertise to education professionals (Hindle, 1993). Specialists who use a particular group process or management technique may work with schools to suggest ways to improve decision-making processes, organizational approaches, and management.

- *Information.* Businesses can provide students with a concrete lesson in understanding possibilities, skills, and requirements of potential jobs and occupations (Hindle, 1993). Summer internships for high school students, field trips to particular sites, and guest speakers provide vital information as young people make decisions about their future occupations.

Businesses are very interested in helping schools in their communities succeed. School–business partnerships provide businesspeople with a way to contribute to their community, support special education projects, and help students learn about careers and occupations.

- *Volunteers.* Businesspeople may be encouraged to become actively involved in specific school projects. People who manage and work in business may volunteer, become partners, and work directly with schools to change and enhance educational programs. Some enlightened companies give employees time off to help schools with activities.

Of course, many of the activities sponsored by business and industry are specifically related to the focus of their work. Some may hope that their involvement will produce competent future workers—or at least future customers. In other cases, businesses will partner with schools as an altruistic gesture of civic duty to support the community. Often, however, the emphasis of particular businesses and the goals of schooling are very much aligned.

Business has in fact been involved in the school reform debate, supporting changes in curriculum to more closely align learning with skills and knowledge needed by business. In the mid-1990s, the School-to-Work Opportunities Act established a national framework to broaden the educational, career, and economic opportunities for all youth through partnerships among businesses, schools, community-based organizations, and state and local governments. The intention of school-to-work programs was to change the way teachers teach and students learn. The basis of the change was to refocus on identifying and classifying the skills workers need to perform successfully in the workplace and to coordinate curriculum developed from the skills of workers with school curriculum. The school-to-work opportunities systems were designed to create a transition between classrooms and the workplace or other educational settings. Creative transition programs that many people are already familiar with (such as youth apprenticeship, cooperative education, and career academies) were the foundations on which school-to-work systems were built. Although the federal support for this program has been greatly reduced, remnants of the school-to-work program still exist at several sites.

Business tends to have a greater influence over educational changes than do other groups (Myers & Myers, 1995). Businesspeople are usually active in government and therefore exert some influence over local and state decisions. Having a preference for curricula that reflect workforce needs, business has positioned itself to influence educational processes. Business can therefore directly affect how schools spend tax money and public attitudes toward education.

During the past decade, business and labor have paid particularly close attention to educational reform (Farris, 1996). Business (as prominent community institutions) often have a great deal of influence during school reform efforts (Hindle, 1993). In some instances, business has leveled particularly harsh criticism at education, schools, and teaching. In particular, businesspeople question the effectiveness of school management and operations. They also support better teaching of basic skills. Most people associated with business believe it is in their best interest that teaching and learning produce students who are proficient, knowledgeable, and able to be successful in the workforce after graduation from high school.

▶ *Interprofessional Partners*

> There is no great mystery about what it takes to help a troubled child or family. In study after study, we find that two things stand out in the histories of kids who make it against the odds. . . . The first fact is access to a second chance to succeed at something the person failed at before—going back to school, being helped to pass a class (as opposed to being either punished or excused for it). . . . The second is the intervention of just one caring person from outside the family . . . that person's role is . . . to get involved in the child's life. (Coontz, 1995, p. K16)

Children and young people often face personal and social difficulties that affect their academic achievement. Teachers commonly mention that the toughest problems they face when working with students are related to social, personal, and health issues. Poverty, violence, drug abuse, and homelessness are major problems in schools, and even the best teachers and the best-planned curriculum cannot overcome them. Children cannot learn unless their basic needs are met. One way to combat social issues and the many demands that children and families face is to develop collaborative relationships between education and health and human services professionals. Nurses, doctors, social workers, community health professionals, and others can become partners who focus on the welfare of children and can provide a wide range of social service activities and programs to help parents help their children. A collaborative effort among professionals who care about children is one of the best ways to offset at-risk behavior. Many feel that collaboration by professionals who work with children and families, called interprofessional collaboration, is one trend of the future that holds a great deal of promise for improving the lives of children and young people.

The number of services designed to help troubled children and families—and the red tape necessary to access those services—are overwhelming to even the most savvy person. When children and families are in trouble, they may need to contact several agencies to receive the help they need. The offices where the families could get help are often located in different parts of town or in unfamiliar areas. Once families find where help can be provided, they must complete many forms, answer many questions, and provide many documents. The health clinic requires one form that asks a multitude of questions, the social worker asks for another form, the social security office requests still another (with notarized signatures), and so on. These documents and instructions are usually written in English that is difficult for native speakers and incomprehensible for families who speak little or no English. Even when families finally access services, the services may be limited and may not accomplish what is needed or may require repeated visits. It is no wonder that children do not receive the services they need to do well in school.

Parents, especially those in low-income, high-risk neighborhoods, are often unaware of the array of social services available to them through the many different organizations working in the community. A school that strives to link social services with academic programs can meet many needs and potentially improve academic achievement in the classroom. Through this link with family support services, schools can address not only the academic problems of students but also their social, psychological, and health problems. Serving as a center for social programs, such a school might offer after-school care for school-age children, day care for three- to five-year-olds, adult literacy classes, teen pregnancy prevention classes, and other services that address the needs of the community it serves.

Efforts that connect social programs with educational outcomes report success stories for students. "Schools, social programs, and caring individuals can compensate for stressful environments and troubled families" (Coontz, 1995, p. K17). Problems facing children and families may seem overwhelming to parents and teachers. At the same time that parents are faced with troubled children, they may be battling their own crises and lack the energy or resources to focus on their children's issues.

Interprofessional programs and activities provide needed support to children and families who find themselves in crisis. Teachers, social workers, community nurses, doctors, dentists, and juvenile workers are among those who generally collaborate to simplify processes. In some cases, police and judges are also involved in these endeavors. These professionals have various objectives, but improvement of children and family situations is at the center of their professional mission. Collaboration can begin by talking together—a skill that must be learned, because even simple tasks linking health and human service agencies can take a great deal of time. In one town in Texas, professionals worked together for a year and a half to devise a single form that could be used by several social service agencies. The result was that families and children could access services with a bit more ease than before the professionals sat down to talk.

The physical facilities supporting interprofessional activities may be based in schools, housing projects, community development corporations, or childcare centers. Sometimes collaborative efforts result in school-based clinics or family centers designed to encourage interprofessional collaboration. These efforts help parents and other interested adults promote their children's learning and give parents the training and self-confidence necessary to be involved in their children's educational processes.

Interprofessional activities—such as job counseling and training, health care, substance abuse treatment, nutrition, housing, transportation, referral centers for family social services, and before- and after-school programs for working parents—are examples of support systems that can aid learning and teaching. Activities that result from collaboration among individuals from different professions to provide integrated services may be called community-based services, school-based services, "one-stop shopping," or interprofessional activities.

Interprofessional collaborations focus on three major activities:

1. *Parent education and parent involvement in the education of their children.* Programs focusing on schools may include the family, the school, childcare and youth programs, and health care agencies.

2. *Intersections between health and human services.* These programs encourage parents to take greater responsibility for their children's primary health care. Parents learn more about health care services: how to access services and how to make them work for the betterment of their children's lives. Programs assess health needs of children and youth, link families and health care providers, and help improve health education in the school.

3. *Professional training of teachers and other professionals.* The professional development of individuals who are trained to work across professions is crucial. University faculty involved in professional training of teachers, social workers, and other health and human service professionals design curriculum and develop field experiences that help future professionals learn about this work.

The importance of interprofessional support is that public and private community resources and public school resources can be combined to focus on prevention and early interventions that address the needs of all students. Different professional groups work together to identify and remove unnecessary regulations and obstacles to coordinating efforts and to provide a strong support system to students. Professional collaboration increases students' access to social services, health care, nutrition, related services, and childcare services. These partnerships can help parents and

Voice of a Parent

I am Maria Sanchez. I live with my husband and two children just up the block from the Family Center. I want to tell you about my experience.

I've been coming here [to the Family Center] for a year now. It is a great place to come and learn about resources around the community. Everything is in one place.

Let me tell you how I got started coming here. I used to walk my boys to the school cafeteria [next door to the Family Center] for free lunch during the summer. I had to walk by here and I noticed things going on. I peeked in and saw flyers telling about activities and meetings that were planned here in the Family Center. To be honest, I was bored and spent much of my time sitting in my apartment in front of the TV. It was summertime and it was hot. I had no air conditioning and this was a cool place to bring my children. I would bring my children here to the programs or to play with toys or read books or just to talk to people. I started coming a lot in the daytime. I came to CPR classes, jewelry classes, and the one I liked best was taught by the School District Parent Educator. It was a program about how to buy a house from the city. It raised my hopes for the future.

I am thirty years old now and I have been out of school for fourteen years. I don't know why I have not thought about doing anything much to improve myself, but I guess I just lacked the drive. Now I have completed and passed my GED and I have a job with the Family Literacy Program, where I get to work with and help other parents.

If it hadn't been for the Family Center, I would not have my job. The Family Center Program Manager knew my capabilities, and she recommended me to the Family Literacy people for this job. At the time I didn't have any intention to get my GED, but since it was a requirement for the job I went ahead and took the GED test. I passed right away. Now I plan to go back to school. I want to take courses at the community college.

I love my job. As I said, I like working with parents. I get to plan trips to the library for parents. Let me tell you about one mother who had never had a library card before. It was a very exciting thing for her to get a library card. I made a photocopy of her library card to keep in her file so that she could have a memento. It was so special.

And since I know about the Family Center, I bring new people from the Literacy Program down here to see what's going on.

I want to add that since I have been coming here to the Family Center, and since I have joined Community Voices [a neighborhood action group that meets at the Family Center], I have become more involved with my children's school. I feel more confident about just going to see what is happening.

FIELD-BASED ACTIVITY

10.4

Locate a community facility that has more than one service (social services, law officials, community health facilities) in one place. It will probably be a community or family center. Choose one of these activities to help you learn about the activities in the center: (1) interview the professionals and/or the children and families, (2) volunteer to help with a project, or (3) sit in the reception area of the facility and take field notes.

INTASC Principles 9 and 10

families by locating such services in schools, cooperating service agencies, community-based centers, or other convenient sites designed to provide "one-stop shopping" for parents and students (U.S. Department of Education, 1994).

Addressing some problems may require interprofessional efforts among individuals. Intervention and help for individual children and their families occur when a teacher, a social worker, a community nurse, or a police officer talk and work together on one issue. Interprofessional work can be embedded in a larger program with a national focus or small programs emerging from grassroots efforts to solve particular problems. To better understand the range and impact of collaborative effort, let's look at three examples in more detail:

Healthy Learners in School Program

This kindergarten-to-grade-five school program focuses on helping children learn about their health so they can make healthy life decisions. The program places public health nurses in schools, where they act as catalysts for collaborative efforts among teachers, students, parents and caretakers, service providers, and community groups. The collaborative partnerships have established over 1,400 school-based health centers. Healthy Learners sponsors varied health-related activities, including free screenings for asthma and other childhood afflictions and an awareness campaign to promote healthy messages schoolwide to students and parents. The school-based health centers provide resources for students to have physical examinations, immunizations, asthma care, counseling, and other essential services.

www You can learn more about the Healthy Learners in School Program at the following Web site:

http://www.district18.nbed.nb.ca/district/ed-services/healthy-learners/default.asp

URLs may change over time. For up-to-date links to relevant Web sites, visit our Companion Web site:

http://education.wadsworth.com/wiseman3e

School Families

A middle school and a university in Texas developed a program to involve community volunteers, university professors, and teachers in a mentoring relationship that provided middle school students with support during the school day. A cornerstone activity at the Texas site has been the School Families program, which provides an academic and social support system for the students along with opportunities for preservice and inservice teachers, school counselors, administrators, and community volunteers to collaborate. Once a week, five adults meet with one classroom. The session begins with whole class discussion and then students and adults break into small groups, where they discuss social, academic, and personal issues.

Accomplished teachers participate in the coordination of services to students. They understand what is available to assist children and families who are under stress, and they know how to access support systems that will contribute to their students' classroom success.

School Development Program

The School Development Program (Comer, 1999) is a large, comprehensive effort that uses an interprofessional approach to oversee students' school experiences and overall development. Schools that implement this program replace traditional school organization with three teams, each with a specific focus:

- The School Planning and Mangement Team focuses on developing a school plan; setting academic, social, and community relationship goals; and coordinating school activities. It includes school administrators, school staff, and parents.

- The Student and Staff Support Team focuses on social conditions and relationships and connects the school's student services with teachers and administrators. It includes school administration staff and professionals with expertise in child development and mental health (such as social workers, psychologists, and nurses).

- The Parent Team develops activities that support the school's social and academic programs. It also has a representative on the School Planning and Management Team.

You can learn more about the School Development Program at the following Web site:

http://info.med.yale.edu/comer/

URLs may change over time. For up-to-date links to relevant Web sites, visit our Companion Web site:

http://education.wadsworth.com/wiseman3e

Schools that embrace the Comer process place students' academic, physical, and emotional needs at the center of the school's agenda. Interprofessional teams and parents work together, make decisions, and share the responsibility for students' school experiences and successes.

Churches and Religious Groups

Churches provide an important community link. For many students, the church is a crucial component of family life. Church ministers are often considered members of the extended family and can be valuable in making school–home connections. In some communities, churches and schools work together to provide day care and after-school programs, organize parent support groups, and improve education for their children (Freedman & Negroni, 1992; Lawson & Briar-Lawson, 1997). Constitutional law may prohibit churches from influencing public school curricular decisions, but their impact on families and children must be considered as part of the context of schooling.

President G. W. Bush has attempted to eliminate barriers that have kept faith-based charities from collaborating with many state and federal

© Jeff Greenberg/The Image Works

Schools are part of the larger community, in which individuals and organizations outside the school contribute to students' personal, social, and academic development. Religious leaders may serve as role models, teachers, and counselors for students.

You can find out more about faith-based initiatives at the following Web site:

http://www.whitehouse.gov/news/releases/2003/09/20030922-1.html

URLs may change over time. For up-to-date links to relevant Web sites, visit our Companion Web site:

http://education.wadsworth.com/wiseman3e

supported institutions. Recent regulations allow faith-based charities to receive federal funds. The new regulations focus on church efforts that "better serve Americans in need," and recent legislative efforts may provide even more flexibility in how public schools and churches work together. Church-based tutoring activities are examples of how faith-based initiatives might provide educational services.

Challenges of Collaboration

Many potential partners may be involved in the complex job of educating students. Collaboration is difficult, but when it is successful, students benefit. The challenges to developing broad-based community collaboration are many.

One factor that prevents collaboration from occurring among different professions is role specialization. Professional specialists ranging from nurses to librarians are trained to understand a particular area and to control and manage different parts of the school system. Educators' roles usually are based on specialization and on understanding certain parts of the educational processes. Science teachers want to teach science, nurses are trained to provide health services, and social workers are experienced in social services. These professionals have not been exposed to ways of working together and connecting their work across professions. This specialization often results in a lack of understanding of the possible contributions others could make.

To begin this work, professionals often have to learn how to work collaboratively, not worry about their own turf, and take the time to understand other people's contexts and professional lives. Collaborative work among schools, families, and communities requires a great deal of negotiating to ensure an effective level of cooperation among professionals.

Involving others in the educational experience may seem an overwhelming task at first. Including input from parents, family members, community, and health and human service professional personnel in the schools adds to the existing complexities and ambiguities. However, if teachers and administrators judge the involvement of others in the day-to-day routine of schools to be vital to their mission and consider it a resource to supplement ongoing school activities, they will view collaboration with such available partners positively. The results of involving the community in students' learning are recognizable yet difficult to measure. It takes time to see changes brought about by collaborative interventions, and schools and business often lack the patience to support an initiative for the five to seven years it may take. Nevertheless, the benefits of collaboration are worth the time and effort educators invest.

Beginning teachers can probably be convinced that working with families, the community, businesses, and other professionals is a good idea, but actually getting involved in collaborative efforts is quite another matter. You may need several years of teaching experience before you understand how you might develop your skills and contribute to these efforts. The first step for beginning educators is to become comfortable with your students' families and the community where you work. Volunteer in community projects, serve on a citywide committee, or visit boys' and girls' clubs in the neighborhoods that surround your school.

A second step is to understand the potential of collaborative efforts and to be open and flexible to ideas that involve partners outside the school walls. Reading and hearing about community-based projects established in schools will provide you with a basic understanding of who might be involved in such activities. Community involvement can be as simple as inviting community members into the classroom or as complex as working with several social services. Once you become aware of the potential of community involvement, you will notice many exemplar options.

Learning to talk and communicate with individuals from other professions will help you develop the capacity for understanding how to collaborate. Participating in ongoing discussions and planning at school will help a new teacher understand the potential of partnerships. When new teachers see a way that they can become involved, they can participate in a way that seems appropriate in their own lives. Take the time now to complete the Self-Reflection exercise on page 350 and to think about what you have learned.

New teachers need to develop the skills associated with good collaboration. Collaborative skills are useful in many areas of daily life, and many teachers already possess them. Listening to others, rephrasing what others have said, remaining flexible, accepting new ideas, and accepting that conflict will emerge when people work together are just a few of the valuable skills needed to collaborate with others productively.

It is difficult to become involved with other individuals and professionals when you are a novice in your own role as a teacher. Although a teacher cannot always single-handedly marshal resources on behalf of his or her students, new teachers will have opportunities to take part in discussions with others who may be able to help. Once new teachers gain information about what is available to help them teach and students learn, they can begin helping to plan cooperative ventures and participate with others to provide the best possible educational environment for their students.

Family and Community Collaborations

Read the following statements about activities that involve you with families and communities. Check any that you have done. If you have been involved in other activities not listed, add them to the list.

_____ **1.** Visit local community centers

_____ **2.** Work with boys' and girls' clubs

_____ **3.** Coach a community sports team

_____ **4.** Serve on a neighborhood committee

_____ **5.** Tutor in adult or child literacy programs

_____ **6.** Attend community functions and celebrations

_____ **7.** Tutor in an after-school program

_____ **8.** Volunteer at a homeless shelter

_____ **9.** Volunteer in low-income childcare facilities

_____ **10.** Read to children at the local library

_____ **11.** _____

_____ **12.** _____

Count the number of checks you have. If you have three or more, you are well on your way to understanding and appreciating the potential contributions of family and community to your work with students. If you have very few checks, you may want to plan ways to learn more about the community where your school is located.

PORTFOLIO REFLECTIONS AND EXHIBITS

Review the Field-Based Activities in this chapter. Adapt and expand one of the activities, design your own exhibit, or complete this suggested portfolio exhibit to represent your learnings and understandings from this chapter.

Suggested Exhibit 10: Experiences with Families and Communities

Your portfolio representation for this chapter should include

1. A summary of all the Field-Based Activities you completed for this chapter

2. Selection of and a rationale for the activity that was most important to you

3. A representation of your experiences and assumptions about the families of students

Decide on the medium you will use to represent your ideas. Review and summarize in writing your ideas about family involvement based on your own experiences. Add narrative explaining what the students and families at your school have taught you about family involvement. Finally, include a description of a community activity you have encountered. Draw a picture, make a collage, graph, continuum, or cut articles from magazines and newspapers that demonstrate your learning from this chapter. Limit this illustration to two pages.

E-Portfolio Entry 10

Develop a two-part E-Portfolio Entry. The first part is the development of a map of the community where your school is located. You may use a map that you find online. Include some of the important sites, such as where your students receive health care, attend church, and engage in recreational activities. If possible, include sites where parents work on the map. Secondly, produce a collage about what you have learned about the families in the community that surrounds the school where you are located. Find online newspaper articles and other online images that characterize the community.

You may also want to visit the following Web site: http://www.community schools.org/partnerships.html#nine

Read the descriptions of the community schools. Write a brief description of how you might bring community resources into the school where you are currently observing. Save your suggestions to a file in your portfolio.

INTASC Principles 9 and 10

ANSWERS TO GUIDING YOUR READING

1. What are the school's and teacher's roles in encouraging collaboration with parents and others?

   Schools should be a welcoming place for parents and offer a range of activities that encourage parents' involvement. Teachers contribute to family involvement by understanding how to include parents and caregivers in students' educational experience. Teachers should be comfortable talking with families and emphasize the benefits of family involvement to parents and others. Schools and teachers who are involved in successful family involvement share the basic assumption that collaboration with others provides benefits for all children.

2. How can multiple partners help students, and what are the benefits of collaborative educational efforts?

   Everyone in the community should be concerned about children and young people and the schools they attend. Explicit connections between schools and other interested partners influence the way that students feel about themselves, improve overall attitudes toward education, and have been linked to improved academic achievement. Including multiple partners in educational processes increases the options and opportunities for students' enrichment and exploration related to learning. An additional benefit of involving multiple partners in school activities is the resultant good public relations between schools and others.

3. How can beginning teachers involve others to improve the success of students?

   Learning how to involve others in students' school success requires an attitude in which others' contributions are accepted as valuable to student learning. Beginning teachers can develop their ideas about family and community involvement by observing family interactions in the school where they are learning to teach, learning and reading about successful community and parent involvement activities in other settings, and becoming involved in community-based activities.

 INFOTRAC COLLEGE EDITION EXTENSION

Log on to the InfoTrac College Edition Web site and use the skills you have gained throughout the semester to find the answers to these questions about collaboration:

1. What are the names of some journals that feature articles and research about collaboration between schools and other agencies or people?

2. Judging from the titles of recent articles in this area, what kinds of collaboration appear to be the most common?

3. What are some benefits and barriers to collaboration between schools and others?

RELATED READINGS

Clinton, H. R. (1995). *It takes a village to raise a child.* New York: Simon & Schuster.

Hillary Rodham Clinton describes her own upbringing and her view of raising children. She explores the responsibilities of communities, in addition to families, to watch after children.

Hechinger, F. M. (1992). *Fateful choices: Healthy youth for the 21st century.* New York: Carnegie Corporation, Council on Adolescent Development.

This book portrays the complex risks and opportunities of the adolescent years. The author believes that, if adolescents are to make wise choices, families and communities must provide support while teenagers are making the transition from childhood to adulthood.

Kralovec, E., & Buell, J. (2000). *The end of homwork: How homework disrupts families, overburdens children, and limits learning.* Boston: Beacon Press.

This book questions the value of homework in light of how it affects overworked parents and discriminates against children who do not have computers, libraries, or well-educated parents.

Lareau, A. (2000). *Home advantage: Social class and parental intervention in elementary education.* Lanham, MD: Roman & Littlefield.

Lareau illustrates how parents try to help their children succeed in school. She points out that working-class and middle-class parents differ in the type and number of resources they bring to the task. Her descriptions help us understand the many small ways parents make sure their children get a good education.

REFERENCES

Epigraph: Meier, Deborah. *In schools we trust: Creating communities of learning in an era of testing and standardization* (p. 44). Boston, MA: Beacon Press.

Ayers, W. (1993). *To teach: The journey of a teacher.* New York: Teachers College Press.

Briar, K. (1993). Response sheet: Program information on integrated services and interprofessional education. Unpublished raw data. Florida International University, Miami.

Chiang, R. A. (1994). Home–school communication for Asian students with limited English proficiency. *Kappa Delta Pi Record,* 30(4), 159–163.

Coalition for Community Schools. (2003). *Making the difference: Research and practice in community schools.* Washington, DC: Author.

Comer, J. (1994). Home, school, and academic learning. In J. I. Goodlad & P. Keating (Eds.), *Access to knowledge: The continuing agenda for our nation's schools* (pp. 23–42). New York: The College Board.

Comer, J. P. (Ed.) (1999). *Child by child: The Comer process for change in education.* New York: Teachers College Press.

Coontz, S. (1995). The American family and the nostalgia trap: Kappan special report. *Phi Delta Kappan,* 76(7), K1–K21.

Epstein, J. (1993, April). Make parents your partners. *Instructor,* 103(1), 73–76.

Epstein, J. (1995). School/family/community partnerships: Caring for the children we share. *Phi Delta Kappan,* 76(9), 701–712.

Engein, J. T. (2003). Guiding school/business partnerships. *Principal Leadership,* 3, 36–39.

Farris, P. J. (1996). *Teaching: Bearing the torch.* Dubuque: Brown & Benchmark.

Flaxman, E., & Inger, M. (1992). Parents and schooling in the 1990s. *Education Digest,* 57, 3–7.

Flores, B., Cousin, P. T., & Diaz, E. (1991). Transforming deficit myths about learning, language, and culture. *Language Arts,* 68(5), 369–386.

Fredericks, A. D., & Rasinski, T. V. (1990). Working with parents: Involving the uninvolved—how to. *Reading Teacher,* 43(6), 424–425.

Freedman, S., & Negroni, P. J. (1992). School and community working together: Community education in Springfield. In L. E. Decker & V. A. Romney (Eds.), *Educational restructuring and the community education process* (pp. 111–120). Charlottesville: University of Virginia.

Hamilton, D., & Osborne, S. (1994). Overcoming barriers to parent involvement in public schools. *Kappa Delta Pi Record,* 30(4), 148–152.

Henderson, A. T., & Berla, N. (1994). *A new generation of evidence: The family is critical to student achievement.* St. Louis, MO: Danforth Foundation and Flint, MI: Mott.

Hollifield, J. H. (1994). *High schools gear up to create effective school and family partnerships.* Baltimore, MD: Center on Families, Communities, Schools, and Children's Learning, Johns Hopkins University. (ERIC Document Reproduction No. ED 380 229)

Hindle, W. R. (1993). The business–higher education link: Consider the possibilities. *Educational Record* (Summer), 33–38.

Ladson-Billings, G. (1994). *The dreamkeepers.* San Francisco: Jossey-Bass.

Lawson, H., & Briar-Lawson, G. (1997). *Connecting the dots: Progress toward the integration of school reform, school-linked services, parent involvement and community schools.* Oxford, OH: The Danforth Foundation and the Institute for Educational Renewal at Miami University.

Myers, C. B., & Myers, L. K. (1995). *The professional educator.* Belmont, CA: Wadsworth.

National Board for Professional Teaching Standards. (1994). *What teachers should know and be able to do.* Detroit: Author.

Rioux, W., & Berla, N. (1994). The necessary partners. *Education Week,* 13(17), 31.

Rutherford, B., & Billig, S. (1995). Eight lessons of parent, family, and community involvement in the middle grades. *Phi Delta Kappan,* 77(1), 64–68.

Scott-Jones, D. (1988). Families as educators: The transition from informal to formal school learning. *Educational Horizons,* 66(2), 66–69.

Sheldon, S. (2003). Linking school-family-community partnerships in urban elementary schools to student achievement on state tests. *The Urban Review,* 35(2), 149–165.

Southwest Educational Developmental Laboratory. (2002). *A new wave of evidence: The impact of school, family, and community connections on student achievement.* Austin, TX: Author.

Spaulding, A. M. (1996). The politics of primaries. In A. Pollard, A. Flier, & D. Thiessen (Eds.), *Children and the curriculum: The perspectives of primary and elementary school pupils* (pp. 132–148). London: Falmer Press.

U.S. Department of Education. (1994). *Changing education: Resources for systemic change.* Washington, DC: Author.

Wilson, S. M., & Wilson, J. D. (1994). Kentucky parents respond to primary education reform. *Dimensions of Early Childhood,* 22(2), 28–31.

Your Professional Portfolio

Portfolios may be a requirement for completion of your teacher education program. If your program requires you to keep a portfolio, it may also include specific suggestions for how you go about collecting evidence about your teaching. Hopefully, the suggestions in this book will fit in with what you must do in your program. Portfolio evidence can link to state or national requirements and may be used to provide examples that your performance as a new teacher meets established standards. Even if your program does not require a portfolio, you may decide that it is a good thing for you to do. Portfolios assist you as you reflect upon your own growth as a teacher and can be used as you move through the profession. As you will see, they can be used when you search for your first position or could be required for your evaluation once you are hired. The suggestions in this book can help you get started, contribute to required portfolio assignments, or help you start a portfolio on your own. Because a portfolio is more than a collection of exhibits, following are some basic suggestions about how you can develop, organize, and present the portfolio activities associated with this book.

Preparing Your Portfolio

You have completed Portfolio Reflections and Exhibits for each chapter and worked through a series of Field-Based Activities. The products that have emerged from these activities can become part of your professional portfolio. The exhibits and artifacts included in a portfolio should be carefully selected to help you describe your own teaching. More than a simple collection of work, a well-developed professional portfolio is a representation of your philosophy of teaching and growth and development as a teacher. Portfolio exhibits also provide an opportunity for you to demonstrate your own unique skills and creativity. Here are several suggestions that you may find helpful as you begin to develop your professional portfolio.

Establish the Purpose of Your Portfolio

A portfolio presents picture of you as a teacher and benchmarks your developmental accomplishments. How you set it up will depend upon how you plan to use it. Your portfolio may serve one of at least four different purposes (Constantino & DeLorenzo, 2002), as follows:

Admission Portfolio. Some teacher education programs require a portfolio for admission. A portfolio designed as a admittance requirement should provide information about your prior experiences related to teaching and the skills and dispositions you have developed that will suggest potential in teaching.

Working Portfolio. This may be used to document your work and growth as you complete your teacher education requirements. The exhibits in a working portfolio document your experiences at various benchmarks in your program—for example, evidence that you have interacted with your professors, teachers in the schools, and other supervisors and used the portfolio documents as a basis for discussing teaching performance.

Exit Portfolio. This selection of artifacts illustrates that you have met the goals and standards of your teacher education program. Exit portfolios are often evaluated by rubrics and required as part of your successful completion of a program.

Interview Portfolio. Many future teachers collect their best work and compile it to be used as an interview portfolio. The portfolio used during the interview has a limited number of artifacts and illustrates the best work of the future teachers.

Link Portfolio Development to Teaching Standards

You will notice that each of the Field-Based Activities and Portfolio Exhibits suggested in the textbook was related to specific INTASC principles that establish what beginning teachers should know and be able to do (shown in Figure 3.1, page 81). INTASC and other professional standards are based on common views within teacher education and provide a framework upon which to develop your portfolio. It is possible that your program will use other standards, but they should easily correlate with INTASC standards. Any standards will encompass the knowledge, dispositions, and skills needed for effective teaching and establish a framework for organizing your portfolio. Most standards can be divided into the following categories (Constantino & DeLorenzo, 2002; Rieman, 2000):

- Knowledge of subject matter
- Planning
- Delivery and assessment of instruction
- Classroom management and organization
- Human relation skills
- Professional qualities

Collect, Select, and Create Documents

Determine what characteristics of your own teaching philosophy and practices you wish to convey and select examples and artifacts that will present this view of your work. One way to start is to review all the exhibits you have prepared during this course. The Field-Based Activities, Portfolio Reflections, and E-Portfolio Exhibits suggested in this textbook will provide you many artifacts that might be appropriate. However, you will need to be somewhat selective about what is included in your portfolio. Consider all your experiences from the course and select one that best represents your philosophy and view of teaching. Choose activities that cover the categories as listed above.

Once you select an exhibit, write a narrative, produce a collage, and prepare a graphic or electronic representation that describes the growth you have experienced as you were introduced to teaching and education. The portfolio exhibits you select to represent this phase of your university program should describe the experiences and growth that have occurred as a result of this course. You may even want to develop a chart to cross-reference your artifacts with standards used in your program.

Write an Introduction

Write an introduction for each portfolio that describes what you have included. The introduction can state the purpose of your portfolio and your philosophy of education. Explain the exhibits you included, how each was developed, and why you selected it. Use the exhibits to help you write a reflective self-evaluation of your growth. What have you learned, and how do the exhibits demonstrate that knowledge?

Organizational Format

You will need some organizational format that is easy to understand and reflects your individuality. A table of contents should be provided to guide anyone reviewing your portfolio. A color-coded table of contents is a logical and highly effective approach to organizing and categorizing your exhibits. Your format should be flexible so that your portfolio will continue to expand throughout your college and teaching career.

Portfolio Displays

Your exhibits will be best shown off in an attractive and appealing visual display. There is no right or wrong way to present your portfolio. Three-ring notebooks, file crates, or book bags are often used to collect portfolio artifacts. Many individuals compile electronic portfolios, develop collections on a Web site, or produce a multimedia presentation. Whatever your choice, the substance and relevance of documentation is much more important than how you present your work. Your portfolio display and its content should reflect your unique approach to teaching and learning, demonstrate your ability to reflect on the teaching process, and help a reviewer understand the experiences you have had as you learn to teach in a field-based setting.

REFERENCES

Constantino, P. M., & DeLorenzo, M. N. (2002). *Developing a professional teaching portfolio: A guide for success.* Boston: Allyn & Bacon.

Rieman, P. L. (2000). *Teaching portfolios: Presenting your professional best.* Boston: McGraw-Hill.

Index

Photo Credits

TO THE OWNER OF THIS BOOK:

We hope that you have found *Becoming a Teacher in a Field-Based Setting,* 3e useful. So that this book can be improved in a future edition, would you take the time to complete this sheet and return it? Thank you.

School and address:_____

Department:_____

Instructor's name:_____

1. What I like most about this book is:_____

_____

_____

2. What I like least about this book is:

_____

_____

3. My general reaction to this book is:

_____

_____

4. The name of the course in which I used this book is:

_____

5. Were all of the chapters of the book assigned for you to read?_____

   If not, which ones weren't?_____

6. In the space below, or on a separate sheet of paper, please write specific suggestions for improving this book and anything else you'd care to share about your experience in using this book.

_____

_____

OPTIONAL:

Your name: _____ Date: _____

May we quote you, either in promotion for *Becoming a Teacher in a Field-Based Setting,* 3e, or in future publishing ventures?

Yes: _____ No: _____

Sincerely yours,

Donna L. Wiseman, Stephanie L. Knight, Donna D. Cooner